'FINAL SOLUTION'

# 'FINAL SOLUTION'

## Nazi Population Policy and the Murder of the European Jews

### GÖTZ ALY

*Translated from the German by*
*Belinda Cooper and Allison Brown*

A member of the Hodder Headline Group
LONDON • NEW YORK • SYDNEY • AUCKLAND

First published in Great Britain in 1999 by
Arnold, a member of the Hodder Headline Group
338 Euston Road, London NW1 3BH

http://www.arnoldpublishers.com

Co-published in the United States of America by
Oxford University Press Inc.,
198 Madison Avenue, New York, NY 10016

Published in German as 'Endlösung': Völkerverschiebung und der
Mord an den europäischen Juden © 1995 by S. Fischer Verlag
GmbH, Frankfurt am Main

English translation © 1999 Arnold

A contribution towards the translation costs of this book has been
made by

**Inter Nationes, Bonn**

and

*ejps* **The European Jewish Publication Society**

The EJPS is a registered charity which gives grants to assist in the publication
and distribution of books relevant to Jewish literature, history, religion,
philosophy, politics and culture. EJPS, First Floor, 37/43 Sackville Street,
London W1X 2DL.

*British Library Cataloguing in Publication Data*
A catalogue entry for this book is available from the British Library

*Library of Congress Cataloging-in-Publication Data*
A catalog record for this book is available from the Library of Congress

ISBN 0 340 67757 0 (hb)
ISBN 0 340 67758 9 (pb)

1 2 3 4 5 6 7 8 9 10

Production Editor: Liz Gooster
Production Controller: Helen Whitehorn
Cover Design: Terry Griffiths

Typeset in 10/12pt Sabon by J&L Composition Ltd, Filey, North Yorkshire
Printed and bound in Great Britain by MPG Books, Bodmin, Cornwall

# Contents

German AS
Eastern European AS
Western european AS
Christian As

# Acknowledgements

I have many people to thank. Topping the list, the archivists who supported my work during the last year and a half included, among others, Kyrill Chernienko (Moscow), Annegret Schöttler (Koblenz), Danuta Kołakowska (Warsaw), Heinz Fehlauer (Berlin), and Torsten Zarwel (Potsdam). The footnote references hardly do justice in crediting their knowledge and helpfulness.

I could not have written this book without many books by other authors. Unlike the archivists, their names are mentioned in the text. Nevertheless, I would like especially to mention Andreas Hillgruber. His questions and theories have been as stimulating as they are different from mine. Hillgruber may have been mistaken in the 'historians' debate' (*Historikerstreit*) shortly before his death, but this did not affect his life's work. In retrospect, the controversy seems a remarkable anachronism, but it continues to have an impact even today. Unfortunately, the ideological walls around the various 'camps' have since grown even higher, and mutual ignorance has taken root. One detail makes this plain: I had Hillgruber's most important work, *Hitlers Strategie*, on loan from the hopelessly overcrowded library of Berlin's Free University for two years. It was the only copy. In all that time, not a single library user filled out a request for it.

The manuscript for the German edition of this book was edited by Walter H. Pehle and Oliver T. Domzalski. Klaus Hartung, Morlind Tumler, Ulrich Hausmann, Susanne Heim, Hans-Heinrich Wilhelm, and Zofia Zyła read the rough draft, out of interest and personal friendship. I thank all of them sincerely. They encouraged me, discussed it with me, and contributed to making the text more precise. I would like especially to thank Peter Witte and Christian Gerlach for corrections to the second edition of the German volume.

My wife, Monika Aly, and our children accompanied the work with loving composure. Fortunately, they kept their distance from the subject and emphasized the present.

Götz Aly
Berlin, September 1994

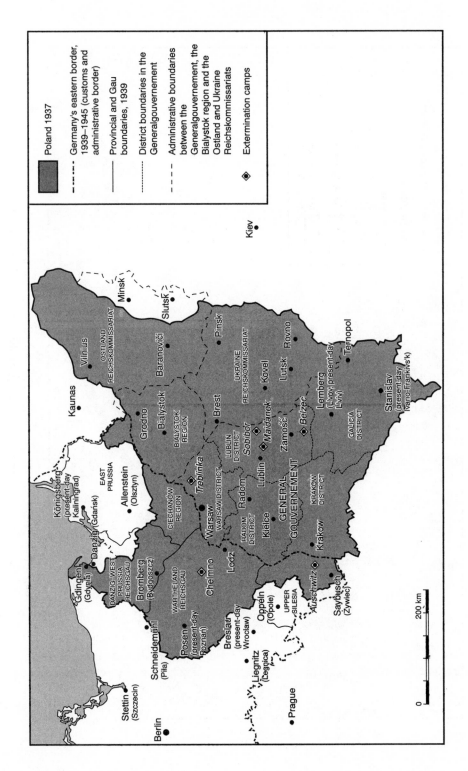

Map 1 Divided Poland, 1939–1945

Poland 1937

Germany's eastern border,
1939–1945 (customs and
administrative border)

Provincial and Gau
boundaries, 1939

District boundaries in the
Generalgouvernement

Administrative boundaries
between the
Generalgouvernement, the
Bialystok region and the
Ostland and Ukraine
Reichskommissariats

Extermination camps

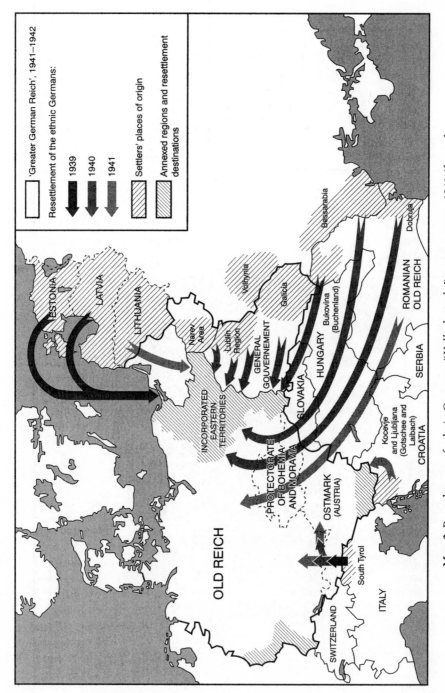

Map 2 Resettlement of ethnic Germans ('Volksdeutsche') up to autumn 1941 (from the
German Foreign Institute (Deutsches Auslandsinstitut, DAI), Stuttgart, 1942)

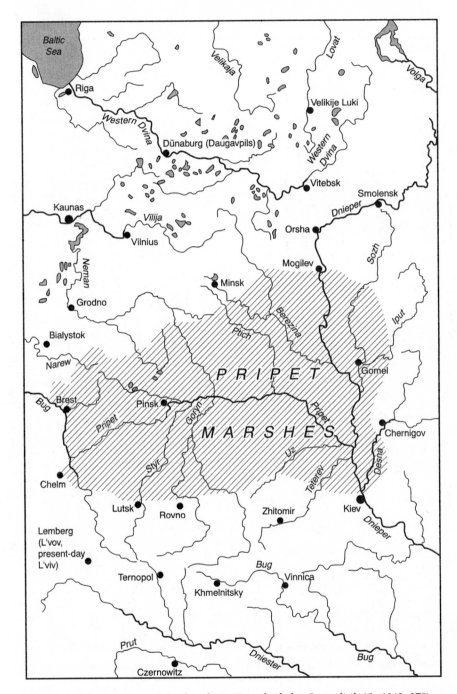

**Map 3** Pripet, Dnieper, Mogilev (from *Zeitschrift für Geopolitik* **19**, 1942, 279)

# Introduction

## The war

This book demands something difficult of its readers; namely, they are forced to become involved with the inner workings of the perpetrators: their logic, their thought processes, calculations, and actions. On the following pages, details will be discussed – statistics, attempts to side-step issues, etc. – that in light of the outcome, the Holocaust, seem trivial and sometimes confusing. But this unreasonable demand is a necessary one, for there is no other way to analyse the political processes that preceded the decision to undertake the 'Final Solution'.

My analysis starts with events of 1 September 1939 and ends with the Wannsee Conference of 20 January 1942. As amoral and racist as the anti-Jewish politics already were in 1933, the most important prerequisites to the Holocaust did not emerge until the war began. Far beyond the level reached in the first six years of Nazi dictatorship, the war promoted a non-public atmosphere, atomizing individuals and destroying any ties they still had with religious and legal traditions. Because foreign policy considerations became virtually non-existent, a situation emerged that the perpetrators referred to as a 'unique opportunity'. It became necessary that 'the operation', as a confidant of Heydrich termed the mass deportation of 1 million individuals planned for 1941, be carried out during the war, 'because the war affords the opportunity to take relatively rigorous action without regard for world opinion'.[1] When at the same time Hitler spoke of the 'Jewish question' with his closest associates, his reasoning was ambivalent; on the one hand, 'the war accelerated the resolution of this question; on the other hand, it brought with it many additional difficulties'.[2] Finally, Goebbels noted in March 1942 on the same issue:

This is making use of a rather barbaric procedure, not to be described here in greater detail, and not much of the Jews themselves will remain. . . . Thank God that in the course of war, we now have a number of options that would not be open to us in time of peace. We must take advantage of these options.[3]

In the first two years of World War II, the Jews who came under German rule became victims of the same discriminatory policies that had already been experienced by Jews in Germany and Austria. In occupied Poland, Holland, and France, the dependent states of Slovakia, Romania, and Hungary, Jews were disenfranchised and robbed of their property as they had been in Germany.

Josef Bürckel, Reich Commissioner of Austria and a zealous Aryanizer, had already thought the inherent consequences of such marginalization through to their logical conclusion by the autumn of 1938. He wrote:

Let us never forget, if we are intent on Aryanizing and removing from the Jews their means for survival, then the Jewish question must be resolved entirely. Namely, to view them as dependants of the state . . . is inconceivable. Hence conditions must be created such that they be sent out of the country.[4]

Forced emigration was difficult enough with respect to foreign policy. On top of that, the German leadership itself created additional obstacles by going to war. As a result of the war, the number of Jews who came under German rule grew by incredible proportions. After the destruction of Poland alone, there were no longer merely a few hundred thousand, but more than two and a half million Jews under German jurisdiction. Moreover, the situation of the persecutees became more and more threatening starting in October 1939, since they were subjected to new, comprehensive policies that aimed to 'ethnically segregate', i.e., deport and resettle, many millions of people in the ever-expanding German-occupied part of Europe. The systematic murder of European Jews was preceded by various deportation projects conceived by the Reich Security Main Office (*Reichssicherheitshauptamt*, RSHA). They emerged under specific basic conditions, and they failed for reasons I shall explain below.

In the autumn of 1939, Hitler, Himmler, and Heydrich had wanted to create a 'Jewish reservation of Lublin' on Poland's eastern border. They then filed away the plans and abandoned the project, since it proved incompatible with other military and economic goals. There is extensive documentation of plans to deport European Jewry to Madagascar. This arose out of Hitler's Continental Block plan, which had several prerequisites: victory over England, the existence of the Hitler–Stalin pact, and collaboration by the Vichy regime in France. A 'German Central African colonial empire' was supposed to be established as an 'economic sphere of influence'. In retrospect, the plan seems completely absurd, but if one considers the fact that the 'Axis Powers' – i.e., Italian troops – had already occupied Addis Ababa and Mogadishu for quite some time, and that

Algeria, Morocco, and Tunisia were part of a defeated France, it becomes more understandable that, in the summer of 1940, discussion was already under way in Hitler's Chancellery regarding future governorships in 'German East Africa'.

In summer 1940, Heydrich justified the Madagascar project in military and foreign policy terms as follows:

> The Jews are considered hostile to us because of our standpoint on race. For this reason they are of no use to us in the Reich. We must eliminate them. Biological extermination, however, is undignified for the German people as a civilized nation. Thus after the victory we will impose the condition on the enemy powers that the holds of their ships be used to transport the Jews along with their belongings to Madagascar or elsewhere.[5]

I agree with Hans-Günter Adler's assumption that although the phrase 'Final Solution' already existed in the summer of 1940, it did not yet refer to extermination in the sense of systematic murder.[6]

Not until spring 1941 did Heydrich, Eichmann, and others begin planning the 'biological extermination' of the Jews. Those unfit for work were to die of hunger and deprivation on reservations, and all designated fit for work were to be deported to unknown destinations 'in the East' to drain swamps and build roads, 'whereby a large proportion', according to Heydrich later, would 'without a doubt drop out owing to natural reduction'. At the same time, it was resolved to liquidate all able-bodied Jewish men in the territories of the Soviet Union that were to be occupied. The plan fitted into the new imperial programme for 'The Move Eastward' (*Ostraumlösung*, literally 'Eastern Territorial Solution'), and it included the aim of exterminating European Jewry within the foreseeable future using so-called biological, yet – in comparison with subsequent practice, as horrible as this sounds – 'conventional' means. Although the programme far exceeded the terms of the Madagascar Plan, and contained all the elements of genocide, it was still fundamentally different from death in the gas chambers, which became the favoured method of extermination a short time later.

The plans devised in early 1941 also failed, in autumn of the same year, since the Red Army – despite great losses – set clear limits to the German offensive. But the protagonists of the Third Reich had long since incorporated the 'forced migration' (*Abwanderung*) of European Jewry into their plans, making deportation the foundation of their planning for wartime and the post-war period. They continued to view the individual projects – unrealistic as they might have been – as having a basis in fact. Faced with the 'imminent total solution', they robbed Jews of all means of subsistence and forced them into improvised ghettos or camps, all the time assuming it was a temporary solution for a few months, in preparation for a final deportation. These temporary conditions started to become a more and more lasting 'burden'; from the murderers' point of view, real political conditions for the 'Final Solution' were developing step by step.

In the book *Vordenker der Vernichtung* (Pioneers of Destruction), Susanne Heim and I revealed the obvious connections between 'ethnic redistribution' (*völkische Flurbereinigung*),* on the one hand, and the extermination of minorities, on the other. We were able to show how different groups of experts, with very different motives, had considered reducing the (Eastern) European population by several tens of millions. Some devised plans to 'deport all Poles' in order to gain 'settlement space' (*Siedlungsraum*). Others suggested 'reducing the population density' of vast expanses of Eastern Europe in order to rationalize agriculture, since successive partitioning of land due to inheritance had eliminated market surpluses. Still others preferred to let 30 million Russians die in an artificially triggered famine, in order to render continental Europe 'blockade-proof', with the help of Ukrainian grain. The murder of European Jewry seemed to us to be part of even broader plans for extermination – in fact, the part that was given priority under wartime conditions and implemented to the greatest extent.

The criticisms levelled at that book could also be raised against this one: the plans were both unrealistic and megalomaniac, and could never have succeeded. It is a moot point whether and how these projects, designed for the immediate future, could have been implemented in the absence of Churchill's steadfastness, the anti-Hitler coalition, and the Red Army. Rather, as the Tower of Babel demonstrated, projects on a titanic scale unleash destructive force not because they are realistic, but because they are regarded as feasible.

## Analytical approach

Whereas in *Vordenker der Vernichtung* we viewed the events from the perspective of a planning elite that thought in terms of *tabula rasa,* here we are dealing with the complement to that, the reactions and plans of the practitioners. I seek here to determine how the difficulties the Germans faced in the war they were waging and their policies of annexation, resettlement, and establishment of a new order affected plans for the 'solution of the Jewish question'.

Relevant documents contain numerous references to this. It is obvious, for example, when Eichmann's subject reference for an entire series of deportations of Jews was: 'Re: Making room for Lithuanian Germans'. Nevertheless, the connection between resettlement of ethnic Germans and the murder of the Jews has never yet been examined, even though projects

* *Völkische Flurbereinigung*: derived from an agricultural term for the consolidation of splintered landholdings, the Nazi distortion referred to the territorial consolidation and mutual separation of different ethnic groups.

entitled 'Settlement policy/*Lebensraum*' and 'Solution of the Jewish Question' reflected the main goals of the Third Reich, and both were combined institutionally under one and the same person – Heinrich Himmler. This seemed logical from a Nazi perspective. Both involved population policies aimed at the restructuring of Europe in terms of demography and political control. These policies presupposed military victory and the unity of settlement and expulsion. Theoretically, this was supposed to proceed 'step by step'. In fact, however, megalomaniacal projects aimed at 'ethnic redistribution in Europe', on the one hand, and the 'territorial final solution of the Jewish question', on the other, began facing difficulties in October 1939. They began to obstruct each other and to face limitations caused by the war, which was originally merely a means to achieve their ends.

In addition to his office as Reichsführer SS and Chief of the German Police, Heinrich Himmler took on another, albeit lesser-known, position in 1939, shortly after the war started – that of Reich Commissioner for the Consolidation of German Nationhood (*Reichskommissar für die Festigung deutschen Volkstums*, RKF). In that office, Himmler brought some 500,000 ethnic Germans 'home to the Reich' (*Heim ins Reich*) in the following years, with the help of several thousand employees and a dozen institutions created for that purpose. The ethnic Germans came from the Baltic states and South Tyrol, from Volhynia and Bessarabia, from Bukovina and Dobruja. Their property there, worth approximately 3,000,000,000 Reichsmarks, was exchanged by the treasury of the German Reich – for the benefit of the foreign trade balance – with the Soviet Union, Romania, and Italy, for oil and food. The 'ethnic German settlers' received the homes, farms and businesses, tools and equipment, livestock, and household goods of the Jews and Poles whom Adolf Eichmann had deported or ghettoized in his capacity as coordinator of the Central Resettlement Office (*Umwandererzentralstelle*, UWZ) in Posen/Litzmannstadt (Lodz).

The resettlement policies were focused from the very beginning on occupied Poland. Hitler and Stalin had divided up the country amongst themselves. The Germans split their section into the 'incorporated eastern territories', i.e., the economically most significant annexed western region, and the Generalgouvernement, the area of central Poland between Warsaw, Krakow, and Lublin. In 1940 roughly 12 million Poles were living in that central region, including 1.5 million Jews. In the annexed western region, there were 8 million Poles, 550,000 of whom were Jews. From the latter region, about half the Poles and all the Jews were forced into the eastern Generalgouvernement to make room for German settlers.

Contemporary German historians were concerned with devising plans to carry out this task. Supported by an understanding of themselves as 'past-oriented [*rückwärtsgewandte*] prophets' (Leopold von Ranke), an idea still familiar to us today, they contributed to the formulation of the political goals of the time, as specialists of past structures that were to be either 'restored' or destroyed. For example, on 18 September 1939, Breslau medievalist and *Volkstum* scholar Hermann Aubin wrote the following to Albert Brackmann, historian for Eastern European history, in Berlin: 'The questions of ethnic nationality [*Volkstum*] in the East have reached a decisive stage. After having received approval for our proposal for regulation from the highest authorities last week, there seems now to be an obstruction.' He continued that it seemed advisable to discuss the issue again with the Ministry of the Interior, in order for 'the questions of *Volkstum* to be put on the right track when re-establishing the German administration in Poland'. 'Scholars', Aubin concluded, 'cannot simply wait to be asked; they must speak up of their own accord.'[7]

Only three days later, Brackmann met Werner Essen, officer for *Volkstum* issues in the Ministry of the Interior, who later worked on the General Plan for the East in Riga.[8] Obviously encouraged in their plans, the activist scholars met on 28 September in Breslau and drafted a working plan 'for a memorandum on the eastern German Reich border and ethnic boundary'. It explained 'the historical prerequisites and conditions for the success of a large-scale settlement policy in the eastern territories'. Theodor Schieder, a 31-year-old assistant also present at the meeting, was assigned to draft the memo. Schieder presented his draft on 7 October. In it, he developed possible alternative contours for the new eastern boundary of the German Reich and commented as follows on the second, more far-reaching alternative: 'Creation of a contiguous German ethnic region [*Volksboden*] in these territories necessitates extremely extensive population shifts. Such a development requires not a programme for a few years, but very long-range planning.' Among the 'immediate measures', Schieder included confiscation of land, resettlement of a portion of the Polish population, construction loans for the ethnic Germans and 'settlement of German persons', but 'under no circumstances should developments be left uncontrolled'. To the problem of 'how and where to direct the expected flow of Polish emigrants', Schieder responded:

> increased migration to 'rump Poland' appears possible under two conditions: (1) if the Jewish population is removed from Polish cities, and (2) if agriculture is intensified such that the food production margin in Poland is raised and the agrarian overpopulation is at least decreased through far-reaching land improvement and separation.[9]

The notion that annexation and resettlement formed a consistent whole was formulated here, with all its implications: the expulsion of the Poles, their resettlement in 'rump Poland' at the expense of the Jews living there, and the creation of an increased 'food production margin' by reclaiming swamplands. All of these suggestions were implemented at least in part in 1940–41 – and all of them failed.[10] It was precisely this failure that led to the second step, the erection and operation of extermination camps, as will be shown in the following chapters.

Schieder's draft never attained the status of a formal 'memorandum for

Adolf Hitler'. Since 'events' then happened so quickly, Schieder's superiors sent the results of their brainstorming session in unfinished form 'to a few officials we knew personally in the Foreign Office and the Ministries of the Interior, Science, and Agriculture, for their personal use' on 16 October, nine days later.[11] This example serves to demonstrate how, between 1939 and 1942, the murderous ideas spread osmotically, rising through a type of capillary action. And it shows how, to this day, respected and – taking their work as a whole – commendable scholars have examined these ideas, successfully reformulating the Nazi 'worldview' into a mercilessly instrumentalized form of rationality and transforming it into practice-oriented programmes.[12]

As can be seen by Schieder's expulsion plan, which was only one among many, the resettlement policies affected the Jews as a whole incomparably more severely than they did the Poles. Jewish property was almost completely expropriated very early on. Moreover, the Jews had to make room not only for ethnic German settlers, but for Polish exiles. Whenever problems arose in the subsequent months in the *Heim-ins-Reich* programme to bring approximately 500,000 ethnic Germans 'home' to the Reich; if homes, money, household goods, or jobs were needed for 'resettled' Germans, 'displaced' Poles, or 'exchanged' Romanians, members of Europe's Jewish minority were robbed still faster, crowded still closer together, and forced to the periphery of their respective cities and regions.

Since the settling of Germans was always linked with economic rationalization, two or even three 'ethnically alien' (*fremdvölkisch*) families – in the official terminology – often had to make way for one German family. In addition, huge military training grounds were to be set up and approximately 300,000 small farmers and their families from the poverty-stricken rural areas of the Reich were to be 'transplanted' onto roughly 50-acre farms in the eastern territories. From all of these different projects, in the winter of 1940–41 alone, a total of 5 million people were to be forced from their homes within a short period of time.

The staff of the Central Resettlement Office accomplished far less than that goal. According to Eichmann, they had 'evacuated a total of 408,525 Poles and Jews in the period from October 1939 to March 1941 from the incorporated eastern territories and sent them to the Polish General-gouvernement'.[13] Consequently, by winter 1940–41 there were already a quarter of a million ethnic German 'returnees' in 1500 resettlement camps that had to be established in the eastern and southern regions of the German Reich. The pact with Italy, too, in which the resettlement of 200,000 South Tyroleans had been agreed upon, could only be partly satisfied. As a result, pressure was continuously growing – brought about by Himmler and his staff themselves – to develop more and more comprehensive plans for expropriation and deportation.

For those who had to implement the plans, it was never clear how, when, and to where these deportations were to take place. As a result, in

September 1941, when mass deportations to the newly seized Soviet 'areas' were already on the agenda, the director of the Central Resettlement Office of Posen/Litzmannstadt asked Eichmann, 'It is essential [to] be totally clear . . . what is to be done in the end with these displaced populations that are undesirable for the Greater German settlement areas. Is the goal to permanently secure them some sort of subsistence, or should they be totally eradicated?'[14]

Reinhard Heydrich, like Himmler, held two positions. His special responsibility to implement the 'solution of the Jewish question' is well known and has been described in numerous accounts. Examined in less detail have been the overlapping tasks of the Central Immigration Office (*Einwandererzentralstelle*, EWZ) and the Central Resettlement Office, both of which were under his direction. Heydrich participated in the *Heim-ins-Reich* programme for the ethnic Germans from eastern and southeastern Europe and also organized the 'evacuation measures' necessary to enable their settlement.[15] This is the reason he created Eichmann's section IVD4 (later IVB4) in December 1939. The section, in 1940 called 'Emigration and Evacuation Matters' (*Auswanderungs- und Räumungsangelegenheiten*), was responsible for the resettlement of Poles and later Serbs, Croats, and Slovenes, as well as the deportation of Jews, until the summer of 1941.

Oswald Pohl was not only in charge of the entire concentration camp administration and an ever-expanding SS economic empire; in 1940–41, he was also the ambitious head of the board of the German Settlement Company (*Deutsche Ansiedlungsgesellschaft*, DAG). Here he was faced with the growing problem of 'making room' for those interned in resettlement camps and had to confront the dissatisfaction of the ethnic Germans. It is no coincidence that the same people who had spent months supervising the forced expulsion of Poles helped organize the murder of European Jews in the years that followed. Eichmann's staff member Dieter Wisliceny, who later became the 'Jewish advisor' to the German embassy in Pressburg (now Bratislava), organized the removal of Poles from Gnesen (Gniezno) in the Warthegau in early 1940. Franz Abromeit, who was later the 'Jewish advisor' in Zagreb, led the relocation of Poles from Danzig–West Prussia from 1939 to 1941. Siegfried Seidl, staff member at the Lodz Central Resettlement Office (Lodz UWZ), who was responsible for 'making room for the Volhynian Germans' throughout 1940, became the commandant of the Theresienstadt concentration camp in 1942. His direct superior, Hermann Krumey, travelled to Budapest in 1944 with Eichmann and Wisliceny to supervise the deportation of Hungarian Jews to Auschwitz. Herbert Otto, another member of Krumey's staff, was sent to the 'Central Office for Jewish Emigration' in Prague in July 1942.[16] In late 1941, several members of the Lodz UWZ staff were transferred to the nearby Chelmno (Kulmhof) concentration camp, where they were directly involved in the murder of Jews.[17] Both tasks, the removal of the Poles and the 'implementation of appropriate measures against Jews and asocials', as it was put by one of the SS men working there, were combined under the 'jurisdiction of the UWZ'.[18]

When, beginning in the autumn of 1941, German authorities spoke of 'deportation', 'displacement', 'resettlement', or 'evacuation' of Jews while now in fact meaning murder, this should not be seen merely as an effort to camouflage their actions; it also serves as an indication of the evolution of events leading up to the Holocaust.

# Sources

The connections have been obscured up to now in part because Himmler's actions as Reich Commissioner for the Consolidation of German Nationhood (RKF) have never been examined systematically. The unsatisfactory study of the RKF offices and departments, and of their cooperation with one another and with other authorities, is all the more surprising since extraordinarily good source materials are available.[19] Furthermore, it is remarkable how close the directors of the resettlement authorities and planning offices were to the highest authorities, Hitler, Göring, and Himmler.[20] Since it is clear that the Germans responsible for population policies sought to solve the problems that arose in implementing the *Heim-ins-Reich* programme for the ethnic Germans at the expense of the Jews, the entire policy of 'ethnic redistribution' must be examined in order to trace the political process that led, in the end, to the murder of much of European Jewry. As early as 17 January 1940, Eichmann referred to 'the difficulties arising from the interaction between resettling ethnic Germans and evacuating Poles and Jews'.

An investigation of that interaction was also obstructed for historians – myself included – who have researched the subject of the Holocaust, because we regarded the ethnic Germans brought 'home' from Eastern Europe as members of the perpetrators' camp. At best, we considered them to have unthinkingly profited from history. Their fate was presented by only a few historical researchers, often in connection with the local history of individual ethnic groups. These almost always ignored the circumstances of their settlement, treating the expropriation and expulsion of 'ethnically alien (*fremdvölkisch*) elements' as taboo.[21]

Conversely, the very notion that something could be learned of the decisions affecting the Holocaust by analysing the resettlement of ethnic Germans appeared absurd. Such reservations, though understandable, have impeded the advancement of research, resulting in countless extant documents on the resettlement of German minorities not even being read with an eye to the murder of European Jews. Even if many ethnic Germans forced to resettle sympathized greatly with the Third Reich and were themselves active Nazis, they were nevertheless objects of power politics.

Individual ethnic Germans living in eastern and southeastern Europe were not given a choice. Their so-called 'option for Germany' did not truly involve any freedom to decide. These 'returnees', as Himmler liked to call them, were shunted about in the interest of population policy as were the Jews, albeit with categorically different procedures and in opposing directions.

The success experienced by those under Himmler's command who were responsible for resettling ethnic Germans was directly dependent on how fast Eichmann was able to transport out the 'ethnically alien elements'. Until autumn 1941 he was never able to meet either deportation deadlines or target figures; he constantly had to concede and recalculate them in countless meetings with the staffs of both the Central Immigration Office and the 'Human Deployment' (*Menscheneinsatz*) Department of the RKF. These calculations always included the Jews.

Thus it proved useful to work through the comprehensive written archival materials on the displacement and resettlement of ethnic Germans with this question in mind.[22] One of my aims was to reconstruct a concrete context tied to the history of events, as this was absolutely necessary for the analysis. I also wanted to determine a procedure based on the sources. Since Eichmann's main files for the period after 1939 had been destroyed completely by fire, all documents on the activities of his department had to be sought in the existing files of other authorities and offices. It made sense to look for them among the records of those who constantly attempted to accelerate the deportations. Upon closer examination, the following also became clear: representatives of the authorities in charge of resettling the ethnic Germans did not merely keep records of the 'Emigration and Evacuation' Department; they also developed their own ideas about how to accelerate this evacuation.

Though similar approaches were tried in Alsace-Lorraine and later in annexed parts of Slovenia, by far the most significant as well as controversial site of German resettlement policy was occupied Poland – and here, above all, the Warthegau. For this reason, the most meaningful documents and files, from which the further development of policies regarding Jews during the course of the war can be reconstructed, can be found in the legacies left by the offices in Posen (Poznań), Lodz, Warsaw, and Krakow that were responsible for carrying out the resettlement.

The most important documents – approximately 1000 items from the UWZ in Posen/Litzmannstadt (Lodz) – have been preserved in the Warsaw archives of the Main Commission for the Prosecution of Hitler's Crimes. They contain hundreds of memoranda, telex messages, and reports by Eichmann and his staff. The files have been accessible to the public for decades, but they were evaluated in the 1960s from a Polish, expressly non-Jewish perspective. And for some inexplicable reason, Hans Safrian, author of the extraordinarily helpful book *Die Eichmann-Männer* (Eichmann's Men), which is cited many times in the following pages, entirely failed to consult this major source in his research. This means that for different reasons, historians have isolated individual questions from the overall context, thus forfeiting the chance to analyse Himmler's race and resettlement policies in their complex totality and on the basis of their inner logic.

What is true for the sources in Warsaw also applies in principle to the comprehensive inventory of the German Federal Archives. This includes materials from the Ethnic German Liaison Office (*Volksdeutsche Mittelstelle,* or Vomi), the Central Office of Immigration (EWZ), the Staff Main Office (*Stabshauptamt*) of the RKF, and the German Foreign Institute (*Deutsches Auslandsinstitut*), which Himmler commissioned in 1940 to document the entire 'settlement project'. In addition, the extensive files of the German Resettlement Trusteeship Company (*Deutsche Umsiedlungs-Treuhand GmbH,* DUT), located in the Potsdam office of the Federal Archives, have now become available. Archive administrators in East Germany had kept them under lock and key in order to prevent any possible Polish claims for compensation. These files, too, were read at most within the context of historical questions involving specific national groups or institutions, but were not evaluated or understood as a complement to source materials on the decision-making process leading up to the Holocaust.[23]

# Presentation

In contrast to the specifically ideologized language of German ethnocrats, 'Baltic Germans', for example, referred to themselves as 'German Balts'. 'Ethnic Germans' viewed themselves over centuries as (loyal) citizens of the countries in which they lived. Up to 1918, residents of Meran, Lemberg (Lvov), or Czernowitz, for instance, saw themselves as belonging to Austria-Hungary, not a 'German nation'.

The term 'resettlement' virtually reeks of Nazi ideology. Of course, the Volhynian Germans, for example, who were 'transplanted' to the Warthegau, were neither 'brought home' nor 'repatriated'. Nevertheless, I have utilized such wording as the jargon of the period. Only occasionally – as a reminder, as it were – do I establish the necessary detachment from the vocabulary of the nationalist *Volkstum* politicians.

The following text is interrupted four times by chronologies. I felt this was necessary for several reasons. First of all, I am convinced that the history leading up to the Holocaust must be reconstructed in as much detail as possible. Moreover, my approach is a new one. For this reason, too, I felt it was important to provide a thorough presentation of the empirical material. The chronologies also serve to reveal parallels involving different events, as well as the contradictory yet parallel reactions of different officials within the political apparatus.

The chronological presentation of historical material is also helpful in view of yet another consideration. If the decision to exterminate European Jewry was not the sudden, voluntaristic act of a dictator and his henchmen, but a political decision-making process stretching over a period of many months and involving the participation of individuals holding various functions and hierarchical positions, then each individual stage and every argument is significant.

In the winter of 1944–45, the perpetrators burned most of the evidence of their murderous actions. Only a very few offices were prevented from obeying the orders from above to destroy all files. And only by chance did one of the 30 copies of the record of the Wannsee Conference survive. The existence of a 'Memorandum on the Expulsion of all Poles', a plan drafted in March 1941 to deport European Jews to the areas of the Soviet Union to be occupied, has been confirmed, yet the documents themselves have disappeared. Also, the files contain numerous references to the fact that important matters were often decided verbally for the purpose of confidentiality and were expressly not recorded in writing.

To the extent that perpetrators were interrogated at all after the 'collapse' of the Third Reich, they were quite successful in adopting a common strategy of lies, denial, and silence. They were nevertheless unable to destroy all the essential, sometimes minute, pieces of evidence completely. If these are interpreted correctly, it is possible to draw conclusions about the intricate motives and the division of labour in the not-always-smooth cooperation of those involved in the discussions and political decisions that in the end led to the murder of much of European Jewry.

# Notes

1 Bruno Streckenbach, 15 January 1941; Frank diary, BAK, R52/II/233, 4060–76.
2 Engel, 94ff.
3 Goebbels diaries, Reuth, 1777ff.: entry on 27 March 1942.
4 Quoted in Safrian, 36. For a detailed discussion, see Aly and Heim, 21–68.
5 This was a statement by Heydrich, according to testimony by Herbert Strickner given in 1948 (no exact date is available) during a hearing by the public prosecutor's office in Poznań; AGK, SOP/154, 288.
6 Adler, 74.
7 Ebbinghaus and Roth, 78f. There is also mention in the letter of future use of the Polish Institute for Silesian Ethnology. Aubin: 'One must ask, for instance, whether we should turn around the "Silesian Institute" and thus fire upon Poland.'
8 Aly and Heim, 427ff.
9 The memorandum appears in Ebbinghaus and Roth, 84–91.
10 This can be found in the Frank diary and the diary of Adam Czerniaków.
11 Ebbinghaus and Roth, 93.
12 Whereas doctors at the German Society for Gynaecology and Obstetrics have since issued an official apology to victims of forced sterilizations of any kind

(see *Frankfurter Allgemeine Zeitung*, 7 September 1994), members and the board of directors of the Association of German Historians have not even considered any comparable action.

13 Letter from Eichmann to Sandberger, 3 April 1941; AGK, UWZ/L/838/2, 4.

14 See Chapter 10, p. 221 and note 28.

15 Heydrich strongly identified with these tasks, assigned to Himmler in his capacity as RKF, as shown by a secret speech he held on 2 October 1941 in Prague, reprinted in Kárný and Milotová, 98ff.

16 Letter from Krumey to Günther (RSHA IVB4), 3 July 1942; AGK, UWZ/L/205, 27.

17 According to Fritz Ismer and Karl Goede. See Ismer's testimony of 9 November 1960; ZStL, 203/AR/7/69/59, vol. 4.

18 Letter from Heinrich Kinna, staff member of the Litzmannstadt UWZ, to the main SS personnel office, 13 July 1943; BDC, PA/Kinna. In the letter, Kinna gave a report of his earlier activities.

19 Deserving of special mention is the work of Robert L. Koehl, which was published in 1957 in Cambridge but received little attention in Germany. It was based on a collection of documents from the Nuremberg trials that was not very comprehensive on this subject. Regarding regional studies, the most significant publications are those by Pospieszalski (western Poland), Ferenc (Slovenia), and Madajczyk (the Zamość region). Two excellent individual studies on the resettlement of ethnic Germans are those by Stuhlpfarrer (on South Tyroleans) and Jachomowski (on Germans in Bessarabia, Bukovina, and Dobruja).

20 Bracher, 409f.

21 This situation has recently started to change, albeit slowly. For example, the 1993 yearbook of the German-Baltic *Landsmannschaft* (cultural association for Germans born in the Baltic states) included, for the first time, recollections of settlement in the Warta region (Warthegau), some of which dealt with the issue of the related deportation of the local population; *Jahrbuch des baltischen Deutschtums* 41 (1994) (Lüneburg and Munich, 1993), 59–150.

22 This was only feasible to a limited extent, considering the mountains of extant files. Further research along these lines is necessary.

23 I cite the inventories of the German Federal Archives according to the location where I viewed the material. As there has since been considerable reorganization, which is still ongoing, many of the files I viewed in Koblenz are now located in Potsdam. Among the complications connected with the research is the fact that, half a century after the end of the war, there is insufficient funding for search aids for the extensive inventories of either the RKF or the DUT. In contrast, Polish and Russian inventories were evaluated at a very early date and are of good quality.

# 1

# Policy towards the Jews, war, and resettlement

## Deportation zones

Up until the start of the war, German authorities constantly attempted to increase the 'pressure to emigrate' felt by German and Austrian Jews. By wanting not only to expel the Jews, but to expropriate their property, the Reich government itself blocked the path to achieving its goal,[1] since foreign governments were increasingly turning away refugees, especially those totally without means. This was even more the case once Germany invaded Poland.

Faced with this situation, Heydrich did an immediate about-face. Instead of forcing the Jews to emigrate, he gave absolute priority to deporting them to the most remote reaches of the German sphere of influence. This meant that the Jews – plundered and humiliated as they were – could not even reach the territory of another sovereign state; they remained totally marginalized and subject to German measures.

In his guidelines of 21 September 1939, Heydrich spoke clearly, albeit indirectly, of the planned formation of a 'Jewish reservation'.[2] He ordered the exclusion of Jews from a certain region near the new southeast Polish border from the general 'concentration', since he planned to deport all Jews and Gypsies to a 'Jewish state under German administration near Krakow'. On the same day, Heydrich defined four goals:

(1) Jews to be moved to the towns as quickly as possible; (2) Jews to be moved out of the Reich into Poland; (3) the remaining 30,000 Gypsies also to be moved to Poland; (4) Jews in the German [i.e., formerly Polish] territories to be systematically deported by goods train.[3]

On 19 September, Heydrich was present at a meeting of the ministerial council for Reich defence, chaired by Göring. At that meeting, plans were discussed that went beyond the guidelines laid down in writing two days later, but they were opposed by the military. The brief minutes of the meeting mention 'the question of the population of the territory of the future Polish protectorate and accommodation of Jews living in Germany'.[4] On the same day, Heydrich spoke with Eduard Wagner, General Quartermaster of the army, about the possibility of deporting all Jews from Germany to a remote corner of carved-up Poland.[5] But on 22 September, only one day after Heydrich's guidelines on future policy towards the Jews were approved, Walther von Brauchitsch, Commander in Chief of the army, expressly demanded that population transfers be discontinued for the time being and that, in the future, they be carried out under the direction 'not of the civil authorities', such as the SS, but 'by the military'.[6] In view of the resistance he knew he faced from the military, Heydrich refrained from discussing in writing his plan also to deport German, Austrian, and Czech Jews to a southeastern or eastern corner of the future Generalgouvernement. In order to circumvent Brauchitsch's objections, he made a tactical distinction between the final goal and short-term, interim measures, allowing the 'concentration' of Polish Jews as a (temporary) alternative to 'immediate clearance' of the area. But Brauchitsch once again expressed his disapproval. On 1 October, Himmler personally revised Heydrich's orders of 21 September, allowing the SS *Einsatzgruppen* (Special Units) to 'initiate *only* preparatory measures' for the concentration and deportation of the Jews; all further action would have to wait 'until a later time'.[7]

The transition from a military to a civilian administration in occupied Poland, which became official on 26 October 1939, boded no good for the Jews. The change greatly increased the scope of action of the (civilian) Reich Security Main Office.[8] In Goebbels' words, 'the military administration in Poland should be replaced by a civilian administration as soon as possible. Military offices are too weak and accommodating. Only force works with the Poles.'[9]

Thus once the war started, policies towards the Jews changed fundamentally. Forced emigration was replaced by a policy of deportation or, to be more precise, plans for deportation. This did not occur primarily because of the approximately 350,000 Jews still living in the 'Greater German Reich (including the Protectorate)', but because with every step of military and economic expansion, more and more Jews entered the German sphere of influence – no longer hundreds of thousands, but millions.

Between September 1939 and September 1941, the Germans expanded the area they controlled four times. The conquest and partition of Poland in September 1939 were followed – aside from the occupation of Denmark and Norway, which is not significant to the context of this book – by the victory over the Benelux states and France early in the summer of 1940, and then the 'peaceful' conquest of southeastern Europe as the 'economic sphere of the German nation' in summer 1940 (with the subsequent war against Yugoslavia and Greece in spring 1941), and finally, the war against the Soviet Union, concrete preparations for which had begun in winter 1940–41. All four expansionist steps directly affected plans for policy towards the Jews and 'ethnic cleansing'. Occupation plans for Poland, France, and later the Soviet Union were – despite numerous differences – all similar as regards one point in the initial phase. In each case, the conquered countries were divided into three sections: one was annexed, or at least plans existed to Germanize it; one was occupied; and one became a peripheral zone of lesser interest. In occupied Poland, this was manifested in Germany's incorporated eastern territories, the General-gouvernement, and the planned eastern reservation for 'undesirables'. In the same way, parts of France and Belgium were immediately annexed by Germany – albeit not de jure; other parts (e.g., Burgundy) were supposed to be annexed; and in addition to the occupied zone, an unoccupied zone was also established. The occupation strategies developed in spring and summer 1941 for the Soviet Union were similar.[10]

Residents of the peripheral zones were to be left to their own resources, in so far as they were not used for slave labour. Without the Germans taking any concrete responsibility for their subsistence, but definitely within the limits of military and police restrictions imposed by the victors, the people there were expected to eke out an existence under miserable conditions. In addition, German population policy experts hoped to deport 'surplus', 'burdensome', and 'undesirable' persons to these less important zones. Former Krupp director Wilhelm Muehlon noted on 19 July 1940 from Swiss exile:

> France looks with horror and fear at the unoccupied zone, in which millions of refugees and demobilized soldiers cannot return to their homes in the occupied zone, separated by a 'Great Wall of China'. The Germans are unmoved by the fact that the French have to suffer the consequences of their sins, reminding them of France's harshness in starving Germany after the World War.[11]

The periphery of the German imperium was also always conceived as a deportation site for the Jews. In this sense, it was entirely logical that a few thousand Viennese and Stettin (Szczecin) Jews, and several tens of thousands of western Polish Jews, were deported to the eastern General-gouvernement in 1939–40 and that Jews from Baden, Saar-Palatinate, Alsace, and Lorraine were deported in the autumn of 1940 to the unoccupied zone in France. German ethnocrats did not carry out these deportations in isolation, but parallel to more extensive plans to force certain segments of the Polish and French populations from their homeland.

But in both occupied Poland and unoccupied France, German occupation officials quickly changed this strategy. They did this for economic reasons, with the goal of making these regions useful to the German wartime economy. In the process, the Germans reduced their own options for deportation and tried to overcome the conflict of interest, at first, through more and more extensive plans for conquest and deportation.

Though they are very different from Auschwitz, it is important to note that all German deportation plans between 1939 and 1941 took for granted the death of tens of thousands, and later hundreds of thousands, of people. Among the planners of the deportations, consensus prevailed that many Jews would die under wretched conditions in the course of their resettlement – under the cover of war – from hunger or from slave labour, insufficient medical care, or the measures of a German police state. Complete physical exposure, travelling in winter on foot or in unheated freight cars, and finally, abandonment in uncultivated, infertile regions – these were not intended to protect and preserve human life. This was desired and ordered quite openly by those who prepared the deportations and continued to discuss them in hastily constituted *ad hoc* working groups.

On 20 November 1939, during an inspection tour by Deputy General-gouverneur Arthur Seyss-Inquart, SS Brigadeführer Schmidt expressed his opinion that a certain eastern Polish area was suitable as a reservation for Jews, since 'its very marshy environment' could 'possibly lead to considerable decimation of the Jews'.[12] At about the same time, Himmler remarked about the Polish Jews that 'it is high time that this riff-raff be herded together in ghettos; then bring in epidemics and let them rot'.[13]

Hans Frank, head of the administration of the Generalgouvernement in Krakow, told his staff on 25 November 1939 in Radom how he imagined the 'large concentration area . . . east of the Vistula', which he was supposed to – and indeed at the time still wished to – establish.

> The winter will be a harsh one. If there is no bread for Poland, don't come with complaints. . . . Don't waste any time on the Jews. It is a joy finally to be able to deal with the Jewish race. The more that die, the better.[14]

Eduard Könekamp of the German Foreign Institute reported in December 1939 from occupied Poland to his colleagues in Stuttgart:

> Many Germans are seeing such masses of Jews for the first time in their lives. . . . The extermination of these subhumans lies in the interests of the whole world. But this extermination is one of the most difficult problems. We will not get by with executions. And we cannot allow the shooting of women and children. Here and there one reckons with losses during the evacuation transports; and during the transport of 1000 Jews from Lublin that was set in motion, 450 died. . . . All offices dealing with the Jewish question are aware of the inadequacy of all these measures. But no solution to this complex problem has yet been found.[15]

As early as 24 October, the London *Times* had reported and – in every sense – realistically interpreted the fact that in well-informed quarters in this country, the German Government's apparent intention to form a Jewish State in Poland is regarded as a remarkable example of political cynicism. . . . Herr Hitler now proposes to concentrate the 3,000,000 Jews of Poland in a State which is to be cut out of the body of Poland and will have Lublin for its centre. . . . To thrust 3,000,000 Jews, relatively few of whom are agriculturists, into the Lublin region and to force them to settle there would doom them to famine. That, perhaps, is the intention.[16]

## 'Ethnic redistribution'

With respect to their goals, all deportation projects failed. Heydrich and Eichmann were not able to achieve more than the very basics of their plans. Instead of 30,000 Gypsies, only 2800 were deported by the end of April 1941. The ghettoization of the Jews was achieved very inconsistently.[17] Of the 350,000 'Reich Jews,' only 15,000 had been deported by summer 1941; of the 550,000 living in the incorporated eastern territories, the figure was about 110,000.

The deportation of Jews to the border between the German and Soviet spheres of influence, scheduled for the autumn of 1939, not only ran into considerable technical problems and increasing resistance from the German civilian administration in the Generalgouvernement. In addition, the original plans were foiled by unforeseen obligations to bring ethnic Germans from Eastern Europe and South Tyrol 'home to the Reich'. German leaders had bound themselves by treaty in the summer of 1939 to resettle half a million so-called ethnic Germans over the next 15 months in the Greater German Reich, expanded through annexation. From that point on, the task of 'making room' for them fell to Heinrich Himmler and Reinhard Heydrich and, a short time later, to Adolf Eichmann as well. In his Reichstag speech of 6 October 1939, Hitler announced and explained the new ethnic policy goals. Although he propagated them as an independent, 'high priority' task, the power politics involved were obvious from the term 'sphere of interest' he used to introduce the subject. The resettlement of the South Tyroleans, although already agreed upon, was not yet definite enough to speak of publicly. Hitler thus concealed the issue behind the concept of 'a far-reaching order of European life'. In the speech, he said:

The goals and tasks that have emerged as a result of the fall of the Polish state are basically the following, as concerns the German sphere of interest:

1. To establish a Reich boundary that does justice to historical, ethnographic, and economic conditions.
2. To pacify the entire region in the sense of creating tenable order and peace.

3. To guarantee absolute security, not only in the territory of the Reich, but throughout the entire sphere of interest.
4. To create a new order for and to restructure economic life, transport, and thus also the development of culture and civilization.
5. But the main task is to create a new ethnographic order; i.e., to resettle the nationalities so that in the end, better lines of demarcation exist than is today the case.

In this sense the problem is not limited to German territory; rather, the task extends much farther, for the entire eastern and southeastern regions of Europe are filled with *in part untenable splinters*[18] of the German nation. Precisely therein lies a reason for continued disturbances between nations. In the age of the principle of nationalities and the notion of race [*Rassegedanke*], it is utopian to believe that these members of a high-quality nation could simply be assimilated. It is thus one of the tasks of a far-sighted ordering of European life to carry out resettlements, in order thus to eliminate at least some of the potential for European conflict.

Germany and the Union of Soviet Republics have agreed to support each other to this end.

In this initial declaration of principle, Hitler had already gone beyond the scope marked out for him with the 'fall of the Polish state'. In the second part of his speech, he formulated further plans for the 'area west of the German–Soviet Russian demarcation line recognized as within the German sphere of influence'. According to Hitler, this included:

1. The establishment of a Reich boundary that, as already emphasized, corresponds to historical, ethnographic, and economic conditions.
2. The ordering of the entire *Lebensraum* [living space] according to nationalities, i.e., a resolution of those minority issues that affect not only this region, but beyond that, almost all southern and southeastern European states.

Hitler also announced that 'in this context, an attempt to order and regulate the Jewish problem' would be necessary.[19]

On the day of his speech, Hitler ordered the formal annexation of those western Polish areas that were to be 'united with Germany', irrespective of the fact that the exact borders had not yet been determined. He was obviously influenced by the resettlement of the Baltic Germans, which had already started. The next day, Hitler transferred all authority for the organization and implementation of the 'ethnic new order' – initially restricted to the soon-to-be annexed regions of western Poland – to Heinrich Himmler. Himmler was given the title of Reich Commissioner for the Consolidation of German Nationhood (RKF), and he set up an office to organize and implement population policy.[20] At the same time, diplomats in the Foreign Office were working feverishly on the wording of appropriate resettlement agreements with the independent (in name only) Baltic republics, with the Soviet Union, and with Italy.

On 6 October, Hitler issued a statement of intent as regards population policy that surprised the officials for Jewish and *Volkstum* (nationhood) issues at the Reich Security Main Office. On 26 September, two days before signing the 'secret protocol' to the Nazi–Soviet treaty, Himmler had met Erhard Kroeger, leader of the Latvian Germans, and informed him of the pending political agreement between Germany and the USSR. At this time it was certain that Latvia and Estonia would go to the Soviet Union. Himmler was not yet planning to resettle *all* Baltic Germans. He intended to bring only a group of 'directly threatened Germans' – active Nazis and 'fighters for nationhood' – to safety. He also wanted to 'place young Baltic Germans fit for service in the Waffen SS'. It was Kroeger who told Himmler that there was a great fear of Bolshevism in Riga, and that the Germans there vividly remembered the massacre of 22 May 1919 'committed by the retreating Bolsheviks in the final hours'. Kroeger

> finished by assuring that a large majority of Baltic Germans had to be regarded as highly threatened by the Bolshevik occupation. . . . It would be irresponsible for any national leadership to characterize a segment of the population, no matter how small or large, as not at risk and thus excluded from emigration.

Himmler promised to inform Hitler the following evening. The spontaneous decision was made as Kroeger had recommended. However, power politics and military considerations caused Hitler to condition his approval on the requirement 'that the entire operation take place in cooperation with the Soviet government'. Furthermore, it was already clear to Himmler on that morning of 27 September that the present state of affairs allowed 'settlement only in the new regions of the Reich that had previously belonged to the Polish state'.[21]

The next day, following a hectic exchange of telegrams between the Foreign Office and the German embassy in Moscow, Ribbentrop and Molotov signed the 'secret protocol' to the Nazi–Soviet non-aggression pact that had been concluded on 23 August 1939. The agreement provided for, on the one hand, the 'resettlement' of the ethnic German population from the Soviet sphere of influence, including the Baltic republics, which were still formally independent, and in return, the 'corresponding' resettlement of 'persons of Ukrainian and White Russian descent' from East Prussia and the German-occupied part of Poland. The wording of the annex suggested a 'minority exchange' between German and Soviet spheres of power. On the surface this called for Germans living within the future borders of the Soviet Union to be exchanged for Ukrainian and White Russian minorities on the German side of the German–Soviet demarcation line. In fact, however, the term 'minority exchange' veiled the signatories' true intentions. German negotiators had sought a choice of words 'that would suggest emigration to the Soviet Union in a gentle, non-discriminatory fashion'. 'The sole purpose' of this wording was 'to allow the Soviet Union to save face and thus to facilitate agreement. In truth, however, no Ukrainian or White Russian was enthusiastic about returning to the Soviet Union.'[22] Himmler later commented on this secret agreement as follows:

> Germany and Russia declared boundaries to their spheres of interest in an agreement that expressed political reason in a most realistic sense. It clearly laid down that Germans who *lived* on Russian soil would be sent to Germany and, vice versa, that Russians and Ukrainians who *wished* to go to Russia, were *permitted* to do so. It was a pact expressing a most simple and natural matter of course, a natural sense of reason.[23]

Though absolutely no preparations had been made, the resettlement of 60,000 people was virtually forced ahead within a mere eight weeks in late autumn 1939. It could not fail to radicalize annexation plans and proposed forms of racist discrimination that had been considered up to then. For example, the Lodz region was not originally slated for annexation. On the eve of the war, approximately 500,000 Poles and more than 200,000 Jews lived in the city of Lodz. After Göring had declared in early November that he 'agreed to let the cities of Kutno and Lodz remain within the General-gouvernement',[24] Werner Lorenz, one of the highest-ranking officials involved in the resettlements, successfully pushed for Lodz to be added to the Warthegau region. The entry of 13 November in Frank's diary says that

> Reich Minister Seyss-Inquart reports on the drawing of the borders: The final decision has been left to the Führer. The Reich Ministry of the Interior has thus declared only a provisional administrative boundary. With respect to Lodz, the General Field Marshal [i.e., Göring], the OKW, and the Reich Ministry of the Interior were in favour of including it within the Generalgouvernement; SS Obergrup-penführer Lorenz was opposed.[25]

The latter headed the Ethnic German Liaison Office (*Volksdeutsche Mit-telstelle,* or Vomi). At this time, he was organizing the '*Heim ins Reich*' programme to resettle the Baltic Germans in the Reich. Since he did not think Posen would be sufficient to settle 60,000 mostly urban ethnic Germans, he wanted Lodz to be 'incorporated' into the German Reich. *De facto* he got his way.

For different reasons, the situation was similar in Upper Silesia, where this time it was Göring who put the pressure on. After an extended dispute with the administration of the Generalgouvernement, German economists finally drew the border so that the cities of Sosnowiec, Będzin, and Dąbrowa became part of the German Reich. The motive in this case was the coalmines there. Historical developments had also caused more Jews to live here than in all of the rest of Upper Silesia.[26]

Nine months later there still had not been a 'final' decision on whether Lodz and the Dąbrowa region belonged to the Reich or not.[27] Hitler never made an official decision. Even Himmler's powerful representative in Posen, Higher SS and Police Chief Wilhelm Koppe, had to resort to indirect reasoning in trying to achieve the deportation of the Jews of Lodz. In July 1940 he said the following to Hans Frank: 'Since the Führer has given the name Litzmannstadt to the city formerly known as Lodz, all are convinced that this city has finally been made part of the Warthegau and will stay there.'[28]

This process demonstrates how German leadership at that time made 'provisional' decisions, how Hitler tried to overcome real differences in interests as, one could say, an ideal 'total polycrat', and how the consequences of such 'non-decisions' in the case of Lodz were imposed upon the large Jewish minority of the city.

In autumn 1939, Hitler 'established' the authority of the future Generalgouverneur, Hans Frank, in the same manner. The 'Edict from the Führer and Reich Chancellor' of 27 September 1939 comprised nine short paragraphs. In paragraph 3, Hitler declared 'the Generalgouverneur is directly responsible to me'; paragraph 5 states that the Council of Ministers for Defence of the Reich and the Plenipotentiary for the Four-Year Plan [along with Frank] 'can enact laws by decree'; in paragraph 6, Hitler allowed all senior Reich authorities to 'issue orders that are necessary for planning the German living and economic sphere, even in areas within the jurisdiction of the Generalgouverneur'; paragraph 7 required that the budget of the Generalgouverneur, who was supposedly 'directly' under Hitler, be 'approved by the Reich Finance Minister'; and finally, paragraph 8 declared that the 'main official for the occupied Polish territories is the Reich Minister of the Interior'; he was to enact 'all legal and administrative measures necessary for the implementation and supplementation of this edict'.[29] The most important point is not even mentioned in the edict, namely, that hundreds of thousands of 'ethnic aliens' (Fremdvölkische) were to be deported to the Generalgouvernement in the foreseeable future with only a blanket and a few days' supply of food. But this had already been decided upon on 27 September 1939, when the rapid resettlement of the Baltic Germans had been resolved within only a few hours. Heydrich declared:

Developments in former Poland have been initially planned such that the former German provinces become German Gaus and that an additional district be formed with a foreign-language-speaking population with its capital in Krakow. . . . RFSS [i.e., Himmler] shall be named settlement commissioner for the East. Deportations of Jews to the foreign-language district [i.e., what later became the

Generalgouvernement] has been approved by the Führer. However, the entire procedure will take place in the course of one year.

This delay was new, a consequence of the sudden decision to resettle the Baltic Germans.

However, at this time Heydrich was still assuming he would have roughly 170,000 Jews to deport from the newly annexed Polish regions to the Generalgouvernement. Only a few weeks later, the annexation of the Lodz and Dąbrowa regions – for reasons that had nothing to do with policy towards the Jews – had raised the figure to 550,000. The number of Jews to be evacuated from the 'new Reich areas' had tripled within six weeks because of these decisions, while at the same time the territory they were to be deported to, the Generalgouvernement, had been reduced in size. On top of that, it had been economically weakened to a greatly disproportionate extent.

Whereas the Polish elite, estimated by Heydrich at about 3 per cent of all Poles, was 'to be taken care of' in concentration camps, the procedure regarding the majority of Poles varied from region to region and had not yet been determined in detail: 'Leaders of the *Einsatzgruppen*', according to Heydrich, 'are to consider how to incorporate primitive Poles into the labour force while deporting them at the same time. The goal is for the Poles to remain permanent seasonal and migrant labourers, with permanent residence in the environs of Krakow.'[30]

Two days later, Heydrich remarked that no 'Jewish reservation' would be built 'southeast of Krakow', as originally planned; instead a '"nature preserve" or "Reich ghetto" [was] to be created' in the 'area beyond Warsaw and around Lublin', for 'all *Polish* and Jewish elements . . . who have to be evacuated from future German Gaus'.[31] The original idea for a reservation had already been modified on 29 September as part of the new resettlement policy, so that it no longer pertained only to 'Jewish elements', but to non-Jewish Poles who were to be evacuated as well. In the beginning, the latter were even given preference, since Heydrich wrote on 9 October that in view of the pending arrival of several tens of thousands of Baltic Germans in Gdynia ('Gotenhafen'),

> it will be necessary largely to clear the city of its Polish population . . . to acquire the required housing. The Polish population, or some of it, is to be deported without delay to the eastern parts of the Polish region occupied by German troops.[32]

The politics of speedy ethnic 'redistribution' began in September 1939 in an extraordinarily rushed, improvised form, because the power and alliance politics of war preparations had yielded the 'resettlement' of, initially, about 500,000 ethnic Germans as a by-product. The hastily resolved resettlement of the Baltic Germans marked only the beginning, followed in the course of the German–Soviet and German–Italian agreements by the evacuation of an additional 440,000 ethnic Germans. This had a lasting impact on Heydrich's attempts to quickly drive out the Jews. The planned deportations of German, Austrian, and Czech Jews were a consequence of racist policies and deliberate economic expropriation. Jews in the incorporated eastern territories, on the other hand, were – at first – to disappear and be shipped to a 'Reich ghetto' merely because they were Jews. But then another motive emerged: the necessity of making room for Baltic Germans 'returning home' in only a few weeks' time. This required not only that Jews be deported, but that certain cities, living quarters, farms, estates, businesses, and jobs be 'cleared' on short notice; also, household goods, cash, and loans had to be made available.

Bringing the Baltic and, a few weeks later, the Volhynian and Galician Germans 'home to the Reich' affected both Jews and non-Jewish Poles. The evacuation procedures were no longer solely a means towards the ends of a more or less separate policy towards the Jews; in addition, and indeed increasingly (as will be shown), the evacuations had become responses, necessitated by other motives, to quickly accommodate the ethnic Germans – who had already started arriving – according to their accustomed standard of living or even better.[33]

## Resettlement Commissioner Himmler

The story behind Heinrich Himmler's appointment as Reich Commissioner for the Consolidation of German Nationhood started in the spring of 1939. After the annexation of Austria and in the interests of a lasting alliance with fascist Italy, Germany's leaders discussed a 'final solution of the South Tyrolean problem'. In contrast to the cases of Austria, the Sudetenland, and the First Vienna Award,[34] however, they did not follow the principle of correcting the Paris peace treaties of 1919–20 according to *völkisch* (ethnic national) considerations. Rather, as regards South Tyrol, the Reich government explicitly refrained from making any territorial revisions. This was done for overriding considerations of power and alliance politics. The so-called German–Italian steel pact of 22 May 1939[35] was a prerequisite for war, as was the subsequent Hitler–Stalin pact of 23 August 1939. Leaders of the German Reich viewed both agreements as diplomatic, material, and military safeguards for their war preparations. They saw minority issues as less significant, since these hindered efforts to secure German expansionist aims through alliances. Instead of revising borders, as it had preferred to do up to that point, the German leadership now wanted a mass exodus, an 'organized migration', to 'resolve once and for all' the minorities issues, which went far beyond German minorities, dominating European politics throughout the 1920s and 1930s. From that point on, German minorities were to be evacuated from the regions in question and permanently brought 'home to the Reich' *only* in cases where their presence interfered with international agreements.

Against this background, in May 1939 Heinrich Himmler devised a plan to resettle the approximately 200,000 South Tyroleans in the Reich, in a 'perhaps historically unique, generous procedure'.[36] Ulrich Greifelt, who later became head of RKF headquarters, was already involved in preparations, as was the Vomi under the direction of SS General Werner Lorenz.[37] In preparation for 'solving the South Tyrolean problem', Himmler created virtually all the resettlement authorities in summer 1939, though some of them were not officially established until later and then quickly expanded. The question *where* to put the South Tyroleans remained largely unanswered. However, German Consul General Max Lorenz had already determined back in March 1939, when German–Italian relations had become somewhat precarious after the annexation of Austria, that the future resettlement of all South Tyroleans would require the creation of *Lebensraum* in the East.[38]

On 23 June 1939, German and Italian negotiators met for the Berlin Conference, with Himmler presiding. Many controversial details could not be resolved, not even the definition of which South Tyroleans were actually considered ethnic Germans. The delegations were nevertheless agreed in their willingness to resettle the South Tyroleans.

On 2 August 1939 in Bayreuth, Hitler gave Himmler 'written authorization' concerning the 'treatment of all issues relating to the South Tyrol problem'. This authorization, which was very broad and vague, was written by Hans Lammers, chief of the Reich Chancellery. It was worded as follows:

Reichsführer Himmler is hereby authorized to issue all necessary orders and instructions in Germany, to negotiate with the Italian authorities, and to make contact with inhabitants of South Tyrol. He is further authorized to take all steps necessary for the resettlements and return of Reich and ethnic Germans presently living in South Tyrol.[39]

The brevity and vague wording of the text resembled the 'euthanasia' authorization issued by Hitler a short time later. But in contrast to the later authorization, Reich Chancellery officials took another look at this one because of the great influence it would give Himmler on both domestic and foreign policies. They deemed it too imprecise and too comprehensive, and instead formulated an 'edict from the Führer',[40] containing considerable restrictions. It required Himmer to 'utilize existing authorities and facilities' and permitted him to negotiate with representatives of the South Tyroleans and Italian authorities only 'in cooperation' with the Foreign Minister. In addition, he was required in cases of dispute to 'ascertain Hitler's decision through the Reich ministers and the chief of the Reich Chancellery [i.e., Lammers]'.[41]

Himmler's new area of competence had hardly been agreed upon and put to paper in the summer of 1939 when Hitler expanded his 'settlement and ethnic national policy [*volkstumspolitisch*]' responsibilities only a few weeks after the start of the war. On 28 September, precisely the day when Ribbentrop and Molotov signed the secret protocol on reciprocal population exchange in Moscow, Lammers wrote the following to the Reich Finance Minister:

> The Führer has given the Reichsführer SS the task of resettling the Reich and ethnic Germans returning to the Reich from abroad (starting with the South Tyroleans), as well as that of placing agricultural settlers in previously Polish areas. An edict on the subject will be issued by the Führer within the next few days. The Führer requests that 10 million Reichsmarks, initially, be made available immediately to the Reichsführer for his activities.[42]

As had previously been announced, the Reich Chancellery issued an 'edict from the Führer and Reich Chancellor on the consolidation of German nationhood' on 7 October. It was not intended for the public eye. The edict required Himmler 'to adapt [the resettlement measures] to the needs of the military leadership', but at the same time it gave him a specific new task: 'Eliminating the influence of ethnically alien populations that present a threat to the Reich and the ethnic German community.'[43]

# Authorization to kill

Even if such edicts from the Führer continually led to disputes, they nevertheless regulated the administration's actions while at the same time granting it extreme flexibility. The most classic example is 'Operation T-4', i.e., the murder of mentally handicapped Germans. Since this crime was very significant in the decision-making process that led to the murder of European Jews, the preceding events – even though they are now relatively well known – need to be summarized here.

Various committees predominantly comprising physicians and professors of medicine met in summer 1939, and plans for this project started taking on definite contours by the following autumn. The 'legal basis' for it was a simple, four-line confidential letter from Hitler, written after the fact under pressure from the Minister of Justice. It was neither a command nor an edict; it 'authorized' the killing. Hitler delegated the implementation and monitoring of the new political task to two of his closest personal advisors, Dr Karl Brandt, in charge of health policy, and Reichsleiter Philipp Bouhler, responsible for domestic policy issues. Of course, neither was able to complete his new tasks with the resources at his disposal. They were thus forced to delegate work further, taking advantage of traditionally available institutions, especially the Medical Administration, at that time still located within the Ministry of the Interior. They also created a new, small special bureaucracy at Tiergartenstrasse 4 in Berlin (hence the code name 'Operation T-4').

Hitler's letter of authorization was vaguely worded and did not place any limitations on the plans of the various committees. Rather, it set free existing planning energy, ambition, and practical imagination. The scope of the 'operation', selection criteria, and long-term goals were decided by those who had planned it. As far as is known, Hitler intervened four times in the 'euthanasia' murders. He authorized the 'operation' in the summer and autumn of 1939; he prevented the promulgation of a completed euthanasia law for interesting, but in this context irrelevant, reasons; he interrupted the murders on 24 August 1941 for pragmatic reasons; and he allowed them to resume a short time later, albeit under the totally different conditions of war and in a more discreet, though soon all the more widespread, form.[44]

Of course, the specialists' arguments and pressure influenced the decision to murder mentally ill Germans, as did Hitler's motives and his willingness in principle – already documented in 1935 – 'to take up and carry out the euthanasia issue' in case of war, but not before.[45] In any case, it is certain that the views of Hitler and his advisors – the opinions of his personal physician Theo Morell are known – overlapped with those of the specialists. Together, they led to the decision to murder chronic care patients in psychiatric institutions. It is possible to distinguish which portion of the expert advice was conceptual and decisive for the 'Führer authorization'. Operation T-4 was thought out, written down, and justified – down to the last detail – by leading psychiatrists and administrative experts, under the supervision of Max de Crinis.[46] The individual aspects can be outlined as follows:

1. In July 1939, Hitler's personal physician Theo Morell drafted a memorandum, certainly after consultation with Hitler. It stated:

> ultimately this concerns the notion of human rights. . . . There is something right about the notion, but it is wrong as a principle. A subjective right of this kind, with an unrestricted individual sphere, exists no more here than for property. . . . The pressing needs of the community cannot develop from a momentarily favourable situation; instead, they must be put aside for an extended period of time and, in particular, must take into account future options as well. Five thousand idiots at an annual cost of RM 2000 each equals RM 10 million per year. At 5 per cent interest, this corresponds to a capital reserve of 200 million.

Morell concluded that it was also necessary to 'evaluate the resulting availability of domestically grown foodstuffs and a certain reduction in demand for imports'.[47]

2. About thirty leading psychiatrists argued in July 1939 in a similar fashion, albeit from their expert perspective. According to the later testimony of Hans Hefelmann, who had organized the conference in the Reich Chancellery, the group reached the following consensus:

> One doctor's suggestion that curable cases be given better treatment than incurable ones was rejected by the others. The doctors also suggested a nurse–patient ratio of one to approximately three or four in serious cases and eight to ten in other cases; thus, in spite of the departures of nursing staff for military service, if euthanasia were administered to the most serious cases, it would ensure a peacetime level of therapeutic care for less severe cases.[48]

3. On 9 October 1939, physicians discussed the questions 'who and how?'. They also set the target number of murders that were to take place by 24 August 1941, marking the end of the first phase of the 'euthanasia' murders. The record of the meeting states that 'the figure [was] yielded by a calculation based on a ratio of 1000: 10:5:1. This means that of 1000 people, 10 require psychiatric treatment, five of these as in-patients. Of these, one patient will be involved in the euthanasia programme.'[49] According to these calculations, the target was initially to kill 60,000–70,000 chronically ill patients.

Viktor Brack coordinated the departments involved in the murders from Hitler's Chancellery, under the supervision of Brandt and Bouhler. He did not respond to the estimates as though he had strict orders from the Führer to kill as many people as possible. His closest associate, Hans Hefelmann, reported in 1961 on the reaction of coordinating officer Brack, who had long since been executed: 'Brack, who was initially very taken with the task he was given, had reservations after the doctors told him that about 60,000 patients were being considered for the operation; the necessary secrecy[50] appeared impossible with such a high figure.'[51]

On top of this came the well-documented complaints, which went on for years, by the Conference of Mayors (*Gemeindetag*), about the excessively high costs of institutional patients and the number of military hospital beds that the military medical inspector said would be needed in the case of war. When on 3 April 1940 Brack spoke to the assembled mayors in the *Gemeindetag* about the killings, he summarized all the major lines of reasoning that had emerged in the debate.

In notes on Brack's speech that happened to survive, it was written that

> in the many psychiatric hospitals in the Reich there are endless numbers of incurable patients of all kinds who are of no use to humanity. They take food away from the other healthy people and often require two or three times the care. The rest of the public must

be protected from them. Since measures are already needed today to preserve healthy people, it is all the more necessary to first eliminate these creatures, even if it is initially only to improve the care of curable patients in mental hospitals. The space thus made available is needed for all sorts of war-essential things: military and other hospitals, auxiliary clinics. Moreover, the operation greatly relieves the municipalities, since for each individual case the future costs of accommodation and care would be eliminated.[52]

The series of decisions that determined the course of Operation T-4 incorporated pragmatic goals of different kinds: clearing out institutional space for various purposes, reducing the social services budget, assuring the food supply in wartime, releasing medical personnel, better care of the mentally ill regarded as curable. A purely ideological explanation, such as a programmatically necessary 'cleansing of the German national body of everything of inferior worth', did not play any significant role in the actual decisions made. Ideology did, however, remain important in so far as it sufficiently undermined the moral and legal barriers in the minds of the perpetrators, serving as a justification for their murderous acts.

The actual organization of the murders was left to technocrats. They were the ones who determined the concrete course of their so-called 'operation' on the basis of comprehensible considerations of *realpolitik*. It is certain that the 'operation' was not carried out by spineless functionaries. At intermediate and lower levels, there were committed people involved who were convinced of the necessity and rightness of their actions. They did not view themselves as tools, but as active, recognized protagonists.

# Notes

1 See Heim, *passim*.
2 Express letter from Heydrich to the heads of the *Einsatzgruppen* of the security police on the 'Jewish question in the occupied territories', 21 September 1939, printed in FGM, 37ff.
3 Quoted in Krausnick, 52.
4 IMG, vol. 31, 230ff.
5 Pohl, 26.
6 Quoted in Krausnick, 53.
7 Heydrich, in FGM (my emphasis); on population shifting and the slowing down of evacuations, see also Heydrich's express letter to the heads of the *Einsatzgruppen*, 30 September 1939, reprinted in Pätzold, 241.
8 See Krausnick, *Einsatzgruppen*, 65ff.; Broszat, 30f.
9 Goebbels' diary, I/3, 609 (entry of 14 October 1939).
10 In a slightly different form, this occupation strategy also applied to the division of Yugoslavia in 1941. People classified as 'undesirable' in the annexed area of northern Slovenia were deported to the Belgrade region.
11 Muehlon, 142.

12 IMG, vol. 30, 95; quoted in Safrian, 88.
13 Quoted in Pohl, 49.
14 Quoted in FGM, 44.
15 Quoted in Aly and Heim, 204.
16 'New Jewish State in Poland,' *The Times* (24 October 1939).
17 Dieter Pohl wrote the following about the attempt to create ghettos in the district of Lublin:

> Ghettoization was begun in Chelm at the end of October (1940), and soon after, a ghetto was formed in Wisznice. In many cases, district heads tried in vain to set up a ghetto. This is indicated by extant files of the district head of Lublin-Land: 'The building of ghettos is still being hindered by the virtually insurmountable shortage of construction materials.' In Piaski, in particular, ghetto construction dragged on for months for this reason. The German administration also complained that Polish governors did not cooperate in building the ghettos, even though in some cases they, too, wanted to isolate the Jews. Thus comprehensive ghetto construction had not been completed by 1941.
>
> (p. 67)

18 My emphasis. It was precisely Hitler's deliberately vague wording that led to both excessive expectations and great concern on the part of the southeastern European Germans – among the Danube-Swabian population in Yugoslavia, for example (Wehler, 68f.). The German Foreign Office thus saw the need to make the following, widely circulated, 'secret' declaration on 13 December 1939:

> Regarding resettlement, we have been in contact only with Italy, Soviet Russia, Estonia, and Latvia. Additional resettlements are not urgent and are not under discussion. . . . Announcements in the press are not intended at this time, since we have a compelling interest in keeping debate on the resettlement as minimal as possible and not going into depth.
>
> (reprinted in Loeber, 159f.)

Representatives of the Ethnic German Liaison Office (Vomi) interpreted Hitler's speech with similar reserve (letter from the Vomi [signed by Rimann] 'on the resettlement issue', 18 October 1939; BAK R59/323, 116; see also Ernst von Weizsäcker's memorandum of 3 November 1939, Loeber, 149f.).
19 Reprinted in *Der großdeutsche Freiheitskampf* (Berlin, 1942), 67–100.
20 On the history and structure of this office, see Koehl, *passim*; Broszat, 62ff.; Aly and Heim, 125–87.
21 Kroeger, 41ff. See also Hehn, 75–87; relevant documents are reprinted in Loeber, 14–78.
22 Kroeger, 60. Of 750,000 Ukrainians in the Generalgouvernement, 'approx. 11,000 [were] resettled in the Soviet Union' within the scope of the Nazi–Soviet pact. At the same time, roughly 40,000 ethnic Ukrainians emigrated from the Soviet-annexed part of Poland to the German-occupied part of the country (Fritz Arlt, ed. *Die ukrainische Volksgruppe im Deutschen Generalgouvernement Polen* (Krakow, 1940), 32ff.; library of the Herder Institute in Marburg, 32/III/C/121).
23 Himmler's 'speech to the Bessarabian Germans in the Jahrhunderthalle in Breslau' on 2 March 1941 (my emphasis); BAK, NS/19/4008, p. 5 of the manuscript.

24 Eisenblätter, 24ff.; Frank diary, 60.
25 Frank diary, BAK, R52II/174, 34. As an incidental note, the Baltic Germans strongly resisted being settled in Lodz; in February 1940, Himmler said on the subject, 'In this regard it is often necessary to dictate what must be done' (speech of 29 February 1940, in Himmler, *Geheimreden*, 135ff.).
26 The environs of both Lodz and Sosnowiec had belonged to the Russian part of Poland until 1918. The Jews there were forced to remain in the newly created Polish state and were not allowed to opt to immigrate to Germany, as were the Jews in the formerly Prussian regions ceded to Poland in 1918.
27 On the unclear boundaries, see Frank diary, 60, 92, 111, 123, 151, 193, 197. On 3 November 1940, the dispute between Frank and Greiser was put aside for the time being; Frank diary, government meeting of 6 November 1940.
28 Meeting of Frank, Koppe, and others; Frank diary, 262. The city's name was changed on 12 April 1940, not of Hitler's own volition, but 'at the recommendation of Greiser', administrative and party head in the Warthegau (Goebbels diary, I/4, 71, entry of 13 March 1940).
   I have tried to use exclusively the spelling *Lodz,* commonly known and used until 1939, for the Polish city of *Łódź.* The spelling *Lodsch,* which was used for a short time in the autumn of 1939, has been changed in citations to *Lodz* without further mention. The name *Litzmannstadt* will be used in citations where it so appeared; in cases where the documents are cited not as direct quotes, but paraphrased, *Litzmannstadt* has been replaced by *Lodz.*
29 RGBl 1939/I, 2077. See Frank's sarcastic commentary on these regulations, 19 December 1941; Frank diary, 313f.
30 Note on a meeting on 21 September 1939 between Heydrich and office and *Einsatzgruppen* leaders; quoted in Pätzold, 239ff.
31 Heydrich's note of 29 September 1939 (my emphasis), reprinted in Pätzold, 240.
32 Report of 9 September 1939 by the chief of the RSHA, appendix 1 on the 'Transport of the ethnic German populations from Latvia and Estonia to Gotenhafen'; reprinted in Loeber, 122ff.
33 See Burrin, 73ff.
34 The foreign ministers of Italy (Ciano) and Germany (von Ribbentrop) negotiated this arbitral award on 2 November 1938, settling disputes between Czechoslovakia and Hungary on border and minority issues. The regions on the southern border of Slovakia and the Carpathian Ukraine, which were populated predominantly by Hungarians, were ceded to Hungary. In 1947 the peace treaty of Paris re-established the *status quo ante.*
35 Germany used this pact to confirm the Brenner Pass as the Italo-German border. The two powers agreed that their expansionist plans should be implemented, with neutrality of interests on both sides, in a southern and a northern 'greater region' (*Grossraum*), respectively, linked by an economic and military 'axis'.
36 Stuhlpfarrer, 63.
37 The Ethnic German Liaison Office (Vomi) was founded in 1936 by the NSDAP in order to better integrate ethnic Germans into Nazi policy. With the change in policy in 1939, it became *de facto* one of Himmler's many resettlement offices. In June 1941, the Vomi then officially became a main SS office.
38 Stuhlpfarrer, 38ff. This was not merely Lorenz's personal opinion, as indicated by the special relationship he had to the SS; Döscher, 116ff.
39 Draft authorization; BAK, R43/II/1412, 3ff.
40 'Erlass des Führers und Reichskanzlers über die Aufnahme der Volksdeutschen aus Südtirol in das Gebiet des Deutschen Reiches' (Edict of the Führer and Reich Chancellor on Receiving the Ethnic Germans from the South Tyrol into the Territory of the German Reich) (draft), ibid. 15f.

41 The draft was minimally revised again on 16 August 1939 after a consultation between Lammers and Himmler. Lammers intended to 'present it for implementation to the Führer as soon as possible' (letter from Lammers to Himmler, 17 August 1939, ibid. 17f.). On the history of the edict, see especially Stuhlpfarrer, 246–60; cf. also Broszat, 62ff.; Rebentisch, 163ff.

42 Letter from Lammers to Schwerin-Krosigk, 28 September 1939; BAK, R43/II/1412, 45.

43 Quoted in *Doc. Occ.*, vol. 5, 176ff. Himmler endeavoured in vain in summer 1940 to have the edict published and to give himself a positive right to carry out 'evacuations'. (See Reich Chancellery memo of 26 June 1940; BAK, R43/II/141, 509f.; Greifelt's draft edict [sent on 19 July 1940], ibid. 519ff.; Kleinschmidt's [DUT] memo of 13 July 1940 about a conversation with Greifelt; BAP, 17.02/146). Efforts to gain law-making rights for the RKF also failed initially (DUT memo of 28 August 1940; BAP, 17.02/217). Nevertheless, in addition to resettlement, discrimination against Eastern European slave labourers – varied, but to some extent grounded in law – was later regarded as an RKF activity. This included, for example, the 'classification of Poles and eastern labourers in the Reich, special wage and tax rates, limitation of marriage and sexual relations, residence restrictions, limited allotment of rationed consumer goods' (RKF progress report [end of 1942]; BAK, R49/26, 34).

44 See Aly, *Aktion T4*, 168–82. A well-documented example of the hollowness of such 'Führer Directives' is the 'special authorization' that Hitler issued on 19 September 1940 for extralegal abortions; see Aly, 'Medicine', 54–5. On the decision-making process of the 'euthanasia' murders, see also Aly, 'Hinweise', 195–204.

45 According to Hitler's autumn 1935 statement to Gerhard Wagner, then Reich Head Physician; cited in Schmuhl, 180ff.

46 De Crinis succeeded Karl Bonhoeffer at the Berlin Charité University Hospital, holding the most prominent German department chair, for psychiatry and neurology; at the same time, he worked as a security service agent and consulting psychiatrist for the Wehrmacht. As state secretary in the Reich Education Ministry, he was responsible for medical department appointment policy.

47 Quoted in Roth and Aly, 125ff.

48 Testimony by Hans Hefelmann; quoted in Aly, 'Progress', 157–8.

49 Quoted in Aly, 'Medicine', 37–8.

50 On the considerations that led Hitler to keep the operation secret, see Chapter 11, 'An open secret', pp. 243–5.

51 Testimony of 30 January 1961 by Hans Hefelmann, 8; Sta. Ansbach, 1 Js 1147/62 (supplementary file).

52 Quoted in Aly, *Aktion T4*, 50.

# 2

# 'Making room' for ethnic Germans

## Chronology: September 1939–April 1940

Introductory note: the following chronology covers the months from September 1939 to April 1940, when the Lodz ghetto was sealed off. It documents the 'interplay' (Eichmann) between the general policy of ethnic cleansing, on the one hand, and policy towards the Jews, on the other, clearly demonstrating how the intention of deporting Jews in the shortest possible time to the eastern border of the German sphere of influence collided with pressures arising, suddenly and with constantly renewed force, from the resettlement of ethnic Germans.

There is occasional divergence among the population figures – classified according to racial principles – provided by Nazi leaders or SS generals, calculated by demographers, and presented by those actually carrying out the resettlements. Thus the estimated or actual statistics on the Jews in the incorporated eastern territories, the Generalgouvernement and the city of Lodz, in particular, could fluctuate within a given time period by up to 50 per cent. This was a result, first of all, of contradictory interests that led various participants to either exaggerate or play down 'the problem', and second, of the empirical sources used by the German ethnocrats. Such inconsistencies are generally of minor significance to the analysis as a whole. Nevertheless, the figures are important as such; they provide insight into the protagonists' ideas and, as a rule, show the extraordinary discrepancy between planning, on the one hand, and implementation, on the other. The figures provided in the deportation plans were almost always far higher than the number of people actually deported; the time frames set out in the plans were almost always exceeded; and many plans were never carried out at all, or were delayed and modified to such an extent that they barely resembled the planners' original intentions.

**18 September 1939:** In Moravská Ostrava, the commander of the security police in Prague, Franz Walter Stahlecker, holds out the prospect of the 'deportation of several thousand Jews to Galicia [the region around Krakow]'.[1]

**21 September:** Heydrich issues guidelines for concentrating the Jewish population in occupied Poland and outlines a plan for the creation of a Jewish reservation east of Krakow.

**22 September:** Heydrich informs the supreme commander of the army that all Poles living in the formerly Russian areas of Poland are to be 'gradually pushed to the east' and that a 'Jewish reservation' is to be created near Krakow, to which 'all Gypsies and other undesirables' will also be deported.[2]

**27 September:** Creation of the Reich Security Main Office (*Reichsicher-heitshauptamt*, RSHA) under Heydrich's leadership.[3]

**28 September:** Secret German–Soviet protocol signed on the 'resettlement' of the ethnic German population from the Soviet sphere of influence.

**29 September:** Hitler discusses his future plans for Poland with his closest associates. The German-controlled area is to be divided 'into three strips'. 'All Jewry [including those from the Reich] as well as all in any way unreliable elements' are to be concentrated 'between the Vistula and the Bug'. An 'impregnable eastern rampart – even stronger than in the west' is to be erected along the Vistula. Beyond the current borders, 'a broad belt of Germanization and colonization' is planned, and 'a Polish "state entity" [*Staatlichkeit*]' is to be erected between the territory of deportation and the zone of settlement. According to Hitler, 'The future will tell whether the belt of settlement can be shifted further over decades.'[4] After only a few weeks, the border of the 'settlement belt' will already shift much farther east than is intended at this time.

**6 October 1939:** Eichmann's superior, Heinrich Müller, authorizes him to conduct talks with the Gau leadership in Katowice 'Re: the deportation of 70–80,000 Jews from the Kattowitz district'.[5]

**6–7 October:** Hitler publicly declares his intention to reorder 'ethnographic relationships' in Europe with the help of resettlements, and also, in this connection, to seek a 'settlement of the Jewish problem'. He assigns Heinrich Himmler the task of planning and coordinating the new ethnopolitics, making him 'Reich Commissioner for the Consolidation of German Nationhood' (*Reichskommissar für die Festigung deutschen Volkstums*, RKF).

**9 October:** The Reich Ministry of the Interior distributes registration forms to all German psychiatric institutions to compile a list of potential 'euthanasia' victims. On the same day, a group of leading psychiatrists determines that roughly 70,000 patients should be murdered.

On the 'transfer of the Baltic German population from Latvia and Estonia to Gotenhafen',[6] Heydrich notes that, because of the resettlements, a segment of the city's Polish population – the figure later mentioned is 40,000 people – 'is to be deported without delay to the eastern parts of the Polish regions occupied by German troops'.[7]

**10 October:** Franz Walter Stahlecker, commander of the security police and SD in Prague, predicts 'very gratifying prospects for the solution of the Jewish question in Austria' in a letter to Reich Commissioner Bürckel in Vienna: 'There is reason to hope that a large number [of Austrian Jews] can be deported' and thus 'this issue can shortly be resolved once and for all'.[8] At this point, some 80,000 people of Jewish extraction are still living in Austria.

**11 October:** Instead of a Jewish reservation 'east of Krakow', one is now planned south of Lublin.[9] The first deportations are to be started immediately and a 'report issued' on them, after which there will be a pause 'until the general deportation of the Jews is ordered'.[10]

**12 October:** Hitler signs an edict 'on the administration of the occupied Polish territories'. In it, without establishing the date of implementation or the location of the borders, he states that 'the territories occupied by German troops will be under the control of the Generalgouverneur for the occupied Polish territories, if they are not incorporated into the German Reich'.[11] In the same edict, which goes into force on 26 October, Hans Frank is appointed Generalgouverneur.

**13 October:** The head of the Reich Criminal Investigation Office, Arthur Nebe, inquires of Eichmann 'when he [can] send the Berlin Gypsies' to the planned reservation.[12] Heydrich forms the Central Immigration Office Northeast (*Einwandererzentralstelle Nord-Ost*, EWZ). It is responsible for the 'racial screening', naturalization, and initially also the temporary housing of German settlers. Martin Sandberger is appointed head of the EWZ.[13]

**15 October:** The German Reich and Estonia conclude a resettlement agreement. Pursuant to this agreement, Estonian Germans – a total of 12,868 people – are resettled by ship between 18 October and 15 November 1939.

**16 October:** Eichmann assumes that the deportation of the Jews from Moravská Ostrava, Vienna, and Katowice to the Generalgouvernement will begin immediately, while for those from the 'Old Reich' [i.e., Germany within its 1937 borders] it will not begin for another three to four weeks.[14]

**17 October:** Hitler tells the supreme commander of the Wehrmacht, Wilhelm Keitel, that 'any signs of a consolidation of the situation in Poland must be quashed. The "Polish economy" [meaning "mismanaged economy"] must flourish. The leadership of the region must enable us to cleanse the Reich territory, as well, of Jews and Polacks. Cooperation with new Reich Gaus (Posen and West Prussia) only for resettlement purposes (cf. Himmler assignment).'[15]

**18 October:** With a view to the creation of a 'Jewish reservation', 901 Jews from Moravská Ostrava are deported to Nisko, south of Lublin. Eichmann's colleague Brunner notes, regarding the deportation of Vienna Jews that would begin two days later, 'The resettlement operation [begins] with the first transport from Vienna's Aspang train station on 20 October 1939 at 2 o'clock a.m. with 1000 Jews fit for work. . . . Further transports leave regularly every Tuesday and Friday with 1000 Jews each. . . . From the fourth transport on, entire families will be assigned to the transports. . . . Gypsies located in the Ostmark [Austria] will be included in the entire resettlement operation, in special cars.'[16]
Resettlement of the Baltic Germans begins the same day.

**19 October:** In his capacity as plenipotentiary for the Four-Year Plan, Göring creates the Main Trusteeship Office in the East (*Haupttreuhandstelle Ost*, HTO). This agency administers, transfers, liquidates, and sells the assets 'forfeited to confiscation [*der Beschlagnahme verfallen*]' in the incorporated eastern territories,[17] including the property of all Jews living there and that of the expelled, escaped, arrested, or murdered Poles. This is used to compensate ethnic German settlers for property they have left behind and to finance the various resettlement offices at no cost to the state.

**20 October:** Deportation of 912 Jews from Vienna to Nisko. This is followed on 24 October by a 'partial transport' from Moravská Ostrava, which, however, never reaches its goal, as the deportations are abruptly halted. The interruption in the 'emigration operation to Poland'[18] is expected to last until all Baltic, Galician, and Volhynian Germans are resettled – until February 1940, according to plan.
Nevertheless, on 20 and 27–28 October, two more transports with a total of 2500 Jews leave Katowice for Nisko. Fifteen hundred Jewish men and women from Sosnowiec are to be deported subsequently, to the same destination. Although all preparations have been made and the intended deportees already placed in an assembly camp, this transport is also cancelled at the last minute.[19]

**21 October:** Representatives of the German and Italian governments sign a resettlement agreement. They set 31 December 1942 as the final deadline. By the end of 1939, 86 per cent of ethnic German South Tyroleans – roughly 200,000 people – have opted for resettlement in the Reich.

By the first half of October, Himmler has selected the Polish Beskids as the location of a 'group settlement area' for the South Tyroleans. For this reason, the planned Jewish reservation is suddenly no longer to be established southeast of Krakow (in the foothills of the Beskids), but instead south of Lublin.

**26 October:** Hans Frank takes office in Krakow as Generalgouverneur. The precise borders of his realm are still not defined. On the same day, an 'Edict on the Introduction of Forced Labour for the Jewish Population in the Generalgouvernement' is issued 'to take effect immediately'.[20]

**30 October:** In line with the German–Latvian resettlement agreement signed on this day, 48,868 Latvian Germans are brought out by ship from 7 November to 15 December and temporarily housed around their destination ports, Gdynia ('Gotenhafen'), Szczecin (Stettin), and Świnoujście (Swinemünde). For this purpose, the psychiatric hospitals in the area around the port cities are cleared and several thousand patients murdered.[21]

The same day, Himmler orders the deportation, in the coming four months, of all Jews – that is, 550,000 people – from the annexed western Polish provinces, all Congress Poles from the province of Danzig–West Prussia,[22] and in addition 'an as yet undetermined number of especially hostile Poles' from the other areas.[23] Himmler estimates a million people in all. The German, Czech, and Austrian Jews and Gypsies are not mentioned, as a result of the new priorities of settlement policy.

**1 November 1939:** First meeting between Ulrich Greifelt (chief of the newly formed RKF staff headquarters), Ernst Fähndrich (head of the 'Human Deployment' Department of the RKF), Otto Ohlendorf (head of the domestic SD), Hans Ehlich (SD), and Martin Sandberger (SD).

The higher SS and police chiefs are named Gau representatives of the RKF,[24] and in this capacity are responsible for 'transport and accommodation of Baltic Germans arriving on ship transports, from port to final accommodation'.[25]

The same day, the higher SS and police chief in Krakow, Friedrich Wilhelm Krüger, states, according to Frank's diary, 'In the eastern region, between the Vistula and the Bug, a particularly heavy concentration of Jews would emerge, about which the Wehrmacht has misgivings. This makes it necessary to take the 22,000 ethnic Germans east of the Vistula out of the region.'[26] This will occur in autumn 1940 – 'after the grain harvest'.

**3 November:** Himmler is forced to concede that the Baltic Germans will first have to be accommodated in winter quarters in Pomerania, West Prussia, and the Warthegau, as his staff does not feel capable of organizing the 'clearing' of homes, farms, and businesses at the same pace as the 'home to the Reich' programme is progressing.[27] Himmler forms the German Resettlement Trusteeship Company (*Deutsche Umsiedlungs-Treuhandgesellschaft mbH*, DUT). The company serves as the RKF's in-house bank, responsible for the 'legal settlement of the returnees' assets' – that is, appraising the value of property left behind, determining compensation, and distributing business loans.[28] Such loans are made with the help of property and money confiscated by the HTO.

**8 November:** Wilhelm Koppe, the Higher SS and Police Chief in Posen, and his Krakow colleague Friedrich-Wilhelm Krüger conclude a 'basic agreement' on future resettlement.[29]

Bruno Streckenbach (chief of the Sipo and the SD in Krakow and confidant of Heydrich) explains, 'on the basis of a sketch indicating the expected sizes of the groups of ethnic Germans to be resettled and Poles to be evacuated', that 'the resettlement and evacuation must be accomplished on a different basis [than] Himmler had initially intended'. This means they are first to be aimed solely at the exigencies arising from the process of 'making room' for the ethnic German settlers. That is, the Jews are only to be removed if this appears useful to achieving that goal.[30]

In addition to the Baltic Germans, Streckenbach announces, an additional 150,000 settlers are to be expected in the near future – from Eastern Galicia, Volhynia, and the Lublin region. The removal of the 300,000 Jews living in the Lodz area is not yet planned at this time. His express words are that the city of Lodz, which has not yet been definitely assigned to the Reich Gau of Posen (that is, the Warthegau), 'is for now not yet to be taken into account in the evacuation, not even with regard to Jews'.[31]

The same day, Himmler issues an edict that 'all Jews who are evacuated in the near future from the former Polish parts of the German Reich territory' are to be 'brought east of the Vistula'.[32]

**9 November:** The Kutno–Lodz region is joined to the annexed Warthegau in order to make additional room for the settlement of Baltic Germans. This quadruples the number of Jews to be deported from the Warthegau to the now-reduced Generalgouvernement, to about 400,000 people.[33]

**11 November:** Koppe, the Higher SS and Police Chief in the Warthegau, sets up two special offices, one 'for local housing and occupational placement for Baltic and Volhynian Germans' and one 'for the evacuation and deportation of the Poles and Jews in the Generalgouvernement'.[34] The latter soon bears the title 'Office for the Resettlement of Poles and Jews' and is renamed 'Central Resettlement Office' (UWZ) in April 1940.[35]

**12 November:** At Koppe's direction, fewer than one-third of the people whose expulsion Himmler ordered only 13 days ago are to be deported by 28 February: 'initially 200,000 Poles and 100,000 Jews'. This expulsion affects, above all, the residents of the cities of Posen, Lodz, Gniezno, and Inowrocław, because these are cities preferred for settlement by Baltic Germans. In selecting Poles, according to the order, 'the aspect of acquiring housing and workplaces for the immigrant Reich and ethnic Germans [has to be] borne in mind in every respect'. 'Manual labourers, clerks and civil servants', as long as they are not considered criminal or particularly active politically, will be 'excluded from the evacuation, as they are urgently needed as workers.' According to Koppe, 'We are striving to begin the deportation operation several days before the Baltic Germans begin to arrive.'[36]

A draft of the order states, 'The aim should be to couple the deportation operation directly with the immigration of Reich Germans, Baltic Germans, Warsaw Germans, Volhynian Germans and Galician Germans.' Should there be delays in the transport of Poles to the waiting scheduled trains, the danger of 'gaps and delays' as a result 'should be effectively addressed by substituting the Jewish residents of the Warthegau, including the city of Lodz, in order to guarantee continuing deportations'.[37]

**13 November:** Koppe prohibits Jews and Poles in the Warthegau from changing residences.[38]

**16 November:** The Soviet Union and the German Reich conclude an agreement on resettlement of ethnic Germans from the areas of eastern and southeastern Poland annexed by the Soviet Union (Narev area, Volhynia, Eastern Galicia).

**23 November:** Directive on 'Identification of Jews and Jewesses' in the Generalgouvernement.

**24 November:** Decree by Koppe on 'deportation of Jews from the Wartheland Reichsgau'. According to this edict, 'half Jews' count as Jews (in contrast to the Nuremberg Laws), and Aryan wives are also to be deported 'if they do not wish to be separated definitively from their families'. Jewish councils of elders are to 'immediately submit a list of local Jews in multiple copies'.[39]

**28 November:** Heydrich divides the resettlement programme into a short-term and a long-term plan. Eighty thousand people are initially to be expelled in December within the scope of the first short-term plan.[40] In the period from 1 to 17 December, 87,838 people are in fact deported from the annexed western Polish provinces to the Generalgouvernement within the framework of this plan, including all Jews living in the western – that is, the former Prussian – part of the Warthegau.[41] The bureaucratic short-hand for the entire 'operation' is 'Re: settlement of Baltic and Volhynian Germans and evacuation of Poles and Jews'.

**29 November:** According to an edict issued by Himmler, Jews and Poles who cross back into the Generalgouvernement at an uncontrolled border point are to be 'summarily executed'.[42] The Poles are not aware of this instruction, but the elders of the Jewish community are 'informed verbally'. It is aimed primarily against the Jews.[43]

**End of November:** Around this time, a 'long-term plan for resettlement in the eastern provinces' comes into being, probably out of Department III of the RSHA. It contains the following aims, later often revised, yet also retained, even in the modified form:

> The goal of resettlement is the depolonization and de-Jewing of the German eastern provinces. To avoid economic harm to the eastern provinces, it must take place in the following stages:
>
> 1. First of all, all Jews and those Poles who have stood out as political leaders are to be deported to the Generalgouvernement. (Compulsory service for men from 18 to 60 years of age.)
> 2. Poles residing in the eastern provinces are to be subjected to a racial screening.
> 3. In order to weaken the Polish nation [*Polentum*], the need for labour in the Reich, especially for farm workers, should be satisfied primarily by racially sound Poles who shall be utilized in the Reich for the duration. This selection should also be carried out in the Generalgouvernement.
> 4. Qualified workers, starting with skilled labourers, artisans and shopkeepers and extending to civil servants at the railroad, post office, in construction, etc., in so far as they seem racially sound and assimilated, should be replaced little by little by comparable workers from the Reich.[44]
> 5. A certain number of Polish workers should remain behind in the eastern provinces for menial duties, thereby guaranteeing labour for industry and agriculture.
> 6. Poles who cannot be used in the Reich or the eastern provinces are to be deported to the Generalgouvernement.[45]

**4 December 1939:** Arthur Greiser, Gauleiter of the Wartheland, appoints Koppe 'the party comrade alone responsible' for all resettlement measures. 'The pace of the evacuations that are becoming necessary, on the one hand', according to the justification, 'and the speed with which resettlement measures for the Baltic Germans are being implemented, on the other', require 'a central concentration of all offices of the party and state that are active in this area'.[46]

**10 December:** The provincial governor responsible for Lodz drafts the first plan for 'concentration of all Jews in a sealed ghetto'. He views the measure as both provisional and necessary. Because 'immediate evacuation [is] not possible', he closes with the following declaration of intentions:

> The construction of the ghetto is of course only a transitional measure.
> I shall determine the time when and means with which the ghetto, and thus the city of Lodz, is to be purged of Jews. In any case, the final goal must be that we burn away this plague spot completely.[47]

**13 December:** The resettlement authorities in Posen set the beginning of the second short-term plan for 21 December.[48] In accordance with this plan, 220,000 Poles and Jews are to be resettled in January and February 1940. They are the ones who would remain of the 300,000 named by Koppe on 12 November, after 'fulfilment' of the as yet uncompleted first short-term plan – that is, the deportation of 80,000 people.[49]

At this time, Himmler declares that, in addition to the already completed resettlement of Estonian and Latvian Germans and immediately following the resettlement of Galician and Volhynian Germans, the home-to-the-Reich programme for some 50,000 Lithuanian Germans will begin on 15 March 1940.[50] By February, this resettlement will already have been postponed 'until further notice'.[51]

**17–23 December:** On Himmler's instructions, a first census is carried out in the 'newly incorporated eastern territories'. Among the reasons given for this census is the following: 'Questions relating to occupation, national affiliation, mother tongue and religion are intended to facilitate the resettlement of national groups.'[52]

**19 December:** Consultation among department heads at the Reich Security Main Office on 'the question whether a Jewish reservation in Poland should be created . . . or if the Jews should be sent to [be spread throughout] the future Polish Gouvernement'.[53] The prevailing view is that a very provisional reservation should be created, to be used as 'pressure' so that 'perhaps, with the end of the war, the question of a worldwide solution [of the Jewish question] [can be] raised'.[54]

On the same day, Heydrich appoints Adolf Eichmann 'special officer' for the 'clearing of the eastern provinces,[55] i.e., for the central processing of security police matters in the implementation of the evacuations in the eastern territories'.[56]

**21 December:** Heydrich presents his staff with a revised second short-term plan drawn up by Eichmann. He makes it clear that the conflict between the goal of deporting the Jews, on the one hand, and of 'freeing up space for ethnic Germans', on the other, has not yet been settled. In contrast to the 13 December version, instead of 220,000 Poles and Jews, 'roughly 600,000 Jews [will be] deported' and their entire assets confiscated.[57] In Heydrich's words, the 'clearing operation, working from the north and from the west in the direction of the territory of the Generalgouvernement, is to comb, as it were, the new eastern German Gaus'.[58] The expulsion is to be completed in April and to 'begin around 15 January 1940'. From this point on, the Reich Ministry of Transport is to make trains 'available for deportation of some 5000 Jews daily from the eastern Gaus'. 'Deferrals of deportations are not to be undertaken, owing to basic considerations and in view of the sufficient number of unemployed Poles available. Instead, attention must be paid to clearing the areas entirely of Jews.' The deportees are not, as was discussed only two days previously, to be taken to a Jewish reservation of Lublin, but instead are to be distributed among the districts of the Generalgouvernement. 'Should opportunities be available, . . . male Jews between approximately 18 and 60 are to be assigned to work brigades there and utilized accordingly.'[59] About further ideas, Heydrich writes the same day that, since the 'purge of the German East' would be 'carried out [according to] a plan thought out in all its details', 'a long-term plan [had been] drafted in the matter of clearing space'. 'This long-term plan will be divided where necessary into several short-term plans.'[60]

**23 December:** The first trainload of Volhynian German settlers arrives in Lodz. By 9 February 1940, a total of 128,000 Volhynian and Galician Germans are transported to Germany from former east Poland, now annexed by the Soviets. Because at first there is no accommodation available in the Warthegau, 101,690 settlers are temporarily assigned to 'camps in the Old Reich' – especially in Saxony and the Sudetenland.[61] (Originally, they were to have been housed 'in winter camps' in the Generalgouvernement and then settled in the Warthegau in spring, but Frank refused to accept this as early as November, owing to the food supply situation and the fact that the Generalgouvernement was crowded with refugees.)[62]

**4 January 1940:** Meeting chaired by Eichmann 'on the evacuation of Jews and Poles in the immediate future'. Participants include representatives of the security police from the annexed western Polish provinces as well as representatives of the HTO and the ministries of the economy, transport and finance. Those assembled agree that 'immediate evacuation of Jews' should be planned for the incorporated eastern territories. In Eichmann's words, this is 'urgent', will occur 'at Himmler's instructions', and will affect, according to the calculations of the 'responsible officer', 350,000 people – that is, 250,000 fewer than announced by Heydrich on 21 December. Furthermore, it does not concern only Jews, again in contrast to Heydrich's wishes only two weeks earlier. According to Eichmann, in the Warthegau and in the Danzig–West Prussia Gau, 90,000 Poles have been 'chosen for immediate evacuation . . . in order to make room for ethnic Germans from Galicia and Volhynia'. However, Eichmann adds the caveat that the date for the start of the deportations cannot yet be announced, and certainly cannot be expected before 25 January.[63]

**5 January:** There is now a considerable shortage of labour in the Reich – especially in agriculture. The first slave labourers are thus already being transferred from the Generalgouvernement to Germany. Therefore, Otto Ohlendorf (Reich Security Main Office) and Helmut Kästner (Reich Ministry of Labour) agree to change the process of resettlement of Poles in the future. Those removed from annexed western Poland are no longer to be deported, as a general rule, to the Generalgouvernement; instead, depending on need and, as already included in the long-term plan of late November, on ability and 'racial suitability', they will be selected for labour in the Reich.[64] As a result of this agreement, a meeting takes place on 11 January between representatives of local employment offices and the RSHA (Ehlich) in Posen. The subject is the problem of 'double resettlement':[65] some of the Poles deported from the annexed areas of Poland to the Generalgouvernement are immediately deported further into the Reich for slave labour (subjected, that is, to a 'double resettlement'). This makes double railway journeys necessary – something to be avoided. From now on, the functionaries of the UWZ will deport to the Generalgouvernement not only people stripped of all their worldly goods and means of production, but also, increasingly, people not entirely, if at all, fit for work.

**8 January:** Himmler once again issues instructions that 'the evacuation of all Jews' from annexed western Poland is to be 'accomplished with urgency'.[66]

**9 January:** In contrast to Eichmann's announcement on 4 January, the RKF in the Danzig–West Prussia Gau, where very few Jews live, intends to evacuate 400,000 Poles as quickly as possible.[67]

The same day, the representative of the RKF in Posen writes to his colleagues at the UWZ:

> The Baltic Germans intended for Lodz are already on their way to Posen, so that the homes in Lodz must be available in a few days. The evacuation of Jewish homes and the transfer of homeowners to the [not yet sealed off] ghetto must therefore take place immediately.[68]

**11 January:** Thirty-seven thousand Jews from Inowrocław and 280,000 from the Lodz region are 'earmarked for evacuation'.[69]

**12 January:** Meeting with the responsible officials in the Reich Transport Ministry on resumption of the deportations, which were halted on 17

December. According to a proposal by Koppe, the higher SS and police chief in Posen, two trains daily should 'depart carrying 1000 people each, specifically Poles from Posen and Jews from Lodz, in order to make room for arriving Baltic and Volhynian Germans'.[70]

**14 January:** According to information from Koppe, the resettlement of 600,000 Jews will not begin on 15 January, as planned by Heydrich, but on 1 February 1940. No deferments are to be granted Jews for economic or other reasons. At the same time, Koppe hints at a modification of the plan:

> The second short-term plan, which is now coming into force, basically includes only the deportation of the Jews. The deportation of Poles is planned under the second short-term plan only to the extent that the deportation operation is directly connected with the arrival of Baltic and Volhynian Germans.[71]

**16 January:** Martin Sandberger, head of the Central Immigration Office, stipulates, 'attracting Baltic Germans to Schneidemühl is again to be strongly encouraged'.[72] On 12 March, 160 Jewish men, women, and children from the city, which belonged not to the incorporated eastern territories, but to the Old Reich, are deported to the eastern General-gouvernement.[73]

Also on 16 January, representatives of the Wehrmacht inform representatives of the RKF and the Generalgouvernement of plans to build huge military training grounds, and of the resettlement of several hundred thousand people that this will necessitate.[74]

**17 January:** Ehlich and Eichmann discuss an 'interim solution to the second short-term plan', which is soon after implemented as the 'interim plan'. From Ehlich's notes on the meeting, it emerges that, so far, 'some 25,000 Baltic Germans [have been] brought to the Warthegau'. 'Approximately 30,000 Baltic Germans in Pomerania' are still housed in camps because no suitable homes could as yet be cleared for them, nor is a single farm yet available for the first Volhynian and Galician Germans now arriving. 'This means', according to Eichmann and Ehlich, 'that space must be made, no matter what, in the form of an evacuation.' But here they encounter obstacles. The German administration in the General-gouvernement 'refuses to take in additional Poles and Jews'. Only the commander of the security police and the SD, Bruno Streckenbach, 'sees the necessity of urgent evictions in the Warthegau', and – 'despite the difficulties with which individual district heads will counter the plan' – is willing to take in 40,000 people at short notice. But it is uncertain that even this minimal project can be achieved, as the Reich Ministry of Transport has 'for now refused any transports' owing to a shortage of locomotives.

According to his calculations, at this time Eichmann must still house some 150,000 German 'returnees'; to do so, in accordance with the RKF's stipulations, he must remove double that number of Jews and Poles. Thus the interim plan, with an 'eviction figure of 40,000, [is] under all circumstances to be viewed only as a pressure valve for extreme emergencies, since it would only make room for roughly 20,000 ethnic Germans'. In closing, Ehlich and Eichmann conclude, 'the difficulties arising from the interplay between settling the ethnic Germans and evacuating the Poles and Jews will have to be resolved at the meeting already arranged by C. ['Chef', or boss – i.e., Heydrich]'.[75] The meeting will take place on 30 January.

**18 January:** Representatives of those brought 'home to the Reich' report from the temporary camps for Baltic Germans in Posen,

> The hope of finally finding work in Posen is immediately destroyed for most people. The people, lacking any more exact knowledge of the overall situation, feel themselves 'at the mercy of' the camp commandant. . . . The worst discipline is in the Gneisenaustrasse camp; the camp commandant goes through the rooms armed with a riding crop. The old ladies shudder; the young people are rebellious. The small camp on Bossestrasse is all right. Occupants (from Windau) are in depressed spirits, but quiet and patient. Parkstrasse camp (from Riga) – restless. Much unjustified grumbling. Ziethen camp – overcrowded. Mood nevertheless quite good. Camp leadership good. Hochstrasse camp – overcrowded. Mood bad. Martinstrasse camp: occupants (Riga suburbs) undisciplined and demanding. Camp leadership excellent. Töpfergasse camp – okay. . . . The camp on Pestalozzistrasse and the one on Naumannstrasse are occupied, at the moment, by Volhynian Germans. The camps are disinfected before the Baltic Germans enter them.[76]

**19 January:** Statement of principles by Frank on a new economic policy in the Generalgouvernement. Under this policy, quite in contrast to Hitler's intentions as announced on 17 October 1939, the country will no longer be simply treated as booty and robbed; instead, 'new means of production' will be built up and placed 'in the service of the Reich'.[77]

At the same time, the staff of the UWZ agrees on a provisional alternative to deportation to the Generalgouvernement, which is now being refused by the authorities there. Since 'the number of Baltic Germans to be settled in Lodz has been fixed at 15,000', the 'Office for Baltic Placement' establishes an evacuation office 'to free up suitable Jewish homes'. The Jews thus robbed of their homes will 'be placed for now in Lodz', in a northern section of the city, 'which is supposed to become a ghetto'.[78]

**20 January:** Koppe announces the issuance of an 'interim plan', so that 'the number of Poles and Jews who must give up homes and jobs for the placement of Baltic Germans can be deported, according to the guidelines provided here'. The second short-term plan – now once again for the purpose of the originally intended deportation of 600,000 Jews – would be carried out *after* that.[79] For this reason, representatives of the UWZ in Lodz make preliminary preparations for a 'future Jewish evacuation' to the Generalgouvernement.[80]

**22 January:** Reporting on a visit to Lodz and the opportunities for settlement there, a representative of the Baltic Germans writes, 'Seven hundred apartments of two to three rooms each are available for immediate occupancy. A reconstruction plan exists. The Jewish quarter is to be completely levelled. In addition, a major cleansing operation will be undertaken.'[81]

**23 January:** Eichmann reports that the commencement of the evacuation of Poles and Jews from the Warthegau planned for 25 January will have to be postponed, as a corresponding scheduling conference will not be held until the 28th of the month in Leipzig. (In fact, it is held on 26 and 27 January.) Eichmann explains this as follows: because railway lines are overloaded, the evacuation transports 'from Lodz can begin no earlier than 15 February, and those from other loading stations no earlier than 5 February', since 'difficulties have arisen' in Lodz 'as a result of the Volhynian transports', which require 16 trains a day.[82]

The same day, Konrad Meyer, head of the planning department of the RKF, proposes a 'general plan' for settlement of the incorporated eastern territories. As 'a goal that can be achieved in the coming years', he demands that 'first of all . . . 3.4 million Poles be deported little by little'.[83] This goal describes the 'long-term plan'. Meanwhile, Meyer ascribes the deportation of the Jews to the first part of the short-term plan: in a draft for the future, he assumes 'that the entire Jewish population of this area, roughly 560,000 people, is already evacuated, or will leave the area in the course of this winter'.[84]

**24 January:** The mayor of Lodz complains of 'unannounced transports of Jews' from the surrounding towns, and telegraphs the UWZ: 'Refuse acceptance, as accommodation impossible because of settlement of Volhynian Germans and Balts.'[85]

**25 January:** Himmler travels to Przemyśl to receive a trainload of Volhynian Germans, and the next day holds a welcoming ceremony for the settlers.[86]

**26–27 January:** Train scheduling conference in Leipzig. The representatives of the Reich Ministry of Transport and the Reichsbahn find themselves unable, 'although good will is very much in evidence', to resume the resettlement transports – which were halted on 17 December – before 10

February. The reasons are as follows: '1. Volhynian operation;[87] 2. Coal transport; 3. Shortage of locomotives; 4. Shortage of personnel.' The representatives of the railway administration, in particular, do not feel capable of 'allowing transports to depart from Lodz', because of the strain on the railway stations.[88]

**30 January:** Meeting in the RSHA on resettlement of Jews, Poles, and Gypsies to the Generalgouvernement. Heydrich informs those present that, from now on, 800,000 to 1,000,000 Poles are to be sent to work in the Reich.[89] Furthermore, he announces that, within the scope of the 'interim plan', another 40,000 Poles and Jews are to be deported to the Generalgouvernement 'in the interests of the Baltic Germans', followed by 120,000 Poles, 'in the interests of the Volhynian Germans'. Heydrich announces that these 'evictions', which will soon be known as the 'second short-term plan', will start in March. Immediately afterwards – following further delay due to other priorities – 'the deportation of all Jews in the new eastern Gaus and 30,000 Gypsies from the Reich territory to the Generalgouvernement [will] take place', along with the deportation of 1000 (Reich German) Jews from Szczecin (Stettin).[90] The same day, Eichmann travels to Lodz.[91]

**31 January:** A representative of the Baltic Germans reports from Lodz:

> The evacuation is progressing very well there. By 12 February there will be an end to the eviction of Jews; then it will be the Poles' turn. Provision of jobs is also progressing well. In any case, one can only be advised to go to Lodz.[92]

**January:** First murders of German psychiatric patients in Grafeneck using poison gas.

**2 February 1940:** Ehlich submits a proposal to Heydrich on work methods at the not yet officially established Central Resettlement Office. The proposal, which is immediately approved, provides for the initial selection of roughly 100,000 Poles, who are to be expelled in order to settle Volhynian and Galician German farmers. Under the plan, the staff of the UWZ will send the Polish 'settlers' to camps for a short time, where they will subject them to 'a very thorough racial and political screening'. According to Ehlich, the important thing is to 'utilize the Resettlement Office as a filter in the evacuation process, in order to redirect the racially valuable portion of the Poles to the Old Reich', where they will be assimilated and later perhaps naturalized.[93]

**8 February:** In Lodz, beginning of 'the relocation of the Jews within the city, with the purpose of creating living space for Balts'. The protagonists see this as a prelude to the 'impending large-scale evacuation of Poles and Jews'.[94]

**10 February:** From now until 15 March, a total of 40,128 Poles and Jews will be transferred from western Polish cities and towns to the General-gouvernement, within the scope of the interim plan.[95] This will take place 'only to procure homes for and final settlement of the Balts'. At this point, resettlement for any other reason is expressly prohibited.[96]

**12 February:** Göring meets department heads to discuss the future of the Generalgouvernement. A report on the meeting includes the following:

> All important persons involved in the four-year plan were present, among them Reich Minister of Finance Schwerin-Krosigk himself, as well as the undersecretaries, and also the regents and Gauleiters of the areas bordering the Generalgouvernement. . . . Further, the General Field Marshal [Göring] attacked the uncontrolled resettlements in harsh words. He said no unannounced transports could be sent to the Generalgouvernement. . . . Concerning the resettlement of Poles, the General Field Marshal voiced the opinion that this resettlement was not at all urgent, because Poles are needed as farm workers. . . . Regarding resettlement of the Jews, the General Field Marshal said that this resettlement should be set in motion systematically.[97]

Himmler explains to the assembled officials that he has to 'make room' for the 200,000 already relocated Germans. In particular, 'Polish peasants in Posen [meaning the Warthegau], West Prussia and Southeast Prussia [must be] resettled.' He has already postponed the 'transfer' of approximately 40,000 Lithuanian Germans, 80,000–100,000 Bukovinian Germans, and 100,000–130,000 Bessarabian Germans.[98] However, some 30,000 ethnic Germans from the Lublin area, 'which is intended as the Jewish reservation', have to be taken into the 'new eastern Gaus', where space has to be made for them.[99]

**12–13 February:** Deportation of Szczecin Jews to the Lublin area in order to procure homes for Baltic Germans 'in maritime occupations'.[100]

**14 February:** The SS and police chief of the Lublin district, Odilo Globocnik, suggests a procedure for dealing with the evacuees: the 'Jews and Poles should feed themselves and be supported by their compatriots, as these Jews have enough. Should this not succeed, they should be allowed to starve.'[101]

**19 February:** Otto Wächter, head of the Krakow district, complains of the inadequate organization of the RSHA resettlement transports and of the fact that overwhelmingly 'unsuitable persons' are being sent 'for work details'.[102]

In a survey, district leaders suggest deporting an additional 137,413 Poles and 290,845 Jews to the Generalgouvernement.[103]

Heydrich writes to Göring on his conception of a 'solution of the Jewish question':

> Plans exist, as we know, to evacuate Jews living in the new eastern German territories in a short time to the Polish Generalgouvernement. Because normal emigration of the roughly 500,000 Jews living in these territories to such countries abroad as could be considered for Jewish immigration appears impossible at this time, the following guidelines must be followed in order to avoid complications:

> 1. Jews living in Reich territories, including the Protectorate of Bohemia and Moravia, cannot be evacuated to the Generalgouvernement at this time, aside from special cases.
> 2. Jews living in the new eastern German territories are to be denied permission to emigrate, as they will soon be deported to the Generalgouvernement.[104]

**25 February:** Rudolf Barth, director of the Office for the Resettlement of Poles and Jews in Lodz, proposes the creation of a concentration camp to which 20,000 people 'from the Jewish and Polish criminal population' in the city could be sent, in order 'to create additional room for the massive influx of Balts, ethnic Germans and Reich Germans'.[105]

**29 February:** Himmler explains to the Gauleiters the difficulties of his 'modern-day mass migration'. He emphasizes its unexpected commencement and gives his word – soon to be broken – not to begin the resettlement of Lithuanian, Bessarabian, and Bukovinian Germans until the conclusion of peace, although this had long since been agreed upon in the German–Soviet pact of 23 August 1930 and the secret protocol of 28 September 1939. He qualifies the goal he had supported only a few weeks previously of deporting western Polish Jews to the Generalgouvernement as quickly as possible:

> This year, the most I am planning – assuming that the war continues throughout the year – is to begin with the emigration of the Jews, to the extent it can be dealt with numerically. This, in turn, depends on the food supply options in the Generalgouvernement, and thus on the reception capacity and transport situation.[106]

**1 March 1940:** Arthur Greiser, the chief of the Warthegau, directs that Volhynian and Galician Germans be settled in the eastern Warthegau in order to 'form an impenetrable bastion of German people against the

Polish nation [*Polentum*]'. 'The settlement [is to] be accomplished in the shortest time possible.'[107]

**1–2 March:** In Lodz, Poles and Jews continue to be relocated within the city to 'create considerable living space in which to place Balts'.[108] A Baltic German observer reports, 'The housing issue [in Lodz] has been resolved better than in Posen. The evacuation of Jews and Poles is progressing according to plan; they are being removed in blocks and may only live in certain sections of the city.'[109]

**2 March:** Koppe orders preparations for the relocation of Polish farmers, in particular, to enable the resettlement of Volhynian and Galician Germans.[110]

**7 March:** Barth augments his proposal of 25 February. Now the planned concentration camp near Lodz is to hold not 20,000, but 30,000 inmates. He suggests fencing in the nearby village of Tuszyn and turning it into a concentration camp. Because all of the 'roughly 4000 Poles and Jews' living there are 'suited for evacuation', they should 'simply remain in Tutschin [Tuszyn] and be fenced in as well'.[111]

The same day, Hermann Krumey, head of the Lodz office of the (not yet so named) UWZ, writes to Eichmann that, with the end of the interim plan on 15 March, 'which included the deportation of 40,000 Poles and Jews, the majority of Balts [could be] placed in housing'. However, he says it had not yet been possible 'in all cases to place [the Balts] in jobs'. Krumey therefore demands the provision of 'at least five transport trains for the evacuation of Poles in the appropriate occupations. . . . Not until then can it be guaranteed that every last Balt is placed in his occupation or in a job that ensures him a livelihood.'[112] Eichmann categorically rejects this, as well as later deportation plans, since he cannot accomplish even the already promised deportations within the prescribed period.[113]

**8 March:** Creation of a ghetto in Warsaw is postponed, 'as the General-gouvernement is considering the idea of declaring the Lublin district a collection point for all Jews in the Generalgouvernement, especially the evacuated Jews and Jewish refugees arriving here'.[114]

As a consequence of the economic rationalization he himself has promoted, the head of the Main Trusteeship Office in the East (which is under Göring's charge) demands that Polish shopkeepers and artisans 'who will lose their livelihoods through the closing of their businesses in the near future' be resettled to the Generalgouvernement.[115] Eichmann rejects this idea as well, referring expressly to Göring's statements of 12 February. At the same time, he informs his staff in Posen that the resettlement train schedule for the second short-term plan cannot come into force before 1 April.[116]

**13 March:** Goebbels notes:

Lorenz reports moving scenes from the trek of the Volhynian Germans. This is indeed a great modern-day mass migration. Greiser tells of his resettlement operation. From 2000 Germans in Posen to 50,000. This is the only way to reach our goal. We must extend the borders of the Reich, both to the east and to the west.[117]

**21 March:** The mayor of Sosnowiec in eastern Upper Silesia declares, 'the evacuation of the Jews will be entirely completed this year, or no later than the coming year. At that time, the former ghetto will be an area empty of people.'[118]

**24 March:** At Frank's insistence, Göring prohibits 'until further notice, any evacuations' to the Generalgouvernement.[119]

**1 April 1940:** Actual start of the second short-term plan. Instead of the deportation of 600,000 Jews from annexed western Poland to occupied central Poland, planned as recently as December and January, the figure is now 130,000 Polish peasants and several thousand Jews (a total of 133,506 people). The purpose of this plan is no longer the 'solution of the Jewish question' in the incorporated eastern territories, but 'making room' for Volhynian and Galician German peasants. The plan will not be carried out until 20 January 1941, rather than within a few weeks, as originally intended.[120] Taken together, both short-term plans and the interim plan have by now resettled a total of 261,517 people.[121]

Also on 1 April, representatives of the Reich Ministry of the Interior, the Finance Ministry, the Food and Agriculture Ministry, the Office of the Four-Year Plan, and the RSHA meet together to discuss the planned ghetto in Lodz. 'The preliminary character of the ghetto [was] emphasized.' Those at the meeting agree to pressure Göring and Frank and to create an 'overall plan' to ensure 'that the Jews of Lodz are definitely the first to be evacuated'.[122]

**3 April:** At a meeting of the German Conference of Mayors [*Gemeindetag*] in Berlin, senior representatives of local governments in Germany are informed of the 'euthanasia' programme.[123]

**8 April:** Waldemar Schön, head of the Resettlement Department in Warsaw, once again urges a ghettoization of the Jews, as there is no longer any thought of 'planning the Lublin area as a collection point for the Jews'.[124]

**9 April:** Germany attacks Denmark and Norway.

**19 April:** The Gestapo in Katowice determines that

because Jewish property has largely been confiscated by the Trusteeship Office, the roughly 100,000 Jews in the Kattowitz administrative district are gradually becoming impoverished. All the funds of the organized Jewish communities have been exhausted. This situation has already made it necessary to close Jewish soup kitchens and welfare facilities. In the interests of maintaining order, and in particular for the sake of the health of Germans living in the area, it is absolutely necessary that the Jewish soup kitchens and welfare facilities be kept open until deportation and sanitary facilities maintained. . . . To avert the greatest dangers, an additional monthly sum of 100,000 Reichsmarks is urgently needed until the final deportation of the Jews of eastern Upper Silesia.[125]

**23 April:** Herbert Backe, state secretary in the Reich Ministry of Food and Agriculture, visits the Generalgouvernement and demands that, despite the prevailing shortages there, wheat, sugar, and meat be sent to Germany. Frank explains the supply situation to him and adds, 'I'm not at all interested in the Jews; whether or not they have anything to eat is the least important question to me.'[126]

**24 April:** Eichmann visits Posen.[127] The same day, the 'Office for the Resettlement of Poles and Jews' is renamed the 'Chief of the Security Police and the SD – Central Resettlement Office in Posen' (*Der Chef der Sicherheitspolizei und des SD – Umwandererzentralstelle in Posen*, UWZ). It is subordinate to Departments III and IV of the RSHA (Ehlich and Eichmann, respectively). The responsibility of this institution remains the 'evacuation of people of alien descent [*Fremdstämmigen*] in the Warthegau'. To accomplish this, the UWZ uses all local police and SD offices. The expenses of the UWZ are paid from the RKF budget – that is, from the property confiscated from the expellees.[128]

The Reich Security Main Office reduces emigration opportunities for Jewish men 'fit for military and labour service' to the point of a *de facto* prohibition. At the same time, it declares that 'until further notice, no deportation of Jews . . . from the Reich territory to the Generalgouvernement will take place'.[129]

**27 April:** Heydrich orders the deportation of 2500 'Gypsies' from western Germany to the Generalgouvernement (2800 are in fact deported).

**30 April:** The Lodz ghetto is sealed. The 160,000 Jews locked into it are to be deported to the Generalgouvernement by October of the same year. On 8 May, Werner Ventzki is named mayor of Lodz; until now, he has been head of the 'welfare' department in Poznań, responsible for 'care of the ethnic German population' and their 'housing in mass accommodations'.[130]

# Notes

1 Letter from the Gestapo in Moravská Ostrava, 19 September 1939, quoted in Safrian, 73.
2 Notes on discussion between Heydrich and von Brauchitsch, printed in *Okkupationspolitik in Polen*, 122ff.
3 The office was formed from the main office of the security police, the SD main office, the state secret police office and the Reich criminal justice office. It was headed by Heydrich.
4 Seraphim, 80ff.
5 Note by Eichmann, 6 October 1939, quoted in Safrian, 73.
6 This refers to Gdynia.
7 Draft by chief of the security main office on the relocation and settlement of Latvian and Estonian Baltic Germans, 9 October 1939, reprinted in Loeber, 122–30, here 127. Heydrich's short-term goal was more or less achieved with regard to the size of the deportation, but not with regard to its goal. Madajczyk writes on this (407):

> thus by 25 October 1939, 8000 residents of Gdynia had left for Warsaw; an additional 5000 went to Poznań [Posen], 10,000 to the environs of this city, and approximately the same number were settled in the area around Kielce. In all, 38,000 Poles were expelled in this way, and 50,000 remained for the time being.

8 Letter from Stahlecker to Bürckel, 10 October 1939, quoted in Safrian, 74.
9 Note by Theodor Dannecker (RSHA), 11 October 1939, quoted in Safrian, 74ff.; on the reasons, see below, 21 October.
10 Note by Günther, 11 October 1939, quoted in Safrian, 75.
11 RGBl., 1939/I, 2077f. See also Hitler's decree of 8 October 1939, ibid. 2042ff.
12 Telex from Nebe, quoted in Safrian, 77.
13 BAK, R43/II/1412, 53. The title 'Central Immigration Office Northeast' was later changed to 'Central Immigration Office', Staff Order No. 9 (signed by Tschierschky), 8 October 1940; AGK, EWZ/L/2, 7.
14 Telex from Eichmann to Nebe, quoted in Safrian, 77.
15 Record of the results of the 'Führer's meeting with head of the OKW on the future structuring of the Polish relationship with Germany (on 17 October 1939, evening)', 20 October 1939, reprinted in *Doc. Occ.*, vol. 6, 27ff.
16 Quoted in Longerich, 52ff.
17 Göring's decree is reprinted in *Okkupationspolitik in Polen*, 132ff.
18 Safrian, 80f.; Benz and Moser, 69.
19 Konieczny, 94.
20 Quoted in FGM, 203.
21 See Chapter 3, p. 70.
22 See Chapter 3, p. 67.
23 This refers to Directive I/II, which Himmler issued in his capacity as RKF, reprinted in FGM, 42ff.
24 This authority was changed on 10 August 1940, with the exception of the Danzig–West Prussia Gau. From then on, each Gauleiter was also the respective representative of the RKF. (Note by Ehlich, 15 August 1940; BAK, R69/493, 60ff.)
25 Ehlich note, 1 November 1939; BAK, R69/493, 8ff.
26 Frank diary, 56.

27 RKF Directive no. 4/II (signed by Himmler), 3 November 1939; AGK, UWZ/P/5, 3.
28 See the relevant correspondence between Keppler and Himmler in late autumn 1939; BDC, SL/55, SS-HO/2460.
29 Retrospective remarks by Koppe in his report on the resettlement of Poles and Jews, 26 January 1940, reprinted in FGM, 48ff.
30 See note 67 in this chapter.
31 Record of the results of a meeting with Frank on 8 November 1939 on 'Accommodation and settlement of ethnic Germans from the Baltic countries, Volhynia etc.; evacuation of the Jews and Congress Poles from the Old Reich, the Danzig and Posen Reichsgaus, and East-Upper Silesia and Southeast Prussia', reprinted in *Doc. Occ.*, vol. 8, 3ff.
32 Letter from Department IV, 8 November 1939, UWZ/P/104, 15.
33 See Chapter 1, p. 23.
34 Secret edict by Koppe as representative of the RKF, 11 November 1939; AGK, UWZ/P/5, 8.
35 Broszat, 87.
36 Memorandum by Koppe on 'deportation of Jews and Poles from the "Wartheland" Reichsgau', 12 November 1939, reprinted in FGM, 43ff.
37 Proposal by Rapp for Koppe's 'Order no. 1', which Koppe then issued in his new capacity as representative of the RKF; AGK, UWZ/P/95, 4–7.
38 The decree was reprinted in *Ostdeutscher Beobachter*, 15 November 1939.
39 AGK, Greiser trial/13, 12.
40 Safrian, 87; Broszat, 90.
41 Final report on relocation within the framework of the settlement of Volhynian, Galician, and Chełm Germans (2nd short-term plan) in the Wartheland Reichsgau, AGK, Greiser trial/13, 141. (Few Jews lived in the part of western Poland that had been part of Prussia until 1918, as most of them had opted for Germany in 1919–20 – not least due to fear of Polish anti-Semitism – and had been transferred there.)
42 FGM, 47.
43 Such a summary judgment is reprinted in *Okkupationspolitik in Polen*, 169.
44 Here the groundwork was already laid in brief for the programme on forced 'Germanization' of apparently 'racially sound and assimilated' Poles, which would only later take effect. It is also plain how much the supposedly racial assessment was linked with economic necessity and the concrete scarcity of occupational groups.
45 'Long-term Plan for Resettlement in the Eastern Provinces', BAK, R69/1146, 1–13. The plan bears neither a signature nor a date. I have dated it on the basis of its contents. Thus the author does not yet count the Upper Silesian Jews in Sosnowiec and environs to the Jews of the incorporated eastern territories, and the census of 17 December 1939 is still to come. In my opinion, it can be ascribed to Department III of the RSHA because of the comprehensive selection programme targeting the Poles that was later implemented on Ehlich's authority.
46 Memorandum from Greiser to all Nazi Party and government offices in the Warthegau, 4 December 1939; AGK, Greiser trial/13, 17b.
47 Letter from provincial head Friedrich Uebelhoer on 'creation of a ghetto in the city of Lodz', reprinted in FGM, 78ff.
48 List by UWZ/P of the directives issued up to then, 16 April 1940; AGK, UWZ/P/145, 1.
49 Letter (dictation reference: 'Mgr./Schr.'), 13 December 1939; AGK, UWZ/P/197, 6f.
50 Letter from Gradmann to the DAI, 17 December 1939; BAK, R57neu/627.

51 Letter from Behrends to Himmler, 25 June 1940; BDC, SS-HO/961.

52 Quoted in Aly and Roth, 80ff.

53 Quoted in Pätzold, 253.

54 Here, too, the deportation of all German, Austrian, and Czech Jews was planned. The planning document is headed 'Final Solution of the German Jewish Problem'. BAK, R58/544, 218f.; quoted in Safrian, 81.

55 Order by Heydrich, 21 December 1939, with reference to the official meeting on 19 December 1939; BAK, R58/240, 26.

56 Letter from Heydrich to responsible SS offices, 21 December 1939, reprinted in *Biuletyn* 12 (1960), 32F. On 30 January 1940, Heydrich described Eichmann's activities as 'central direction of evacuation tasks', ibid. 66F.

57 Because of 'the small number of Jews living in West Prussia . . . some 10,000 Poles [were to be] also deported' from there. This, according to Heydrich, resulted in 'complete utilization' of the trains and 'the possibility of gaining experience for later transports of Poles'.

58 The way in which Eichmann and Heydrich successively developed the expressions later found in the minutes of the Wannsee Conference is noteworthy. There the wording was, 'In the course of the practical implementation of the final solution, Europe will be combed through from west to east.'

59 Relocation plan of 21 December 1939 (signed by Heydrich); AGK, UWZ/P/97.

60 Order by Heydrich on 'evacuations of the eastern provinces', 21 December 1939, AGK, UWZ/L/5, 83. This apparently refers to the above-mentioned long-term plan, which was unveiled in November 1939.

61 Alfred Thoss, 'Die Umsiedlungen und Optionen im Rahmen der Neuordnung Europas', *Zeitschrift für Geopolitik* 18 (1941), 127–54, here 129.

62 Meeting between Frank and Dr Scholz (Vomi), 9 November 1939, Frank diary, 63.

63 Note on 8 January 1940, reprinted in *Biuletyn* 12 (1960), 37Fff. According to this, Eichmann wanted to deport 30,000 Jews from the formerly Polish district of Ciechanów (which had been added to East Prussia), 120,000–125,000 from Upper Silesia, and 200,000 from the Warthegau, especially from Lodz. Of the 90,000 additional Poles to be relocated, 80,000 lived in the Warthegau.

64 Telex from the RSHA (signed by SS Oberstuf. Lorenz), 5 January 1941, reprinted in *Biuletyn* 12 (1960), 35F.

65 Telex from RSHA to SS Oberführer Döring in Posen, 5 January 1940; AGK, UWZ/P/146, 1; see also telex from Heydrich to security police in Posen, 12 January 1940, reprinted in *Biuletyn* 12 (1960), 41Ff.

66 Quoted in Pätzold, 257.

67 Report by Hildebrandt on the activities of the 'Eimann' SS guard regiment, reprinted in *Okkupationspolitik in Polen*, 150f. Hildebrandt, the higher SS and police chief and RKF representative responsible for Danzig–West Prussia, had already mentioned this plan on 26 November 1939 on the occasion of a speech 'on settlement and new settlement' in Bromberg. According to him, 'In 1940, the Gau [will] deport 400,000 people to the Warsaw–Lublin area attached to it.' (BAK, R75/13, 1.)

68 Letter from Döring to Rapp, 9 January 1940; AGK, UWZ/P/114, 12.

69 Statement by Rapp on the occasion of a discussion in Posen on 11 January 1940 on the use of Polish farm workers in the Reich; AGK, UWZ/P/146, 4.

70 Telex from Heydrich to the Sipo [security police] in Posen, 12 January 1940, reprinted in *Biuletyn* 12 (1960), 41Ff.

71 Directive from Koppe, 'Räumung der Ostprovinzen, hier: Umsiedlung der Juden' (Clearing the East Provinces, here: Relocation of the Jews), 14 January 1940; AGK, UWZ/L/5, 101ff.

72 Telex from Central Immigration Office Northeast (signed by Sandberger), 16 January 1940; BAK, R69/854, 61.

73 On the terrible conditions of this deportation, see report on the 'death march from Lublin', 14 March 1940; BAK, R43/II/1412, 108ff.

74 Müller, 125–9.

75 Ehlich's note on discussion, 17 January 1940; BAP-DH, ZR 890 A 2, 218–20.

76 Report from the Vomi in Posen on visit to camp on 18 January 1940; StA Poznań, Vomi/P/23, 39ff.

77 Frank diary, 93ff.

78 Special orders and daily reports from January and February 1940; AGK, UWZ/P/218, 36–54.

79 Directive from Koppe, 'Umsiedlung von Polen und Juden, hier: Zwischenplan' (Relocation of Poles and Jews, here: Interim Plan); AGK, UWZ/L/5, 105ff.

80 Letter from Barth to Rapp, 20 January 1940; AGK, UWZ/P/99, 34f.

81 Report by Lakenfeld, 22 January 1940; StA Poznań, Vomi/P/23, 47f. Representatives of the ethnic Germans not only issued such reports, but also got involved. Thus in January 1940, the office for registration and screening in the evacuation staff of the 'Office for the Resettlement of Poles and Jews' in Poznań employed 35 Baltic Germans in addition to six Reich Germans. (AGK, UWZ/P/83, 2ff.)

82 Note of 23 February 1940 on a meeting between Eichmann and Seidl in Berlin, reprinted in Biuletyn 12 (1960), 44Ff.

83 Meyer's memorandum is reprinted in Mitteilungen der Dokumentationsstelle zur NS-Sozialpolitik 1 (1985), no. 4, and in Müller, 130–8.

84 Roth has recently sown confusion in the distinction between short-term and long-term plans in this phase of planning for the eastern territories. His contribution to this problem is imprecise and sometimes incorrect (Roth, 'Gesamtplan', 33–8).

85 Telegram from mayor of Lodz to Reichstatthalter [regent] in Poznań, 24 January 1940; AGK, UWZ/P/197, 11.

86 Himmler's appointment calendar; BAK, NS19/3954.

87 This refers to the transport of Volhynian Germans from the eastern border of the Generalgouvernement to temporary camps in the Reich.

88 Krumey report 'on the consultation on train schedules that took place in Leipzig on 26 and 27 January 1940'; AGK, UWZ/P/197, 14ff.

89 Cf. the above-mentioned meeting on 5 January 1940. The resettlement authorities hoped that deportations for forced labour would give them leeway for their projects. In practice, however, the additional opportunity for deportation was not enough. In addition, this practice, as already mentioned, led to renewed protests on the part of the government of the Generalgouvernement. On the use of Polish (slave) labourers during this period, see Herbert, 67–95.

90 File note on the meeting on 30 January 1940 at the RSHA, chaired by Heydrich; Nuremberg Doc., NO-5322, reprinted in FGM, 50ff.

91 Note, AGK, UWZ/P/85, 1.

92 Fircks report, 31 January 1940; StA Poznań, Vomi/P/23, 63f.; see also Koskull report of 1 February 1940, ibid. 68.

93 Ehlich memorandum on 'creation of central resettlement offices', 2 February 1940; BAP-DH, ZR 890 A 2, 210–17.

94 Letter from Office for Resettlement of Poles and Jews, Lodz office (signed by Barth), 8 February 1940; AGK, UWZ/P/22, 9ff.; see Gilbert, Holocaust, 143f.

95 Final train schedule for transport trains within the scope of the interim plan, reprinted in Biuletyn 12 (1960), 61F.

96 Letter from Rapp to provincial heads in Kalisz, 6 March 1940; AGK, UWZ/P/96, 35.

97 Frank diary, 109–11.
98 Although the corresponding agreements were not negotiated until summer
   1940, and the resettlement of southeastern European ethnic German minorities was not carried out until autumn 1940 and winter 1940–41, additional
   Soviet annexations and the resettlements they led to had apparently by this
   point long been discussed with representatives of the Soviet Union (see also
   Himmler's speech of 29 February 1940).
99 'Meeting on eastern issues, chaired by Minister President General Field
   Marshal Göring' (minutes of outcome, signed by Gramsch, 12 February
   1940), IMG, vol. 36, 299–307. On 15 February, Frank reported in Krakow
   on the results of the meeting (Frank diary, 109ff.) Engel (75) writes on this,
   'Frank spoke about the situation in the Generalgouvernement of Poland.
   Reports on resettlements and concentrations of Jews.'
100 See Chapter 3, p. 60.
101 Minutes of district meeting, quoted in Pohl, 52.
102 Wächter's progress report for January 1940, reprinted in FGM, 52ff.
103 Itemization by the Office for Resettlement of Poles and Jews of the 'number of
   Poles and Jews so far suggested for evacuation by district heads'; AGK, UWZ/
   P/229, 3.
104 Directive from Heydrich of 19 February 1940, quoted in letter from Göring
   (signed by Galke) to the Trusteeship Office in the annexed eastern territories,
   4 March 1940; StA Poznań, Vomi/P/161, 153.
105 Letter from Barth to Höppner, 26 February 1940; AGK, UWZ/P/193, 1.
106 Himmler, Geheimreden, 138ff.
107 Letter from Greiser to provincial leaders of Kalisz and Inowrocław, 1 March
   1940; AGK, Greiser trial/36, 549ff.
108 Telex from Barth to Rapp, 7 March 1940; AGK, UWZ/P/129, 1.
109 Damberg report, 13 February 1940; StA Poznań, Vomi/P/23, 87; see Zorn,
   94ff.
110 Letter from Koppe, 2 March 1940; AGK, UWZ/P/130, 30.
111 File note by Barth on 7 March 1940 on such a discussion with Kroll, representative of the HTO in the East; letter from Barth to Höppner, 8 March
   1940. The plan to build a Tuszyn camp was not pursued further, as Higher SS
   and Police Chief Koppe considered 'several smaller camps to be more
   efficient'; AGK, UWZ/P/193, 2ff.
112 Telex from Krumey to Eichmann, 7 March 1940; AGK, UWZ/P/197, 25ff.
113 File note, Posen UWZ, on a telephone conversation with Eichmann, 11 March
   1940; AGK, UWZ/P/197, 27.
114 Review by Waldemar Schön, resettlement expert in the Warsaw district, 21
   January 1941, quoted in FGM, 108ff.
115 Telex from Eichmann to Rapp rejecting his suggestion, 14 March 1940; AGK,
   UWZ/Posen/130, 35. Overall, in the course of the desired economic rationalization, the Main Trusteeship Office in the East closed down 45,000 of 60,000
   businesses in 1940. Thus these businesses had been distributed right after the
   Baltic Germans were resettled. For later groups of ethnic German resettlers,
   the subjective legal right to compensation in kind in their old occupations
   could no longer be satisfied, at least in this respect (report by DUT director
   Kulemann to a meeting of the board of directors on 20 March 1941; BAP,
   17.02/34, 9).
116 See note 113: AGK, UWZ/P/197, 33.
117 Goebbels diary, I/4, 71ff.
118 Letter from mayor of Sosnowiec to Main Trusteeship Office in the East, 21
   March 1940; StA Katowice, HTO/1397, 47.
119 Quoted in Pätzold, 262.

120  On the early time schedule, see Rapp's file note, 3 April 1940; AGK, UWZ/P/ 197, 28ff.
121  Final report on relocation within the framework of the settlement of Bessara- bian Germans (3rd short-term plan), 21 January 1941 to 20 January 1942 in the Wartheland Reichsgau; AGK, UWZ/L/13, 95ff.
122  Copy of a record of the meeting on 1 April 1940, appendix 5, on an expert opinion from the Reich Auditing Office, quoted in *Dokumenty*, 167ff.
123  Minutes of the meeting are quoted in Aly, *Aktion T-4*, 50–2.
124  FGM, 86.
125  Letter ('very urgent') from Katowice Gestapo to Main Trusteeship Office in Katowice, 19 April 1940; StA Katowice, HTO/1397, 55.
126  Frank diary, 186ff.
127  AGK, UWZ/P/22, 13.
128  Letter from head of the security police and the SD (signed by Best), 24 April 1940; AGK/UWZ/L/1, 13f. Ernst Damzog, supervisor of the security police and SD in Posen, became head of the UWZ and appointed Rolf-Heinz Höppner as his 'deputy and secretary' (letter from Damzog, 21 May 1940; AGK, UWZ/L/1, 18). On 2 February 1940, Ehlich had already written up a note on the subject of 'creating central resettlement offices' for Heydrich and Eichmann; it contained some of the structural elements of the decree of 24 April (BAP-DH, HAIX/11/ZR/890/A.2, B.210–217).
129  In this context, the phrase 'Reich territory' certainly does not include the incorporated eastern territories. Decree by RSHA on 24 April 1940 on increased 'Jewish emigration', quoted in Pätzold, 262ff.
130  Testimony by Ventzki at trial of Höppner on 19 April 1968; ZStL, V 203 AR 690/65, 135.

# |3|

# 'Himmler is shifting
# populations . . .'
## '. . . not always successfully'

In view of the German crimes, it is one of the greatest achievements of historians since World War II to have made the victims' perspective their own. Thus the view from the perpetrators' perspective is bound to be upsetting. But the subject matter – the decision-making process leading to the Holocaust – forces us to look inside the minds of the administrators and planners. What to the victims must have seemed the horrible efficiency of the bureaucracy of death appeared very different in the eyes of the perpetrators. In the contemporary view of the deporters, the same story was seen as an unbroken series of defeats, an inability even to approach their goals, once established.[1] The economists and ideologues of nationhood (*Volkstum*) constantly demanded far more comprehensive and rapid mass resettlements than the men of the settlement headquarters were ultimately able to supply.

But even when drastically reduced and delayed, the plans, when measured against the actual results, quickly proved to be armchair gameplaying, far removed from reality. They required further compromise and hastily improvised interim solutions. The activities of Himmler, Heydrich, and Eichmann can thus be described as a chronology of failure. As early as 24 January 1940, as Himmler sought in vain to resettle the Baltic Germans in the time allotted, Goebbels noted, 'Himmler is presently shifting populations. Not always successfully.'[2]

Additional requests for resettlement, for a variety of reasons, from the members of various staff offices of the Wehrmacht, local and regional governments, health departments and police authorities, had to be refused, despite the ideology of Germanization. Such refusal was, in fact, one of Eichmann's jobs, as one of his members of staff, Hermann Krumey, recorded in late 1940:

> If all the requests for resettlement made to field offices by district
> heads, mayors, and other offices had had to have been met, at least

seventy to eighty new transport trains [each carrying 1000 people] would have been necessary; unfortunately, they were not available.[3]

By 30 January 1940, Heydrich was no longer referring to the ambitious goals of 'Jewish deportation'; instead, he announced an interim plan, the 'urgent' deportation of '40,000 Jews and Poles'. They were to make room for the Baltic Germans, the large majority of whom were settled in the few cities of the Warthegau. Immediately thereafter, according to Heydrich, 'a further improvised evacuation, in the interests of the Volhynian Germans to be resettled in the eastern Gaus, [is to be] carried out'. This applied to Polish peasant families, as the Volhynian Germans were also peasants.[4] Heydrich assumed that 'the number of Poles to be evicted for this reason [can] be expected, initially, to be roughly 120,000'. By this point, '4000–5000 Poles and Jews [had been] collected in camps'; they had to make room for the Baltic Germans, but could not be deported.[5]

By 30 January, after the Volhynian Germans had been brought in for settlement and the Poles simultaneously moved out, Heydrich still intended to follow this with a 'final mass movement' in early summer: 'The deportation of all Jews in the new eastern Gaus and 30,000 Gypsies from the Reich territory to the Generalgouvernement' – a total of more than half a million people. Heydrich kept to this plan, although it had taken great effort for him to deport even 125,000 people with the help of the first short-term plan and the interim plan, and although it was becoming clear that the second short-term plan, which was to involve 120,000 people, would be even more difficult to accomplish than the first. But Heydrich waved aside the objections raised on 30 January 1940 by Seyss-Inquart, representative of the Generalgouvernement, who opposed the deportation of an additional 600,000 Jews and 30,000 Gypsies for reasons relating to transport and food supply. Heydrich hinted at forced labour camps, and did not even mention the organizational aspects of the plan.

Concretely, Heydrich merely announced the deportation of '1000 Jews from Stettin [Szczecin]' whose homes were 'urgently needed', supposedly 'for purposes of the wartime economy', but actually for the Baltic German settlers.[6] The relevant report states, 'The homes of expelled Jews are available for the Baltic Germans who have found work in Stettin.' The same was true for Baltic seamen, whose home port would now be Szczecin: 'The families of the same have moved into the emptied Jewish homes.'[7] In his speech to the Gauleiters on 29 February 1940, Himmler justified the move as follows:

> In one single Gau, I transferred Jews from the Old Reich to the Generalgouvernement. This is the Pomeranian Gau, because Pomerania has no more room for the Baltic Germans, especially the old Baltic Germans. Therefore, I had to make room.[8]

Just as the deportation of Jews from Vienna, Moravská Ostrava, and

Katowice was halted as a result of the Baltic resettlement, the reverse process – namely, the expulsion of the Szczecin and Piła (German: Schnei-demühl) Jews – can be explained as a consequence of the resettlement of special groups of ethnic Germans.

In February and March, the resettlement offices discussed in detail which farms were to be vacated when and where for the now dissatisfied Volhynian and Galician German 'returnees', who were living in numerous camps. Timetables were drafted, commandos assigned and, at the end of March, two 'test settlements' and 'evacuations' attempted. In the process, a new problem arose that became increasingly serious: the Poles had not yet organized systematic resistance to the expulsions, but they evaded them, thus disrupting one aspect of the German plans. 'SS Oberführer Döring has informed me', complained Koppe after the second test resettle-ment, 'that a large number of Polish peasants who were to be evacuated have already left their farms and gone into hiding. This is, of course, an untenable situation, as the Poles absolutely must leave their locations.'[9] Although Koppe ordered 'that comprehensive precautions be taken to keep our opera-tions from becoming known in the future', the problem remained. During the following months, an average of up to 40 per cent of the people on the resettlement lists went underground in the days and nights prior to the 'operations'.[10]

A further problem arose from the test resettlements. Because, 'for tactical reasons, evacuation and placement' had to take place 'little by little', since the same vehicles and escorts had to be used and farm chores – especially feeding and milking the livestock – could not be interrupted, the organizers of the population exchange also had to consider the psycho-logical aspects of the process. According to secret guidelines:

> The Volhynian and Galician German settlers, with their families, should be housed on a neighbouring farm for a short time during the evacuation, so that they are spared the sight of the evacuation. This is not insignificant for the psyche of the Volhynian and Galician Germans. . . . Only when the evacuated Polish family is out of sight should the installation of the settlers occur.[11]

In other words, the Galician and Volhynian farmers, coming from simple backgrounds and speaking fluent Polish, did not fit as easily as the Baltic Germans into the 'master race' behavioural pattern assigned to them.

At the end of February 1940, the resettlement strategists still believed that 'the resettlement of the Volhynian Germans must be completed before spring planting, so that these Volhynian Germans can still parti-cipate in the battle for the harvest'.[12] (In general, Himmler's ethnopoli-ticians strove, as far as possible, to complete each intended 'population exchange' in winter, in consideration of the sowing and harvest seasons. Thus, for example, wheat farmers could be resettled earlier than potato farmers.)

This intention proved to be pure illusion in the case of the Volhynian Germans. When this became clear, Heydrich ordered that the second short-term plan begin on 15 April and finish by July 1940. On 4 May 1940, while visiting a settlers' camp at Kirchberg (Wiśniowa Góra), near Lodz, where 8000 Volhynian German settlers were waiting for the settlement they had been promised, Himmler spoke reassuringly: 'You must understand that you have to wait. Before you get your farm, a Polack must first be thrown out. Often they are such holes that we first have to put the buildings in order or combine two farms.' And then Himmler assured them, 'By summer you will walk on your own land.' The speech reflected the settlers' dissatisfaction. Apparently, they had complained of the lack of pocket money and were worried that the farms intended for them would be too small and the soil bad; they also feared possible acts of revenge by the Poles. Himmler promised that their farms would be 'rounded out by a few acres by next spring', and that new buildings would be built as soon as the war was over. Further, every Pole should know that 'if you so much as touch a hair on a [German] family's head, you and all male Poles in your village will lose your lives'.[13]

On 10 May, Himmler wrote to Koppe, referring expressly to his promises at Kirchberg, that 'being confined in the camps' was 'very bad, in terms of both health and spirits, and the length of the stay should be shortened in every possible way'.

> The present placement cannot be a final settlement, but must be accomplished as unbureaucratically and as quickly as possible. The goal is to settle 100 peasant families a day, and to complete the entire resettlement by approximately the end of August.

This was urgently necessary, he said, so that the people would forget as quickly as possible what they had been through: 'The whole shock of departure from their homes, the migration and the trek in winter, the long wait in the camps, the sickness and sometimes the death of a child.'[14]

On 5 June, Eichmann informed his Posen member of staff Siegfried Seidl that, under orders from Himmler, the resettlement of the Volhynian Germans 'has to be completed by 31 August 1940'.[15] On 1 July, in a letter to the UWZ in Posen, Eichmann's deputy, Günther, hinted at difficulties in keeping to the timetable, though he outwardly confirmed it, noting

> that on the basis of the agreement concluded on 12 June 1940 between the chief of the security police and the SD and the General-gouverneur, in consideration of the pressure under which the Generalgouvernement finds itself, it cannot be expected that more settlers will be taken in than the figures listed on the occasion of the discussion on 30 January 1940. Considering the present situation, therefore, it will hardly be possible at present to carry out more operations than the current Volhynian operation and the Jewish

evacuation operation that will probably begin in August of this year.[16]

Only eight days later, on 9 July, Himmler ordered a 'halt to the evacuation of Jews to the Generalgouvernement' in view of the Madagascar Plan.[17] The Madagascar Plan thus came to seem more real, and the organizers of 'human deployment' in the RSHA and the staff main office of the RKF immediately derived a dual advantage from it: for one, they now had to deport fewer people from the incorporated eastern territories to the Generalgouvernement; for another, since the Jews would be shipped from there to Madagascar, room would be made available for further deportation of Poles.

Only now did Eichmann and his colleagues continue the deportation of those Poles who had to make way for the Volhynian Germans.[18] On 22 July, the resettlement bureaucrats in the Warthegau assumed that the resettlement of Volhynian German families could be completed by September; in September, they postponed the deadline to the beginning of October,[19] only to discover on 18 October that nothing had happened as yet.[20] At the time, 4000 Volhynian German families – more than 20,000 people – were still stranded in camps, idle and disappointed. According to RKF logic, this required the removal of at least twice as many Poles. On 28 October, Eichmann pointed out that, within the scope of the second short-term plan, only another 11,000 people could be evacuated, since no more trains were available; that would 'have to do'.[21]

Eichmann's categorical attitude can be easily explained. The third short-term plan was already in preparation, because the decision to resettle an additional 250,000 ethnic Germans had already been made in summer 1940. This number came, first, from the German–Soviet resettlement agreement, and second, as a consequence of 'ethnic new order' policies in southeastern Europe. Thus, as will be described in the next two chapters, at the end of 1940 the Bessarabian, Bukovinian, Dobruja, and Lithuanian Germans had to 'return home'. However, the third short-term plan could not be tackled before the second short-term plan had been completed. Therefore, Heydrich and Eichmann concluded their second short-term plan – the project of 'making room for the Volhynian and Galician Germans' – pro forma on 20 January 1941 and began implementing the third short-term plan.[22] In fact, statistics show that, as late as 1 April 1941, 'only [!] 8640 people from Volhynia and Galicia were still in the camps'.[23]

## Eichmann, plenipotentiary for evacuation

Adolf Eichmann, the organizer of expulsion, was at times little concerned with the 'field' for which he is generally known – 'Jewish matters'. Next to Himmler and Heydrich, he represents the increasingly close political and organizational links between general 'ethnic redistribution' and the 'solution of the Jewish question' as it gradually presented itself, contrary to the original intentions of the protagonists. On 19 December 1939, Heydrich had appointed Eichmann, his 'official in charge of Jewish matters', to be 'special officer' for the 'evacuation of the eastern provinces', assigning him 'the central coordination of evacuation tasks'.[24] In the Reich Security Main Office's first task allocation plan, of February 1940, Eichmann's section was given the official designation 'IVD4'; its responsibility was described as 'emigration and evacuation'.[25] In the previous weeks, the section had been part of IVR (for '*Räumung*', or 'evacuation'). The cluster of offices designated 'IVD', to which Section 4 was answerable, was also responsible for the occupied territories. Overall, Section 4 combined the political and executive functions of the security police and the Gestapo.

Within the scope of his new functions, Eichmann naturally retained responsibility for the 'Central Offices for Jewish Emigration' in Vienna and Prague, which he had held since 1938–39. These functions were included within the new programme.

In addition to Eichmann's office, there still existed the 'field of Jewish matters'. At first, this 'field' was expected to be handled by Section IVD3, in charge of minorities, foreigners, and Jews within the Reich. But by 29 February 1940, Heydrich had changed this assignment, giving the 'field of Jewish matters' to Section IVA5 ('Emigrants') and transferring the directorship to Walter Jagusch. He, it should be noted, handled not emigration itself, but the surveillance of emigrants abroad.[26] Overall, the shifting back and forth of 'responsibility for the Jews' in winter 1939–40 suggests that Heydrich at this point reckoned with the impending deportation of all German, Austrian, Czech, and western Polish Jews, and thus changed his office's task allocation as a precautionary measure.

The next, revised RSHA task allocation plan came on 1 March 1941. Here the shorthand for Eichmann's office was changed from 'IVD4' to 'IVB4'. But why? The new task allocation plan was adapted to the responsibilities of the RSHA, which had been changed and augmented owing to the war, but included no general reorganization under which Section IVD4 could simply have been relabelled.

The description of its responsibilities now read, 'Jewish matters, evacuation matters'. In 1940, Eichmann's office had been assigned to the cluster of offices designated 'D', whose personnel, as mentioned, dealt mainly with the occupied territories – for example, with 'Protectorate and Generalgouvernement matters'. Now he again took his place in the 'B' group of offices, where he had worked, *de facto*, before the creation of the Reich Security Main Office in autumn 1939: in the 'research and combat' of religious and racial adversaries within the Reich (and in 'areas of German habitation'). In addition, there were offices for 'political

Protestantism, Catholicism, Freemasonry, etc.'.[27] A Jewish office no longer existed, not even on paper.

Because Eichmann's activities did not suddenly change, but were subject to several shifts of accent from 1939 to 1941 between 'Jewish' and 'evacuation matters', the simple change in bureaucratic shorthand should not be overestimated. Nevertheless, it is significant for the creeping change in purpose it reflects, and therefore should not be passed over as a mere formality. In a survey of Department IV in November 1941, at a time when the 'Final Solution' had already begun, Section IVB4 bore only the brief designation 'Jews'.[28] In the task allocation plan of 1 October 1943, the title of the office was changed according to the Eleventh Decree on the Reich Citizenship Law as follows: 'Jewish Matters, Evacuation Matters, Seizure of Assets Hostile to *Volk* and State, Revocation of German Citizenship'.[29] In fact, however, Eichmann had barely concerned himself with general resettlement matters since late summer 1941. This is evidenced by the fact that until then he had carried on a lively correspondence on this issue, which suddenly broke off. His last letter, to my knowledge, on resettlement of non-Jewish persons was written on 20 August 1941.[30]

The changes in the tasks handled by Eichmann, according to the task allocation plan and in reality, reflect one thing: in 1940, Heydrich apparently considered Jewish policy to be part of general resettlement policy. One year later, at the latest, and probably *de facto* with the development of the 'Madagascar Plan' in summer 1940, he again increasingly separated Jewish policy from the organization of general resettlement. However, the overall institutional structure persisted in the form that had originally been laid out: Eichmann's deputy, Rolf Günther, continued to handle general resettlement matters; until 1944, the staff of the UWZ in Posen participated in both the further deportations of Poles and the extermination of the European Jews. This is confirmed by the later testimony of Franz Novak, transport officer in Section IVD(B)4: 'All this experience in transport techniques, incidentally, was already gained during the evacuation, before the Jewish transports, of roughly 500,000 Poles from the areas of the Wartheland and Danzig–West Prussia to the Generalgouvernement of Poland.'[31]

In the period from December 1939 to autumn 1941, Eichmann did not conduct resettlement on his own. Rather, he shared power, in many respects, with the office cluster designated 'IIIB', which was part of Department III ('Areas of German Habitation') of the RSHA and was headed by Otto Ohlendorf. The IIIB cluster was formally restructured on 21 March 1940 as the '*Volkstum*' group, but it had been labelled 'III ES' ('Immigration and Settlement') since 31 October 1939 and was headed by Hans Ehlich, a surgeon and racial hygienist.[32]

The Central Resettlement Office in Posen and its office in Lodz were answerable to both Eichmann and Ehlich. Letters from the local offices were generally addressed to both men. Because Ehlich was responsible for 'racial screening' – that is, selections – and Eichmann for the organization of the deportations themselves, the latter had greater influence as far as Jews were concerned: they were not subjected to so-called suitability tests by Ehlich's envoys. On the other hand, Ehlich's office led the research on the moods and desires of Germans abroad and ethnic German settlers. Ehlich knew quite well that the promises made by Hitler and Himmler to those brought 'home to the Reich' were constantly being broken, that ridicule, sarcasm, and discontent were developing among the settlers, and that more and more ethnic Germans were even expressing a desire to return to their old homes. For these reasons, Ehlich had to be interested in forcing the removal of Jews in any way possible, in order to extend the increasingly narrow latitude for resettlement.

## Blocked New Order

Heydrich used the Central Resettlement Office, formerly called the Office for the Resettlement of Poles and Jews, to relocate the native population of annexed western Poland; he had created the Central Immigration Office (EWZ) for so-called repatriation of ethnic Germans. The two institutions operated simultaneously in five successive 'operations'. Though the numbering was somewhat confusing, as well as indicative of constant improvisation, they were called '1st short-term plan', 'interim plan', '2nd short-term plan' (April 1940 to 20 January 1941), '3rd short-term plan' (21 January 1941 to 20 January 1942), and '3rd expanded short-term plan' (21 January 1942 to 20 January 1943). All these short-term plans were understood to be *ad hoc* resettlements for the purpose of bringing in specific groups of ethnic Germans. The first short-term plan and the interim plan applied to the Baltic Germans, the second short-term plan to the Galician and Volhynian Germans; the third expanded short-term plan was essentially a continuation of the third short-term plan, which had been halted at the outset, and its purpose, too, was to bring in Bessarabian, Bukovinian, Dobruja, and Lithuanian Germans.

Hermann Krumey, head of the Central Resettlement Office (UWZ) in Lodz, wrote in October 1941 in retrospect:

The major long-term planning . . . was converted of necessity to a short-term plan and limited to the clearance of accommodation for ethnic Germans returning to the Reich. Thus at the end of the interim plan, for which, by late March 1940, forty transport trains had been routed to the Generalgouvernement, the Baltic Germans were by and large placed in homes and jobs.[33]

On the practice of resettlement that followed, he commented elsewhere:

After settlers from Volhynia, Galicia, the Cholm [Chełm] area,

Bessarabia, and the Buchenland [Bukovina] began to arrive in April 1940, the categories of people to be removed had to be increased accordingly. The number and time of arrival of the assigned settlers were now determined by the number and speed of removals.[34]

On 30 October 1939, Himmler had ordered that '*all* Jews from the formerly Polish, now Reich German, provinces and territories' be resettled. In addition, '*all* Congress Poles' from the areas of Danzig–West Prussia were to be expelled, as well as 'an as yet undetermined number of hostile Poles' from the provinces of Posen and South and East Prussia. To the deporters, this meant, in particular, the Polish intelligentsia. The reasons for deportation thus varied; as one of the participants formulated it, they included 'a biological, a political and a social component'.[35] The various points of view immediately found themselves in competition; thus the German ethnic policy experts considered 'Congress Poles' to be those who had emigrated since 1919 from the formerly Russian to the formerly Prussian part of Poland. Their expulsion was considered urgent, for *völkisch,* ideological reasons. But problems immediately arose, as it was precisely the 'Congress Poles', as a rule, who were 'simple workers . . . involved in economic life and to an extent indispensable'. Because their housing was therefore relatively modest and unsuitable for the Baltic Germans, their rapid, collective deportation was not at issue. The actual priority in resettlement targeted 'people with good housing'.[36]

The first systematic deportation operation, the 'first short-term plan', began not in November, as intended, but in December 1939. Instead of the projected figure of a million deportees, the talk at first was of '80,000 Jews and Poles'.[37] The pragmatic change in resettlement practices became even more evident in the interim plan that followed. Heydrich had to insert this plan in mid-January 1940, at short notice, before the already-drafted second short-term plan at the instigation of Koppe, who had not succeeded in settling the Baltic Germans in the Warthegau in time. Implementation began on 10 February and ended on 15 March.[38] The 40,128 deportees came from western Polish cities. Like the first short-term plan, the purpose of the interim plan was nothing more than 'creation of housing and work opportunities for the Baltic German settlers'.

The second short-term plan, in the version laid out by Heydrich on 21 December 1939, was supposed exclusively to fulfil the purpose of expelling all 600,000 Jews in the annexed western Polish provinces to the General-gouvernement – not, for example, to the Jewish reservation in Lublin, favoured by Heydrich, for different opposition had already formed against that by November. A draft 'long-term plan for resettlement in the eastern provinces' of November 1939 explained:

> The Supreme Command of the Wehrmacht does not wish for a concentration of Jews to occur near the German–Soviet Russian border. Security reasons also to a certain extent militate against

allowing the pressure of population density in the Generalgouvernement, especially in the eastern regions, to become too great, since the
masses eking out an existence there under the most miserable living
conditions only too easily represent a breeding ground for
Bolshevism.[39]

Whatever resistance or problems the resettlement experts of the RSHA had
expected before the fact, in reality it was mainly a shortage of transport
capacity that hindered implementation of the plans.

In addition, resistance began to develop within the German administration of the Generalgouvernement in January 1940. Most importantly,
though, the organizers of the resettlement programmes had to give up their
goal of deporting the Jews as rapidly as possible to the 'Lublin area',
because the ethnic Germans arriving from Eastern Europe took priority,
and great effort was required to find sufficient railway capacity even for
them. The second short-term plan plainly had to be changed.

Nor did it begin, as originally hoped, in mid-January, but instead not until
early April 1940. Instead of being directed against 600,000 Jews, it targeted
not only considerably fewer people, but also completely different ones:
120,000 Poles. The 'clearing' of farms in the Warthegau alone took centre
stage, as the ethnic Germans from Volhynia and eastern Galicia – formerly
Polish, now annexed by the Soviets – were almost exclusively farmers.
Heydrich had subordinated his plan for the rapid deportation of Jews, *de
facto*, to the pragmatic demands and possibilities of overall resettlement
policy, although well into June 1940 he would continue trying, albeit without
success, to carry out his original intention of deporting all Jews from the
incorporated eastern territories to the Generalgouvernement.

Furthermore, a new procedure was introduced along with the second
short-term plan: the non-Jewish victims of deportation were chosen not
only for their jobs and farms, which would now be assigned to Volhynian
Germans; in a second selection, 'some were deported to the Generalgouvernement, others sent to the Old Reich to be Germanized or for
labour'.[40] In this way, three things could be accomplished: differentiated
treatment of Poles; mitigation of the labour shortage in the Reich caused
by the war (especially in agriculture, at the time); and a reduction in
deportations to the Generalgouvernement.

While the Jews were, from the beginning, to be expelled without
exception, for Poles the criteria for the selections varied by region and
changed constantly over the course of the war. Overall, so-called racial
criteria increasingly diminished in importance. Ultimately, apart from
those they considered members of the Polish nationalist intelligentsia,
the Germans decided not on the basis of rigid ethnic criteria, but
according to opportunity.

It remained crucial whether an individual Pole worked as a miner or – far
more unfavourably for him – as a farmer, whether he was an irreplaceable

railway worker or a tuberculosis patient unfit for work, or whether he was adaptable or rebellious.

But the differentiation itself, originally seen as a relief, brought forth new conflicts. The occupation authorities in the Generalgouvernement were soon complaining that almost all the Poles being deported were those unable to work, sick or elderly, and that they thus 'became a burden' upon the public welfare system there. A typical report went as follows:

> On 12 December 1940, meanwhile, a resettlement transport of 1000 persons – this time from eastern Prussia – arrived in Neu Sandez [Nowy Sącz]. It is sufficiently known what a burden these transports represent for the overpopulated area, but it must be borne. . . . The resettlement transport that arrived here was, in addition, a train of pure misery. According to the labour office, of the 1000 people, forty at most (including women) were fully capable of work deployment. No fewer than 215 persons required medical examination and treatment. Aside from acute illness (sixty cases), thirty skin and fifteen tooth ailments, there were twelve cases of pulmonary tuberculosis, six cripples (blind, lame, etc.), and even two cases of mental illness in the transport. Among those with lung disease, there was one woman with open pulmonary tuberculosis who had five children with her. In addition, some fifty-one people suffering from the usual symptoms of age (weak heart, swollen lungs, etc.) had to be treated; nine people were found completely incapable of transport. Six patients had to be hospitalized immediately, and forty-two people, among them thirty-three of the infirm aged, had to be housed in a dwelling confiscated for the purpose. Eight of them died by Christmas.[41]

The property of all Poles and Jews deported to the Generalgouvernement was confiscated beforehand. They arrived with 50 kilograms of baggage, 25 Reichsmarks in cash, and – if they had any at all – enough food for a few days. Finding housing for them necessarily caused difficulties for the occupation authorities. But the situation worsened even further when, starting in January 1940, 'a new economic policy' for the Generalgouvernement – now called the 'neighbour of the Reich' – was introduced. Its aim was 'development', productivity, and German order. Thus the 'Führer's will', as expressed by Hitler as recently as 17 October 1939, according to which there was to be no economic consolidation in the Generalgouvernement, became a farce only months later. Hitler did refer once again to this concept, in winter 1940–41, but it had in fact been obsolete for months. Göring and his advisors had long since set different economic priorities, and the regents of the Generalgouvernement under Hans Frank had developed the ambition – like their colleagues in the incorporated eastern territories – to 'make productive' and 'create a new order in' the conquered land.[42] This, too, is why they had to oppose turning the land they governed into a 'catch-all for undesired Volkstum', and was also a reason why they soon gave up their original, common goal of creating a Jewish reservation in Lublin. They were successful; on 12 March 1940, Hitler declared semi-publicly that 'the solution of the Jewish question is a question of space'. In explanation, he pointed out that

> even the creation of a Jewish state around Lublin would never be a solution, because there, too, the Jews lived too close together to achieve a relatively satisfactory living standard. Anywhere that people live more than 70 per square kilometre, life was difficult and confined.[43]

The area around Lublin could hardly be given to the Jews, according to Hitler, because that would take too much from the Poles.[44] In fact, the issue was German interests. But with the recognition of the economic importance of the Generalgouvernement, the territory was lost for Jewish deportation.

## Gas vans and resettlement

The first systematic mass murders occurred during the first phase of the resettlement of ethnic Germans. In a causal connection with the bringing of 60,000 Baltic Germans home to the Reich, two SS commandos murdered more than 10,000 mentally ill people from October 1939 to spring 1940. At first, the victims were patients of the psychiatric hospitals located around the ports of Gdańsk (Danzig), Świnoujście (Swinemünde), and Szczecin (Stettin). Somewhat later came the murder of patients in Warthegau psychiatric institutions; here, too, the aim was to create accommodation and transit camps for ethnic German settlers – both from the Baltic states and from the part of eastern Poland annexed by the Soviets.

A special commando unit under police superintendent Herbert Lange murdered these patients with the help of gas vans; mass shootings were the responsibility of a special commando unit under Sturmbannführer Kurt Eimann.[45] Eimann began his activities near Wejherowo (German: Neustadt), West Prussia. Lange and his men drove their gas van to each hospital. The murdered were German patients from Pomerania,[46] Germans and Poles from West Prussia, and Polish, Jewish, and German patients from the Warthegau – a total of at least 10,000 people.[47]

> From October to December 1939, near Neustadt (Wejherowo)
> in West Prussia, patients from the Pomeranian hospitals at
> Stralsund, Lauenburg (Lębork), Ueckermünde, Treptow on
> the Rega were executed. The victims roughly totalled      1,400
>
> In the same period, the following were murdered:
> In Konradstein, West Prussia (Polish: Kocborowo), between
> 22 November 1939 and 4 January 1940      1,692[48]

| | |
|---|---:|
| plus patients whose deaths cannot be individually confirmed | 216 |
| In Schwetz (Świecie near the Vistula) in October 1939 | 1,068 |
| In Gnesen (Dziekanka–Gniezno) between 7 December 1939 and 12 January 1940 | 1,043 |
| In Owinska (Treskau) near Posen, from October to December 1939, roughly | 1,000 |
| In Chełm/Lubelski on 12 January 1940 | 441[49] |
| In Kosten (Kościan) between 15 and 22 January 1940 and from 9 February to March 1940, patients from Brandenburg and Pomerania | 532 2,750 |
| In Gasten (Gostynin), between 3 February and 3 April 1940 | 48 |
| In Lodz (Jewish community home for the mentally ill), in March 1940 | 50 |
| In Kachanówka (near Lodz), between 13 and 27 March 1940 | 540 |
| Total: | 10,780 |

This list is undoubtedly incomplete. Thus in 1962, a witness testified that gas vans were first used in Stralsund to kill the mentally ill.[50] It can be gathered from a report by T-4 doctor Robert Müller on 11 December 1942 that, of a total of 7500 patients in Pomerania, some 5000 were transferred at the beginning of the war, and most were probably murdered.[51] The situation was similar in the Warthegau. There, of a total of 4650 beds in psychiatric hospitals, 2800 were 'freed up' in the years 1939 and 1940.[52] In Danzig–West Prussia, roughly 2500 beds were 'made available for different purposes' in the winter of 1939–40.[53]

To organize the murders, the authorities in the Warthegau first created the 'Central Office for Transfer of Patients' in Kalisz, then an institution of the same name in Posen, headed by medical officer Hans Friemert.[54] This was also the location of a special registry office whose head, Inspector Otto Fischer, enjoyed good relations with the security service and himself belonged to the SS; he entered falsified causes of death on the death certificates of murder victims.[55]

On 23 October 1939, Martin Sandberger, head of the Central Office for Immigration, demanded urgently that 'at least 5000 beds, mattresses, bedding, and eating utensils be made available' for the arriving Baltic Germans.[56] On 2 November he reported that 'in Posen, at present, only processing accommodation for 6000 people is available'. Because the emigration of 60,000 ethnic Germans from Latvia had to be accomplished by 15 December 1939 under the resettlement agreement, he said it was necessary to house the settlers for the time being in alternative accommodation.[57]

On 29 October, officials of the Central Office for Emigration in Gdynia met to discuss the 'care of sick and infirm Baltic Germans'. This referred to 1000 people occupying – or, from the perspective of the Nazi politicians, blocking – hospital beds at the time in Danzig and the surrounding area. The outcome of the discussion was that the 700 infirm among them were to be 'transported out' and 'immediate efforts made to free up the former institution at Neustadt'. According to the minutes of the meeting, the same was to happen in the area around the Pomeranian ports at which the next settlement ships were to arrive, because 'all our experience shows that further people in need of care will most likely arrive with each transport'. The fact that this actually occurred can be gathered, for example, from a petition by a Baltic German settler, whose 'very fragile' daughter 'was first transferred to the Stralsund hospital' and 'from there to Meseritz-Obrawalde'.[58] The same has been documented for the Ueckermünde psychiatric hospital; some ill and infirm Baltic Germans were temporarily quartered there.[59] A telex to Ehlich summarized this as follows:

> Quartering [them] in other areas of the Reich is not considered expedient, because many of the people to be accommodated will return to their relatives once they have achieved a secure footing. . . . The question of the transport of the infirm to accommodation in Pomerania and Mecklenburg is being handled by the Gotenhafen [Gdynia] Central Office.[60]

At the beginning of their 'operation', in autumn 1939, the SS collected the patients from the hospitals in Pomerania and brought them directly to West Prussia for execution. Soon after, the transfer and killing of patients were organized to take place in a complicated, disguised fashion, similar to the procedure used for the murder of the mentally ill within the scope of 'Operation T-4': those destined for death were temporarily housed in so-called interim hospitals, in order to camouflage their disappearance and sudden death and to erase the traces of the crime, at least to some extent.

In later testimony, a nurse from the Lębork (German: Lauenburg) institution in Pomerania reported:

> It is true that the first patient transports left the Finkenbruch railway station at the beginning of October 1939. . . . After the first or second transport, rumours had already started that the transports were being taken to Neustadt in West Prussia. There was also a mental hospital there, which people said had already been evacuated. The pastor of Lauenburg, who had some connection or other to Neustadt, supposedly had said that there were many mass graves in Neustadt and the population had been warned that [military]

exercises were being held at night. Then I learned officially from head nurse Jobst, who served in Tiegenhof [the Gniezno hospital in the Warthegau], that these patients had been shot. . . . Further, I must mention that the transports at first came to Neustadt and then suddenly ceased. It was generally said that Gauleiter Forster of Danzig no longer tolerated these transports. The transports then went to the Warthegau, to Kosten [Kościan], and were no longer collected by the SS, but brought there by nursing staff.[61]

This practice was also confirmed by nurses from Meseritz-Obrawalde: 'In February 1940, a transport of psychiatric patients left for the Kosten hospital in Poland. The Stralsund hospital was closed, and some of the staff and patients came to Obrawalde. Once again, lists were made of names of patients.' Then, the testimony continues, buses came and collected the patients over the course of several days; 'an escort . . . took the valuables and the sandwiches we had prepared for the trip'. Exactly the same thing happened, according to the testimony of the above-mentioned nurse from Lębork, when the Kückenmühle hospital near Szczecin (Stettin) was closed:

Once again, we received some of the staff and patients. . . . Right after the transports to Neustadt, some transports left for Kosten in the Warthegau. . . . I know from the nurses who went along that the SS received the patients and brought them to a large hall, where they first were fed. Then the nurses were dismissed and returned to Lauenburg.[62]

After that, the SS murdered the patients in the gas van. The same occurred in the other psychiatric hospitals in the Warthegau. The nurse quoted above was transferred to Tiegenhof in Gniezno on 1 March, when the Lębork (Lauenburg) hospital was 'turned over to the SS'. There she experienced the following practices:

Here, too, I received complete lists from the administrative office. The people on the lists were mainly old and infirm. These people had to assemble at the infirmary. Then a large van came by with the SS men mentioned above, who drove up to the machine house and the infirmary. . . . The van was like a small furniture van. The driver and one SS man sat in front; the second SS man drove behind in his private car. At the time, it was said that Himmler had invented a gas van. I also recall that this van had no windows. . . . In the van there were benches. But the very seriously ill were seated on straw. Back then, no one dared to say anything. However, I suspected that this means of transport was a gas van. The van also did not drive, as was usual, in the direction of the city of Gnesen, but instead towards the large forest. I never again heard anything from the patients.[63]

From 10 to 20 December 1939, approximately 30 Pomeranian nurses were
involved in 'collecting the mentally ill from Riga by ship'. They accompanied the transport to the port of Świnoujście (Swinemünde).[64] No doubt
these Baltic German patients were not directly murdered. But the Baltic
German doctor Vladimir Nikolayev, who had found a new position as a
psychiatrist in the Tiegenhof hospital, later testified, 'In connection with
the resettlement, the mentally ill Germans from Latvia were brought to
Arnsdorf near Dresden, and those from Estonia to Meseritz-Obrawalde.
Later on, these patients were transferred back to where their relatives were
located.' This occurred at the direct behest of the RKF.[65] In all, after 'room
was made' in the now usual way, roughly 400 men and women were
transferred to Tiegenhof. The Baltic Germans were not, however,
murdered with poison gas like the native patients; in this connection,
the German authorities were very cautious, then as later, about dealing
with the mentally ill relatives of the settlers. However, according to
Nikolayev's testimony, in summer 1941 the Baltic Germans in the hospital
were systematically undernourished. Their mortality rate was 'very high'
at the time. 'These patients' especially, added Nikolayev, 'died off like
flies.'[66] The RKF had long since written off these people legally, and on
22 February 1940, in response to a query, the office wrote, 'There is no
intention of giving pocket money to the mentally ill and infirm settlers
housed in the hospital. Nor is there any intention of granting them Reich
citizenship.'[67]

The connection between resettlement and murder is illustrated with
great clarity in the example of the Schwetz (Świecie) hospital, through a
note in a file of 4 November 1939:

> At the behest of SS Hauptsturmführer Schöneck, office of public
> health, negotiations were held on 2 November 1939 with the liaison
> for the German Reichsbahn, Reichsbahn legal counsel Hölzel, and
> later with the deputy head of the public health office, SS Untersturm-
> führer Dr Masur,[68] on the transport of mentally ill Poles and the
> corresponding transport of infirm Baltic Germans. The transport of
> mentally ill Poles is to occur on Friday, 3 November 1939, from
> Schwetz to Prussian Stargard. This involves 700 mental patients
> who are to be diverted from the Schwetz mental hospital to the
> mental hospital at Konradstein [Kocborowo], near Prussian Stargard.
> The accommodation that will be freed up in the process will be
> newly occupied on Saturday, 4 November 1939, by 200 infirm Baltic
> Germans from Neustadt and 500 infirm Baltic Germans from
> Danzig.[69]

It is worth mentioning in passing the memoirs, published in 1993, of the
German-Estonian official Otto von Kursell. On the subject of Schwetz, he
writes, '[I wrote] a second complaint about the initially horrible conditions
in the former Polish mental hospital in Schwetz, in which the residents

of the Reval old age home in Katharinenthal [Marienstift], among others, are supposed to be housed.' After the memorandum was 'personally handed to Hitler via Professor Haushofer', there was 'immediate and surprising success': 'Only a few days later, the renovation and cleaning of the many buildings in Schwetz and the landscaping for the garden facilities were already in full swing.' Von Kursell was soon convinced 'that this dirty, dilapidated, huge mental hospital had become an attractive, cultivated estate for our old people, where the residents felt comfortable'.[70]

This was also the impression of the staff of the Ethnic German Liaison Office in Gotenhafen (Gdynia) in March 1940; they therefore suggested copying the 'extraordinarily fortunate solution' for accommodation at Schwetz. 'Because additional former insane asylums, such as Riesenburg and Neustadt, are available in West Prussia', the question arose 'whether these, too, could not be transformed into old-age homes' where 'an additional 1600 infirm Baltic Germans could be housed'.[71] At the same time, the head of the Department of Hereditary and Racial Maintenance (*Abteilung Erb- und Rassenpflege*) in the Lodz department of health, Herbert Grohmann, visited the Kochanówska psychiatric hospital near the city and ordered, according to a later Polish report, 'that an SS unit be quartered in one of the hospital departments, and that three pavilions be cleared for reception of repatriated Germans from the East'. On 13, 14, and 15 March, 540 of the hospital's patients were murdered in gas vans.[72]

The extent to which the practice of murder was camouflaged, from day one, in discussions even among its top officials is shown in a letter from the higher SS and police chief of Danzig–West Prussia to Himmler. In this letter, declared a 'confidential Reich matter', Hildebrandt defended the Eimann guard regiment, which Himmler wanted to dissolve. In the process, he referred obliquely to the systematic murders, the orders, and, at the same time, the existing taboo in telling fashion:

When you, Reichsführer, visited my department officially a few weeks [after the beginning of the war], I had the opportunity to give you a very thorough report on the Eimann guard regiment. I emphasized especially how valuable this unit was, in view of the varied responsibilities you had assigned me in the interests of the Reich.

Only the accompanying 'Report on Selection, Deployment and Activity of the SS Eimann Guard Regiment' referred expressly to the fact that the unit had taken care of 'eliminating' 2400 psychiatric patients.[73]

In 1962, a former SS mechanic responsible for the gas vans testified on the period under discussion here: 'Additional gas vans from Sachsenhausen went to the Sauer Battalion in Posen and the so-called evacuation staff, also in Posen.'[74]

In the few publications on these murders up to now, all the authors fail to recognize the obvious connection with resettlement policies. Hans-Walter Schmuhl, in particular, argued speculatively and even maintained that the northeastern German Gauleiters murdered more or less on their own, against the will of Philipp Bouhler, the official in the Reich Chancellery responsible for 'euthanasia'.[75] This is out of the question.

Even for these initial mass murders, it is indicative that no concrete order existed to murder the mentally ill. Although the forced resettlements at the time are well documented, there are no documents explicitly proving the linkage between the murder of thousands of German and Polish patients and the resettlement of the Baltic and Volhynian Germans. Nevertheless, the participating organizers, murderers, and beneficiaries obviously worked hand in hand, and for that, all that was needed was verbal prescriptions of expediency, possibly only vaguely expressed. All the perpetrators, however, could note one thing: mass murder was possible, requiring only mild camouflage. No one hindered the progress of events; no one demanded justification, though many knew about it. Thus a model was created for the future murder of the Jews.

At the time, the Gniezno branch of the 'Office for the Resettlement of Poles and Jews' (*Amt für die Umsiedlung von Polen und Juden*) was located very near the Tiegenhof psychiatric hospital. It was directed by Dieter Wisliceny – one of Eichmann's closest associates – at just the time patients were being killed in gas vans.[76] It may be assumed with near certainty that Wisliceny, too, participated, or at least knew what was happening; that he reported to Eichmann, to the extent this was even necessary; and that he henceforth considered this type of 'evacuation' to be one option among many.

But it was not only in psychiatric hospitals that murder took place for the benefit of the resettlement authorities. After August 1942, at least, 'patients and cripples [in the resettlement camps of the Litzmannstadt (Lodz) UWZ] were often selected and deported'.[77] In July 1943, Krumey, the head of the Litzmannstadt UWZ, stated decisively, 'The mentally ill and incurably ill encountered during the [resettlement] operation are offered to the RSHA for special treatment. Permission has been granted in all cases.'[78]

# Jewish reservation or ghetto

In September 1939, Himmler and Heydrich still planned to deport all Jews in the former western Polish provinces to a new zone on the far side of the Vistula; the German, Austrian, and Czech Jews were to follow soon after, as well as the Gypsies. A few weeks later, the deporters were suddenly forced to coordinate their plans with the resettlement of the Baltic Germans. They abruptly took on increasing responsibilities that were subject to other 'exigencies'. Eichmann therefore had to break off the deportations of Jews from Vienna, Moravská Ostrava, and Katowice almost before they had even begun.

Nevertheless, Himmler and Heydrich held fast even in October to the plan to resettle at least the Jews of the incorporated eastern territories – more than half a million people – to 'rump Poland' within a few weeks. The plan was not without complications: on 9 November 1939, the Lodz region was retroactively added to the Warthegau, in order to gain a second large city for the thoroughly urban Baltic Germans. The decision meant, as already mentioned, that the number of Jews in the expanded Warthegau more than doubled, so that deportation took on new quantitative and qualitative dimensions, while the destination of the deportations simultaneously became even smaller and economically even poorer.

Himmler and Heydrich at first overcame this new, self-created problem maximalistically. They enlarged the planned extent of rapid ethnic cleansing in linear fashion. They now planned the immediate deportation of around a million people within only four months – 'by February 1940'.[79] On 8 November 1939, Friedrich Wilhelm Krüger, the Higher SS and Police Chief in Krakow, even remarked that 'in daily transports of 10,000 people, 600,000 Jews and 400,000 Poles from the eastern Gaus, and later also all Jews and Gypsies from the Reich territory, would be sent to the Generalgouvernement'.[80]

But by 28 November, Heydrich already found himself forced to make the first cutbacks in his programme. As in his guidelines of 21 September 1939, he also divided the new, now much larger deportation project into a short-term and a long-term plan:

An evacuation plan has been designed by the Reich Security Main Office, consisting of a short-term and a long-term plan. The short-term plan is to be carried out by the beginning of the census on 17 December 1939. Under it, enough Poles and Jews are to be deported so that the incoming Baltic Germans can be accommodated. The *short-term* plan will be carried out only for the Warthegau, since Baltic Germans will only be brought there at first. . . . The *long-term* plan will be drafted from here and definitively established for all the eastern provinces after consultation at my office.[81]

In this way, Heydrich was already qualifying the goal, formulated in September and October, of rapidly deporting all Jews within the German sphere of influence, or at least the western Polish Jews, to the eastern part of the Generalgouvernement. He did this in order not to delay settlement of the Baltic Germans, already waiting in resettlement camps, until the achievement of his ambitious goals.

Although with the start of the second short-term plan, the Jews from the incorporated eastern territories actually stopped being expelled, their living conditions worsened dramatically. The Germans treated Poles and Jews quite differently in their deportation to the Generalgouvernement, especially with regard to material expropriation; it affected the Jewish population, right from the beginning of the occupation, incomparably more severely than the Polish. The general expropriation of Jewish property, the theft of all their assets, their household goods, even their clothes, was one of the material prerequisites of the entire resettlement programme. The expropriation was directed by the Main Trusteeship Office in the East – that is, the very institution that Göring had created to ensure the enrichment and economic rehabilitation of the new eastern territories, as well as property compensation for the ethnic German settlers. The economic experts structured the financial side of the resettlement business as a combination of theft and game of chance – a combination that often characterized German policy at the time.

In autumn 1939, the following mechanism came into play: the Foreign Office concluded bilateral treaties with Italy, the Baltic republics, and the Soviet Union regulating the 'repatriation' of ethnic Germans. The RKF and the Ethnic German Liaison Office organized the resettlement. The property that the settlers had to leave behind in their homelands was estimated by auditors on behalf of the DUT. On the basis of these appraisals, the countries of origin paid 'compensation' for the settlers' abandoned property to the treasury of the German Reich. This occurred in a lump sum and, as a rule, not in cash, but in the form of raw materials and food supplies – for example, oil and wheat. Actually, the Reich Ministry of Finance should then have paid out to the settlers the value of their property. But in fact, it used the income from the resettlement deal for the German war effort and to cope with supply bottlenecks, thus benefiting the German population. The resettled families were 'compensated' almost exclusively with the assets of Jews and Poles, and later those of the French and Slovenes. In the end, those expropriated were the 'superfluous eaters' – a 'burden' on the Reich budget.

Thus an additional motive was created for expulsion and later extermination. The German state, especially the Four-Year Plan authorities responsible for raw material and food imports, improved its balance of payments, which was already running a constant deficit, in this triangular exchange; this could only succeed on the basis of the expulsion and expropriation of minorities.[82] The situation developed exactly as the Hungarian newspaper *Magyarság* had predicted on 24 October 1939: Germany could, with the help of this resettlement operation and property transfers by settlers, ensure 'the procurement of food and raw materials over the long term' and settle these people in Poland without any major financial expense, since they 'would take over the vast region there . . . that was mainly in Jewish hands until now'.[83] At the end of 1942, the staff main office of the RKF reported, not without pride, 'Essentially, the repatriation of the ethnic German settlers was financed through the uncompensated use of formerly alien property – that is, without utilizing Reich funds.'[84]

The functionaries of the Main Trustee Office in the East and the DUT stripped the Jews of their property immediately and entirely.[85] They used it to create financial reserves, pay cash allowances and reconstruction loans, and finance the entire resettlement apparatus, and they allotted Jewish workshops and factories – if they were not liquidated for insufficient productivity – to suitable settlers. But the expropriation of Jewish property, in contrast to that of the majority of Poles, was not dependent on concrete resettlements; it was anticipatory. That is, the Jews – and only the Jews – were robbed of almost their entire means of subsistence and thus turned into a 'superfluous', 'unproductive' population; but, because of a lack of deportation opportunities, they at first remained in the country. Thus was the material basis for the image of the filthy, loafing Jewish black marketeer created.

By March 1940, it was clear that there would be no Jewish reservation in Lublin and thus no concrete possibility of deporting Jews to the Warthegau. Instead, on 30 April 1940 the Germans sealed off the Lodz ghetto. At the time, local authorities were given the 'firm promise' that by 1 October 1940 – that is, within five months – 'the Jews [would be] completely removed from the Litzmannstadt ghetto'.[86] In the following weeks, such a goal was already proving illusory.[87]

The organizers of the deportations considered the ghettos to be provisional, a sort of mass detention pending deportation that would end immediately as soon as the original resettlement plans could be carried out. Conversely, of course, the ghettoization would put pressure on other participating authorities, who might still be reluctant due to technical concerns or contrary partisan interests, to organize the deportations rapidly and ruthlessly.

Once the plan to set up a 'Jewish reservation of Lublin' had failed, the organizers of the resettlement programme had to find another solution to the problem they themselves had created. They did this, once again, by surmounting conflicts of purpose in maximalist fashion. Soon the catchword 'Jewish reservation of Lublin' was replaced by the 'insular "Madagascar solution"'; not long after, 'Madagascar' was replaced by 'deportation to a territory yet to be determined'.

In accordance with the inner logic of this process of restructuring, eviction, displacement, and resettlement, on 24 June 1940 Heydrich argued vehemently with Ribbentrop for a 'territorial final solution'. He justified it by pointing out that 'the overall problem of the approximately three and a quarter million Jews' under German jurisdiction can 'no longer be solved by emigration alone'.[88] This was expressed even more clearly in an August 1940 planning paper on the Madagascar project: 'With the addition of the masses from the east, a resolution of the Jewish problem through emigration has become impossible.' Also, the 'solution of the Jewish problem in Reich territory, including the Protectorate of Bohemia and Moravia, by way of emigration . . . [will be] hard to bring to a conclusion in the foreseeable future'.[89] Whereas the inventors of the 'Jewish reservation of Lublin' intended to resettle roughly a million German, Austrian, Czech, and western Polish Jews to the area 'east of the Vistula', the second project, conceived after the defeat of France – the 'insular solution' of Madagascar – now involved 4 million people. In addition, all Polish Jews were now supposed to be resettled, as well as the Slovak, French, Dutch, and Belgian Jews. The Madagascar Plan, as illusory as it might have been, had very concrete consequences: it legitimized further ever more radical steps towards ethnic segregation.

Thus in summer 1940, the 'repatriation' of a further 250,000 (south)-eastern European ethnic Germans had been decided upon, even though those who had already been resettled were still far from receiving permanent accommodation, and deportations were not even close to keeping pace with settlements. As well as the 'home to the Reich' policy for southeastern European ethnic Germans, which had been agreed upon in new German–Soviet pacts, the Reich government simultaneously began the ethnic and economic new order in southeastern Europe and, in addition, annexed parts of France and Belgium. At the same time, German population politicians agreed to reduce the number of inhabitants of the General-gouvernement, and not only there, in order to 'resolve the most pressing social problem – overpopulation'.[90]

In addition, the German leadership further accelerated the spiral of resettlement, expropriation, and expulsion by formulating additional economic goals that can only be outlined briefly here. From the beginning, they intended to 'break up' the internal German population structure with the help of the annexations in the east (and later also in the west). In particular, a million people were to be relocated from the impoverished rural regions of the German Reich, thus shutting down some 250,000 farms that were considered unproductive because of successive divisions of land due to inheritance.[91] This would fundamentally change – that is, 'improve' – the economic structures of the western Polish areas through the settlement of German small farmers. Thus, as a rule, two or three Polish or Jewish families had to make way for one German family.[92]

On top of this, there were the interests of the Wehrmacht. The chiefs of the army and air force demanded early on the removal of hundreds of thousands of people to 'free up' huge military training grounds, safety zones, and bridgeheads. It was 'desirable', according to the planners in January 1940, 'as far as possible, to settle only ethnic Germans – in any case, no Jews or Poles – within 50 km of military facilities'. This preference implied the removal and settlement of more than a million people. As similar as they might have been, the military concepts collided with Himmler's resettlement plans. The Wehrmacht's demands further reduced the already diminished opportunities for the Generalgouverne-ment to accommodate evacuees from the incorporated eastern territories; at the same time, the military themselves increased the pressure for rapid removal, since they wished to build colossal military training grounds not only in the Generalgouvernement, but also in the incorporated eastern territories. Some of these grounds were indeed built later.[93]

By the close of 1939 the resettlement plans, with their varied motives, had added up to the prospective expulsion of several million Poles and Jews. Their motivations and goals remained incompatible, as shown by the running battles among various offices. If one planner found the 'repatriation' of the ethnic Germans important, for another the creation of an enormous artillery testing range took centre stage; if one wanted a rapid, uncomplicated solution to the 'Jewish question', another spoke of structural improvements in the impoverished rural regions of the Reich. These completely divergent ideas inevitably acted as mutual obstructions. No one ordered the abandonment of certain projects, or even set priorities. The participants sought refuge in fragile, short-lived compromises and unrestrainedly placed their bets on their projected ability to overcome bottlenecks and conflicts of interest during the imperialist war.

The organizers of resettlement soon found a code for this: 'Madagascar'. This plan, they speculated in summer 1940, would succeed in 'relieving' the new greater European territory first of 4 million, then, in December 1940, of 5.8 million people. The Jews were to be forcibly resettled, in the course of the 'territorial final solution', to the actual or – beginning with the Madagascar Plan – the projected periphery of the German sphere of influence. The Madagascar project did not emerge in isolation. Rather, it was a consequence of the plan, earnestly discussed by the Wehrmacht, Hitler, and the Foreign Office, of creating a German 'Central African colonial empire' after the presumed defeat of France. It would serve as a 'Central African sphere of influence', with the 'final goal' of securing 'provisions for 150 million people' in the European 'greater economic sphere'.[94]

Just as the failure of the 'Jewish reservation of Lublin' project had led to the ghettoization of the Lodz Jews, the failure of the Madagascar Plan led to the ghettoization of the Warsaw Jews in late autumn 1940. The Warsaw ghetto was sealed off on 15 November 1940. Frank had postponed this twice previously, once on 8 March 1940, in view of the fact that the Lublin district was to become 'the collection area for all Jews'. Once this plan, never really pursued in earnest, had been officially laid to rest a few days later, on 9 May the local occupation authorities resumed preparations for the confinement of the Warsaw Jews. At the beginning of July, Frank stopped work on the ghetto walls because Hitler intended 'to settle the Jews in Madagascar after the end of the war'. Therefore, the following chronology includes the period from the total sealing off of the Lodz ghetto to the walling off of the ghetto in Warsaw – that is, from spring to late autumn 1940.

# Notes

1 Burrin agrees, 73.
2 Goebbels diaries, vol. I/4, 21.

3　Final report by Krumey 'on relocations within the scope of the placement of Volhynian, Galician and Chelm Germans (second short-term plan) to the Wartheland Reichsgau' (1940); BAK, R75/6, 8.

4　The Jews earned their living almost exclusively as workers, artisans, tradesmen, and self-employed professionals. In contrast, the SD found the following occupational structure among the Volhynian German settlers: 'Five per cent urban population, 5 per cent village artisans, 8 to 10 per cent farm workers, approx. 80 per cent independent farmers' (Reports from the Reich, 26 January 1940, 688).

5　Note on the discussion by Eichmann on 30 January 1940; *Biuletyn* 12 (1960), 66F–75F.

6　Quoted in Pätzold, 259; on the delays in Baltic resettlement and the immense pressure under which the organizers had placed themselves, see the correspondence between the Vomi branch in Gotenhafen (Gdynia) and the RKF; StA Poznań, Vomi/P/161, *passim*.

7　Activity report of the Vomi office in Szczecin for the period from 1 January to 30 April 1940, ibid. 173, 11f.

8　Himmler, *Geheimreden*, 139. See also sources in Benz, Arndt and Boberach, 40.

9　Telex from Koppe ('Re: 2nd Volhynian German resettlement'), 28 March 1940, to Erich Spaarmann, head of the SS settlement staff in Lodz; StA Lodz, UWZ/L/L-3636, 62. See also *Okkupationspolitik in Polen*, 182.

10　Far more, in certain cases; *Okkupationspolitik in Polen, passim*.

11　'Merkpunkte für die Arbeitsstäbe der Kreise im Bezug auf Vorbereitung und Ablauf der Ansiedlung von Wolhynien- und Galiziendeutschen' (Guidelines for the District Staffs Regarding Preparation and Implementation of Settlement of Volhynian and Galician Germans), 2 March 1940 (signed by Koppe); AGK, UWZ/P/130, 30.

12　Letter from Koskull to Hoffmann, 1 March 1940; StA Poznań, Vomi/P/34, 19.

13　Speech by Himmler to internees of the camp at Kirchberg, near Lodz, on 4 May 1940, quoted in a letter from the settlement staff at Litzmannstadt, 21 May 1940; BAK, R49/20, 5, 18.

14　Letter from Himmler to Koppe, 10 May 1940; AGK, UWZ/P/130, 81f.

15　Note from Seidl to Höppner, 6 June 1940; AGK, UWZ/P/161, 4. How precarious Eichmann's situation had become is shown by his request to have reports on new difficulties in this resettlement addressed to him directly 'as "secret"' – 'telexes are not desirable'.

16　Telex from Günther to Höppner, head of the Posen UWZ, on new demands for evacuation in the Warthegau, 1 July 1940, *Biuletyn* 12 (1960), 94F. The same deadline for deportation also applied to the Jews from Upper Silesia: on 19 April 1940, the state police office in Katowice reported that the 'beginning of deportation' of Jews to the Generalgouvernement was 'not to be reckoned with before the end of August of this year' (quoted in Konieczny, 94).

17　Note on discussion between Günther and Höppner on 9 July 1940 in Berlin, *Biuletyn* 12 (1960), 96Ff. (See Ch. 4, 8 July).

18　Ibid.

19　Telex from Krumey to Eichmann, 12 September 1940, reprinted in *Biuletyn* 12 (1960), 108F. The letter speaks of 1000 families, downplaying the problem.

20　Telex from Krumey to Eichmann, 18 October 1940, 'Re: Volhynian Operation', *Biuletyn* 12 (1960), 111F.

21　Telex from Eichmann to the Posen UWZ, 28 October 1940; AGK, UWZ/P/130, 108. In the telex, Eichmann provides an overview of the transports of the second short-term plan which had been processed so far. According to it, 1000 people each had been deported with the following number of trains to the Generalgouvernement: 20 from Saybusch (Żywiec) in Upper Silesia (see

Chapter 6), five from Danzig–West Prussia, three 'Gypsy transports' (see Chapter 2, 27 April) from the Reich, and 81 transports in connection with the 'Volhynian Operation'.

22 See the list of 'transport trains that have departed from the Warthegau with evacuated Poles from Litzmannstadt [Lodz] to the Generalgouvernement within the scope of the second short-term plan – Volhynian Operation', *Biuletyn* 21 (1970), 98ff.

23 Monthly statistical report by the Resettlement Office Altreich (Old Reich)/Ostmark (Austria), 21 April 1941; BAK, R49/2639.

24 According to Heydrich at a meeting on 30 January 1940, FGM, 50. Eichmann, who worked until September 1939 in the Jewish Matters section of the SD (reference: II/112), had proved himself in particular as founder and head of the 'Central Office for Jewish Emigration' in Vienna (see Safrian).

25 BAK, R58/840, 281. On Eichmann's function until 1939, see Drobisch, *passim*; Heim, *passim*.

26 Internal memorandum from Müller, 29 February 1940; BAK, R58/240, 32, according to which Section IVA5 was divided into the following areas of specialization: 'IVA5a: Emigrants; IVA5b: Jewish matters (incl. Reich unification)'.

27 RSHA task allocation plan of 1 March 1941; BAK, R58/840, 240.

28 Overview of the sections in Department IV, November 1941; BAK, R58/240, 159.

29 RSHA task allocation plan of 1 October 1943; BAK, R58/840, 323.

30 Letter from Eichmann on the resettlement of Slovenes, Ferenc, 356.

31 Handwritten notes by Franz Novak while in investigative detention, 7 January 1974, quoted in Pätzold and Schwarz, *Auschwitz*, 157.

32 Task allocation plan, BAK, R58/840, 225. On the personnel and structural changes in the section, not significant here, see ibid. 238.

33 Report by Krumey, 18 October 1941; AGK, UWZ/L/16, 128ff.

34 Note by Krumey on 'the work of the Central Resettlement Office from 1 October 1940 to 8 September 1941'; AGK, UWZ/L/26, 1.

35 Letter from Albert Rapp to RSHA, 16 December 1939, *Biuletyn* 12 (1960), 22F–31F. Rapp headed the Office for the Resettlement of Poles and Jews in Posen, later the 'Central Resettlement Office' (ibid. p. 43F). For the Warthegau, Rapp calculated that 540,000 people (including their family members) could be considered members of the Polish intelligentsia, ibid. p. 30F.

36 Note on a meeting between Eichmann and Seidl on 22–23 January 1940, *Biuletyn* 12 (1960), 44Ff. On 20 January 1940, the Office for the Resettlement of Poles and Jews issued 'Statistics on the Quality of the Dwellings to be Evacuated'. It found 63.9 per cent of the homes to be 'bad or unhabitable', 26.3 per cent 'average', and only 9.8 per cent 'good or very good'. AGK, UWZ/P/7, 14.

37 Letter from Heydrich, 28 November 1939, *Biuletyn* 12 (1960), 18F. The destination of the deportation was the Generalgouvernement. According to Heydrich's orders, 'the deportation . . . is to occur such that 5000 persons are deported daily from the Warthegau'. This (greatly reduced) goal was in fact achieved within the planned time period. See the report by Rapp cited above, 30F.

38 See 'final schedule for transport trains involved in the interim plan', *Biuletyn* 12 (1960), 61F.

39 Long-term plan for resettlement in the eastern provinces; BAK, R69/1146, 1–13.

40 Final report on resettlement within the scope of the settlement of Bessarabian Germans (third short-term plan) from 21 January 1941 to 20 January 1942 in the Wartheland Reichsgau; BAK, R75/8, 1.

41 Status report by the district chief of Nowy Sącz, 31 December 1940, *Doc. Occ.*, vol. 6, 373ff.

42 See Aly and Heim, 276–86.

43 Notes by Hewel on a meeting between Hitler and journalist Colin Ross on 12 March 1940; ADAP, series D, vol. 8, 714ff.

44 However critically the discussions between Hitler and Ross may be viewed, the statements documented here were confirmed by Hitler's later behaviour in summer 1940.

45 The 'Eimann SS Sturmbann' was formed in Danzig (Gdańsk) shortly before the outbreak of war. The task of this special unit consisted, at first, in 'securing and purging the districts of Prussian Stargard, Berent, Karthaus and Neustadt (Wejherowo)'. In the process, according to Broszat (28), 'in the second half of September, many hundreds of members of the Polish intelligentsia (pastors, teachers, lawyers, doctors, property owners) were executed on the spot, while others were taken to camps or arrested . . . on the orders of the Higher SS and Police Chief of Danzig and with Himmler's express approval'. Shortly thereafter, Eimann was assigned the task of 'clearing' the psychiatric institutions. The close connection between this murderous activity and the arrival of the Baltic Germans is documented by the fact that Eimann was ultimately awarded the 'Baltic Cross'; BDC, PA/Kurt Eimann.

46 This included patients from Brandenburg in Pomeranian hospitals on the basis of appropriate agreements.

47 Among the German-language portrayals, the most accurate is Jochen August, 'Das Grab Nr. 17 im Wald von Piasnica. Die Tötung der Geisteskranken begann im besetzten Polen', *Antifaschistsches Magazin. Der Mahnruf* 28: 193 (1984), 6–8. A detailed study has since been published that at least provides some information on the number of the murdered and the dates of their deaths: *Pacjenci Pracownicy Szpitali Psychiatracznych w Polsce Zamordowani przez Okupanta Hitlerowskiego i Los Tych Szpitali w Latach 1939–1945*, ed. Polskie Towarzystwo Psychiatryczne, Komisja Naukowa Historii Psychiatrii Polskiej, vol. 1: Szpitale (Warsaw, 1989); the second volume contains the names of the murder victims. The authors, because they are mainly concerned with Poland's pre-war boundaries, leave out the parallel events in the Pomeranian and East Prussian hospitals. For Pomerania, the dissertation by Heike Bernhardt is thorough in many respects, but equally unsatisfactory on the questions addressed here.

48 These, like the following figures, are taken from the lists in the above-cited study *Pacjenci Pracownicy*, 94ff.

49 Because it was located in the Generalgouvernement, this hospital does not, strictly speaking, belong on the list. I mention it here nevertheless because it was, in all likelihood, 'freed up' as interim quarters for the Volhynian German settlers who were then sent on from the nearby Dorohusk railroad station. Note (undated) on the corresponding planning by the Reichsbank administration in Lodz, late November–early December 1939; AGK, UWZ/P/218, 15.

50 Statement by Gustav Sorge, 7 March 1962; LG Hannover (Hanover district court), UR 6/61.

51 Report from Müller to Nitsche on psychiatric care in Pomerania, 11 December 1942; BAK, R96/16.

52 Report (signed by Herbert Becker) 'on the Warthegau planning', 12 October 1942; BAK, R96/1/15.

53 Report (signed by Herbert Becker) 'on the Danzig–West Prussia planning', 13 October 1942; BAK, R96/1/15.

54 Aly, 'Medicine', 36. A similar institution apparently also existed temporarily in Schneidemühl (Piła) in Pomerania, Bernhardt, 32.

55 Testimony by Herbert Vollbrandt on 8 May 1963; Sta. Hamburg, 147 Js 58/67, Sonderbände [special volumes on] Tiegenhof, 311ff.
56 Telex on Sandberger's requests, 23 October 1939; BAK, R69/493, 35.
57 Telex from Sandberger to the RSHA, 2 November 1939; BAK, R69/854, 2.
58 Letter from district head of Mogilno to EWZ in Posen, 19 May 1940; StA Poznań, Vomi/P/33, 279.
59 Letter from NSDAP district headquarters to Vomi in Posen regarding 'patient transports to the Reich'; StA Poznań, Vomi/P/123, 43.
60 Discussion on 29 October 1939 between Ehlichs, responsible for health matters at the EWZ in Gotenhafen (Gdynia); Dr Hanns Meixner; and Party Comrade Schram(m)el of the NSV on 'care of sick and infirm Baltic Germans'; telex from Meixner to Ehlich on the same day regarding 'securing old age homes' for Baltic Germans in need of care; BAK, R69/426 (I would like to thank Matthias Hamann for referring me to these documents).
61 Testimony to police by head nurse Maria Lüdtke; 24 September 1962; Sta. Hamburg 147Js58/67/Sonderbände [special volumes on] Tiegenhof, vol. 1, 173ff.
62 Correspondence from Margarete Danielsson and Lila Klobo to Berlin-Moabit district court, 27 January 1961, ibid., not paginated.
63 Lüdtke testimony, ibid. 181; testimony of Klara Wiedenhöft, ibid. 193ff. Administrative Secretary Wilhelm Heiden described the same procedure at the Kosten (Kościan) and Tiegenhof (in Gniezno) hospitals, ibid. 187ff.
64 Testimony of Frieda Wilke, 16 April 1963, ibid. vol. 2, 299.
65 Letter from Foreign Department of the Reich Physicians' Chamber (signed by Zietz) to Reichsstatthalter (regent) in Posen, 23 April 1940; StA Poznań, Vomi/P/129, 73ff.
66 Testimony of Vladimir Nikolayev, 6 May 1963, Sta. Hamburg 147Js58/67/Sonderbände [special volumes on] Tiegenhof, vol. 2, 325ff. It is not surprising that the director of the Tiegenhof hospital, Viktor Radka, became an official evaluator for T-4 in summer 1941 – 'a new one working with us', as his colleague Mennecke put it on 3 September 1941 (Chroust, vol. 1, 198; Klee, 228f.). Carrying out the 'transports of the mentally ill' was – like other, later resettlements – the responsibility of the Reich Chamber of Physicians. In a letter on 23 February 1940, it was stated:

> The Foreign Department of the Reich Chamber of Physicians takes this opportunity, within the scope of the return migration operation, to once again thank the Reich Transport Ministry, the government offices of the provinces of Brandenburg and Pomerania and the city of Berlin for support and implementation of the two transports of the mentally ill from Latvia and Estonia.

Special thanks for the fact that 'these two unusual transfers took place smoothly' were offered to the chief physicians of the Berlin psychiatric institution of Wittenau and the captain and officers of the ship *Bremerhaven*. StA Potsdam, Brandenburgische Landesanstalt Neuruppin, Rep. 55C/50, 262, 267. A trip by the *Bremerhaven* is documented in Loeber (234). It set out from the Latvian port of Ventspils (German: Windau) on 11 November 1939 with 537 passengers. A second transport set out from Riga on 4 December 1939. See the report by the director of the transport, Chief Physician Schreiber of the Berlin-Wittenau hospital, 18 December 1939; StA Poznań, Vomi/P/123, 112ff.
67 This letter from the RKF is quoted in a letter from the foreign department of the Reich Physicians' Chamber (signed by Zietz) to the hospitals at Arnsdorf on the Saale and Meseritz-Obrawalde, 27 February 1940; StA Poznań, Vomi/P/

129, 75. The leaders of the Baltic Germans did not intervene against this method. Instead, one of them, Andreas von Koskull, voiced regret that they had 'unfortunately not been able to leave behind the inferior portion' of their own national group. This would 'naturally continue to bring no joy to us and the authorities here'. Letter from Koskull to Drescher, 19 April 1940; StA Poznań, Vomi/P/34, 11.

68 The correct name is Masuhr (Fritz).

69 File note from the EWZ (Transport and Housing Office), 4 November 1939, 'Re: Transport of 700 mentally ill Poles on 3 November 1939 and 700 infirm Baltic Germans on 4 November 1939'; BAK, R69/426. The Polish patients were removed in 18 freight cars; the infirm Baltic Germans 'in third-class and some second-class passenger cars'. Beforehand, the 'higher SS and police leader, Gruppenführer Hildebrandt, [wanted] precise information on departure times'. The Schwetz hospital was then officially transformed into an old-age home and rebuilt at considerable expense – 400,000 RM, which had to be raised by the RKF. See memos and letters from the RKF, 3, 21 and 22 March 1941; BAK, R49/2609.

70 Kursell, 314ff. (I would like to thank Wilhelm Lenz for referring me to this report).

71 Letter from the Vomi in Gotenhafen (Gdynia) (dictation symbol 'Ha', for Hans Handrack) to Conti, head of the Reich Chamber of Physicians, 7 March 1940; StA Poznań, Vomi/P/161, 161f.; the response from the Reich Physicians' Chamber can be found ibid. 199. Despite extensive efforts to achieve such an 'ideal solution', the proposal foundered as a result of the interests of the military and the regional administrator.

72 *Zagłada*, 115ff.

73 Letter from Hildebrandt, higher SS and police leader of Danzig–West Prussia, to Himmler, 9 January 1940, with enclosure; BDC, SS-HO/2140.

74 Testimony of Gustav Sorge, 7 March 1962; LG Hannover, UR 6/61.

75 See Klee, 95–8, 112–15; Schmuhl, 240ff.

76 Memorandum from Koppe, 20 January 1940; AGK, UWZ/P/96, 10.

77 Judgment of the LG (district court) Frankfurt/Main, 29 August 1969 in the trial of Krumey and Hunsche; ZStL, 502 AR-Z 60/58, 7, 24ff.

78 Ibid. 12.

79 Quoted in Adler, 109. Edict 1/II of 30 October 1939 is published in *Biuletyn* 12 (1960), 9F.

80 Quoted in Adler, 109.

81 Telex from Heydrich, 28 November 1939, *Biuletyn* 12 (1960), 15Fff.

82 Aly and Heim, 153ff.

83 Quoted in Stuhlpfarrer, 147, which contains descriptions of what the corresponding German–Italian agreements on property compensation looked like.

84 RKF activity report (as of the end of 1942), BAK, R49/26, 39.

85 For greater detail, see Hilberg, 239–45.

86 According to the provincial head of Lodz in summer 1941, in hindsight, *Dokumenty*, vol. 3, 177ff.

87 Report from SD leadership section in Litzmannstadt to Section IIIB4 (Ehlich) of the RSHA, 24 June 1940; AGK, UWZ/P/129, 3.

88 Notes by Luther, a deputy state secretary in the Reich Foreign Ministry, on the development of the 'Final Solution of the Jewish Question' from January 1939 to the Wannsee Conference, 21 August 1942. Under point four, he wrote, 'by a letter of 24 June 1940, Gruppenführer Heydrich informed Mr Ram [short for Reichsaussenminister, or Reich Foreign Minister] . . .' Quoted in Pätzold, 350.

89 'Reich Security Main Office: Madagascar Project', drafted at the end of July–beginning of August 1940, PAA, IIg/177, 201.
90 For greater detail, see Aly and Heim, 69–279.
91 Aly and Heim, 398ff. Comprehensive documents on this are located in BAK, R49/1001, *passim*.
92 Aly and Heim, 159ff.
93 Report on discussions held in Lodz on 16 and 17 January 1940 on Wehrmacht planning for the new eastern territories, Müller, 125–9; see also 133.
94 See Hillgruber, *Strategie*, 242–55.

# |4|

# 'The Madagascar Plan'

## Chronology: May–September 1940

**10 May 1940:** Germany invades France, Luxembourg, Belgium, and the Netherlands.

**17 May:** The first Polish 'families scheduled for assimilation in the Old Reich' are transported to Germany from the annexed region of western Poland.[1] In the course of the second short-term plan, a total of 2399 're-Germanizable persons' are 'released' into the Old Reich;[2] within the scope of the third short-term plan – from 21 January 1941 to 20 January 1942 – the figure is 7327 persons.[3] A similar procedure is developed in the autumn in Lorraine,[4] and later in northern Slovenia.

**19 May:** Second order to ghettoize the Jewish population in Warsaw. Ghetto construction is to begin on 1 July 1940; German authorities are assigned this task as a result of the failure of plans for a 'Jewish reservation of Lublin'. However, 'in the early stages of preparation', in early July, Frank issues instructions 'to abandon all ghetto construction plans in view of the Führer's plan to send the Jews to Madagascar after the war'.[5]

**20 May:** Himmler writes to high-ranking SS and police officials in the annexed area of western Poland about the planned 'Germanization' of Poles:

> Germanization in the eastern provinces can only be implemented in accordance with racial standards if the population in these provinces is screened. The racially worthy. . . must be transplanted to Germany as individual families in the Old Reich. . . . The other segment, which cannot be integrated racially, shall remain in the country as long as we can use them in the labour force to build up the provinces. Over the next 5–10 years, without any mercy or exceptions whatsoever, they

shall be deported to the Generalgouvernement, which will serve as a collection point for all those who are racially of no use in Germany.[6]

During this time, Himmler writes his well-known report 'on the treatment of ethnically alien elements [Fremdvölkische] in the East', which Hitler deems 'very good and correct'. In it, Himmler outlines how Poles are to be subjected to 'racial screening' and how individual families are to 'be integrated with confidence into German life after changing their names'.[7] A large majority of Poles in the Generalgouvernement, including 'the deported population from the eastern provinces' and segments of the 'inferior population' of Germany ('e.g., Sorbs and Wends'), are to become a 'leaderless nation of labourers, . . . called upon to work' on the 'eternal cultural sites and edifices' of the Germans, 'perhaps, in view of the amount of heavy labour required, enabling their construction in the first place'.

About the Jewish minority, Himmler writes, 'I hope to see the term *Jews* totally eradicated through the opportunity for a mass emigration of all Jews to Africa or another colony.'[8]

On 24 June, Himmler writes a postscript to this memorandum. In response to reservations that emigration plans could prove counter-productive to labour force needs, Himmler insists that, of the native Polish population, 'seven-eighths must continue to migrate eastward to the Generalgouvernement'. For heavy labour, 'millions of subsistence-seeking individuals' in the neighbouring states to the east are to be used as seasonal migrant labourers. In doing this, any and all 'economic and social equality' is prohibited, particularly 'any interbreeding between these racial aliens and Germanic individuals'. 'Any racial alien who seduces a German woman or girl will be hanged.' In summary, Himmler refers to his principles as 'socialism of good blood'.[9]

**21 May:** For the first time, Grand Admiral Erich Raeder suggests to Hitler the idea of invading England.[10]

Between 21 May and 8 June, members of the Special Commando Unit of Herbert Lange murder 1558 mentally ill patients in the East Prussian psychiatric hospital in Soldau (Działdowo). The facility later becomes a transit camp for Lithuanian Germans being resettled.[11]

**24 May:** Philipp Bouhler travels throughout the Generalgouvernement discussing the 'final solution of the Jewish question'.[12] Bouhler, one of Hitler's closest staff members, coordinates the 'euthanasia' murders, along with Karl Brandt.

**3 June 1940:** Franz Rademacher, responsible for anti-Jewish policies in the German Foreign Office, deals with the question 'Where to put the Jews?' As possible options, he considers the 'conceivable war aim' either to remove all Jews from Europe or to use the Eastern (European) Jews as security for 'the Jews of America', thus deporting only the Western (European) Jews, to 'Madagascar, for example'.[13]

**10 June:** Italy enters the war.

**13 June:** Walter Emmerich, newly named Minister of Economics in the Generalgouvernement, presents a plan for the economic development and rationalization of the region. It is based on the 'compression of the Jewish sector' and its controlled 'replacement by the Polish sector'.[14]

Bruno Streckenbach, Chief of Security Police and SD in Krakow, is given the additional office of representing Heydrich's deputy, Werner Best, who has been transferred to France.[15]

**15 June:** Soviet troops occupy Lithuania. German resettlement authorities immediately start preparations for the 'return' of 50,000 Lithuanian Germans, though this is not carried out until six months later.

**17 June:** Soviet troops occupy Estonia and Latvia.

**18 June:** Ribbentrop mentions the project of 'sending the Jews to Madagascar' to Italian Foreign Minister Galeazzo Ciano.[16]

Hitler mentions the same idea to Mussolini and confirms that Burgundy is being planned as a 'group settlement area' for South Tyroleans.[17]

**19 June:** Luxembourg and Alsace-Lorraine are to be 'annexed' to the German Reich.[18]

**20 June:** Grand Admiral Raeder notes, 'The Führer wanted to use Madagascar to harbour the Jews under the aegis of the French.'[19]

**22 June:** France surrenders. The country is divided into an occupied and an unoccupied zone; Alsace-Lorraine is annexed *de facto*, but not *de jure*.

Göring assigns the Reich Ministry of the Economy the task of preparing for the 'new economic order in Europe'.[20]

**23 June:** Philipp Bouhler, responsible for Operation T-4 in the Chancellery of the Führer, wants to become Generalgouverneur of East Africa, since he assumes the 'Central African sphere of influence' will be conquered shortly; he asks Hitler for 'the colonial task'.[21]

Soon after, Viktor Brack, Bouhler's second-in-command (*Oberdienstleiter*), suggests that the Foreign Office 'use the transport system' that he had set up for the euthanasia action 'to transport the Jews to Madagascar'.[22] At the same time the systematic murder of all Jewish patients in German psychiatric hospitals begins.[23]

**24 June:** The head of the SD command division in Lodz informs the RSHA:

> Deportations from the Litzmannstadt [i.e., Lodz] ghetto, with a total of about 160,000 Jews (according to the most recent count), will require 200 days (incl. delays), or approx. seven months, since only 1000 Jews can be deported per transport. The deportation of Jews from Litzmannstadt to the Generalgouvernement will thus last from August 1940 until February 1941. From a health standpoint [that is, in view of the danger of epidemics] as well as an economic standpoint, the plan is considered untenable in this form, referring once again, particularly in light of the approaching winter, to the only plausible option for deporting the Jews, namely a Jew trek [i.e., foot march].[24]

On the same day, Heydrich pressures the Foreign Office for a 'territorial final solution', since 'the overall problem of the approximately three and a quarter million Jews' under German jurisdiction can 'no longer be solved by emigration alone'.[25]

Himmler notes that

> according to the established guidelines, the selection shall continue such that a ratio of approximately 1:7 racially sound [*gutrassig*] [Polish or other non-German] men and women with their children be transplanted in families or individually to villages and towns in Germany.[26]

**25 June:** Frank refuses to accept more forced deportees into the General-gouvernement than the number laid down in the second short-term plan, since these resettlements, in view of the 'overpopulation' and the 'wretched food supply situation' in the Generalgouvernement, are 'no longer tenable, considering the catastrophic consequences'.[27]

**28 June:** In accordance with the Nazi–Soviet pact of summer 1939, the Soviet Union annexes the Romanian regions of Bessarabia and northern Bukovina. The resettlement of the ethnic German minorities there thus becomes imminent.

**1 July 1940:** The chief of the Jewish Section of the Gestapo in Warsaw informs the head of the *Judenrat* (Council of Jews) that 'the war would be over in a month' and the Jews of Warsaw 'would all leave for Madagascar'.[28]

**2 July:** A 'plan to solve the Jewish question' is drafted in the Foreign Office.[29]

**3 July:** Franz Rademacher, responsible for Jewish affairs in the Foreign Office, notes that he has already spoken in detail with representatives of the Reichsführer SS, the Ministry of the Interior, and the NSDAP about the Madagascar Plan. Rademacher summarizes, 'The desirable solution is: all Jews out of Europe.'[30]

Freiberg geologist Friedrich Schumacher prepares a report, commissioned by the Foreign Office, in which he concludes that Madagascar has no valuable mineral resources, making it sufficiently worthless to be used for the Jews.[31]

Demographer Friedrich Burgdörfer is also commissioned by the Foreign Office to prepare a report. Issued on 17 July, it states that it would pose no problem for 6.5 million Jews to live on the island of Madagascar in addition to the 4 million native inhabitants. Taking then current German Middle East policy into account, Burgdörfer includes the Jews living in Palestine in the deportation plan.[32]

Eichmann tells the heads of the compulsory associations of Jews in Berlin, Prague, and Vienna that after the war is over, 'a comprehensive solution of the Jewish question in Europe will probably' have to be sought, and approximately 4 million Jews will have to be settled in another country. Eichmann gives the representatives of the Jewish organizations the task of compiling a list of 'general points that should be considered in such a plan'.[33]

**5 July:** Meeting between Frank and Goebbels on the situation in the Generalgouvernement. Goebbels' note on the outcome: 'The Jewish question can hardly be solved any more.'[34]

**8 July:** Meeting between Frank and Hitler. Four days later, Frank reports on it to his staff:

> The Führer's decision, at my request, to cease transporting Jews to the Generalgouvernement is very significant. In terms of general policy, I would like to say that there are plans to transport the whole Jewish tribe from the German Reich, the Generalgouvernement, and the Protectorate to an African or American colony in the shortest possible time after peace is declared. Madagascar is being considered. . . . I have made an effort to bless the Jews in the Generalgouvernement, as well, with this opportunity to create a new life in a new country. This was accepted, so that a colossal burden shall be lifted within the foreseeable future.[35]

**9 July:** Hitler orders German armaments production to focus on the air force and navy;[36] i.e., a showdown in the war against Britain is to be sought. This is followed by the creation, on 30 July, of the 'England' military economy staff for special use, which is then disbanded on 28 October 1940.[37] The beginning and end of plans to invade Britain mark the time frame in which the Madagascar Plan is seen as a realistic variant of a 'territorial final solution', since at the very least it required the defeating of British naval supremacy in the Mediterranean.[38]

**10 July:** Ulrich Greifelt, chief of the RKF main office, presents a memorandum on 'thoughts on the resettlement of the South Tyrolean national group into a group settlement area'. He considers Burgundy a likely location.[39] Only three days later, Himmler departs on a two-day trip to view Burgundy, accompanied by Lorenz (Vomi), Greifelt (RKF), Kulemann (DUT), and others.[40]

**11 July:** The trusteeship office in the Generalgouvernement issues orders forcing Jewish property owners to pay rental income into a blocked account.[41]

**13 July:** Representatives of the RKF, Vomi, Four-Year Plan, and the Reich Ministry of Commerce meet to discuss the resettlement of ethnic Germans from the regions of Romania annexed by the Soviet Union.[42]

**14 July:** The French government announces it would be impossible to feed 10 million refugees in the unoccupied zone for an extended period of time, since it comprises only two-fifths of the country.[43]

**16 July:** Forced resettlement of 3000 Jews from the Alsace region to the unoccupied zone of France begins.[44] The deportations last 14 days. Similar actions take place in Lorraine. By mid-September, 24,210 French citizens, including all Jews living there, have been deported.[45]

**19 July:** Under Greifelt's leadership, a commando unit from the South Tyrolean ethnic German minority and the RKF set off on a four-day trip to occupied Burgundy, where the 'group settlement area' for the South Tyroleans is to be established. The affected regions are to be 'cleared of French citizens' in compliance with a stipulation in the peace agreement with France.[46] On 13 August, according to a remark by RKF department head Fähndrich, it is decided that after the war, the South Tyroleans will be resettled in Burgundy.[47] However, the project is shelved in the autumn and later abandoned entirely.

**21 July:** The already occupied Baltic states of Estonia, Latvia, and Lithuania are officially transformed into Soviet republics.

The next day, Himmler orders the acceleration of preparations to resettle the German minority from Lithuania. In September, German–Soviet negotiations on the issue are held in Kaunas. The resettlement agreement, which also includes 'subsequent resettlement' from Estonia and Latvia, is not concluded until 10 January 1941, after some delays due to the resettlement of ethnic Germans from Bessarabia, Bukovina, and Dobruja, which has been pushed ahead. From this point until the end of March 1941, German resettlement commandos bring 48,000 Lithuanian Germans and 12,000 Latvian and Estonian Germans 'home to the Reich'. Although Himmler initially orders the 'subsequent resettlement [of the Lithuanian Germans] to take place directly from village to village only, and not via transit camps',[48] and additionally orders all 'evacuations necessary to enable the settlement' of the Lithuanian Germans,[49] almost all of them are placed in mass camps in West and East Prussia.[50] From 5 to 17 December 1940, 6607 Poles and 3259 Jews are deported from Danzig–West Prussia in anticipation of the arrival of Lithuanian Germans.[51]

**22 July:** High-level meeting presided over by Reich Minister of the Economy Walther Funk on 'the economic new order of Europe'. Goals are:

1. Integration of the areas annexed or occupied by the Reich into the Greater German economy.
2. Economic disputes with the enemy states.
3. Restructuring of Germany's continental economy and its relationship to the global economy.

As indicated in documents accompanying this meeting, planners of the 'new order' in the Ministry of the Economy already start – with explicit reference to Hitler's speech of 6 October 1939 – to include in their ideas 'the removal of Jews [*Entjudung*] from the other European countries' and to examine its feasibility for Alsace-Lorraine. The representatives pressure for 'the organized and faultless implementation of measures to remove the Jews' and propose that economic specialists influence 'the process of removing Jews from significant enterprises' in Holland and Belgium.[52]

Ministerial official Gustav Schlotterer is responsible for further planning of the European 'new economic order'. He explains to German industrial leaders a few weeks later that, in the foreseeable future, 'the Jewish question' will be resolved in the occupied territories as well, and for the economy, the important thing is 'to take over the good Jewish positions, if possible without making any concessions'.[53]

On the same day, the *Warschauer Zeitung* newspaper reports on an address given by Peter-Heinz Seraphim, expert on Jewish affairs, at the Institute for German Activities in the East, in Krakow. According to Seraphim,

> One must thereby keep in mind the essential realization that, by itself, a restriction of Jewry is not sufficient. Rather, the limitation of Jewish influence and the isolation of Jewry must be replaced by a constructive solution through which these measures will be effectively supplemented.[54]

At the same time, sociologist Fritz Arlt, head of the Population and

Welfare Department in Krakow, justifies the deportation of Jews from the Generalgouvernement:

> If, after the new order is established in Europe, the great plan of relegating the Jews to their own sphere outside of Europe succeeds, then the *Lebensraum* of the Generalgouvernement would be rid of around 1,500,000 Jews. . . . First of all, this would provide a large number of employment options for the local non-Jewish population, i.e., un- or underemployed within the Polish population would experience significant relief. . . . In the course of sociological restructuring, some of these people could take on positions in industry, commerce, and the trades that had been previously held by Jews. This would contribute greatly to the recovery of the Polish rural proletariat. At the same time, relieving the burden of a surplus of rural workers would offer a further option in constructively confronting the problem of overpopulation.[55]

**23 July:** The director of the Lublin employment office reports that he 'would like to reduce Jewish employment considerably, since changes are to be expected shortly'.[56]

**26 July:** In a conversation with Hitler, Romanian Prime Minister Ion Gigurtu comments that the 'solution of the Jewish question' has indeed begun in Romania, 'yet it is not possible to proceed to its final settlement without the help of the Führer, who will have to implement a comprehensive solution for all of Europe'. Hitler's goal in the discussion is to convince the Romanian Prime Minister to cede part of Transylvania to Hungary in order to reduce minority problems between the two countries and prevent a regional conflict. Hitler and the Romanian representatives agree

> that the new border will have to be established such that Hungary and Romania each have the same number of members of the other nation on their respective territories to ensure that a subsequent exchange of these alien populations could resolve the situation entirely. . . [in a] 'one for one' exchange.[57]

**31 July:** Frank, Greiser, Koppe, Krüger, and Streckenbach meet in Krakow. The participants view the Madagascar Plan as more of a vague option that in any case will not help them overcome the current stagnation of the resettlement programme as a whole. Streckenbach reports that he has been assigned by Heydrich 'to determine how many Jews are in the entire area presently occupied by Germany'.[58] Hitler makes his first comments regarding an 'approximately five-month campaign' against the Soviet Union, scheduled to begin in early 1941.[59]

**1 August 1940:** Walter Emmerich, Minister of the Economy in the Generalgouvernement, anticipates 'certain, [yet definitely justifiable] turbulence' within the economy as a result of the impending evacuation of the Jews.[60]

**5 August:** The first deployment study for war against the USSR is completed.[61]

**7 August:** The RKF continues to adhere to the resettlement goals agreed upon internally in autumn 1939:

> To be evacuated are: (a) all Jews from the incorporated eastern territories [500,000 people]; (b) all Congress Poles from Danzig–West Prussia [400,000]; (c) all other ethnic aliens in the remaining regions whose property is needed for the settlement of the ethnic German 'returnees'.[62]

Eichmann prepares to deport 20,000 Poles from the Upper Silesian district of Żywiec (German: Saybusch) 'for the settlement of Galician German peasant families'.[63] The deportation of Polish peasants is started in October. By 14 December, 17,413 Poles have been deported to the Generalgouvernement to make room for the 'settlement of approximately 800 Galician German mining families'. In early 1941 there are a few additional transports of deportees from Żywiec.[64] The ethnic Germans receive 'an average of 30–40 morgens [of land, 64–84 acres], some of them receiving as many as 100 morgens [212 acres]'. The Polish peasants owned 'an average of 4–6 morgens [8.5–13 acres]'.[65]

On 11 September, Himmler authorizes a proposal by the RKF in Upper Silesia to deport significantly more Polish peasants. He announces his 'agreement' that in addition to the district of Żywiec, the peasant-dominated Polish districts of Teschen, Freystadt, Rybnik, Pless, and Wadowice are to be 'declared settlement zones of the first order'.[66]

**9 August:** Referring to a group discussion with Hitler, Goebbels notes that 'Himmler reported on the resettlement programme. He has already achieved a lot, but there is still much more to be done. Just bring them on in, because we have to settle the empty eastern territories.'[67]

**12 August:** Experts from the Foreign Ministry consider 'an inter-European bank for the utilization of Jewish assets in Europe'.[68]

**15 August:** Eichmann's department presents detailed plans for the deportation of 4 million European Jews to Madagascar. The project has been previously worked through and agreed upon by the Foreign Ministry and other authorities. 'To avoid continual contact between other peoples and Jews, an overseas, insular solution is preferred over all others.' Plans exist to deport the Jewish minorities from the following countries: Germany (including the annexed regions: 743,000 people), the Generalgouvernement (2,300,000), the Protectorate of Bohemia and Moravia (77,000), Belgium (80,000), Holland (160,000), Luxembourg (2500), Denmark (7000), Norway (1500), Slovakia (95,000), and France (270,000).[69]

**17 August:** Goebbels notes:

> The English are now attacking the concentration camps. Let them. There is nothing there but refuse anyway. The judiciary will never be able to deal with them. The Führer plans to deport the real criminal elements to an island sometime in the future. . . . Later on, we want to ship the Jews to Madagascar. They can set up their own state there.[70]

**30 August:** In accordance with the second Vienna Award, which comes into force on this day, Romania has to cede northern Transylvania and the Szatmár region to Hungary. The Foreign Ministers of Germany and Italy 'declare the new borders and dictate the basic stipulations of the arbitral award'.[71] The exchange of populations is not expressly regulated in the award, but is implied.

A supplemental protocol gives the 95,000 Transylvanian and Szatmár ethnic Germans still living in Hungary the option to resettle in the Reich, including the right to 'bring with them all their property'.[72] The Romanian government guarantees Germans living in *German communities* in Romania equal status as citizens and the right to retain their cultural independence.[73] This pertains, however, only to those Romanian Germans living in southern Transylvania and the Banat region – a total of 520,000. Romanian Germans from the northern Dobruja and southern Bukovina regions, as well as the so-called scattered Germans [i.e., those not living in German communities], on the other hand, are to be brought 'home to the Reich'. The German government makes this agreement in order to facilitate Romania's acceptance of far-reaching territorial concessions to Hungary, Bulgaria, and the Soviet Union.[74] The resettlement treaty is not officially concluded until 20 October. Between 15 October and 15 December 1940, 76,902 Romanian Germans are transported to the Reich and interned in camps there. In the subsequent weeks, Romania is forced to accept, at short notice, approximately 250,000 (Romanian) refugees and forced 'settlers' from northern and southern Bukovina, northern Transylvania, and Bessarabia. On German recommendation, a 'settlement organization' is established: 'The material element', as is later recorded, 'now amounts to 260,000 hectares [ca. 640,000 acres] of arable land that has been transferred to state ownership through resettlement of ethnic Germans and expropriation of Jews.'[75]

In response to a Foreign Office request, Greifelt has already announced on 15 August that he is prepared 'to allow a Romanian commission to examine the resettlement efforts'; he has 'no reservations about informing Hungary and Bulgaria in basically the same way'.[76] Interest has been sparked by Hitler, who on 26 July advised Romanian Prime Minister Gigurtu as follows regarding the forthcoming boundary modification:

> With respect to the extent of the sacrifice to be made, the agreement must do justice to all sides in terms of ethnography. This can be accomplished in the long term by an exchange of populations, which eliminates the harshness of the territorial concessions, leading in terms of ethnic identity to 100 per cent satisfaction of all wishes.[77]

**31 August:** In the Warthegau, problems continue regarding the settlement of the Baltic Germans, even though the procedure has long since been completed. 'Herr Greifelt let it be known that he would have to consult with the Reichsführer personally on the issue, should final progress not be achieved in the general question of assignment of accommodation.'[78]

**2 September 1940:** Resettlement of ethnic Germans from the General-gouvernement commences, a procedure which has been planned since May and then set for a time 'immediately following the grain harvest'. A total of 30,275 ethnic Germans[79] from the regions around Chełm (German: Cholm) and Lublin are relocated by 14 December.[80] In order to settle them, 28,365 Poles are transported out of the Warthegau on the same trains.

In August, Himmler has already given his authorization that, contrary to the original plans, in addition to Poles deported from the West, Ukrainian and German-Ukrainian families that have been evacuated together with Germans from Soviet-annexed eastern Poland will also be settled on the evacuated farms.[81]

**5 September:** German–Soviet pact on the evacuation of German minorities from Bessarabia and northern Bukovina. The resettlements continue from 23 September[82] to November 1940 and involve 137,077 people, who are transported to Germany by ship along the Danube, or by rail or on foot. Like the Lithuanian Germans who are resettled later, almost all are interned in camps. The Bessarabian Germans are supposed to be settled in both the annexed western regions and the incorporated eastern territories,[83] a decision which serves to accelerate the forced resettlements to Luxembourg and the annexed French *départements*.

**7 September:** Romania cedes southern Dobruja to Bulgaria, pursuant to the Craiova Accord. Like the second Vienna Award, this (still valid)

Table 1

| | Jews | Others[84] | Germans |
|---|---|---|---|
| Hungary | 700,000[85] | 200,000 | 800,000 |
| Romania | 300,000 | 300,000 | 613,000 |

treaty is an outcome of German 'new order' policies. It also encompasses the forcible resettlement – within three months – of 65,000 Bulgarians from the northern to the southern Dobruja, and the reverse resettlement of 110,000 Romanians.[86]

On the same day, the RKF publishes statistical material for internal use only on the minorities in Hungary and Romania after the second Vienna Award.[87] This provides the picture summarized in Table 1.

**12 September:** Himmler issues an edict 'to check and isolate the population in the incorporated eastern territories'. Consequently, a 'maximum of one million' of 8,530,000 Poles are to be Germanized. Candidates for the 'recovery of German blood' are to be screened by the UWZ 'according to racial, health-related, and political criteria' and, in cases judged positively, entered onto the 'List of Ethnic Germans' (*Deutsche Volksliste*). On this list, the Poles to be Germanized are divided into four categories of worthiness and, depending on the category, are to be given either Reich citizenship (*Reichsbürgerschaft*), German citizenship (*Staatsangehörigkeit*), or revokable German citizenship. All other Poles are considered 'protected members of the German Reich with limited [*Inländer*] rights'.[88]

**14 September:** In a note 'on the future structure of the Bohemian–Moravian region', Heydrich asks what to do with the 'remaining non-Germanizable Czechs'. His answer is that, since it is 'presently an imaginary goal to evacuate these remaining Czechs to an as yet imaginary Gouvernement', a temporary reservation is to be established 'until the entire region can be cleared of remnants of a Czech nation'.[89] This corresponds to far-reaching Germanization plans for the Protectorate of Bohemia and Moravia.[90]

**18 September:** Registration begins for issuance of ethnic German passports to Hungarian Germans.[91]

**25 September:** Meeting between Hitler and Martin Bormann, on the one hand, and Josef Bürckel and Robert Wagner, on the other. (Bürckel and Wagner are the heads of the civilian administrations in Lorraine and Alsace, respectively.) Hitler demands that the two Gauleiters report to him in ten years that their respective regions are 'German, purely German';

he says he will not ask them 'what methods they had applied in making the region German'.[92]

Between 11 and 21 November, some 60,000 Lorrainers and 10,000 Alsatians, predominantly peasants, are deported to unoccupied France.[93] In late 1942, the population statisticians of the RKF report the balance: '295,000 Alsatians, Lorrainers, and Luxembourgers have been deported to France or [in so far as they fled prior to the German attack] have been prevented from returning.'[94]

**End of September:** Warsaw district governor Ludwig Fischer orders the establishment of a 'Jewish quarter'. Preparations have been under way for about three weeks; on 15 November the ghetto is sealed.[95]

# Notes

1 Telex from Ehlich to Höppner, 15 May 1940; AGK, UWZ/P/251, 1ff. (These transports, too, were organized by Eichmann.)

2 See Majer (317ff.); RKF order 17/II for the 'selection of Germanizable Poles' (signed by Himmler), 9 May 1940 (cited in *Menscheneinsatz*, 52ff.); RKF instructions (signed by Greifelt) on concrete 'use of Germanizable Poles', 3 July 1940 (AGK, UWZ/P/259, 11ff.); and Himmler's order on the 'selection of Polish families to be Germanized', 30 October 1940 (AGK, UWZ/L/1, 31). According to a telex of 5 July 1940 from Ehlich, these families could not be placed in the eastern German 'national–political danger zones', but only 'beyond the Elbe or within the jurisdiction of the Nordmark employment office' (AGK, UWZ/P/259, 14) (Nordmark refers to Schleswig-Holstein as the northern borderland).

3 Appendix to the final report on relocations within the scope of settlement of Bessarabian Germans (3rd short-term plan) from 21 January 1941 to 20 January 1942 in the Wartheland Reichsgau; AGK, UWZ/L/13, 117. The notion of assimilating Poles was familiar even to Hitler. As early as 1 October 1939 he had said, 'It would be best if vast segments of the Polish population could be resettled, specifically, to places where they would be swallowed up. Typical of this is the Ruhr valley, where the Poles have been almost entirely Germanized' (Engel, 64, also 62ff.).

4 In his letter of 13 November 1940 to the RKF representative in Metz (BAK, R49/2603), Stier (RKF) states, 'In response to your request, . . . preparations have been made to accommodate 1000 racially sound [*rassisch wertvolle*] Lorrainers.'

5 Retrospective comments by Waldemar Schön, head of the resettlement department in the district of Warsaw, 20 January 1941; FGM, 110. As early as 10 May 1940, Adam Czerniaków, head of the Warsaw Council of Jews, wrote, 'I received today the *Skizze des Sperrgebietes Warschau* [sketch of closed-off area of Warsaw]. A ghetto in spite of everything' (Czerniaków diary, 148).

6 Letter written by Himmler, 20 May 1940, quoted in Pätzold, 264.

7 On the later implementation of these ideas of Himmler's, see Wasser, 133ff.

8 Reprinted in VZG 5 (1957), 194–8.

9 BAK, NS 19/3282. Himmler evidently typed the eight-page document himself – as suggested by the numerous errors – on the so-called 'Führer typewriter',

with oversized letters. The document has no title, but it refers to archival report no. 14 on the subject of 'Evaluation of German Settlements in the East up to the Seizure of Power.' Himmler noted on the cover page that he presented the paper on 30 June 1940 to 'the Führer in the train from Freiburg/Br. to Appenweier', and that Hitler deemed it 'important, point for point'.

10 Hillgruber and Hümmelchen, 30.
11 See Chapter 5, p. 120.
12 Frank diary, 206; Czerniaków diary, 155–6; brief entry 'Generalgouvernement' in the periodical *Die Judenfrage* (9 June 1940).
13 Quoted in Döscher, 215. The idea of 'security' had already been mentioned by Heydrich on 19 December 1939 (see Chapter 2, p. 41) and had been spoken of even earlier (Heim, 67, note 78). The notion of different deportation plans for Jews in the East and the West was taken up again in October 1940, but was quickly abandoned because of resistance from the Vichy government.
14 Conversation between Frank and Emmerich, Frank diary, 244; for details, see Aly and Heim, 222ff.
15 Memorandum by Heydrich, 12 June 1940; BAK, R58/240, 61.
16 Ciano diary, 249.
17 Döscher, 216; Stuhlpfarrer, 651.
18 Note on the meeting on 19 June 1940 in Göring's headquarters, IMG, vol. 22, 30ff.
19 Burrin, 77.
20 Aly and Heim, 331.
21 Hillgruber, *Strategie,* 246 and 252.
22 Aly and Heim, 161f. The representative of the German Foreign Office welcomed the suggestion, since 'an existing system that has acquired considerable expertise' could be implemented much more quickly 'than a corresponding new one'. File note by Rademacher, 30 August 1940; excerpts printed in Klee, *Dokumente,* 265.
23 For sources and an interpretation, see Chapter 5, pp. 120–1.
24 Telex from the SD Litzmannstadt to RSHA section IIIB4 (Ehlich); AGK, UWZ/p/129, 3. The letter was evidently a response to Koppe's demand for the rapid 'evacuation of the Litzmannstadt Jews' (letter from Höppner to Eichmann, 27 June 1940, ibid. 2).
25 Letter from Heydrich to Ribbentrop, quoted in Döscher, 217.
26 Note by Himmler 'on future German farm settlements', 24 June 1940, quoted in Ackermann, 302.
27 Frank to Lammers; BAK, R43/II/647, quoted in Broszat, 94.
28 Meeting between Czerniaków and SS Oberscharführer Gerhard Mende, Czerniaków diary, 169.
29 Döscher, 217.
30 Ibid. 217f.
31 Aly and Heim, 263.
32 Ibid. 86.
33 Quoted in Safrian, 95.
34 Goebbels diaries, I/4, 229.
35 Meeting of department heads in Krakow, 12 July 1940, Frank diary, 247.
36 Hillgruber and Hümmelchen, 38.
37 Ibid. 40.
38 Even after the defeat of France, Churchill ordered the units of the British navy in the Mediterranean – around half the total battleship fleet – not to return to home waters.
39 Stuhlpfarrer, 653ff.

40 'Reiseprogramm des Reichsführers SS vom 13.–15.7.1940' (Travel plans of the Reichsführer SS from 13 to 15 July 1940); BAK, NS19/1792.

41 Czerniaków diary, 173.

42 BAK, R5/817.

43 Muehlon, 136.

44 Safrian, 95.

45 Ibid.; Kettenacker, 146ff.

46 It was assumed that this would involve half a million people.

47 This was stated in a memorandum from Robert Ernst, general representative of the chief of the civilian administration in Alsace; the memo was adopted by Stuckart, state secretary in the Ministry of the Interior; BAK, R59/233, 19; R69/1152, 23ff.; on Ernst's biography, see Kettenacker, 76–92. The resettlement plan did not include the Ladino-speaking inhabitants of the Grödner valley, who were to be 'dispersed' throughout Carinthia.

48 Letter from Himmler to Greifelt and Lorenz, 2 July 1940; BDC, SS-HO/961.

49 Draft of the order of 27 June 1940 'for the resettlement of the Lithuanian Germans', corrected by hand by Himmler, ibid.

50 Vomi activity report on resettlement in Lithuania, BAK, R59/109 *passim*; diary on the resettlement of the ethnic Reich Germans from the Soviet Republic of Lithuania, BAK, R59/253. See also the anecdotal recollections of Gotthold Rhode, historian and resettlement official under Himmler, which were published on this subject (Rhode, *passim*).

51 List of the Litzmannstadt UWZ of December 1940; AGK, UWZ/L/23, 7; Safrian, 93.

52 Note on the high-level meeting chaired by Reich Minister of the Economy Walther Funk on 22 July 1940 in the Reich Ministry of the Economy; Department 'III WOS 8' appendix of 31 July 1940 on the question 'whether and, if so, how should the economy of the regions to be annexed or incorporated into the Greater German Reich after the war be cleansed of Jews [*entjudet*]'; ZASM, 1485/29/8.

53 Minutes of the meeting of the Grand Council of the Reich industrial group, 3 October 1940, quoted in Eichholtz, 368ff.

54 Quoted in Czerniaków diary, 177.

55 Fritz Arlt, *Übersicht über die Bevölkerungsverhältnisse im Generalgouvernement* [*Volkspolitische Informationen* 3] (Krakow, 1940), 20f. There is a similar paper in the files of the Lublin division of the Department of Population and Welfare. Here it says, evidently using the same statistics, 'Deportation of the Jews, which would reduce the population density to 110. Rural proletariat could assume available jobs previously held by Jews' (quoted in Pohl, 76). On Arlt's activities in the Generalgouvernement, see Aly and Heim, 207–17.

56 Quoted in Pohl, 83.

57 Hillgruber, *Staatsmänner*, vol. 1, 171, 179.

58 Frank diary, 261ff.; see Chapter 5, pp. 105ff.

59 Hillgruber and Hümmelchen, 40.

60 Quoted in Aly and Heim, 225ff.

61 Hillgruber and Hümmelchen, 41.

62 Initial draft of 'guidelines and instructions' for further resettlements, 7 August 1940 (dictation initials: Schr/B); BAK, R49/2602.

63 Note by Eichmann about a meeting with Krumey (Lodz), Jahnke (Posen), and Dreier (Katowice) on the 'settlement of approx. 600 to 800 Galician German mining families in the district of Saybusch [Żywiec]', 7 August 1940, reprinted in *Biuletyn* 12 (1960), 103Fff.

64 Note by Eichmann of 7 August 1940, record of the 'Saybusch operation' of

December 1940; AGK, UWZ/L/23, 1–5; note by the EWZ (Gradmann) about a meeting on 23 July, 25 July 1940; BAK, R68/388, 79.

65 Ibid. In the Żywiec region, RKF structural planners combined up to 40 Polish peasant farms to form one settler farm (Broszat, 99). On the average, six Poles were deported to make room for each ethnic German. According to RFK plans, the resettlement was to begin on 20 August and be completed by 10 September. However, on 23 September Eichmann commented that the Reichsbahn (German railway) had reduced the number of trains available for resettlement purposes to five weekly, and that Frank 'refused to accept more Poles than the agreed upon number'. Theoretically, then, with respect to accepting Poles from the Żywiec district, 'renewed negotiations were necessary'. This could be avoided if one were to view 'the evacuation as falling under the Volhynia operation' (Fähndrich's note about a meeting of 23 July 1940; BAK, R49/2602).

66 Note on a meeting between Himmler, Bracht, Bach-Zelewski, and Greifelt, 11 September 1940; BAK, R49/2639.

67 Goebbels diaries, I/4, 273.

68 Quoted in Pätzold, 268f.

69 Quoted in Adler, 75ff.

70 Goebbels diaries, I/4, 284.

71 Quoted in the diary of the Italian Foreign Minister, Galeazzo Ciano; Ciano, 268. The arbitral award itself became necessary owing to the massive territorial claims made by the Hungarians to the Romanian government, for the revision of the Treaty of Trianon (4 June 1920). The second Vienna Award consisted of a compromise, which Muehlon (180) comments on as follows: 'If the arbitral award is taken for a moment to be that which its authors claim it to be – a just resolution of the dispute between two states on equally friendly terms with the Axis powers – then one must admit that Hungary had as much cut off from its demands as it had received, and that Romania retained as much as it deserved.'

72 Hillgruber, *Carol*, 108.

73 Ibid.

74 This apparently confidential agreement can be assumed from Fähndrich's (RKF 'Human Deployment' Department) report of 7 September 1940 'on the situation of ethnic identity [*Volkstumslage*] in the regions that Romania ceded to Hungary as a result of the Vienna Award of 30 August 1940' (BAK, R69/304, 1–6), which states, 'Romania . . . will lose a large number of ethnic Germans through the cession and the planned resettlements.'

75 Quoted in Aly and Heim, 363ff. The Romanian government expropriated the property of the rural Jews on 5 October 1940 and that of the urban Jewish population on 28 March 1941; ibid. 355; see also Hillgruber, *Carol*, 237ff.

76 Greifelt's response on 15 August to the Foreign Office request of 9 August 1940; BAK, R49/2602.

77 Hillgruber, *Staatsmänner*, vol. 1, 176.

78 Letter from DUT staff member Karl Schneider to Ferdinand Bang, director of the DUT office in Posen, 31 August 1940; BAP, 17.02/204. The author referred to the report of a conversation between Greifelt (RKF) and Winkler (HTO), showing resignation in his conclusion 'that nothing else can be done at the moment'.

79 Statistical report, n.d.; BAK, R69/388, 3.

80 'Aufstellung der im Rahmen des 2. Nahplans – Cholmer Aktion – mit ausgesiedelten Polen von Litzmannstadt in das Generalgouvernement abgegangenen Transportzüge' (List of railroad transports carried out within the scope of the second short-term plan – Chełm operation – taking Poles evacuated from Lodz to the Generalgouvernement), reprinted in *Biuletyn* 21 (1970), 101ff. To a large extent, Poles received the farms of resettled ethnic Germans and vice versa.

This was the only so-called 'farm-to-farm' or 'exchange resettlement'; the trains shuttled back and forth between Lublin and Lodz. (Final report on the evacuations within the scope of the settlement of the Volhynian and Chełm Germans – second short-term plan – in the Wartheland Reichsgau [Warthegau]; AGK, UWZ/L/25, 2.)

81 Litzmannstadt EWZ order, 14 September 1940; BAK, R69/765, 1ff.; R69/145, *passim*. The 'problem' had already been mentioned in March, but no decision had been made at that time; BAK, R69/388, 31f. This was in keeping with the policies of the German administration in the Generalgouvernement, which sought relatively privileged status and strengthening of the Ukrainian ethnic group. Krüger, representing the higher SS and police chief in Krakow, held negotiations with the Wehrmacht on 5 April 1940. He had also considered placing – on precisely these farms – the 60,000–70,000 Poles who had been evacuated from the Generalgouvernement to make room for new military training grounds. At this time, Himmler wanted to consolidate the farms of the resettled Germans into large estates because of the fertile soil, and have them run by the SS. The farms of the ethnic Germans were thus assigned, long before their owners were 'evacuated', to four very different groups: Ukrainians, Polish Wehrmacht settlers in the Generalgouvernement, Polish settlers from annexed western Poland, and SS-operated large estates (letter from Krüger to Himmler, including enclosure, 15 April 1940; BDC, SS-HO/970).

82 Report of the Ethnic German Liaison Office (Vomi)/Resettlement Department on the resettlement of ethnic Germans from Bessarabia and northern Bukovina, 23 November 1940; BAK, R59/14, 45ff.

83 Declaration by Ernst Fähndrich, 13 August 1940; BAK, R69/1152, 23ff.; note by RKF Main Department (HA) II, 16 August 1940, which mentions a letter from Himmler on 2 August 1940 and a note of 12 August 1940 by the planning department; BAK, R49/2602. On later settlement attempts in Lorraine, see Wolfanger, 185ff.

84 This pertains to the Gypsies, in particular.

85 According to the statistical supplement to the records of the Wannsee Conference, the number of Hungarian Jews was 742,800.

86 The treaty served to partly revise the peace treaty of Neuilly (17 November 1919). The scheduled forced resettlements took place the following winter.

87 See note 74.

88 Quoted in *Doc. Occ.* vol. 5 (1952), 114–18; see Majer, 413ff.

89 File note by Heydrich, 14 September 1940, about K. H. Frank's memorandum 'on the treatment of the Czech problem and the future structure of the Bohemian–Moravian sphere'; Král, 74ff.

90 Ibid. *passim*.

91 Note by the EWZ coordination office in Berlin, 18 September 1940; BAK, R69/493, 75.

92 Quoted in Safrian, 102.

93 Kettenacker, 146f.

94 RKF activity report (as of the end of 1942); BAK, R49/26, 34.

95 FGM, 102ff.; Czerniaków diary, 197ff.; Frank diary, 281. The public 'announcement regarding establishment of a Jewish residential district in the city of Warsaw' appeared in the *Krakauer Zeitung* newspaper, 18 October 1940, *Doc. Occ.* 6, 544f.

# |5|

# 'Home to the Reich' – and into a camp

## 'Untenable situation' I

On 31 July 1940, a meeting took place in Krakow centring on a concept that would play a disastrous role until well into the year 1942: the 'untenable situation'. The participants included Wilhelm Koppe and Friedrich Wilhelm Krüger, the two Higher SS and Police Chiefs; Bruno Streckenbach, chief of the security police and the SD in the Generalgouvernement at the time; and Hans Frank and Arthur Greiser, the two most senior political actors. At this meeting, the contours emerged of a situation of mutual obstruction that would be decisive for the ensuing developments. Thus I quote the minutes of the meeting – written in the third person, as is all of Frank's diary – in detail.

By way of introduction, Frank noted, 'He held a discussion of the Jewish problem to be necessary. . . . On the basis of a meeting with the Reichsführer SS, he was able to determine that the intention now exists of deporting Jews overseas to specific areas.' However,

the Jewish problem, to the extent it concerned his Gau, [had to] somehow be settled before the winter. That of course depended on the duration of the war. Should the war last longer, an interim solution would have to be found.

Greiser responded that:

In Litzmannstadt [Lodz], the Jews had been placed in a ghetto. The operation was essentially completed, but was only provisional in character. . . . The plan had been to transport them in an efficient manner to the Generalgouvernement, and the wish had been to settle this manner of transfer today as well.[1] In the meantime, the new decision [the Madagascar Plan and the associated prohibition on deporting further Jews from the Warthegau] had been handed down, and it was very important to him that the transfer be settled, because it would be an untenable situation for the Warthegau, for reasons involving food supply policy as well as, in particular, epidemics control, if the Jews crowded together in the ghetto were to be kept through the winter and beyond. Therefore, an interim solution definitely had to be found, one that made it possible to deport these Jews to another area.

Koppe, the Higher SS and Police Chief of the Warthegau, underlined Greiser's arguments: '[He] pointed out that the situation regarding the Jews was worsening day by day. The ghetto in Litzmannstadt had actually been created only on condition that the deportation of the Jews begin in the middle of this year at the latest.'

Frank countered that the 'transfer of the Polish population, for example from Hungary, Lithuania, Romania and other countries', was already facing great obstacles.[2]

The average population density of the Generalgouvernement was significantly larger than that of the Reich. Under such conditions . . . he could barely continue to take responsibility for ensuring that epidemics and other types of catastrophes, such as starvation, would not ensue.

Streckenbach, Commander of the Security Police and SD in the General-gouvernement, came to Frank's defence:

[He] points out that, in addition to the demands from the Warthe-gau, great demands were made by East and West Prussia and Silesia to take in Poles. . . . The Generalgouvernement had been taken over with a population density of 102 people per square kilometre; today the average is already 136 people. This figure was increasing because huge areas had to be freed up for military training grounds, bridge-heads, etc. After these tasks were completed, one would have to reckon with a population density of 145 people per square kilometre for the Generalgouvernement. In peacetime – that is, before the outbreak of the Polish war – the territory of the Generalgouverne-ment was an area of scarcity in terms of food supply.

Krüger, the Higher SS and Police Chief of the Generalgouvernement, put in a word:

[He] points out that, in a recent discussion with Reichsführer SS Himmler, he had also touched on the question of the Gypsies; all the Gypsies are supposed to go to the Generalgouvernement. This probably involves a total of around 30,000 Gypsies from the Old Reich and other areas.

In the face of the combined arguments of the three representatives of the

Generalgouvernement, Greiser ultimately gave in, saying, 'he had to admit, on the basis of this state of affairs, that the Generalgouvernement is not in a position to take in the 250,000 Jews [from the Warthegau], even if only for the interim'.

Frank summarized:

> The situation was beginning to be disastrous for both territories. Therefore, the question had to lead to a fundamental decision. . . . Should these masses of Poles enter the Generalgouvernement, the necessary food supply would have to be ensured entirely at the expense of the Reich. This would be necessary if only because the Generalgouvernement had an important task to fulfil for the German Reich.

In closing, the minutes state, 'The Herr Generalgouverneur entirely acknowledges the difficulty of the Jewish problem, especially in Litzmannstadt, but once again expresses his opinion that the Generalgouvernement can only help if all questions of food supply policy and economics are fully resolved.'[3]

The progress of the discussion shows, first of all, that all participants were cautious, at best, about placing their hopes in a 'territorial Madagascar solution', which could not, in any case, be expected to happen rapidly. Second, 'the discussion of the Jewish problem' was constantly deferred because of other, more immediate resettlement plans – here, the deportation of Gypsies and Poles. Third, the danger of epidemics, the question of food supply, and the impending winter were central for both sides. Neither Greiser nor Frank expected that any vision for the future would help them deal with the current controversies and requests for deportation. The same arguments with which Greiser sought a rapid 'interim' solution for the Jews of Lodz led Frank firmly to reject the further deportation of Jews and Poles to the Generalgouvernement. The two were thus in agreement to the extent that they came up with the same justifications, sometimes even using the very same wording. This only further deepened their actual conflicts of interest.

The same was true for the three SS generals involved. Although they belonged to the same SS, which appeared so monolithic from the outside, they argued against each other, like Greiser and Frank, and reflected the same respective interests. Koppe, on the one hand, and Krüger and Streckenbach, on the other, also took the concrete problems they faced in Krakow and Posen as their point of departure. They pursued neither abstract SS interests nor the central prescriptions of the Reich Security Main Office. This is especially noteworthy because Streckenbach had a relationship of particular loyalty to Himmler and Heydrich.

# Germans from southeastern Europe

In autumn 1940, the German leadership had to abandon its plans to invade Britain. The 'aerial war' against the British public had proved unsuccessful. British naval forces were operating with undiminished superiority in the Mediterranean and holding their bases in North Africa and Gibraltar, Malta and Suez. The German plan to create an 'economic sphere of influence' in Central Africa thus proved infeasible, as did the Madagascar Plan. In short, 'The Madagascar Plan was born and died of military circumstances.'[4]

Although the hope of a rapid 'insular solution' in summer 1940 might have had little objective justification, subjectively this was seen as a realistic option, thus facilitating the activities of the resettlement functionaries, which were already projective in any case. They had accelerated the confiscation of Jewish property in the German sphere of influence[5] and had taken on the 'repatriation' of an additional 275,000 ethnic Germans; from the Soviet-annexed lands of Bessarabia, North Bukovina, and Lithuania, 93,548, 43,531, and 50,700 people, respectively – a total of 187,779 ethnic Germans – were shipped to the German Reich. These were joined by the so-called subsequent resettlements from Estonia and Latvia, comprising 12,000 people, and the deportation of 52,107 and 15,063 ethnic Germans from the Romanian areas of South Bukovina and northern Dobruja, respectively, as well as 9732 so-called *Streudeutsche* – ethnic Germans not living in German communities, but scattered among the population – from Romania.

Although they attempted to keep their situation quiet *vis-à-vis* the outside world, the German resettlement officials nevertheless found themselves under pressure to justify their actions. They had not deported the Jews, but had instead shut many of them up in open or completely sealed ghettos; it was difficult or impossible to expel the Poles to the General-gouvernement before overcrowding there was 'relieved', at the expense of the Jewish minority.

The resettlement of the first roughly 200,000 ethnic Germans, relocated between October 1939 and February 1940, succeeded only imperfectly, contrary claims notwithstanding, and required extraordinary efforts and a constant downgrading of its original aims. A similar situation was now emerging in southeastern Europe, where the relocation of a segment of the German minority and all Romanian Jews had also been made the *sine qua non* of a major population policy programme. In summer 1940, amid the euphoria of an expected rapid victory, the German government had promised the Soviet and Romanian governments to remove more than a quarter of a million ethnic Germans living in southeastern Europe as quickly as possible in the coming months. The new relocations began in

September 1940 and ended in March 1941. Permanently settling the new-comers would take longer: first months, then years.

Instead of the announced ethnic and economic new order and the associated rapid expulsion of at least 1 million 'ethnic aliens', a quite different reality now took shape. In late autumn 1940, hundreds of thousands of people were languishing in resettlement camps or had been herded into ghettos, robbed of any means of production. Depending on whether they were Jews, Poles, or ethnic Germans, they were to be kept alive in a state of either starvation, misery, or subsistence, but in any case, one of unproductivity – in the midst of a war in which food, housing, and workers were in extremely short supply.

With German expansion temporarily halted, if only for a few months, the ethnocrats of the RKF also found themselves making no headway. The 'difficulties' of which Eichmann had already complained in January, and which he had described as an undesirable, hard to master 'interplay between settling the ethnic Germans and evacuating the Poles and Jews',[6] became greater. These interactions only increased in face of the Madagascar Plan, which had existed for only a few months and was now abandoned owing to lack of military strength.

While Heydrich still planned in winter 1939–40 to deport a maximum of 1 million western Polish and 'Greater German' Jews to the least fertile areas of the Lublin region, by June 1940 he was calling for a 'territorial final solution' for 3.25 million people, including all Polish, German, Bohemian, and Austrian Jews. The Madagascar Plan, which was then developed after the rapid defeat of France, provided for the relocation of 'around 4 million Jews'. The discrepancy between this figure and the one named by Heydrich arose from the fact that Jews living in France, Holland, Luxembourg, and Belgium were now, like the Jews of Slovakia, also at the mercy of the Germans. At the beginning of December, Eichmann was already counting on relocating all European Jews living west of the German–Soviet border – a total of 5.8 million. As he noted for Himmler, they were to be removed 'from the European economic sphere of the German *Volk* to a territory yet to be determined'.[7]

While the resettlement of ethnic Germans from the Soviet-annexed regions of East Central Europe accorded with the secret Nazi–Soviet resettlement agreements concluded in September 1939,[8] the sudden resettlement of Romanian Germans occurred for very different reasons. It can be explained as a result of the ethnic, national, and economic new order in southeastern Europe, which had been driven forward by German economists and population experts since summer 1940.

The second Vienna Award (of 30 August 1940) and the closely related Craiova Accord (of 7 September 1940) arose out of German policies to protect this new order. Both treaties altered borders with the intention of solving minority problems.[9] Including the Soviet annexations sanctioned by the Germans, such alterations took place three times at the expense of

Romania, which was particularly important to the German war economy. Therefore, Hitler promised to ease the situation of the Romanian government by relocating Romanian Germans from places expected, as a result of the surrender of territory, to have the largest number of ethnic Romanian settlers and refugees. At the same time, the German government now also granted ethnic Germans living in northern Transylvania and the Szatmár region[10] – people who were now, against their express wishes, to be transformed from Romanian to Hungarian citizens – the right to opt for resettlement in the German Reich.[11]

This occurred despite the fact that all resettlement projects begun until then had long since flagged, especially the relocation of the South Tyroleans, which was particularly important to ensure peace within the Axis. It should be added that originally, in autumn 1939, the South Tyroleans, like the Poles, were to be settled 'on the northern slopes of the Beskids', and Zakopane was to become the 'Cortina of the north'. With this in mind, Himmler had informed the Italian Police Chief Bocchini on 28 September 1939:

> Through the vast expanse in the east that we will receive within our borders upon conclusion of the conflict with Poland, fate has given us the opportunity to resolve the most difficult issue so far. That is, if they wish to emigrate, the rooted population of the South Tyrol will be able to relocate somewhere as a group (which would not have been possible in the former Germany because of the shortage of space).[12]

In connection with this plan, in the last week of September 1939 Heydrich may also have abandoned the idea of creating a Jewish reservation 'southeast of Krakow';[13] instead, though also merely as an ephemeral plan, it was to be created in the Lublin region. Hitler had assigned Heydrich the task of resettling the South Tyroleans, which had become an annoyance to him, and in spring of 1940 – this is typical of the dictator – still 'did not want to hear any more about the issue'.[14] The 'Beskid Gau' project failed for various reasons, in particular because the South Tyroleans did not want to be 'transplanted' to the barren, harsh northeastern border province. The 'group settlement area of the Free County of Burgundy [Franche-Comté]', which was then chosen for them in June–July 1940, was far better suited climatically. It found acceptance among the potential settlers themselves, and at first the issue seemed to be resolved. In fact, however, Hitler, who had wanted to resettle the South Tyroleans purely for reasons of power politics, now shied away from the tactically undesirable humiliation of France connected with such a resettlement. Once again for reasons of power politics, but now very different ones, he blocked the RKF 'Burgundy' project, since it 'did not comport with the special peace to be concluded between France and the Axis powers', which he still planned at the time.[15]

When Heinrich Himmler met Agostino Podestà in Bolzano on 23

November 1940, the supposedly all-powerful Reichsführer SS was forced to reassure this Italian provincial prefect, who would have liked to see 'more speed'[16] in the South Tyrolean resettlement – that is, who asked nothing more than the fulfilment of old German promises:

> Himmler pointed out the difficulties in the area of resettlement that had arisen as a result of the lack of a group settlement area, but also as a result of the other resettlements from eastern Europe, and informed Podestà 'that it was only natural that migration would now stagnate a bit. He had first of all to gain an overview of the Reich's various relocation plans and make comprehensive preparations.' Podestà had to be content with Himmler's vague promise, 'In a few months, the ongoing resettlements will be tackled on a large scale.'[17]

(In fact, in April 1941 came the succinct announcement, 'South Tyrolean resettlement presently halted.')[18]

A further reaction during these days in November 1940 shows how nervously and coldly Himmler, the Third Reich's chief resettler, responded to the additional 'return of German blood', and how precarious the situation of the German ethnocrats had become. Himmler immediately denied the rather modest request of the Bulgarian government to relocate ethnic Germans living there – a mere 1100 people. This ran counter to the publicly propagated image of the organizer of the 'Great Homecoming'. The justification offered by Himmler to the head German negotiators resembles an oath of disclosure in regard to settlement policies: 'a) the internal German resettlement offices [are] overloaded, b) the settlers . . . [cannot] . . . be placed in the eastern territories immediately, c) the settlers [would have to] remain in the temporary camps until summer 1941.'[19]

In the offices of the Reich, ridicule and disbelief were rife. For example, in Posen the personal assistant and son-in-law of Gauleiter Greiser made fun of Himmler's 'fantasies'. 'You know yourself', he said to an SS resettlement official, 'what has come of all the Reichsführer's grand plans.'[20] The German envoy in Budapest, Otto von Erdmannsdorff, who had been promised in September 1940 that Szatmár Germans who had become Hungarians under the second Vienna Award would be relocated to the Reich, reacted with barely concealed sarcasm: 'We are not aware', he wrote in a letter to Berlin, 'that the Greater German Reich is in such desperate need of human material that it must try everything in its power to resettle as many Szatmár ethnic Germans as possible.' The recipient in the Foreign Office in Berlin, Max Lorenz, made this extremely serious note on 18 September:

> In the view of Kult A,[21] the resettlement must be as comprehensive as possible and must be to an area where the settlers have it as least as good as in Hungary. . . . The 'desperate need for human material' for

Germany arises, among other things, from the fact that we have a large number of enemies and, in the East, a Slavic neighbour with a rapidly growing population of two hundred million. We also have large territories that must be Germanized. Reading *Mein Kampf* would easily enlighten the legation on the urgency of the population problem. Only complete resettlement would straighten out the situation and thus also be politically desirable.[22]

On 3 November, the Foreign Office wrote rather apologetically to von Erdmannsdorff: 'The issue of the resettlement of the Szatmár Germans has not yet been settled. Recently it has been suggested that this resettlement be dispensed with entirely. However, no decision has yet been made.'[23] Nothing else was done in the matter. Again, a self-created problem was taken care of with the help of a non-decision.

In autumn 1940, Himmler not only had brusquely to reject the resettlement of a few hundred Bulgarian Germans, delay the politically important project of bringing the South Tyroleans 'home to the Reich', and break a promise to the Szatmár and northern Transylvanian Germans; in November 1940, he even found himself forced to announce in a public notice, 'During the war, Reich German farmers and applicants for resettlement *cannot* be settled in the new eastern territories.'[24] And although Himmler had also promised the ethnic German settlers that their younger sons who lacked rights of inheritance could also become independent farmers in the annexed East, in January 1941 he had to direct that 'the creation of a new German peasantry must not occur during the war, even for second and third sons of ethnic German farmers'.[25]

Only ten months previously, Himmler, as Reich Commissioner for the Consolidation of German Nationhood, had unrestrainedly propagated the settlement of small farmers and younger sons of farmers from south-western German areas in which inherited plots had become progressively smaller. Under this plan, 110,000 families (more than half a million people) were to be 'resettled to the new eastern Gaus' from Württemberg and Baden alone. The justification, as expressed in a press campaign in January 1940, was:

And thus begins the second great task of the work of domestic development: the restructuring of eastern German *Lebensraum*, for which the farmers and artisans from Estonia, Latvia, Volhynia and Galicia have already laid the foundations. They are being followed, in gradual but long-planned settlements, by the surplus agricultural workforce from the West.[26]

In November 1940, Himmler refused to tolerate southwestern German small farmers seeking to do just what he himself had encouraged them to do – 'resettle in the East'.

At the same time, those Reich and ethnic Germans to whom he had

earlier promised vast spaces and milk and honey were squeezed even more
tightly. On 21 October, the Office for Public Welfare (*Amt für Volkswohlfahrt*) in Karlsruhe informed its subsidiary offices that 20,000 'Bessarabian
German returnees' were to be placed in Baden;[27] on 9 November, an RKF
directive required that in the 'Swabian Gau, some 7000 ethnic Germans'
from southeastern Europe were to be 'accommodated in camp-like
facilities'.[28] The process was similar in other regions of southern Germany,
in Saxony, Silesia, and soon after – with the housing of Lithuanian German
settlers – in Pomerania, West Prussia, and East Prussia. In winter 1940–41,
more than 200,000 were languishing in 1500 camps. Thus an SS function-
ary in Posen who was actually supposed to be carrying out the 'generous
settlement' of ethnic Germans was now faced with quite different, though
no less serious, problems: 'In consideration of the small store of straw as a
result of the general loss of the harvest,' he wrote, 'I direct that each camp
lay in a store of straw large enough to fill the straw sacks once.'[29] A further
order soon followed. If he could not 'present' his 'homecomers' with large
farms and fertile land, Himmler now at least intended to move the 'camp
inmates', as they were now profanely termed, 'as far as possible into
productive work'.[30] The organizers of this 'modern mass migration' had
now been transformed, reluctantly, into camp administrators. The
Madagascar Plan could not be accomplished, yet the deportation of the
Jews nevertheless remained one of the essential conditions of the ever-
expanding plans for 'ethnic redistribution'. Thus a constellation had
developed in autumn 1940 in which all resettlements and deportations
obstructed each other – a regular stalemate.[31]

## Deportation, but where to?

At the start of the mass resettlements, the demographic and economic
planners had demanded the rapid expulsion of some of the Polish and all
of the Jewish population from annexed western Poland to the Generalgouvernement. Heydrich, Himmler, and Hitler initiated these plans.

But since spring 1940, German leaders in the Generalgouvernement had
also been working on the construction of a new administrative and
economic structure. They came from the same intellectual and political
schools as their colleagues in the Warthegau, had similar experiences, and
in principle pursued the same ends. They wanted to make the Generalgouvernement a productive 'neighbour to the Reich', and operated to that
end under the protection of the Four-Year Plan authorities responsible for
the wartime economy – but in explicit opposition to Hitler's concepts and
instructions. To recapitulate, he had demanded on 17 October 1939:

Any signs of a consolidation of the situation in Poland must be
quashed. The 'Polish economy' [Hitler's way of saying 'mismanaged

economy'] must flourish. The leadership of the region must enable us to cleanse the Reich territory, as well, of Jews and Polacks.[32]

Even such statements sounded more definite than they were; after all, even at that time, the German resettlement strategists had 'to take account of the fact that, according to an order from the Führer, hunger revolts in these territories [i.e., the Generalgouvernement] must be avoided at all costs'.[33]

The unique feature of the 'structural model' for the Generalgouvernement that began to be developed in January 1940 was not the model itself, but the region for which it was designed – that is, 'rump Poland', an area not rich to begin with and now further impoverished by German measures. Originally, this 'space' was supposed to 'take in' those people to be relocated from the other areas under German authority. Now, however, the occupation government was doing precisely the opposite, demanding the deportation of 'excess populations'. The German experts calculated the 'overpopulation' of the Generalgouvernement in numerous contemporary studies. The results ranged from 3 to 5 million, out of a population of 12 million living in the region at the time.

The Germans themselves made sure that the social conflicts they had defined as the 'population question' long before the occupation would intensify. Military invasions, annexations, expulsion, the theft of thousands of millions, and finally the systematic rationalization of industry and trades contributed to this.[34] The same experts whose proposals and measures brought the situation to a head then pointed to the consequences of their policies as 'objective requirements', in order to compel a rapid, final 'clearing up' of the 'Jewish question' – a first step towards 'solving' the 'population question' in a more comprehensive sense.

In October 1940, Peter-Heinz Seraphim, the expert on 'Jewry in the eastern European sphere', published an essay in the quarterly journal of the Institute for German Activities in the East (*Institut für deutsche Ostarbeit*) entitled 'The Jewish Question in the Generalgouvernement as a Demographic Problem'. Seraphim, an economist, was at the time stationed in Krakow as an economic command officer and worked informally to help build up the Institute for German Activities in the East, which the government of the Generalgouvernement had created for the purpose of political consultancy. In his essay on the 'Jewish question', he wrote that the Generalgouvernement had 'taken in close to 350,000 Jews from the areas reintegrated into the Reich over the course of the last few years'.[35] In this

> area that is already essentially oversaturated with Jews . . . new Jewish population elements have thus flowed in that . . . almost across the board possess no means of subsistence and represent a serious burden on the Generalgouvernement from an economic and social point of view. Thus the Jewish question . . . has become a first-degree problem of mass population policy. It takes its place next to

the difficult population policy questions involving the agrarian overpopulation of this area, and, over the long term, calls urgently for a
solution. These masses of Jews are today largely without any
productive employment or their own means of subsistence. They
clog the cities, and thus not only inhibit their healthy development
[Seraphim was speaking here not of the healthy development of the
Jews, but of the cities] but also prevent the solution or easing of the
problem of agrarian overpopulation, and are a difficult burden on
the Generalgouvernement, inhibiting development. This gives rise to
one long-term goal: the demographic cleansing of this area, which
need only be hinted at here. Until it can be taken in hand, however,
any further intensification of the structural tensions in population
and economics in the Generalgouvernement is to be avoided, and it is
necessary to prohibit a further influx of Jewish population elements
into the area of the Generalgouvernement.[36]

Here Seraphim was merely formulating the consensus on questions of
population policy that had developed among German experts in Krakow
by autumn 1940, and he reached three conclusions: first, in his opinion,
relocations from annexed western Poland and the German Reich to the
Generalgouvernement should be halted immediately; second, this artificially created region should itself be 'demographically cleansed', for the
sake of economic development; third, Seraphim, like countless other
experts on population and economy, was also eager to link the ideological
goal of 'freedom from Jews' with the concept of 'relieving agrarian overpopulation'.

The plan to combine 'economic development [with] resettlement' in the
annexed eastern territories, in southeastern Europe, *and* in the Generalgouvernement was further developed in light of the prospects for a solution through the Madagascar Plan. Now it was possible to consider the
mass deportation of 2 million people *from* the Generalgouvernement and
half a million from the incorporated eastern territories. This would represent a 'colossal relief', as Frank had put it, and would create conditions
'for large-scale reconstruction' and 'economic penetration'. For a small
space of time, the population policy-makers in Krakow and Posen nurtured
the illusion of a common perspective. This strengthened their fateful
tendency to continue bringing the plans for both German-occupied parts
of Poland into alignment. In summer 1940, both sets of planners placed
their hopes on the deportation of hundreds of thousands of people
considered by them to be 'superfluous', 'burdensome', or 'racially worthless'. Once the Madagascar Plan had been proved a mere chimera, the two
concepts ultimately stood in each other's way.

Against the background of the Madagascar project, and at Frank's
urging, Hitler had in early July 1940 disapproved of further deportations
of Jews to the Generalgouvernement and limited the deportation of Poles.

Only the expulsion that had already begun to make room for the settlement of Volhynian and Galician Germans was still to be completed before the defeat of Britain – that is, before implementation of the Madagascar Plan.

Once these conditions had so obviously failed to be met, the 'Führer's Directive' of July also lost its significance. Thus on 2 October, in a meeting with top aides, Hitler attempted to qualify the prohibition he himself had issued – albeit at the urging of others, rather than on his own initiative. In addition to Frank, Baldur von Schirach, Gauleiter of Vienna, and Erich Koch, Gauleiter of East Prussia, sat at the negotiating table. While Koch complained that his demands for expulsion of Poles and Jews remained unsatisfied, von Schirach concretely demanded the deportation of the 60,000 Viennese Jews to the Generalgouvernement. This deportation had already begun once in autumn 1939, but after a brief beginning it had foundered on the priorities of overall resettlement policy. Trying to mediate, though at the same time taking sides, Hitler called on Frank to abandon his resistance to further relocations. Martin Bormann kept a record of the progress of the discussion: at first, Frank reported that his 'activity in the Generalgouvernement could definitely be described as successful. The Jews in Warsaw and other cities are now sealed into ghettos, and Krakow will be free of Jews within a short time.'

Von Schirach 'remarked that he still had 50,000 (!) Jews in Vienna that Frank had to take off his hands. . . . Party Comrade Frank described this as impossible!' The words were barely out of Frank's mouth when Koch, Gauleiter of East Prussia, pointed out 'that he too had not heretofore deported Poles or Jews from the Zichenau [Ciechanów] region; however, it is obvious that these Jews and Poles would have to be taken in by the Generalgouvernement'. Frank rejected this as well and 'emphasized that it is unheard of that people are sending such masses of Poles and Jews into the Generalgouvernement when no facilities are available to accommodate them'.

From Bormann's record, it is also implicitly apparent that Frank brought into play the concept of 'overpopulation' and the danger of economic disruption of the Generalgouvernement, utilizing Seraphim's arguments, which had in all likelihood been made available to him beforehand. Bormann wrote:

The Führer now took a fundamental position on this overall problem, in the following manner: he emphasized that population density in the Generalgouvernement is irrelevant; population density in Saxony is 347 people per square kilometre, 324 in the Rhine province, and as high as 449 people per square kilometre in Saarland. It is impossible to understand why the population density in the Generalgouvernement should be any lower. . . . The standard of living in Poland has to be low; that is, it should be maintained.

This, he said, would make for cheaper labour, which in turn would

> be an advantage to every German, to every German worker. The
> Generalgouvernement is not to become a closed economic area
> producing its own necessary industrial goods in part or entirely;
> the Generalgouvernement is a reservoir of labour for menial work
> (brickmaking, street building, etc. etc.). . . . The lending agency for
> unskilled labourers . . . a great Polish work camp.[37]

The reason for the meeting was the dispute over further deportations to
the Generalgouvernement. As was often the case, Hitler did not make a
quick decision. Instead, he asked for a report from von Schirach. When this
had been submitted, the head of the Reich Chancellery, Hans Lammers,
responded on 3 December that 'the deportation to the Generalgouvernement of the 60,000 Jews still living in the Vienna Reichsgau would be
expedited, i.e., implemented during the war, due to the shortage of housing
in Vienna'.[38] This promise, as will be shown, at first amounted to little.
Heydrich did include von Schirach's wishes – which had Hitler's blessing –
in his third short-term plan in early January 1941, but for the first phase of
this plan (and only this phase was concretely developed) he provided only
for the deportation of 10,000 Viennese Jews.

Koch had also failed to receive a definite promise on 2 October.
Apparently, Hitler had enjoined him to first make arrangements with his
neighbouring Gauleiter, Albert Forster (Danzig–West Prussia), concerning
which of the two would be the first to deport Poles and Jews to the
Generalgouvernement, and how many would be deported. Because the
adversaries could not agree, they called on Hitler together on 5 November
1940. Goebbels' version of the discussion survives:

> Koch and Forster, East issues. The Führer once more makes peace
> laughingly. Everyone wants to unload their rubbish into the General-
> gouvernement. Jews, the sick, the lazy, etc. And Frank resists. Not
> entirely without justification. Frank doesn't like it, but he has no
> choice.[39]

But in what a way was peace 'laughingly' made! Hitler gave each the same
thing, and far less than either had demanded. Within a short space of time,
10,000 Poles and Jews could now be deported from both East Prussia and
Danzig–West Prussia; from 10 to 20 November 1940, eleven resettlement
transports[40] carrying a total of 10,700 people[41] departed from Mława (in
the part of East Prussia that had belonged to Poland until 1939). Between 5
and 17 December, they were followed by 6607 Poles and 3259 Jews from
Danzig–West Prussia.[42]

On the previous day, 4 November, Hitler had spoken with Frank and
given him a far more important task than he would concede to Forster and
Koch a day later. 'On a specific special issue', Frank reported on the
meeting,

namely, on the issue of the relocation of Poles in the Generalgouvernement, the Führer declared quite generally that the Generalgouverneur,
as his representative, was to carry out political assignments, and
there can be no objections to this from any quarter.

And, looking at Major General Alfred Jodl, who was also present, Hitler
had added, 'The political assignments in the Generalgouvernement take
precedence over the military ones.'[43]

As much as Hans Frank was forced to concede during these weeks, he
succeeded in ensuring that the problems resulting from overall resettlement
policy were not 'solved' arbitrarily at the expense of the Generalgouvernement. This was not due to his negotiating skills. Hitler was also guided in
his decisions, most likely to a significant degree, by the fact that his
generals had already planned the first phase of mobilization for the war
against the Soviet Union. They and their top strategists must thus have
been interested in ensuring calm in the operational area of the Generalgouvernement – and in keeping transit routes clear.

Parallel to these rather half-hearted decisions, Hitler on 5 October 1940
had already rejected far-reaching resettlement visions for the Protectorate
of Bohemia and Moravia, as developed by Heydrich, among others.[44]
Instead of 'relocation of the Czechs and Germanization of the Bohemian–
Moravian region with German settlers', Hitler chose, among three options
offered him, the following, more easily handled alternative:

> the Germanization of the Bohemian–Moravian region through
> Germanization of the Czechs, that is, through their assimilation.
> The latter would be possible for the majority of the Czech people.
> To be excepted from assimilation are those Czechs against whom any
> racial reservations exist or those with anti-Reich sentiments. This
> category is to be wiped out.[45]

It must be noted that Hitler voted, at this point,[46] for the pragmatic
variant. For the 'majority' of the people, this meant forced Germanization;
for the remainder, classified as racially or politically objectionable, it
meant extermination.

The deportation of 6504 Jews from Baden and the Saar–Palatinate to
unoccupied France followed 14 days later, on 22–23 October.[47] At the same
time, the deportation of German, Austrian, and Czech Jews to France
rather than to the Generalgouvernement was apparently considered.
According to a report by the Foreign Office,

> Because of the intention to deport the remaining Jews from the Old
> Reich, the Ostmark [Austria], and the Protectorate of Bohemia and
> Moravia – a total of roughly 270,000 people, mainly of advanced age
> – to France, the Vichy government has expressed its misgivings about
> this measure. As a result, the proposal to send the Jews from Hesse
> has been postponed for the present.[48]

Also on 23 October, new 'Guidelines on the Implementation of Evacuation Operations in the Wartheland Reichsgau' were issued, expressly exempting Jews from the deportations.[49] This apparently also applied to Upper Silesia; on 31 October, Himmler appointed Albrecht Schmelt as his 'Special Plenipotentiary for Ethnic Alien Labour Deployment'. Schmelt organized the initially open form of slave labour for Jewish men and women in Upper Silesia.[50]

The above chain of decisions and contradictory options permits a number of conclusions to be drawn. It is conceivable that at this time Hitler was considering making distinctions in the 'solution of the Jewish question'. There might have been a plan to distinguish between the mass of Eastern European Jews (*Ostjuden*), whom he particularly hated, and the relatively smaller number of Western and Central European Jews, and to expel or deport them to different destinations, using different methods. There is little evidence to bolster such speculation. Even if such a plan may have been considered for a short time, it was abandoned so quickly that it had little significance for further developments; at most, the fact that yet another proposed solution had proven untenable could become an argument, in the logic of resettlement, for more radical ideas.

The political reorientation with regard to the ghettoized Jews in the incorporated eastern territories can be traced far more easily. The repeatedly unsuccessful efforts to deport them to the Generalgouvernement after all, in a rapid 'operation', were abandoned in October 1940 – apparently in favour of a new, as yet indefinite 'territorial final solution' after the war, which was now expected to end in 1941.[51] In practice, since April 1940 Jews had only been deported from the incorporated eastern territories in exceptional cases, as the deportation of Polish farmers to facilitate the settlement of ethnic German farmers always took priority. It was now only too obvious that, in view of the fact that the southeastern European Germans were already awaiting their 'farm assignments', nothing would change in this respect in the near future. Nor would it be helpful to the 'compensation' of the few city people among the settlers to deport the Jews of Lodz, Sosnowiec, and Ciechanów. The Main Trusteeship Office in the East had already confiscated their property and distributed their assets. Refraining from rapid deportation of the Jews demonstrated insight into the normative power of facts – no more and no less.

# Institutionalization of murder

On 24 September 1940, the Ethnic German Liaison Office (Vomi) began planning the construction of barracks for the impending influx of ethnic German settlers from southeastern Europe and Lithuania. The RKF, which was supposed to pay for the barracks, agreed, but with a caveat: such quartering should 'only occur to the extent that lodging in solid buildings is really infeasible'.[52] In fact, the barracks were not built; instead, the Vomi resorted more frequently to existing quarters, including psychiatric hospitals. Though it remains speculation, it is not unlikely that a meeting – noted in Himmler's appointment calendar under 14 September – in the Führer's Chancellery with Viktor Brack, organizer of 'Operation T-4', had already dealt with this subject.[53] In this period, too, the scope of Operation T-4 was perceptibly expanded. While the euthanasia officials had originally considered the murder of roughly 70,000 patients, they were soon talking about 140,000;[54] on 15 August, Werner Heyde, former medical director of T-4, declared, 'In contrast to the previous period, the mental hospitals are not all that necessary at the present time for military purposes, but they must nevertheless continue to be freed up, because one never knows what is to come.'[55] In the period from 21 May to 8 June, 1558 German and some 300 Polish psychiatric patients in the East Prussian psychiatric institution in Działdowo (German: Soldau) had already been murdered; they had been brought there from other psychiatric hospitals in the region, especially the Tapiau and Kortau facilities.[56] Himmler had approved the 'operation',[57] and the hospital later became the central transit camp for Lithuanian German settlers and Poles being relocated.[58] The murders had been organized, using the now-familiar gas vans, by Koppe, the higher SS and police chief in Posen, who was simultaneously a representative of the Reich Commission for the Consolidation of German Nationhood. 'Special Commando Lange, given to me for special tasks,' he later wrote, was 'sent to Soldau in East Prussia and during this period evacuated 1558 patients from the Soldau transit camp.' He did not consider the murder of Polish patients worthy of mention. Elsewhere, Koppe described the same events as follows: 'In June 1940, I removed 1558 troublesome persons for the purpose of other accommodation.'[59]

With the Madagascar Plan in view, all Jewish patients in German institutions – more than 2000 people in all – were deported to the gas chambers in summer 1940. This occurred through Operation T-4, but in a manner that clearly differed from the murder of 'Aryan' patients. While the Germans were killed selectively, according to criteria that included length of hospital stay, ability to work, and medical diagnosis and prognosis, the Jews became victims of 'euthanasia' collectively, solely on the basis of their racial classification.[60]

As vague as the extant documents are, the facts show conclusively how the self-created pressure to house ethnic German settlers in camps now also began to accelerate the murder of German psychiatric patients in the southern part of the Reich as well. Joining the earlier-mentioned justification for Operation T-4, an additional motive had now emerged for clearing psychiatric institutions and killing some of their patients in gas chambers. Events followed the same internal logic with which, in autumn and winter 1939–40, psychiatric institutions in the northeastern part of the Reich had been cleared to make room for Baltic and Volhynian Germans. However, now Himmler was no longer acting on his own. He coordinated the clearing of the hospitals with Operation T-4, now established as an organization and possessing practical experience. A few examples serve to suggest this.[61]

- In the period from 13 September to 20 September 1940, 218 of 452 patients in the Schwarzacher Hof psychiatric facility in Baden were deported to the killing hospital of Grafeneck. The Ethnic German Liaison Office thereupon confiscated the building on 30 October.[62] On 24 October, the local NSV (*Nationalsozialistische Volkswohlfahrt,* National Socialist Public Welfare) group in Unterschwarzach had already inspected the hospital for the purpose of 'housing Dobruja Germans'. An architect estimated that 580 resettlers could be quartered there, 'assuming four square metres of sleeping space per person'.[63]
- On 26 May, the Vomi had relocated 299 mentally ill South Tyroleans from the Pergine hospital near Trento to Schussenried.[64] Another 195 South Tyrolean patients followed on 1 November. Each time, the staff of Operation T-4 had first made room, deporting a corresponding number of patients to the gas chambers of Grafeneck.[65]
- After 320 of the 760 patients from the Stetten psychiatric hospital had been killed in Grafeneck a week earlier, on 15 December 1940 the Ethnic German Liaison Office confiscated the building and occupied it with ethnic German settlers.[66] On 12 October, the responsible medical director in the state of Württemberg's Ministry of the Interior had described this procedure as a 'purely administrative measure . . . which became necessary because many of the patients requiring hospitalization who were brought along by the resettled Russian Germans had to be distributed among the various mental hospitals in the Reich'.[67]
- Also in the second half of 1940, and on 2 December for the last time, T-4's deporters 'transferred' more than 400 patients from St Joseph's Hospital in southern Baden. The Ethnic German Liaison Office subsequently quartered 208 ethnic Germans there, and later 243 Slovenes who were to be Germanized.[68]
- Around this time, T-4 also cleared the Attl hospital near Wasserburg am Inn. Looking back on this in February 1941, Ehlich wrote:

  > This monastery belongs to lay brothers who have until now housed incurable idiots in their institution. Some of these occupants have already 'departed'. The district head has placed this facility at the disposal of the Reichsführer SS to take in returnees.[69]

- Although clearance of the Neuendettelsau hospitals was not prepared until several months later, it will be described here because the motives and the method with which negotiations were held are noteworthy. On 23 April 1941, a representative of the Reich Chamber of Physicians wrote to the Minister of the Interior:

The foreign division of the Reich Chamber of Physicians, which the Reichsführer has charged with the medical care of resettled Germans, requests that the Reich Minister of the Interior apply the Reich Benefits Act to the particularly suitable Neuendettelsau mental institutions for the purpose of accommodating old, infirm South Tyroleans in need of care. It is requested that 1800 beds be cleared.[70]

As with resettlement in general, even with the clearing of psychiatric institutions the assumption was apparently that 'the same amount of room is needed for one South Tyrolean as for two former patients'.[71] On 20 April, the director of the Lutheran Diakonissen hospital in Neuendettelsau declared himself willing to place '550 beds at the disposal of the national comrades [*Volksgenossen*] from South Tyrol'.[72] On 14 July 1941, the Reich Chamber of Physicians reported to the RKF, 'Broad agreement was reached with the directors of the hospital.'[73]

These few examples demonstrate that Himmler no longer knew what to do with all these settlers, whom he greeted with propagandist enthusiasm but could only house in confiscated psychiatric institutions, monasteries and gymnasiums. The officials of the relocation operations – Eichmann, Ehlich, and his UWZ staff – were unable to keep pace with the officials responsible for resettlement projects at the Vomi and EWZ. They were not lacking in brutality, suitable personnel, general good will or money; nevertheless, each of their mass expulsions created all but insoluble conflicts.

As with the murder of the mentally ill during the first resettlement phase in 1939–40, there is no written document on the murders in the second phase that expressly proves the connection, although a comparatively large number of documents have survived on important decision-making processes in the central Berlin T-4 office. This demonstrates the extent to which such decisions were made verbally, so that a written record was avoided even in secret internal correspondence. The same phenomenon can be observed in the secret 'reports from the Reich' written by the SD, which were supposed to provide the top echelons of the state and party with the unadorned truth about the situation. Here, too, the mass murders of German psychiatric patients, and later of Jews, were systematically omitted. However, SD agents without a doubt also regularly studied the 'mood' of the Germans on this issue as well.[74]

Thus although, at least so far, no unequivocal documents are available, it becomes clear from chronological and factual relationships that the members of the resettlement apparatus acted in agreement with T-4, and that a large number of consultations pertaining to this *must* have taken place. With unusual candour and obvious satisfaction, the Würzburg representative of the Ethnic German Liaison Office informed his Berlin superior, 'To accommodate the ethnic Germans from Bessarabia intended for the Main-Franconia Gau, I have, among other things, confiscated several building complexes from the Werneck mental hospital and cleared them by relocating the mental patients.'[75]

Of the 1500 buildings used by the Ethnic German Liaison Office as settlers' camps in 1940–41, 550 were church-run institutions.[76] Himmler had already developed this idea by the end of 1939, when he was confronted with the vacillation surrounding the accommodation of old, infirm Balts.[77] At that time, Greifelt had already established a sort of legal basis for such requisitions for his colleagues at the Ethnic German Liaison Office, in the form of – as he literally put it – an 'authorization to confiscate appropriate camp spaces for temporary group accommodation of ethnic German settlers'.[78]

In autumn 1939, the completely unplanned resettlement of the Balts suddenly created pressure, in the view of Himmler and Sandberger, Heydrich and Eichmann, that they could only overcome, in their opinion, by 'radical means'. However, since May 1940 they had already institutionalized murder with their additional extermination operations: it had now become a standard element in the operating procedure of all resettlement officials. Altogether, by the end of 1940 they had killed more than 20,000 people – based on minimum figures – for the 'purpose of making room for ethnic German settlers'. The way in which this practical experience of murder, which must be viewed in hindsight as an intermediate step on the road to the Holocaust, influenced subsequent procedure is shown in the following example.

At the end of June 1940, in his capacity as representative of the RKF in the Warthegau, Koppe issued guidelines 'on those to be held back in evacuations'. In them, he ordered – under pressure from the authorities in the Generalgouvernement – that 'cripples, the infirm, the sick, those unfit for transport, etc.' should not be deported to the Generalgouvernement, but had to be 'taken in by neighbouring Poles'.[79] This soon led to complaints from district leaders: 'During the resettlement,' complained one of them in October, 'it could be observed that, of the Polish families to be relocated, only able-bodied persons were resettled, while the sick and infirm remained in the Posen district.' Those who remained behind would 'become a burden on the public welfare', so that a situation arose that was 'untenable over the long term'. The district head thus suggested 'also relocating at least those sick and infirm people who belong to families of Poles who are to be relocated'. Höppner, who understood the additional complications this would involve with the leadership of the Generalgouvernement, noted on the margin of the report, 'It is possible that different measures must be taken for persons unfit for transport. For reconsideration 10 November 1940.'[80]

Höppner's marginalia are dated 22 October. On 27, 28, and 30 October, three groups of sick and aged Jews from Kalisz (in the Warthegau) were already being 'resettled' – a total of 290 people. As Isaiah Trunk reported, the German police reassured the patients by telling them they would be taken to a sanatorium to be 'cured'. The same day, they were all murdered in a nearby forest.[81]

## 'Emigration of the Jews – room for Poles'

Having manoeuvred himself into a corner by late autumn 1940, Heinrich Himmler was forced to explain the policy of ethnic redistribution. This occurred in an 'address on settlement' that he delivered on 10 December before the assembled Reichsleiters and Gauleiters in Berlin. The conference began at 10 o'clock a.m. Himmler appeared, as he expressly noted, in 'civilian dress',[82] apparently in order to emphasize his non-police function as Reich Commissioner.

The key words of Himmler's address, noted in his own handwriting, have survived;[83] there are also brief reports on the state of affairs, which he had requested 14 days previously from the chiefs of staff of the various offices responsible for resettlement policies, in order to help him prepare his speech.[84]

At the front of the preparation folder are three reports by Eichmann. One is a list, by year, of the forced emigration of Jews between 1933 and 1940 showing that, up to that point, 341,975 Jews had been forced to leave the German Reich. Eichmann attached to this a second list on the 'evacuation' of Poles and Jews from the incorporated eastern territories, indicating region of origin, number of expellees and reason for expulsion (that is, the settlement of Baltic, Volhynian, and Galician Germans aimed at in each case) – altogether 305,000 people, including the ongoing 'deportation of 10,000 Jews and Poles to the Generalgouvernement'. The two last pages by Eichmann were headed 'The Jewish question'. This memo, written by Eichmann on 4 December, was divided into two points. Under the heading 'I. Initial solution of the Jewish question through emigration', the head of Section VID4 reported that, so far, a total of 501,711 Jews had left Germany, Austria, and the Protectorate; to this, Eichmann had added the 'decline in the number of Jews through natural reduction' by subtracting 'total births' from 'total deaths' and arriving at a total 'death surplus' of 57,036 people. His figures indicated that the 'total number of Jews still residing in the Reich territory' (including the Protectorate, but without the incorporated eastern territories) came to 315,642.

The reason Himmler and Eichmann needed these calculations is obvious: they had to justify their actions. With regard to the deportations begun in December 1939, their results fell far short of their own projections, the 'grand plans of the Reichsführer SS'. Considering the now implemented resettlement of 530,713 ethnic Germans, which was to conclude in the following weeks, and considering their own projections requiring the expulsion of two to three 'ethnic alien' families for the settlement of one ethnic German family, the total of 300,000 evacuated by December 1940 was inadequate in every respect. Therefore, in his speech Himmler threw in the Jews who had fled or been driven out between 1933 and 1939 and noted to himself, 'Great mass migration for the last eight years.' According to such embellished figures, there were 873,483 'emigrants' for the entire period, compared with slightly more than 500,000 'immigrants'. Thus to justify himself, Himmler included – not very convincingly – the entire expulsion of German and Austrian Jewry in his programme of 'making room' for ethnic Germans.

Further, Himmler comforted the at least partially sceptical Reich and Gauleiters by pointing out the great financial profits that the German Reich made on the relocations: the estimated wealth of the resettled ethnic Germans, according to DUT calculations – which can also be found in the preparation folder and in the notes for Himmler's speech – came to 3315 thousand million Reichsmarks. These were sums which the countries of origin, under treaty, were required to pay into the Reich coffers. In contrast, payments to ethnic German settlers had so far amounted to only 65 million. Thus a clear profit of three and a quarter thousand million Reichsmarks seemed possible, assuming that the principle which Himmler referred to as 'natural restitution' – that is, the principle of confiscation and expulsion – could be maintained.[85]

The second point in Eichmann's notes for Himmler on 4 December 1940 was much briefer. It went, 'II. The final solution of the Jewish question. Through resettlement of the Jews from the European economic sphere of the German *Volk* to a territory yet to be determined. Approximately 5.8 million Jews fall within the scope of this project.' This figure encompassed all continental European Jews living west of the German–Soviet demarcation line.

The difference between the 4 million who were to be deported to Madagascar as recently as August 1940 and the 5.8 million Jews now mentioned arose from the territorial description, used here for the first time by Eichmann, of the 'European economic sphere of the German *Volk*'. In August 1940, Eichmann had still employed a very different concept; in formulating the Madagascar Plan, he had spoken exclusively of the Jews who lived 'under direct German jurisdiction' or 'under German military jurisdiction'.

Since now, without another war having been fought, according to Eichmann an additional 1.8 million Jews were to be deported, the new concept of the 'European economic sphere of the German *Volk*'[86] took on great significance. In contrast to the situation at the time of the Madagascar Plan, the planners operating in the Ministry of Economics and the Office of the Four-Year Plan had now clearly defined this concept; they had concrete ideas for the economic, social, and demographic alteration of the various countries, including those that were 'peacefully subjugated' – and the 'solution of the Jewish question' was unquestionably among them.[87]

We should note parenthetically that, because the number 5.8 million marked an interim stage of planning, and because at the point in question – December 1940 – Eichmann was not (yet) considering the systematic murder of the Jews, Wolfgang Benz is obviously incorrect when he writes that this figure was 'an original reference to the number of Jews who were to be subject to a "final solution"'.[88] Lucien Steinberg's formulation is more cautious: 'Ce n'est peut-être qu'une coïncidence, mais ce chiffre est vraiment très proche de celui des victimes de cette Solution Finale.'[89] Any other conclusion would also mean that, at the Wannsee Conference, the murder of not all, but only some of the 11 million European Jews had been discussed. That is out of the question.

Important to the decision-making situation in December 1940 was, first of all, the way in which Himmler used his colleagues' information, including Eichmann's notes on the 'final solution of the Jewish question', in his speech 'On Settlement'. First, he assured the assembled Reich and Gauleiters that he would make no more 'propaganda' during the war for the settlement of peasant families from the Reich in the new eastern territories.[90] Second, Himmler promised that from now on, of the German minorities in Europe, 'only splinters that cannot maintain themselves as an ethnic unit' would be brought home to the Reich; otherwise, however, unlike heretofore, the issue would be the 'consolidation of German nationhood in Europe' (which meant that ethnic Germans would henceforth remain in their homelands). Third, with regard to the impending evacuations to the incorporated eastern territories, which in his view had to be carried out to enable the settlement of the Bessarabian, Bukovinian, and Dobruja Germans living in interim camps, Himmler noted, '*ruthless German authority* [in the Generalgouvernement]; the Generalgouvernement is a labour reservoir for seasonal and one-time jobs; *emigration of the Jews* to make more room for Poles.'[91]

It should be noted that Himmler now promised 'emigration of the Jews' from the Generalgouvernement, originally the territory intended as the end of the line for the deportation of Poles and Jews. Now, as already established in the Madagascar Plan, 2 million Jews were to be deported specifically to make room for Poles, who in turn had to make room for ethnic German settlers in the incorporated eastern territories. Whether Himmler hinted in his speech at the destination of such 'emigration of the Jews' is not clear from the surviving documents. However, it may be assumed that, around this time, he was discussing possible alternatives with his staff and asking for suggestions. How this took place is not known, but it is certain that, soon after, options were being discussed that would emerge from a victorious war against the Soviet Union. They will be discussed in the following two chapters.

With his internal, and soon public, announcements of further deportations, Himmler found himself in sharp opposition to Frank and the leadership of the Wehrmacht in winter 1940–41. Aside from the general reasons leading Frank to refuse additional resettlements, there was now also the Wehrmacht mobilization in the eastern part of the Generalgouvernement. From November 1940 to 15 March 1941, the Wehrmacht had already sent 2500 trainloads of soldiers and *matériel* to the Generalgouvernement. The German military thus set in motion the first phase of deployments for operation 'Barbarossa'. This gave Hans Frank good arguments in his ongoing dispute with the head of the Warthegau, Arthur Greiser. On 3 November, in Krakow, he gave Greiser the following memorandum:

> In view of the labour and occupancy situation in the Generalgouvernement that has arisen as a result of the special order, the Wehrmacht is raising objections in the Generalgouvernement against taking in any additional Poles and Jews in the already completely overcrowded region. I informed Reichsführer Himmler of this fact today. It would be impossible to send additional Poles and Jews to the Generalgouvernement before the end of the war. I have instructed my offices to stop any transports from neighbouring regions and send them back to the Reich territory.[92]

Two days later, Höppner reported to his superior, Eichmann, on Greiser's reaction, on the basis of a discussion with Koppe:

> The Gauleiter is convinced that the Generalgouverneur has such important tasks at the moment that his work is made more difficult by the evacuation transports. He has thus agreed that after completing the train transports already approved by the Generalgouvernement,[93] no further orders for additional trains will be made by him.

Höppner thereupon wrote to Koppe that 'the resettlement staffs should be instructed immediately to cease all demands for supplemental evacuations, especially for improving the status of ethnic Germans'. Höppner's letter continued:

> The thought was expressed by SS Gruppenführer Koppe that for later measures (Bessarabian operation, improvement of the status of ethnic Germans), perhaps a relocation of Poles within the Gau should be considered. As a reservation, I mentioned threats to security.

However, between the lines of his letter to Eichmann, Höppner let it be understood that, unlike his superiors Koppe and Greiser, he would pay less attention to Frank. He wrote, 'If the Reich Security Main Office should not get trains for the Bessarabian resettlement, that is, if it must begin relocation within the Gau, it is my opinion that . . .'[94] This was followed by unimportant suggestions for this extremely undesirable possibility. What is crucial is that Höppner – going over the heads of Koppe, Greiser, and Frank – was requesting that Eichmann make efforts to allow the deportations to continue as usual. The attempt was not unsuccessful.

Together with his experts on resettlement, Heydrich developed the third short-term plan around the end of 1940. The plan is well known. In its concrete form, concluded at the beginning of January 1941, it provided for (in addition to the aforementioned deportation of 60,000 Viennese Jews) the expulsion of 771,000 Poles in order to 'accommodate' the southeastern European ethnic Germans in the incorporated eastern territories of the Reich, and in order to 'make room' for the Wehrmacht and for other purposes – such as the expansion of the Auschwitz concentration camp. To the extent that Jews were also to be expelled from the incorporated eastern territories for these purposes, their deportation was also provided for within the scope of the figures provided by Heydrich. However, the third short-term plan could only affect relatively few Jews; the German authorities had already stolen their property and herded most of them into ghettos, so their deportation would free up neither adequate housing nor jobs for ethnic Germans.

The question of how and when the Jews of the Warthegau, eastern Upper Silesia, and southeastern Prussia could be deported was not answered by the third short-term plan. The few extant documents, however, suggest that in late autumn 1940 Heydrich had developed another plan, independent of the third short-term plan, involving the 'territorial final solution of the Jewish question'. The plan, which was to give weight to Himmler's promise of 'emigration of the Jews to make more room for Poles', will be presented after the following chronology, in the contours that are possible, given the limited source material.

# Notes

1  As already explained, the Lodz Jews were originally to be deported to the Generalgouvernement starting on 1 August by train or, if necessary, on foot (see Chapter 4, 24 June).
2  This involved the return of several tens of thousands of Poles who had fled the approaching German Wehrmacht in September 1939.
3  Extracts from Frank's diary, 261–4.
4  Browning, *Final Solution*, 42.
5  Thus on 31 October 1940, Walter Emmerich, director of the Generalgouvernement's economic council, who simultaneously headed the main economics office in Frank's government, explained, 'Much catching up remains with regard to the elimination of the Jews from the economy.' Emmerich reported that his department was preparing to expropriate Jewish real estate, the value of which he estimated in Warsaw alone as being around two thousand million zloty (or one thousand million Reichsmarks) (Frank diary, 299). The expropriation had been in preparation since the summer.
6  See Chapter 2, p. 45.
7  For an explanation of this figure, see Chapter 9, pp. 195ff.
8  Himmler had already begun to think about this removal around the end of the year 1939, but because of the logistical difficulties facing his resettlement programme, he was forced to give it lower priority. (See Chapter 2, p. 48.) Political considerations may also have played a part; after all, an early

resettlement of the Bessarabian Germans – analogous to the process in the Baltic states – could have been too plain an announcement of the impending annexation of the region by the Soviet Union, negatively influencing the understanding with Romania that was urgently needed for economic reasons.

9 See Muehlon, 170–92.

10 Overall, 95,000 people were involved. See the RKF treatment (Main Department I) 'on the state of *Volkstum* in the territories ceded to Hungary by Romania under the Vienna Award', 7 September 1940, BAK, R69/304, 4. The treatment was thus available a week after the Vienna Award took place and already took into account the resettlement of the Bukovinian Germans.

11 Resettlements in northern Transylvania and the Szatmár region, PAA, R100629.

12 Quoted in Stuhlpfarrer, 621. On the development of the Beskids plan and its rapid abandonment in mid-November 1939, see ibid. 617–49. This is obviously what was referred to in a flyer distributed in autumn 1939 by the minority of so-called 'stayers' among the South Tyroleans, against the 'option for *Volk* and Reich':

> Compatriots, you have been given a free choice – between the homeland and Galicia! . . . You are to live in huts from which Polish residents have been driven, to work on farms from which the owners have been driven with wives and children. Shoved among hostile peoples, surrounded by Slovaks, Czechs and Polacks, with the Russian Bolsheviks right nearby, you are to be 'deployed' in the national struggle against Poland, as intruders, unwanted and hated by them, until you are driven from the country, for the wheel of fortune can turn again; in a not too distant future, the Poles will demand back from you the houses and fields taken from them. Once again, without worldly goods, you will have to go wandering. Where to? No one knows, least of all those who try to lure you from your homeland with their unscrupulous propaganda.
>
> (Quoted in Messner, 246f.)

13 See Chapter 2, pp. 34f., 37.

14 Himmler, *Geheimreden*, 131.

15 This according to Otto Bene, German General Consul, in November 1940, quoted in Stuhlpfarrer, 692. On this, see especially Hillgruber, *Strategie*, 388ff. ('The global political situation at the end of 1940 from Hitler's point of view').

16 Report of Otto Bene to the Foreign Office in Berlin, 5 November 1940, 'referring to impressions of the situation in the South Tyrol', ADAP, series D, vol. 11, 1, 398–402.

17 Notes on the Reichsführer SS's journey through Bolzano on 23 November 1940, quoted in Stuhlpfarrer, 540. Himmler came more or less accidentally to Bolzano, as he had taken part in the funeral of the Italian Police Chief, Arturo Bocchini, in Rome on 21 November.

18 Report on the meeting of VDA directors in Posen on 6–7 April 1941; BAK, R59/28, 338–47.

19 Note by Reich Ministry of Finance of 26 November 1940 on a meeting in the Foreign Office on 22 November 1940 on the subject of 'Resettlement of Bulgarian Germans'; BAK, R2/25096, 7. The minutes of this meeting are found in PAA, R100627. Representatives of the RKF and Vomi at this meeting declared the envisaged resettlement feasible at short notice, subject to Himmler's agreement.

20 Note by Dolezalek, head of the Posen planning department of the SS settlement staff, 12 February 1941, on a discussion with Oberregierungsrat Siegmund and Gauleiter Greiser on 4 February 1941; BAK, R49/Anh. I/34, 43–7.

21 The department of the Foreign Office represented by Lorenz and in charge of Germans abroad.

22 Letter from German legation in Budapest to the Foreign Office in Berlin, 11 September 1940; PAA, R100629.

23 Letter from Foreign Office to German legation in Budapest, drafted on 23 October, sent 3 November 1940; ibid.

24 Instructions (signed by Himmler, November 1940), emphasis in original, reprinted in *Menscheneinsatz*, 62.

25 Note by Höppner, 30 January 1941; AGK, UWZ/L/182, 9.

26 Newspaper clippings on this campaign from January 1940 can be found in BAK, R69/1032, here p. 15.

27 Generallandesarchiv Karlsruhe, 465d/894, quoted in Hans-Werner Scheuing, 58ff. (I thank the author for his kind permission to quote from the as-yet unpublished manuscript). Apparently, this concerned those Bessarabian Germans who, according to a decision by Hitler (in summer 1940), were to be 'settled in the new western territories'. Five thousand of them were in fact 'placed in Alsace and Lorraine' in early 1943 – parallel to the settlement operation in Zamość (report from Himmler to Hitler on 20 January 1943 on the state of his activities as Reich Commissioner for the Consolidation of German Nationhood, quoted in Bach and Jacobsen).

28 Letter from State Welfare Association in Swabia to the St Joseph Congregation in Ursberg, 9 November 1940. Reprinted in Immenkötter, 139. On the basis of this directive, 180 patients were 'transferred' from Ursberg (I thank Peter Witte for this reference).

29 Daily orders from director of Vomi/deployment staff at Litzmannstadt, 4 October 1940; R59/220.

30 Note by Günter Stier on 'Settlement of Bessarabians and Buchenland [Bukovinian] Germans' and on 'temporary labour service by camp inmates', 4 December 1940; BAK, R49/2603.

31 This idea was first developed in Aly and Heim, 276ff.

32 IMG, vol. 26, 377ff.

33 Long-term plan for resettlement in the eastern provinces; BAK, R69/1146, 5.

34 On this, see Aly and Heim, 207–56.

35 The figures were influenced by the interests of the Krakow government; that is, they are plainly exaggerated – in addition to official relocation statistics, they include an estimate of the number of Jewish refugees; in contrast, the RKF functionaries in annexed western Poland did their best to ignore the undoubtedly significant (but as far as I am aware, never precisely calculated) number of Jewish refugees.

36 Peter-Heinz Seraphim, 'Die Judenfrage im Generalgouvernement als Bevölkerungsproblem', *Die Burg* 1: 1 (1940), 63.

37 Note by Bormann on the meeting between Hitler, Schirach, Frank, and Koch on 2 October 1940; IMT, vol. 39, 425ff.

38 Quoted in Pätzold, 279.

39 Goebbels diaries, vol. I/4, 387.

40 Train schedule for Mława; AGK, UWZ/L/16, 135.

41 Listing by Litzmannstadt UWZ on December 1940; AGK, UWZ/L/23, 6.

42 Ibid. 7.

43 Frank diary; BAK, R52/II/179 (minutes of meeting, 6 November 1940).

44 See the deportation plan of 14 September 1940 to an 'imaginary Gouvernement', developed by Heydrich and discussed in Chapter 4, p. 99. In contrast, on 24 September 1940, Goebbels had already noted, 'The Führer, too, is more and more interested in a policy of assimilation in the Protectorate' (Goebbels diaries, I/4, 337).

45 Note by representative of Foreign Office (signed [Kurt] Ziemke) at the Reich Protector in Bohemia and Moravia on 5 October 1940, Král, 88f. On 7 December 1940, the RKF noted, 'An overall resettlement to the Bohemian–Moravian area cannot be considered even for the future'; BAK, R49/2603. The 'settlement of ethnic Germans' in the Protectorate was 'proposed by various offices', among them Department VI of the Reich Ministry of the Interior. Because of the 'overall political situation', Himmler also refrained from deporting Czechs living in the Sudetenland to the Protectorate and replacing them with Bessarabian Germans. (Response from Stier [RKF] to the Reich Ministry of the Interior, 7 November 1940; letter from Himmler to Bormann on the same day; BAK, R49/2603.)

46 One year later, Heydrich accomplished his plans in a second attempt; see Müller, 102f.

47 The administration of the property of Jews who had already been 'evacuated' from Baden, the Saar–Palatinate and Stettin [Szczecin] in 1940 was the responsibility (at least until the end of 1941) of the Reichführer SS (notes by expert Walter Maedel [RMF] of 8 December 1941 on a discussion on 4 December 1941 with representatives of the RSHA, the Ministry of Justice and the Reich Commissioner for Enemy Property; BAK, R2/9172b, 20ff.). It would be interesting to pursue the question whether and to what extent this property – especially houses and apartments – was given to ethnic German resettlers.

48 'Report on Sending Jews with German Citizenship to Southern France', quoted in Klarsfeld, 360f.

49 Guidelines of 23 October 1940 (no signature); AGK, UWZ/L/1, 23ff.

50 Konieczny, *passim*.

51 The deportation, mentioned on p. 117, from Danzig–West Prussia, where few Jews lived, was an exception.

52 Letter from RKF to the Vomi, 28 September 1940; BAK, R49/2602.

53 Himmler's calendar, written by R. Brandt; BAK, NS19/3954.

54 See Faulstich, 288.

55 Report by psychiatrist Gottfried Ewald on the meeting with Heyde on 15 August 1940, quoted ibid., 248.

56 Hilberg, 894f. Even before then, and in the subsequent months, at least several hundred Polish and Jewish patients and people in need of care were murdered in the annexed part of East Prussia; Benz and Golczewski, 431.

57 See the decision by the second penal chamber of the Bonn district court in the investigative procedure against Koppe; 13 Qs 383/60, 21.

58 In East Prussia, at least the Carlshöfer institutions run by the Innere Mission near Rastenburg and the provincial psychiatric institution near Wehlau (present-day Znamensk) were also cleared (a total of 2500 beds).

59 Letter from Koppe to Jakob Sporrenberg, 18 October 1940; letter from Koppe to Karl Wolff, 22 February 1941, quoted in Preliminary Investigation of Wilhelm Koppe, LG Bonn (Bonn district court), 13 UR 1/61 (appendix on final decision of 30 September 1963).

60 On the circumstances of this murder operation, see Friedlander, *passim*.

61 These are taken from the secondary literature, which was available to me with no extensive research, but then is extremely sketchy and always unsystematic on this point. The subject 'Operation T-4 and resettlement policies in the years 1939–1941' requires a systematic empirical investigation.

62 Mosbach, 12ff.

63 Quoted in Scheuing, see note 27; Mosbach, 12f. Indeed, the facility was not used for resettlers, as originally intended. As I was informed by H. W. Scheuing as this book went to press, however, around Easter 1941, 250 to 300 southeastern European ethnic Germans were quartered in the Kehl-Kork facility. (See

70 *Jahre Korker Anstalten. 1892–1962* (Kehl-Kork 1962), 41). The deportation of a corresponding number of patients was already organized in October 1940 (Klee, 272).

64 It is true that many South Tyrolean patients became victims of general neglect during the war and deliberate starvation in German facilities, but the German leadership apparently feared murdering the mentally ill settlers in gas chambers. This did not rule out individual 'transfers' – when no relatives spoke up. (See May *et al.*, 42f.)

65 Ibid., 39ff.; Stuhlpfarrer, 518ff.

66 Schaich, 83.

67 Letter from Stuttgart general prosecutor to the Reich Minister of Justice, 12 October 1940, quoted in Klee, *Dokumente,* 211. (In fact, the issue was not primarily the accommodation of sick ethnic German settlers, but the creation of restricted camps for healthy people.)

68 Wollasch, 359, 365.

69 Letter from Ehlich to SS Standartenführer Max Sollmann, who wanted to turn the institution into a Lebensborn home, 4 February 1941; BDC, SS-HO/5372.

70 Quoted in Gebel and Grießhammer, 13.

71 File note of Bavarian State Ministry of the Interior, 7 April 1941, on the 'Results of the Negotiations in the Führer's Chancellery, Reich Minister of the Interior and Foreign Section of the Reich Chamber of Physicians, as well as the Gau Leadership of Nuremberg and the Provincial Head' on the freeing up of the Neuendettelsau institutions, ibid., 16f.

72 Ibid., 18f.

73 Ibid., 27f. This, however, only occurred after Himmler had decreed on 3 July 1941 that 'the accommodation of old, no longer fit South Tyrolean resettlers is to be tackled immediately'. On 9 September 1941, the 'Human Deployment' Department of the RKF reported that the decree had been carried out, referring to Neuendettelsau (BAK, R49/2606/7).

74 See Aly, 'Hinweise', 195–9.

75 Telex from the Gau staff office leader of the Gau leadership of Main-Franconia, Karl Hellmuth, to the Ethnic German Liaison Office, 24 September 1940; BAK, R59/132, 278. (The Werneck institution was housed in the castle built by Balthasar Neumann that was used for the T-4 propaganda film *Dasein ohne Leben* (Existence without Life) as an example of the supposed excessive care provided to psychiatric patients. See Roth, 'Film', 135ff.).

76 RKF activity report (situation at end of 1942); BAK, R49/26, 33.

77 Letter from Himmler to Hilgenfeldt, 12 December 1939; StA Poznań, Vomi/P/ 123, 102.

78 Letter from Greifelt to Behrends, 12 November 1940; BAK, R49/2603. The date the confiscation power was granted is given here as 30 December 1939.

79 File note by Höppner, 24 June 1940; AGK, UWZ/P/252, 8. The passage is also included in the 'Guidelines for Implementation of Evacuation Operation in the Wartheland Reichsgau', issued by Eichmann on 23 October 1940, and the simultaneously issued 'Guidelines for the Implementation of the Evacuation Operation in the Saybusch District'; AGK, UWZ/L/1, 23ff.

80 Report by the Main SD Branch in Posen on the 'effects of the resettlement in the Posen district', 19 October 1940; AGK, UWZ/P/195, 4f. A similar report on 25 October 1940 is found ibid./225, 5.

81 Trunk, 251; Benz and Golczewski, 431.

82 Himmler's appointment calendar, entry on 10 December 1940; BAK, NS19/ 3954.

83 Himmler's notes for 'speech before the Reich and Gau leaders in Berlin on 10 December 1940'; BAK, NS19/4007.

84 Himmler's collection of materials for an 'address on settlement', BAK, NS19/3979.

85 Overviews on 'property in the charge of' the DUT and 'payments as of 30 November 1940', 7 December 1940 (signatures: Kulemann, Schmölder); BAK, NS19/3979, 12–14.

86 In the minutes of the Wannsee Conference, there is mention of 'forcing the Jews out of the *Lebensraum* of the German people'.

87 Aly and Heim, 350–64.

88 Benz, 2.

89 Steinberg, 10. It is not my intention to find mistakes in Benz or Steinberg. However, these misinterpretations are examples of how documents on the Jewish policy of the Third Reich can be incorrectly interpreted if they are not read within the context of the overall plans for a new order and resettlement.

90 The word 'propaganda' is doubly underlined in Himmler's notes for his speech. At this point, Himmler gave the number of possible 'peasant families' as 480,000 – that is, around 2.5 million people.

91 Emphasis in original. It is remarkable that, in Himmler's notes for the speech, he referred to completely outdated numbers of Jews supposedly living in the southeastern European countries: for Romania, 1 million; for Hungary, 1.5 million; for Yugoslavia, 150,000; for Slovakia, 250,000. These figures are noted in the section of his speech subheaded 'ethnic Germans'. The ethnic German minorities in these countries, who were apparently no longer to be resettled, came to (respectively) 580,000, 845,000, 705,000, 160,000. Possibly – but this must remain conjecture for now – the synchronized naming of the German and Jewish minorities in each case indicated Himmler's intention to strengthen the position of the German minorities in these countries by removing the Jews living there. The outdated figures for the Jews in the four countries could have been mentioned for a number of reasons. Either Himmler exaggerated without restraint to show his audience the considerable 'demographic relief' that the displacement of the Jews would bring for southeastern Europe; or he added the 'others' listed there (mainly Gypsies) and those he suspected of being '*Mischlinge*', of mixed parentage, to the figures determined by the RKF in September 1940 for the Jewish minority in the southeastern European countries, and then simply subsumed all these people, whom he considered 'inferior', under the heading of 'Jew'.

92 The text is quoted in a rush telex from Höppner to Eichmann and Ehlich, 5 November 1940; AGK, Greiser trial/36, 559. The telex, which Frank had sent to Greiser the previous day, is reprinted in *Biuletyn* 12 (1960), 113F.

93 This involved around 20 additional trains – that is, 20,000 people from the Warthegau and Danzig–West Prussia.

94 Note by Höppner for Ehlich, Eichmann, Damzog, and Krumey, 6 November 1940; AGK, Greiser trial/36, 557ff.

# 6

## A major plan fails

### Chronology: 15 November 1940– 15 March 1941

**15 November 1940:** Final sealing of the Warsaw ghetto. Fritz Arlt, head of the RKF field office in Upper Silesia, works for a 'territorial expansion of the Auschwitz concentration camp' and submits relevant plans to the RKF staff main office in Berlin.[1] On 16 January, the 'Human Deployment' Department of the RKF plans the evacuation of 20,000 people for this purpose.[2] On 1 March, Himmler orders the expansion of the camp.

**20 November:** Hungarian Foreign Minister Pál Teleki declares at a meeting with Hitler in Vienna 'that the Jews must be removed from Europe once peace is achieved'. Hitler responds that he sees 'the solution of the Jewish question for Europe as one of the greatest peacetime tasks'.[3]

**22 November:** In a meeting with Hitler in Berlin, Romanian Prime Minister General Ion Antonescu estimates the number of refugees in Romania, which has lost territory three times, at 245,000. The influx of refugees from Bessarabia, Dobruja, and the part of Transylvania now belonging to Hungary 'will not stop'.[4]

**End of November:** The officer for Jewish matters in the Department for Population and Welfare in Krakow publicly demands that Jews quickly disappear from the Generalgouvernement. He explains that

> wartime events and their consequences have greatly restricted the living space and conditions of the Jews. Jewish workers have been replaced by Aryans in numerous enterprises, causing economic and social crowding in addition to physically cramped conditions. These conditions will continue to worsen, demanding that pressure be relieved and a solution found.[5]

**26 November:** Himmler issues guidelines 'for building up the rural areas in the new eastern territories'. They include plans for two-thirds of peasant family enterprises to receive 50–300-acre parcels of land. 'Use of modern technology and extensive automation' are expected to 'increase the productivity of the peasant families.'[6]

**29 November:** First plans are drawn up by the Supreme Command of the Army (OKH) for the war against the Soviet Union.[7]

**30 November:** Franz Halder makes an entry in his war diary about a discussion on the 'Jewish question in France'.[8]

**3 December 1940:** Hitler promises von Schirach 'that the deportation to the Generalgouvernement of the 60,000 Jews still living in the Vienna Reichsgau would be expedited, i.e., implemented during the war, owing to the shortage of housing in Vienna'.[9]

Himmler orders that ethnic German 'camp inmates be integrated as far as possible into productive work'.[10]

**4 December:** Eichmann calculates that there are 5.8 million Jews to be 'removed from the European economic sphere of the German *Volk* to a territory yet to be determined'.[11]

**5 December:** Halder presents Hitler with the plan of the German Chiefs of Staff for the war against the Soviet Union. The Arkhangel'sk–Astrakhan line is to be reached after a five-month campaign.

**10 December:** Himmler's 'address on settlement'.[12]

**17 December:** Meeting with Eichmann 'on the implementation of the so-called third short-term plan (settlement of the ethnic Germans from Bessarabia, Buchenland [i.e., Bukovina], Dobruja, Lithuania, etc.)'. The participants are Rolf-Heinz Höppner (Posen), Hermann Krumey (Lodz), Franz Abromeit (Gdynia), Schlegel (Königsberg), and Riedel (Katowice). No representative from the Generalgouvernement is invited.[13]

**18 December:** Hitler signs 'Directive no. 21 (Barbarossa)': 'The German Wehrmacht must be prepared to defeat the USSR in a speedy campaign, even before the end of the war with England.' Preparations are to be completed by 15 May 1941.[14]

**19 December:** The EWZ in Lodz assumes the RKF will begin resettling the Bukovinian Germans 'within the next few days'.[15] On the same day, Himmler conducts separate, private discussions, in close succession, with Heydrich, Greifelt, Lorenz, and Göring. As suggested by the context, they presumably deal with future resettlement policy.[16]

**21 December:** The RKF orders 'improved (economic) status for the long-standing rural population in the Eastern territories', because the local German population feels disadvantaged in comparison with the newly settled Eastern European ethnic Germans.

This order represents a new form of internal expulsion by those carrying out the resettlement, and one which will become important later. Since the Poles 'to be removed from their farms within the scope of this status improvement operation . . . can no longer be evacuated' because the 'Volhynia operation' has not yet been completed, 'it remains up to them to find refuge'. In other words, their property is expropriated, but they remain in the Warthegau and must seek lodging with friends or relatives. Later, UWZ experts refer to this procedure as 'eviction' (*Verdrängung*).[17] In January 1941, representatives from the Warthegau request that, to 'improve the status' of Germans already residing there, 30,000 Poles be evacuated to the Generalgouvernement during 1941.[18]

**28 December:** Julius Claussen, deputy head of the Reich Ministry for Food and Agriculture, declares:

> Today, problems exist in all areas of food supply. There is a severe shortage in the grain supply. . . . The Warthegau region is unfortunately not in a position to deliver large amounts of grain to the Old Reich. . . . Most Poles residing there must be prepared to leave the country in the near future. The Poles are therefore no longer planting their fields and are trying to sell their property illegally.[19]

**Early January 1941:** Meeting between Hitler and Frank. Hitler provisionally gets Frank to accept Himmler's and Heydrich's resettlement demands in accordance with the third short-term plan. Hitler informs OKW representative Alfred Jodl that 'in the Generalgouvernement, even the Wehrmacht would have to bow absolutely to the political exigencies of this resettlement'.[20]

At the same time, Heydrich receives orders to prepare the 'final evacuation of the Jews' (see Chapter 7, 'Marshlands, White Sea, Siberia', pp. 171ff.).

**6 January:** 'At a fundamental consultation' between Koppe and Krumey, the 'following evacuation figures' are established for the year 1941 for the Warthegau region alone:

| | |
|---|---:|
| For 42,000 Bessarabian Germans | 132,000 Poles |
| For 11,000 Bukovinian Germans | 22,000 Poles |
| For military training grounds | 130,000 Poles |
| To improve status and resettle ethnic Germans | 30,000 Poles |
| For Old Reich German craftsmen and from searches[21] | 16,000 Poles |
| Total | 330,000 Poles[22] |

Heydrich reduces this request two days later by 20 per cent, to 268,000,[23] although the authors consider their statistics to represent minimum figures. He comments that,

> should plans be made to resettle – in addition to the above-mentioned settlers – additional contingents of Dobruja Germans and Baltic Germans, as well as Bukovinian Germans originally scheduled for Silesia, then two Poles must be evacuated for each additional settler.

7 January: Ernst Fähndrich, chief of the 'Human Deployment' Department of the RKF, negotiates with representatives of the RKF offices in Katowice, Posen, Gdańsk (Danzig), and Königsberg 'on the allotment of resettlers from Buchenland [Bukovina], Dobruja, and Bessarabia'. The men try irritably to pass the ethnic German newcomers off onto each other. The main tenor is reflected in the following:

> According to this list, however, which was immediately referred to by Dr Arlt [Upper Silesia] as 'biased towards the Warthegau', 27,000 would be assigned to Upper Silesia from the southern and northern Bukovina. . . . The Warthegau took 18,000 of the Bukovinian Germans, most of whom, however, are tradesmen and only a small minority of whom peasants. Since tradesmen are desparately needed in Upper Silesia as well, Dr Arlt once again lodged a protest.[24]

In addition, other ethnic Germans – a total of 39,000 – are also to be settled in Upper Silesia. By the end of the month, Arlt succeeds in having the number reduced to 23,204.[25]

8 January: Meeting with Heydrich on the third short-term plan and the evacuation prescribed therein of 771,000 Poles from the incorporated eastern territories, including a few not-yet-ghettoized Jews. The purpose of the plan is the 'consolidation of German nationhood'.[26] According to preliminary calculations, the figure also includes the expulsion of 202,000 Poles, who are to be deported to make room for the Wehrmacht to set up military training grounds, and 60,000 Viennese Jews, whose deportation Hitler has promised insistent local politicians. Since the Wehrmacht leadership also wants to set up training grounds in the Generalgouvernement, an additional 200,000 are also to be relocated within the Generalgouvernement. This indicates the intention for more than a million people to be deported to or forcibly 'resettled' within the Generalgouvernement in the course of 1941, half of them in response to requests by Wehrmacht leadership.

According to Heydrich's figures for all of 1940, 'only 340,000 Poles and Jews were evacuated to the Generalgouvernement'. The extraordinary increase in 1941 is a result of the fact 'that an increased number of settlers have to be settled and because, above all, the Wehrmacht is pressing for the immediate clearing of their grounds'. 'The representative from the

Generalgouvernement', according to the records, 'accepted the demand
without batting an eye – there was no discussion of the matter.'[27]

Heydrich's plans, which are not questioned by those present at the
meeting, call for two trains daily with 1000 Poles each to arrive in the
Generalgouvernement in the first phase of the third short-term plan, i.e.,
until 1 May 1941: '30,000 from East Prussia, 24,000 from Silesia, 40,000
from Danzig–West Prussia, and 90,000 from the Warthegau,[28] making a
total of 184,000 persons'. To this, Heydrich adds 54,500 Poles who are also
to be evacuated during the first phase (to the end of April); the Wehrmacht
wants them evacuated in order to build additional military training
grounds: 'a total of 238,500 persons, plus 10,000 [of a total of 60,000]
Jews to be deported from Vienna'.[29] In the course of 1941, a total of 831,000
are to be resettled to the Generalgouvernement. Heydrich summarizes the
reasons for this: '(a) the need to create space for ethnic Germans returning
to the Reich; (b) to build military training grounds; and (c) the deportation
of the [Viennese] Jews'. Heydrich further divides the people to be deported
for each of the three reasons into detailed groups.

**For ethnic Germans to be resettled** in the following areas:

| | |
|---|---:|
| Danzig–West Prussia (53,350 Germans) | 100,000 Poles[30] |
| Warthegau (57,100 Germans) | 148,000 Poles |
| Upper Silesia (39,000 Germans) | 150,000 Poles |
| East Prussia (18,000 Germans)[31] | 46,000 Poles |
| | 444,000 Poles |

**For other purposes**

| | |
|---|---:|
| To improve the status of already-settled ethnic Germans | 50,000 Poles |
| Auschwitz concentration camp[32] | 20,000 Poles |
| Residences for (German) families of state employees | 50,000 Poles |
| Poles who have fled evacuation | 5,000 Poles |
| | 125,000 Poles |

**Wehrmacht plans**

| | |
|---|---:|
| Konin/Pleschen | 80,000 Poles |
| Sieradz | 40,000 Poles |
| Warthe camp (Obornik) | 20,000 Poles |
| Air Force, north (Rippin) | 22,000 Poles |
| Army, north (Mława) | 25,000 Poles |
| Pisia near Bytom | 10,000 Poles |
| Thorn | 5,000 Poles |
| | 202,000 Poles |

**Relocation of Viennese Jews**

| | |
|---|---:|
| | 60,000 Jews |
| | 831,000[33] |

Also on 8 January 1941, at an interministerial consultation on the treatment of Jews with respect to labour law, the suggestion is made 'to exclude Jews totally from German labour law, subjecting them to exhaustive special regulations that could be referred to as "Jewish wage rates"'.[34] The outcome of the meeting is published on 25 February 1941 in essay form in the *Reichsarbeitsblatt*.[35]

**11 January:** Frank, Higher SS and Police Chief Krüger, and Eberhard Westerkamp, the director of the Department for Internal Affairs Administration, meet to discuss 'the question of settling roughly 800,000 Poles and Jews in the Generalgouvernement'. Frank's question, whether 'the prerequisites with respect to food and clothing, etc. for the masses of people to be settled have been satisfied', is answered negatively by Krüger. As an alternative, Frank suggests, on the one hand, 'a massive export of workers to the Reich', where they would be better paid because of the 'constant demand' there and, on the other hand, 'comprehensive employment plans' in the Generalgouvernement.[36] This includes making rivers navigable, constructing roads, and reclaiming marshlands.

**13 January:** Telex from the RKF Staff Main Office in Berlin to the RKF representative in Katowice announcing that 'a total of 8000 Poles' in the month of March and 'a total of 15,000 Poles' in the month of April are to be evacuated by rail from Upper Silesia to the Generalgouvernement. In March and April, 2300 and 3700 Bukovinian Germans, respectively, are to be 'brought from camps in Silesia' and settled on the farms of the evacuees.[37]

**15 January:** After only 180,000 ethnic Germans have been brought to the incorporated eastern territories by 1 December 1940, the RKF publicly announces, in view of the upcoming start of the third short-term plan, that 'an additional approximately 200,000 ethnic Germans will arrive in the new eastern Gaus for resettlement'.[38]

Frank explains to his staff in Krakow that the new 'settlements must take place', since this is a major task ordered by the Führer. The district governor of Krakow reports that his district administrative chiefs are already 'in utter despair'; the local population is 'prepared to resist with violence'. Moreover, he says, 'from their experience, most of those to be settled [are] welfare recipients and sick, weak, and aged persons'. As justification for the third short-term plan, SS Brigadeführer Bruno Streckenbach explains to those gathered that

> in order to evacuate the Poles and Jews from the Germanized eastern territories, it is necessary to resettle the ethnic Germans from Lithuania, Volhynia, etc. . . . And the situation is such that the evacuated ethnic Germans have been in camps scattered throughout

the entire Reich for months; [they are] unused German workers waiting to be settled. As could be expected, their spirits are not very high. Their initial confidence and trust threaten to shatter if they are not settled quickly. . . . It is also necessary to carry out this operation during the war because the war affords the opportunity to take relatively rigorous action without regard for world opinion.[39]

Krüger reports the following on the subject: 'SS Gruppenführer Heydrich explained that the Reich finds it necessary to evacuate the Poles and Jews from the eastern territories as soon as possible, so that the settlement of ethnic Germans from Volhynia, Lithuania, etc. can finally be undertaken.'[40]

**17 January:**  Josef Bühler, Frank's undersecretary, issues an eight-page edict on the 'evacuation of Poles and Jews starting on 1 February 1941'. It prescribes 'the arrival of two trains daily in the Generalgouvernement, carrying 1000 persons each'. 'Evacuated Jews' are to be 'kept separate from the Poles and receive special treatment'.[41]

**21 January:**  Official (not actual) beginning of the third short-term plan for the settlement of Bessarabian, Bukovinian, Dobruja, and Lithuanian Germans. Since from the outset it does not appear that the programme can be implemented with the scope originally planned, a simultaneous RKF order signed by Himmler calls for more than 100,000 ethnic Germans from this camp, as well as those from earlier resettlement operations who are still interned in camps, to be settled in the 'Old Reich' or the 'Ostmark' (i.e., Austria) and engaged 'in useful employment'. For this purpose, a special 'Old Reich' settlement office is formed, led by SS Oberführer Hintze.[42] By 15 November 1941, 99,000 so-called 'A cases' (for 'Altreich', i.e., Old Reich) among the settlers are actually 'placed' in the Old Reich.[43] Compensation for property turns out to be particularly difficult. The HTO reports for the 1942 fiscal year, 'Negotiations with the Reich Minister of Finance and local senior financial officers have led to the identification of objects from confiscated Jewish property, and we have been able to facilitate settlers' acquisition of said objects.'[44]

Also on 21 January, the head of the Resettlement Department in Warsaw announces:

We want to show the world that within the scope of our colonizing effort we are capable of managing the Jewish problem, even if it appears a problem of masses. . . . The development of the Jewish residential area in Warsaw basically represents a preliminary stage in the exploitation of Jewish labour in Madagascar, as planned by the Führer.[45]

**23 January:**  As has already been done in Lodz, Eichmann sets up a Central Resettlement Office (UWZ) in Danzig (Gdańsk). It serves to ensure the 'evacuation of people of alien descent' (*Fremdstämmige*) from the district of Danzig–West Prussia, in view of the resettlement of the Lithuanian Germans, which is starting.[46]

**28 January:** Fähndrich, head of the RKF 'Human Deployment' Department, publicizes detailed 'planning figures for settlement and evacuation for the year 1941'. The plans call for 'two Poles to be evacuated for every settler' in Danzig–West Prussia, 'two to three Poles' per ethnic German in the Warthegau, and 'four to five Poles for a peasant settler and three for an urban craftsman settler' in Upper Silesia.[47]

**January:** Himmler orders the preparation of a propaganda event called 'The Great Homecoming'.[48]

**5 February 1941:** The deportation of Poles and Jews from the Warthegau begins, as part of the third short-term plan.[49]

On the same day, the Wehrmacht official in charge of transport in Krakow makes the following note:

> [The following is] making the overall transport situation more difficult: (a) the major resettlement programme (including, for example, 60,000 Jews from Vienna to the Gen. Gouv.); (b) not yet registered Air Force materials transports for the construction of airports east of the Vistula.[50]

Two days later, the responsible Wehrmacht officers declare that 'conditions of the railways on the territory of the Generalgouvernement are now totally unacceptable, by no means satisfactory in meeting the demands of national defence'.[51]

**7 February:** According to the guidelines for the implementation of the third short-term plan, the evacuation of Jews from the Warthegau to the Generalgouvernement is once again permitted, after having been prohibited for several months.[52]

**14 February:** A Central Resettlement Office (UWZ) is established in Katowice. The office is supposed to coordinate the resettlement of 200,000 people from Upper Silesia, as called for in the third short-term plan.[53] It has already existed since 15 January under the title 'Special Department for Evacuation Preparations'. Rudolf Barth, previously Deputy Director of the Lodz UWZ, is made director.[54]

On the same day, Albrecht Schmelt, who subjected Jews from Upper Silesia to an independent, semi-open system of forced labour with the approval of Himmler, limits the use of Jewish slave labourers to Upper Silesian enterprises. He writes, 'I will only approve the employment of [Jewish] labourers beyond 28 February 1941' if the companies 'do not have ethnic German or, if necessary, Polish labourers assigned to them as replacements by the employment offices'. From this point on, Schmelt has the Upper Silesian Jews sent to the various slave labour camps;[55] starting in the spring of 1942, most of them are deported to Auschwitz-Birkenau, where they are murdered.

**15 February:** The Vienna 'Central Office for Resettlement in the General-gouvernement' begins the long-planned deportation of Vienna's Jews. Of the 10,000 scheduled for the first phase of the third short-term plan, approximately 5000 – most of whom are 'infirm persons over 60 years of age'[56] – are deported by 11 March, after which the transports are discontinued.[57]

**17 February:** Representatives of the German military secret service (counter-intelligence, *Abwehr*) in the Generalgouvernement request an 'immediate halt' to the deportation transports because, among other things, 'a remarkable number [of the deportees are] unfit for labour'.[58] Nevertheless, on 7 March, it is formally decided in Posen to 'suggest Poles for evacuation who are no longer useful' and to fill their homes with 'Poles from the Litzmannstadt (UWZ transit) camp who are fit for labour, to serve as a labour reserve'.[59] The UWZ has already been proceeding according to this principle from the commencement of the third short-term plan. By March, a total of 19,226 'Poles unfit for labour' are deported from the Warthegau 'to the Generalgouvernement', including 2140 Jews and 6468 persons 'classified as asocial'.[60]

**19 February:** The Reich Transport Ministry informs Eichmann 'that for obvious military reasons, the Reichsbahn [railway] is no longer in a position to provide the total number of evacuation trains agreed upon at the time in the first subprogramme of the third short-term plan'. Rolf Günther, Eichmann's deputy, then orders that the remaining special trains be used 'exclusively for evacuation operations for the purpose of making room for ethnic Germans' and not for the 'clearing of military training grounds'.[61]

At the same time, police forces in Upper Silesia are to be removed. Greifelt fears this will hamper 'the evacuation and thus the settlements'.[62]

'A discussion on the forthcoming evacuation of the Jews' takes place at the office of the head of the Danzig UWZ.[63]

**20 February:** Himmler writes to Frank that 'resettlement [of ethnic Germans] from the Generalgouvernement to the territory of the Reich must be discontinued'.[64]

**26 February:** Hitler names Himmler 'his official in charge of all questions of *Volkstum* . . . within the Party as well'.[65]

A local representative of the UWZ in the Warthegau, SS Untersturm-bannführer Ludwig Hahn, receives a telegram from the UWZ in Posen: 'Call everything off'; supposedly, no more evacuation trains have been ordered.[66]

**28 February:** Members of the SS settlement staff in the Warthegau discuss 'the growing resistance to the resettlement of Poles in the Generalgouvernement'. Officials in charge of settlement see themselves forced 'to confront the danger that Poles will remain behind in the Warthegau for the foreseeable future'.[67]

**1–2 March 1941:** Himmler inspects the Auschwitz concentration camp and orders the expansion of the camp for a capacity of 130,000 prisoners.[68] The next day he celebrates the public naturalization of Bukovinian German families as the 'culmination of ethnic German homecoming'. The celebration takes place in the 'Jahrhunderthalle' in Breslau, in front of 12,000 spectators, most of whom are living in resettlement camps. Himmler declares that the nationhood struggle today has to be 'waged with vigour', since it concerns 'solutions for centuries'; to 'thunderous applause' he promises that 'the East will not be settled according to capitalist or outdated methods'.[69] Further, Himmler guarantees the settlers a new, albeit provisional, 'homeland'. He announces:

> Everyone will receive at least as much property as he owned in his abandoned ethnic German homeland. Everyone will have a livelihood the same as or similar to the one he had, whether it is a position as craftsman, a workshop, a business, or a house. At the moment we can offer only provisional accommodation. New, decent homes, as we would like them, cannot be built until peacetime. . . . I repeat one more time: we are still at war. Nevertheless – for there is no standstill – there shall be no unnecessary waiting. Nevertheless, after preparations have been made, we will be sending you to your new homeland, week by week, train by train. . . . You will return to the German East, a German East that does not lie outside German borders, but is part of the mighty German Reich.

'In the next few weeks and months,' Himmler concludes, the settlers can travel to the 'new, beloved homeland'.

> Germans have been brought to Germany, and Poles and Jews to the Generalgouvernement, the living space for Poles and Jews. That is the arrangement that brings some hardship with it, yet also much joy and happiness for you Germans and, above all, endless happiness and peace for the future.[70]

**3 March:** Initial plans by Hitler, Himmler, and Heydrich of 'special tasks' for the security police and the SD in the war against the Soviet Union.[71]

**8 March:** In a meeting with Göring, Antonescu declares that

> the efforts of the Romanian government aim to Romanianize the economy of the country, i.e., to eliminate foreigners, in particular Jews. Romania is not, however, in a position to completely bridge the resulting gaps in terms of capital and technology. German economic influence can be of assistance in this regard.[72]

**11 March:** Express letter from Greifelt to Eichmann, director of the Vomi, the DUT, and all major branch offices: 'We must reckon with a total halt in the evacuation of Poles into the Generalgouvernement, starting next week.' He continues that this leads to the question 'whether this also means that the transport of settlers out of the camps in the Old Reich will be totally halted', writing that for this reason, a conference was being arranged for 19 March to discuss 'local measures (e.g., transfer or other use of the Poles for work purposes)' in the settlement areas.[73]

**12 March:** Eichmann writes to the Foreign Office, informing it that 'in view of the forthcoming final solution of the Jewish question, there is no interest at the present time for Jews with a Reich German passport who are currently in Yugoslavia to be moved farther away'.[74]

**15 March:** Final forced ethnic German settler transport within the scope of the third short-term plan. Instead of deporting the scheduled 250,000 individuals by 1 May 1941, only a total of 25,000 – including this transport – are deported to the Generalgouvernement. Wehrmacht leadership is critical of the 'influx of Jews into the Generalgouvernement'.[75] Heinrich Müller, Eichmann's superior in the RSHA, informs the director of the central office for Jewish emigration in Vienna that from 16 March 1941 until further notice, it will not be possible 'to carry out evacuation transports to the Generalgouvernement from the incorporated German territories in the East or from Vienna'.[76]

# Notes

1   This follows from a letter of 31 December 1940 from camp commandant Rudolf Höss to Gerhard Ziegler, regional planner for Upper Silesia, cited in Aly and Heim, 178. In August, Arlt was transferred from Krakow, where he had built up and run the Population and Welfare Department, to the RKF office in Katowice. Among other things, he was supposed to accelerate the evacuations in Żywiec. He thus knew the problems of the 'other side' in the General-gouvernement very well, and personified a stalemate situation.

2   Fähndrich's statistics of 28 January 1941 on 'deportation and evacuation to the incorporated eastern territories for the year 1941', based on planning status as of 16 January 1941; BAK, R49/Anh. III/26, 17ff.

3   Hillgruber, *Staatsmänner*, vol. 1, 348.

4 Ibid. 355.
5 Heinrich Gottong, 'Die Juden im Generalgouvernement', *Das Vorfeld* 1 (1940), 3rd ser., 20; on Gottong's career, see Aly and Heim, 123.
6 General order of the RKF (no. 7/II), 26 November 1940; AGK, EWZ/L/838, 1–5. The order is signed by Himmler but was definitely prepared by his planning chief Konrad Meyer and Meyer's staff.
7 Hillgruber and Hümmelchen, 51.
8 Halder war diary, vol. 2, 202; Jäckel, *Frankreich*, 4.
9 See Chapter 5, 'Deportation, but where to?', pp. 115ff.
10 Note by Stier on the meeting of the previous day on 'settlement of the Bessarabian and Bukovinian Germans', 4 December 1940; BAK, R49/2603.
11 See Chapter 5, 'Emigration of the Jews – room for Poles', p. 125.
12 Ibid. pp. 124ff.
13 Telegram to the State Police Regional Headquarters in Posen, 12 December 1940; BAK, R75/9a, 97. A meeting between Himmler and Friedrich Wilhelm Krüger, Higher SS and Police Chief in Krakow, had taken place the evening before.
14 Hillgruber and Hümmelchen, 54.
15 Gradmann's 'Information' to the departments of the 'EWZ Litzmannstadt', 19 December 1940; AGK, EWZ/L/838/78, 25.
16 Himmler's appointment calendar; BAK, NS19/3954.
17 General order of the RKF (9/IV, signed by Himmler), 21 December 1940. Resettlement for 'status improvement' purposes had evidently already begun (Höppner's note about a conversation with Koppe, 1 November; AGK, UWZ/L/182, 1ff.).
18 Note by Höppner on 'resettlement to improve the status of ethnic German families', 20 January 1941; AGK, UWZ/L/182, 5ff.
19 Record of a conversation between Claussen and a delegate of the WiRüAmt (Armament Economy Office) (not signed); BA-MA, RW19/473, 299. Claussen also took this occasion to complain that 'returnees', in particular the Bessarabian and Volhynian Germans, had demanded larger special allotments 'since they were accustomed to higher bread consumption and the rations did not suffice' (303). At that time, a reduction in weekly meat rations for the 'typical German consumer' was already being discussed. It became necessary in June 1941.
20 Frank diary; entry of 11 January 1941, 319. It cannot be totally ruled out that Frank was referring to the meeting of 4 November 1940; see ibid. 203.
21 This refers to the deportation of Poles who had gone underground in 1940. The final report of the second short-term plan mentions figures deviating from those above: 'Especially in the summer of 1940, many Poles evaded evacuation through flight. Thus it was necessary to publish a wanted persons list. At the close of the Volhynia operation it comprised 18,500 names. Up to now [i.e., January 1941], 6000 Poles have been apprehended through searches and deported to the Generalgouvernement' (BAK, R75/6).
22 Telex from Krumey to Günther, 6 January 1941, cited in *Doc. Occ.* vol. 8, 84ff.
23 For detailed statistical information, see Dolezalek's note of 10 January 1941; BAK, R49/Anh. I/34, 7f.
24 Butschek's note 'about the meeting on 7 January 1941 in Berlin at Fähndrich's office'; BAK, R49/Anh. III/26, 1ff.
25 Note on a meeting on 29 January between Meyer, Zoch, Arlt, Butschek, Fähndrich, and Stier; BAK, R49/Anh. III/26, 27ff.
26 The following Generalgouvernement representatives attended the meeting: Friedrich Wilhelm Krüger (Higher SS and Police Chief), Eberhard Westerkamp (Internal Affairs), Hansjulius Schepers (Department of Regional Planning [*Raumordnung*]), and Walter Föhl (Section on Population and Welfare). For

the resettlement interests, the following were represented: the RKF, the Supreme Command of the Wehrmacht and Army, the Reich Transport Ministry, and the Reich Economics Ministry; also present were inspectors from the security police in the incorporated eastern territories and the district representative for Vienna.

27 Dolezalek's note of 10 January 1941; BAK, R49/Anh. I/34, 7ff.

28 Hilberg touches upon the history of these deportations very briefly and imprecisely (211ff.); the same is true of Burrin (86). Adam's mention of Heydrich having ordered the deportation of 90,000 Jews from the Warthegau on that day (p. 289) is a distortion of the facts. On page 258, Adam even claims that the plans for the evacuations in the first phase of the third short-term plan involved Jews exclusively, a total of 'a quarter of a million people'. In fact, it was not primarily Jews but non-Jewish Poles who were to be evacuated, because only they still owned property that could be transferred to ethnic German settlers.

29 Krüger's report of 15 January 1941; Frank diary, 327.

30 The term 'Poles' as used here by Heydrich also included a relatively small number of Jews. For a more detailed discussion, see Chapter 7, 'Foot march to the ghetto', pp. 163ff.

31 Figures for the settlement of ethnic Germans are based on the cited note by Dolezalek (see note 27).

32 This refers to the expulsion of people who still lived within the 'sphere of interest' of the concentration camp, such as in Brzezinka, i.e., Birkenau.

33 Quoted from the report of 13 January 1941 by Westerkamp, who participated in the session; Frank diary, BAK, R52II/233, 4077–4081. On 4 November 1940, Hitler was still using totally different, to some extent much lower, figures for the scheduled 'movements in the East' (third short-term plan): 'Danzig–West Prussia: 50,000–60,000 Bessarabian Germans; Zichenau [Ciechanów] (administrative district): 40,000 from Lithuania; Warthegau–Posen: 60,000 Bessarabian Germans; Gouvernement: plus 150,000–160,000 Poles and Jews from the regained territories' (Engel, 90ff.).

34 Note on the 8 January 1941 session, quoted in Pätzold, 280.

35 Hans Küppers, 'Die vorläufige arbeitsrechtliche Behandlung der Juden', RABl. 5: 6 (1941), 106ff.; cited in Maier, 125. On the development of a special labour code for Jews, see ibid. 119–40.

36 Frank diary, 318f.

37 Draft letter of the RKF, n.d., not signed; BDC, SS-HO5058.

38 'Grundtatsachen zur Umsiedlung' (Basic resettlement facts), in Deutsches Blut kehrt heim, ed. Reich Director of Organization of the NSDAP (Main Training Office) (Munich, January 1941), 30. The given figure of 200,000 is 32,000 more than what Heydrich actually planned.

39 Frank diary, BAK, R52/II/233, 4060–76.

40 Information from Krüger about the third short-term plan, quoted in Okkupationspolitik in Polen, 193.

41 BAK, R52/II/52, 9–16.

42 RKF Order No. 26/I, 21 January 1941; BAK, R59/100, 4.

43 Statistical report on resettlement (as of 15 November 1941) prepared by Dept. I of the RKF; BAK, R49/2719.

44 German Resettlement Trusteeship GmbH, Berlin (DUT), 1942 financial report, 7. The DUT monthly report for January 1942 reveals a chronological link to the Wannsee Conference; there, too, negotiations between RKF, DUT, and the Ministry of Finance are mentioned, the goal of which was 'to also make Jewish real estate in the Reich available for "A cases"' (BAP, 17.02/300, 4).

45 Report by Schön, quoted in Okkupationspolitik in Polen, 194.

46 Letter by Heydrich, 23 January 1941; BAK, R58/240, 89.

47 Planning guidelines on 'settlement and evacuation in the incorporated eastern territories for the year 1941, compiled by Main Department I in the Office of the Reich Commissioner for the Consolidation of German Nationhood' (signed by Fähndrich), 28 January 1941; BAK, R49/Anh. III/26, 17–26. Fähndrich's more detailed figures deviated slightly from those provided by Heydrich on 8 January 1941. For example, 792,500 people were supposed to be deported in the course of 1941, instead of the 831,000 previously called for.

48 The preliminary correspondence can be found in BAK, R69/554.

49 Krumey's second report; BAK, R75/8, 9.

50 Report by the authorized transport officer of Army group command B to the Wehrmacht chief of transport, on a 'meeting of 4 February 1940 with Gedob [Head office of the Eastern railway] in Krakow'; BA-MA, H12/131.

51 Letter from the head of the WiRüAmt (Armament Economy Office) to the head of Wehrmacht command, 7 February 1941; BA-MA, RW19/2198, 606.

52 'Richtlinien' (Guidelines), n.d., received by the 'UWZ Litzmannstadt' on 7 February 1941; AGK, UWZ/L/1, 38ff.

53 Letter from Heydrich, 14 February 1941; BAK, R58/240, 95.

54 Letter from Barth to the RSHA, 14 February 1941; BAP-DH, ZA/ZR/512/A.11.

55 Konieczny, 100.

56 Letter from a Jewish transportation supervisor to Marek Alten, deputy representative of the Council of Jews in Lublin, 26 February 1941, quoted in FGM, 62.

57 Safrian, 97ff.

58 Nbg. doc. NOKW-128.

59 Höppner's note of 7 March on a meeting on 4 March 1941; AGK, UWZ/P/146, 26ff.

60 Second report (see note 49), 11. The last transport train, carrying 1000 Poles, arrived in the town of Skierniewice in the Generalgouvernement on 15 March 1941, ibid. 9 (The only two Jewish transports, each carrying 1070 people, left on 8 and 10 March for Zwierzyniec and Krasnystaw, respectively, in the Lublin district.)

61 RSHA letter (Section IVD4, signed by Günther), 21 February 1941; BAK, R75/9a, 94ff. Eichmann withstood the obvious provocation by the military for only one week, then once again ordered that 'clearing for military training grounds should be taken into consideration' (telex from Eichmann, 27 February 1941; BAK, R75/9a, 98ff.).

62 Letter from Greifelt to Kurt Daluege, chief of the regular police, in which he complained about the related announcements of 19 and 24 February by Erich von dem Bach-Zelewski, Higher SS and Police Chief in the Southeast Main Division (*Oberabschnitt*), 27 February 1941; BAK, R49/2604.

63 Telex from the UWZ in Danzig to the Gestapo offices in Bromberg, Graudenz, and Elbing, 18 February 1940; BAK, R75/13.

64 The letter was written by Fähndrich and signed by Himmler. It was cited in a file memo by the Vomi in Warsaw, 26 April 1941; AGK, EWZ/LK/57, 128.

65 Order A 7/41 (signed by Hess), 26 February 1941; reprinted in *Reichsverfügungsblatt der NSDAP*, edition A, 10/41, 8 March 1941.

66 Weekly report by Hahn, 16 March 1941; AGK, UWZ/L/34, 6.

67 Note by the SS settlement staff of the Litzmannstadt planning department (signed by Dolezalek), 28 February 1941; BAK, R49/Anh. I/39.

68 Czech, 79. In addition to arguments based on settlement policy that were presented by the representatives of the Upper Silesian RKF, Göring's and IG Farben's interests with respect to industrial policy and economic command were significant in reaching this decision (see Höss, 96ff., 179ff.; Pressac, 25f.; Aly and Heim, 168–84).

69 Quoted in 'Reichsführer SS Himmler zum Gruß! Buchenlanddeutsche in Breslau', *Breslauer Neueste Nachrichten,* 2 March 1941.

70 Himmler's 'address to the Bessarabian Germans in the Jahrhunderthalle in Breslau', 2 March 1941; BAK, NS/19/4008, 6ff. of the manuscript.

71 See Hillgruber, *Strategie,* 523; Halder war diary, entry of 5 March 1941 ('Sonderauftrag des Reichsführers SS'), vol. 2, 303.

72 ADAP, Ser. D, 12: 1, 185. German participants at the meeting were Erich Neumann (Göring's state secretary), Hermann Neubacher (plenipotentiary for economic issues in southeastern Europe), Alfred Bentz (officer to promote oil drilling with the Four-Year Plan authority), and Ernst R. Fischer (director of the department for the oil industry in the Reich Economics Ministry).

73 Express letter from Fähndrich (signed by Greifelt) to the RKF officers in Königsberg, Posen, Danzig, and Katowice, and as information to the RSHA (for the attention of Eichmann and Dept. 3), the Reich Transport Ministry, Vomi, and DUT; R69/388, 247ff. An invitation to the meeting on 19 March was enclosed with the letter.

74 Quoted in Adler, 28.

75 OKW war diaries, vol. 1, 359.

76 Eichmann documents, quoted in Safrian, 97.

# |7|

# *Ghetto, work, 'The Move Eastward'*

## Transport halt because of 'Barbarossa'

In terms of objectives, the third short-term plan went much further than its predecessors. On the other hand, whereas the first short-term plan, the interim plan, and the second short-term plan were subjected to repeated delays, and whereas the dual objectives of deportation and resettlement had to be constantly postponed, cut back, and modified, the third short-term plan failed totally before it ever really got started. Instead of deporting 770,000 Poles[1] from the incorporated eastern territories and 60,000 Jews from Vienna, the organizers of the population exchange achieved only 3.5 per cent of the target they had set. For them, the deportations were unsatisfactory, perpetually falling below the target figure. In any case, the transports served to better the balance by about 25,000, though the number of Poles who were deported to make room, not for German settlers, but for military training grounds or a concentration camp extension, had to be subtracted. The 5000 Jews from Vienna who were deported to the eastern Generalgouvernement were also insignificant relative to the total RKF settlement figures. Moreover, in view of the fact that two 'ethnically alien' families were deported for each ethnic German one, the deportation of 25,000 people, all things considered, only made enough space for 5000 ethnic Germans. The others, exactly 256,257 'returnees', remained in the camps.[2]

It was a fiasco, as was clear from the fact that, even though figures for the third short-term plan had been set many times higher, they were actually already seen as one of many compromises from the point of view of the organizers. Far from the 'ideal plans' of Konrad Meyer, this project would not have come close to satisfying the prerequisites for a utopia of lasting reform of population policy and economic structures, even if it had been implemented in its entirety. As early as 3 December 1940, Meyer, head of the RKF planning department, had written a memorandum on Himmler's 'address on settlement', demanding a level of population shifting that had never been discussed up to that point. Meyer thus laid the cornerstone for the later 'general settlement plan for the East', which extended far into the Soviet Union. He had written:

> It must be noted that even if a total of 60,000 sq. km. [more than 23,000 sq. mi.] [of *usable*] agricultural land in the new western territories [i.e., Alsace-Lorraine] were used exclusively for the settlement of Germans from the Old Reich, the *entire area of the Generalgouvernement,* with its approximately 60,000 sq. km., would still be needed to achieve healthy agrarian structures in the Old Reich.

Three months before Frank, Himmler, and Hitler had agreed upon such a project, Meyer had calculated, justified, and even initiated a plan to deport all Poles and Jews from the Generalgouvernement. 'If the new area in the West should prove to be smaller, then – in purely mathematical terms – *even the Generalgouvernement* will not be sufficient to satisfy all needs.'[3]

As an aside, the settlement staff were less and less successful in finding farms of adequate size for the ethnic Germans. Thus smaller and smaller farms had to be combined and, as was the case in Żywiec, an increasing number of Polish families were displaced for each German family. This was due not to an absolute shortage of arable land, but rather to a stalemate between wartime food supply economists and settlement planners. Koppe reported in early January 1941:

> The high number of Poles to be deported within the scope of the Bessarabian operation can be explained by the fact that larger estates are not being divided up, as was originally planned. Instead, small and very small farms will be combined, so that for each of a large proportion of the new farms for Bessarabian Germans, five to six Polish families have to be evacuated.[4]

Himmler and Konrad Meyer, his planning chief, had originally taken for granted that large estates in the Warthegau would be divided up for social, economic, and demographic reasons. This plan of theirs failed, among other reasons, because of Greiser. Greiser reported in February to Dolezalek, planning chief of the SS settlement staff, who had long been pressing for the release of more land, that

> the task of the Warthegau, as assigned by the Führer and the Reich Marshal [i.e., Göring], is the production of grain, grain, and once again grain, 'a grain factory'. . . . For that we need our large estates and for that we need a labour force! The labourers must stay in the Warthegau, even though they are Poles. The present agrarian structure cannot be changed. We must bring order to the Warthegau; order to agricultural production.[5]

At this point, planners were still considering structural improvements in the Old Reich with respect to population policy, and they still wanted to settle deserving German soldiers in the East. On the other hand, the practitioners, i.e., those actually implementing the resettlements, had already abandoned such notions. Instead, on 28 January, Ernst Fähndrich of the 'Human Deployment' Department of the RKF had taken into account in the third short-term plan only the minimum amount of population shifting that he and his staff felt was absolutely necessary to carry out the settlement of the southeastern European 'returnees', after the project, which Himmler again and again insisted would be carried out in the near future, had been blocked for months. Brute force was to be used to end the acute embarrassment, fulfil repeated promises, and put an end to the grumbling that was growing louder among the ethnic Germans, who, after being welcomed with fanfare and ceremoniously granted citizenship, were now needlessly interned and robbed of their homeland and property.

But real circumstances and competing projects caused the plan to fail. On 15 January 1941, Hans Frank had already sworn his district governors to the 'great task assigned by the Führer'. In fact, however, all he had announced was the wretched stream of hundreds of thousands of deportees that Himmler and Heydrich had barely managed to achieve.[6] This led to protests from the city and district administrative chiefs, who rebelled against the will of Hitler, Himmler, and Heydrich. It was not political opposition, however, but arose because they wanted to maintain a minimum of occupation order for purely selfish reasons. At the same time, they continued to want to 'relieve pressure in matters of population policy', demanding deportations from the deportation territory itself (on this point they agreed with Meyer, whose ideas were still hypothetical at the time). They maintained their position even though Frank strongly reprimanded his subordinates, urging them to further dehumanize their methods of rule. According to the records of 15 January, 'all criticism' of the new series of deportations 'due to any remnants of sympathy or questions of expediency' should 'be abandoned totally'.[7] Nevertheless, the local officials did not withdraw their protest.

The Wehrmacht commanders directly involved responded similarly. They also had reservations about the new resettlement plans, even though it was the military themselves who had consistently raised the number of people to be deported and had emphatically demanded the displacement of at least 400,000 people in order, finally, to be able to set up their training grounds and prepare for war, the consequences of which would eclipse all deportations up to then by far.[8] But at the same time – for a new, more important reason – Wehrmacht leaders needed precisely the locomotives, railway cars, and track capacities that they would have had to release in order to implement the deportation programme they had in fact devised. This new reason was the mobilization for the campaign in Russia – 'Operation Barbarossa'. And it was assigned absolute priority.

On 4 November 1940, in Frank's presence, Hitler had obligated Wehrmacht commanders to support the politically pressing resettlements in every way possible. Only a few weeks later, Frank was forced to admit that nothing had come of the Führer's order. Frank noted in his diary that, when Keitel requested that he

> see to it that the concerns of the Wehrmacht were given highest priority, that actually contradicted the Führer's statement to General Jodl, when he emphasized that in the Generalgouvernement, even the Wehrmacht would have to bow absolutely to the political exigencies of this resettlement.[9]

On 14 March 1941, one day before the actual end of the third short-term plan, the first preliminary phase for the war against the Soviet Union was concluded. In complete secrecy, 2500 trains filled with soldiers and military equipment advanced to the German–Soviet border.[10] By the end of February, camp commanders had already been instructed to compile lists of ethnic Germans who could be used as interpreters in the impending campaign.[11]

The military until then were making only moderate use of the railway lines towards Warsaw, Lublin, and Radom for the deployment of the Central Army Division, and thus merely showing down the deportations. In contrast, the start of the second deployment phase and the sudden change in attack plans thwarted further implementation of the third short-term plan. On 15 March, the Wehrmacht started assembling not only the Central Army Division in the eastern Generalgouvernement, but the South Army Division as well. According to the original mobilization plan, the latter was to advance through Hungary and Romania towards the Crimea and the Caucasus. The strategy was changed for political reasons and because of engineering problems. On the one hand, there was the instability of the Romanian government; on the other, the breadth of Russian rivers in the south, which meant it would be faster to cross them in the north and would involve fewer losses. In mid-March, German commanders suddenly halted road construction and the reinforcement of bridges in Romania and Hungary.[12]

The third short-term plan failed because of the priorities set by the military for 'Operation Barbarossa' and because its own goals contradicted each other, not to mention the so-called civilian goal of creating an ethnic and economic new order. Even the German general staff was not able to build huge training grounds and at the same time prepare for the 'most atrocious war of conquest, enslavement, and destruction' of modern times.[13] It was certainly not an issue of political obstruction of the settlement policy. On the contrary, Wehrmacht leaders willingly made use, for their own purposes, of the racially ranked, self-interested methods of deportation policy that had already been tried out by Himmler. Thus Lublin district governor Ernst Zörner reported on 25 March that with respect to the situation developing in the district of Lublin, the wishes of the Wehrmacht have been largely fulfilled. In Lublin, too, the Jews had to be evacuated within three days, and 10,000 Jews were relocated outside of the city. Poles were settled in the now-empty former Jewish quarters. . . . The cleared Polish quarters were then made available to the Wehrmacht. The Jewish quarters have also been cleared in the main towns in the district, and the evacuated Jews are now being concentrated. Everything is progressing in great haste according to a particular plan.[14]

At the same meeting, Higher SS and Police Chief Krüger reported that 'the resettlement of Poles and Jews to the Generalgouvernement has presently been halted. Resettlement within the Generalgouvernement for the purpose of making room for military training grounds is proceeding.'[15]

In view of such documents, Rolf-Dieter Müller's comments seem doubtful when he stresses the 'courageous effort of individual local commanders in opposing the deportation and extermination policies of the SS'. Although Müller accurately describes the conflict between settlement policy and military interests, it did not 'slow progress at times', but rather had a generally radicalizing impact, especially because of the military 'wishes'.[16] Not only in the Lublin area, but in the district of Radom as well, the stationing of the Central Army Division supported the ghettoization of the Jewish population in a way that clearly surpassed the methods of persecution practised up to that time.[17] As a consequence of the third short-term plan, the brutal new wave of ghettoization in the Generalgouvernement was triggered in January to 'make room' for Poles. After the plan was terminated in favour of preparations for 'Operation Barbarossa', the Wehrmacht used and accelerated ghettoization – especially in the districts of Lublin and Radom – to support their mobilization effort.[18]

## 'Emergency settlement' instead of Germanization

Four days after evacuations to the Generalgouvernement were stopped, on 19 March 1941, resettlement camp administrators, directors of the settlement staffs, and their colleagues involved in the evacuations all met Ulrich Greifelt, head of the staff main office for the consolidation of German nationhood.[19] Their plans had once again proved unreliable. The Reich Transport Minister, the military, Frank, and, finally, Hitler himself had prohibited any further resettlements. For the moment, no one knew what to do, and the mood deteriorated. According to the minutes recorded by the representative of the Central Office of Immigration (EWZ), 'No substantial, feasible proposals to continue resettlements in the eastern territories were made.'[20] Höppner reported with frustration that 'future steps [were] completely unclear'.[21] Another participant noted that 'nothing is known about the duration of the transport restriction'.[22] Fähndrich suggested using 'the present time . . . to prepare for the settlements, which hopefully will resume shortly'.[23]

Nevertheless, over several hours those present developed proposals for the near, and difficult, future. 'Every Gau', they finally encouraged each other, should now 'take individual initiative, despite all . . . difficulties, to implement appropriate measures – even if not as comprehensive as has been the case up to now – to take settlers from the camps and give them homes.' The staff of the regional Central Resettlement Offices (UWZ) offered their services to organize jobs and accommodation for the 'Poles evicted from settlement areas'; it seemed logical to put 'the Poles to be evacuated' into the camps still housing ethnic Germans awaiting resettlement.[24] Where such measures proved insufficient, 'attempts [were] to be made to create appropriate camps'. As was previously the case regarding ghettos, camps and reservations, too, were now to take up the slack caused by the inter-ruption in deportations – as a short-term solution in anticipation of their projected resumption. In addition, it was resolved that proposals be devel-oped 'that take into consideration the internal transfer of Poles and Jews unfit for work'. Greifelt promised to provide a large number of 'transport-able sheds' – 'especially' for the foothills of the Beskids, i.e., the region around Auschwitz.[25] Other than that, he delegated further responsibility to the staff of his local offices, requesting that they 'immediately inform him of any measures taken'.[26] Krumey, a resettlement practitioner, did not trust such promises. He warned his staff 'to pay special attention to the difficul-ties that could arise while the Polish camps were being established. These difficulties should by no means be underestimated.'[27]

Not only Poles and Jews were supposed to be housed in barracks, but ethnic Gemans as well. On 4 April, the RKF 'Human Deployment' Depart-ment was involved in all aspects of the 'delivery of wooden barracks to accommodate Bessarabian German settlers in Posen'. The RKF wanted to have them 'build the barracks themselves', since materials and labour were available and 'only the finances [were] lacking'.[28]

Barracks had been in the offing for quite some time. On 12 February 1941, the staff of the Ethnic German Liaison Office (Vomi) had developed the same idea for Munich. Since housing was 'the most pressing social issue' for the ethnic Germans – whose accommodation there was wretched in every sense of the word – they had suggested that 'as an initial emergency measure, barracks for families should be constructed in the city (e.g., on the Theresienwiese)'.[29] A critical mass had already been reached in Posen: Dolezalek, head of the planning department of the SS settlement staff in Posen, had been negotiating to have the size of settler allotments reduced as much as possible. On 16 January, he reported that

because the ethnic groups settled comprise almost exclusively farmers . . . the Wartheland Reichsgau is suffering not only a shortage of farms, but a general shortage of land. The settlement staff must therefore take action most exceptional in the history of the German settlement programme and 'settle' the Bessarabian Germans in barracks. It is none the less to be expected that about 1700 Bessarabian German peasant families that have been assigned to the Warthegau will not be able to be settled.[30]

Having got themselves into difficulties, resettlement officials changed their attitude towards the ethnic Germans. All of a sudden, regional RKF representatives started trying to pass 'unproductive settlers' (pensioners, the elderly, etc.) back and forth.[31] One would accuse another of 'deliberately moving the least productive [ethnic German] farmers out of their region'.[32]

As was often the case, Heinrich Himmler avoided uncomfortable meetings. But then, on 19 March, he made a long-distance 'request' that 'regardless of present transport difficulties, the Bessarabian Germans (7800 persons) still in the Lodz camp be settled as soon as possible in the Danzig–West Prussia Reichsgau'.[33] In order to create space for the settlers, the staff of the Danzig (Gdańsk) office of the UWZ were supposed to house several Polish families in a single residence, and – in accordance with the needs of the war – as many Poles as possible were to be referred for slave labour. The procedure was no longer referred to as 'resettlement' (*Aussiedlung*), but as 'eviction' (*Verdrängung*).

The same applied to the Warthegau and Upper Silesia. Representatives of the RKF-affiliated Katowice offices held a meeting there on 14 March to discuss 'changes in the resettlement measures' in view of the announced termination of deportations. They had assumed that 'at this time, no total evacuation of the Poles' was possible, and that 'in order to guarantee the labour process, ethnically alien workers should not be evacuated if at all possible', in accordance with the cited order by Göring. Since the available workers were small farmers who had to leave their farms to make room for ethnic Germans, the resettlement experts intended to build 'ethnic alien reservations . . . at a radius of about 15 kilometres from the planned industrial site'. 'The procedure was [described] on the basis of the example of Auschwitz', where the construction of new industries, both bomb-proof and necessary for the war effort, had been planned several weeks earlier. This had consequences for the local residents. 'As far as possible the reservation area will be cleared of Jews and ballast lives that are unfit for labour. If evacuation trains are not available, then . . . a procedure will be found for partial evacuation.'[34] For the Jews, this meant ghettoization in the part of Upper Silesia that had belonged to Russia until 1918.

Regarding such reservations, it was decided three days later that 'all existing towns and buildings at a convenient transportation distance are to be used only to accommodate Polish workers and their families. Therefore, all unproductive Poles and Jews must first be removed from this area.'

Aside from the labour policy goals of Göring and IG Farben, the RKF saw its aim as 'shortening the settlers' demoralizing and debilitating stays in the camps',[35] and, 'despite the difficulties that arose, . . . to engage them in the productive cultivation of the eastern soil as soon as possible'.[36] By 20 March, personnel of the Upper Silesian RKF office were already involved in the 'internal transfer of Poles unfit for work, [demanding] above all clarification of the issue of Jews in Auschwitz', referring to the Jewish residents of the town. The very next sentence declared that the transport of ethnic German settlers was to be accelerated.[37]

In April, the 6000 Jews still living in the town of Auschwitz were relocated to Dąbrowa in order to make room for Polish workers, who in turn had been evicted from their farms in favour of ethnic German settlers.

In the agrarian Warthegau, the policy of 'eviction' went less smoothly. On 22 March, a responsible district gendarmerie chief reported on such an eviction, which could not be followed by a deportation:

> The Polish residences in question were occupied suddenly. On orders of the SS resettlement staff, the evacuated Polish familes were not to be deported, but were told to leave their residences and seek accommodation with relatives and acquaintances. . . . This form of deportation was used within the district of Sieradz for the first time. It is doubtful if it will prove worthwhile, especially since it must be feared that a large number of Poles will thus have a chance to roam the country aimlessly (security concerns).[38]

A chief constable of the gendarmerie in another community near Lodz reported that

> these people are wandering around aimlessly or are being taken in by relatives or friends who have already been resettled and are living under poor conditions, perhaps, or by relatives who have to reckon with evacuation or eviction any day. This situation is more or less forcing the evictees to engage in smuggling or illicit trading to survive, or even robbery and theft. . . . Identification cards are no longer accurate, since many of these people have to move to other villages. This has made it difficult or impossible to locate these people.[39]

Despite these reservations, German resettlement experts continued their usual practice, for lack of any alternatives. Up to 20 January 1942, a total of 82,093 people were 'evicted from individual districts' in the Warthegau.[40] During the same period, UWZ personnel shipped 17,223 people by way of the employment offices to the Reich for forced labour;[41] 7327 Poles were selected by SS racial examiners to be 're-Germanized'.[42]

To mitigate 'security concerns' about the evictions, the inspector of the security police and SD in Posen ordered that:

In order to be able to monitor the location of the 'displaced' [*ausgesiedelt*] [i.e., 'evicted' (*verdrängt*)] Poles at all times, every evacuated Polish family will be issued a registration card, which they must present at the appropriate gendarmerie or police station once a week at a set time.[43]

It was not until later that the staff of the Lodz UWZ developed this into a closed system, as they prepared the evacuations in the eastern Polish region of Zamość in the autumn of 1942. Shortly after the Jewish population there had been murdered, guidelines were drawn up and then followed for the 'evacuation of Poles in the district of Lublin (Zamość) to make room for the settlement of ethnic Germans'. They precisely described the procedure by which men, women, and children were brought to the transit camp for selection into 'categories'.

The UWZ further specified the emergency eviction measure and started practising a deportation model that functioned without any foreign territory as its destination. It involved a combination of re-Germanization, forced labour, and transport to starvation reservations or Auschwitz:

1. Polish families in categories I and II will be selected and sent to Litzmannstadt to be 're-Germanized'. . . .
2. Children in categories III and IV will be selected along with the over-60-year-old Poles, i.e., generally children with grandparents, and will be placed in so-called pensioner villages. Sick and infirm Poles under 60 years of age will likewise be placed in 'pensioner villages'. . . .
4. Fourteen- to 60-year-olds in category III who are fit for work will be referred for work placement in the Reich, without family members who are unfit for work. In agreement with the general plenipotentiary for labour deployment, they will be used to replace Jews still working in positions necessary for the war effort.[44]
5. Fourteen- to 60-year-olds in category IV will be transported to the Auschwitz concentration camp.[45]

In the spring of 1941, however, the UWZ staff had not yet developed this system of forced labour, selection, and extermination. First they suggested starting the settlement of ethnic German peasants in the Generalgouvernement. They were referring to the districts at the western border, Tomaszów and Piotrków.[46] Frank took up the idea of the 'imminent Germanization of the Vistula valley' a short time later,[47] but the absolute halt to deportation remained. In his edict of 10 May 1941, the Gauleiter of the Warthegau approved and justified what had already become common practice: 'After the UWZ camps became filled with evacuated Poles,' argued Greiser, and it remained prohibited to resettle the Poles in the Generalgouvernement, he then allowed the settlement of ethnic Germans using 'evictions' of the Poles within the Gau territory.[48] The new procedure, even more so than the deportations to the Generalgouvernement, must have quickly reached the limits of feasibility. Only four weeks later, the Katowice department for resettlement reported that 'through the present method of placing displaced Polish families together with other Polish families, the towns that are still Polish will soon be overcrowded, thus halting the settlement operation'.[49] Officials in charge of evacuation and settlement in the Warthegau found themselves confronting the problem that 'options for obtaining additional space have been exhausted' and there were in any case no more 'appropriate farms' available.[50]

This is why the RKF was forced to annul the guidelines stipulating approximately 62 acres as the minimum size of farms for the ethnic Germans. Instead of basing their actions on theoretical efficiency requirements, the focus was shifted, albeit only 'for the time being, . . . to local circumstances'. The Berlin staff main office had to admit in black and white that, despite all their economic and structural requirements and despite the promises that Himmler continued to make to the ethnic Germans, the settlers' farms were being steadily reduced in size. They even had to abandon their previously ironclad principle of reserving 60 per cent of the arable land in the incorporated eastern territories for Reich German settlers and deserving soldiers. 'It has proven necessary that the previous order be abandoned.' This was definitely temporary and provisional in nature, 'with the necessary condition that they may be carried out later'. The planning bureaucrats of the RKF started speaking of 'emergency settlement'.[51] The practitioners had long been acting under such conditions; they took for granted 'a colossal carving up of the arable land', viewing it as 'a temporary wartime measure', which, 'despite all other reservations', had to be implemented in order to settle the ethnic Germans.[52]

Even the new programme, which ran counter to all aspects of the system originally planned, was faced with insurmountable problems. The Reich Ministry of Transport insisted that 'until further notice no special trains, *including those for local transportation,* are to be used for resettlement movements in the East'.[53] This pertained not only to the deportations, but expressly also to the 'transport of settlers from the Old Reich to the incorporated eastern territories'[54] and even to the baggage of the ethnic Germans from southeastern Europe. The resettlement authorities had shipped the baggage up the Danube in the autumn, and it was being stored by Viennese shipping agents. Its transport would have required 3000 freight cars . . . and they were not available.

Plans for the 'total new order of Europe' became mired in grotesque problems of details. The Reich Commission for the Consolidation of German Nationhood (RKF) had to pay exorbitant monthly storage fees and could not even send articles of clothing or linens to those waiting helplessly for them, and they were kept busy 'sorting out perishable foods' and protecting the belongings 'from moths and bug infestation'.[55] Luggage and settlers had to stay where they were – in separate camps.

Instead of the announced, generous compensation in kind for assets they had left behind, Heinrich Himmler put off his 'returnees' with colourful documents called German Reich debenture bonds, at a 4 per cent interest rate.[56] Instead of placing the ethnic Germans, as promised, on flourishing farms, the RKF issued secret orders in March 1941 that 'settlers presently in camps in the Old Reich be given practical employment as soon as possible'.[57] The elderly and those in need of care were to be transferred 'to appropriate care facilities. . . . The difficult question of compensation for assets [was] to be resolved solely' on the basis of the willingness of the respective individuals to work, and 'those obstinately refusing to work [were] to be made aware of the commitment required of them'.[58] 'Without regard to whether they were previously self-employed [as most were] or not', they were to be quickly 'placed in positions of employment', lowering them to the level of factory and agricultural labourers.[59] Commissions fanned out 'in search of settlers fit for work'. However, there was a scarcity of accessible, more or less appropriate positions in close proximity to the resettlement camps. And where there were jobs, homes were lacking. As a result, several thousand ethnic Germans 'from the overpopulated areas were moved to the Gaus', especially Mecklenburg and Pomerania, 'where the necessary dwellings [could be] made available for them and their families'. Due to the freeze on transports, this took place 'in small groups with regularly scheduled trains'.[60] At least 60 settler families eventually received homes there, but they were unfurnished. In any case, the RKF economics department ordered furnishings for 60 kitchens and 60 bedrooms from a 'list of ghetto furniture' and 'housewares that could be spared there (such as china)'. The objects were already stored in the RKF 'baggage centre' in Lodz and were supposed to be sent to an RKF field office in Golnow, in Mecklenburg.[61]

But this could not significantly change the situation for the 250,000 interned 'returnees'. In Lodz alone, '5360 Bessarabian Germans, 3800 Bukovinian Germans, and roughly 25,000 Lithuanian Germans' were stranded in camps.[62] Since any real improvement in their miserable circumstances seemed hopeless, Himmler's staff resorted to occupational therapy. For example, an order on 25 March to the directors of the resettlement camps reported that 'due to transport difficulties that have developed, settlement will come to a standstill in the next few months'. It was thus necessary that the settlers be kept busy, that morning roll calls and early morning sports be 'extended as far as possible', and that schools and nursery schools be 'used to their full capacity', in order to prevent 'camp psychosis' from setting in, as had already been the case among the Volhynian and Galician Germans.[63] It was therefore ordered that

all settlers in the camps are to be kept occupied at all costs. Thus, they are to be employed in the camps. Athletic fields have to be erected (however, no cost estimates may be submitted in this regard, since no expenses will be approved). Also, roads need to be improved, and settlers can be employed to take care of horses and as coachmen.

'Taking into account that the settlers will be remaining in the camps for an extended period of time', the Ethnic German Liaison Office lifted the curfew – or rather 'quarantine' – that had been imposed on their charges, 'effective immediately'.[64]

The situation also had to be justified outwardly. The worried directors of the League for Germandom Abroad (*Verein für das Deutschtum im Ausland,* or VDA) met in Posen on 6 April. No, claimed Alexander Dolezalek at the meeting, the RKF is 'not a human shipping agent'; the 'battle against this mechanization of settlement [has been] victorious'.[65] Back in January, Himmler had already ordered an exhibition on 'The Great Homecoming'. Originally, it was supposed to be shown in Berlin in March, next to the *Neue Wache* memorial on the boulevard Unter den Linden. But there was a difference of opinion about the extent to which the methods of ethnic cleansing should 'reach the public', and Heydrich had all texts for the exhibition panels presented to him for approval. It was very important to Eichmann that 'a special room of the resettlement exhibition be dedicated to the start of the evacuations'. Representatives of the Ethnic German Liaison Office (Vomi) were up in arms about this idea, since they feared negative repercussions from those who read the planned propaganda panels. As Eichmann put it, the Vomi urged that 'the evacuations be removed from the exhibition'. In the end, however, Eichmann got his way.

The exhibition was never shown. At first its completion was delayed. 'In the late afternoon hours' of 9 June 1941, Himmler appeared unexpectedly for a 'preview' and ordered that 'the exhibition not be officially opened in this form'. Instead, in view of the imminent war against the Soviet Union and the assumption that he would have overcome all the resettlement problems by then, Himmler ordered 'the planning of a new, expanded exhibition . . . that [would] probably be set up in the exhibition rooms of the (Berlin) radio tower and which [was] to be completed by March 1942'. Nothing came of that either.[66]

## 'Speedy solution' – after the victory

Hitler and his generals waged a blitzkrieg against the Soviet Union simply because no other strategies were considered, in view of the chronic scarcity of resources. The notion of a fast, overpowering victory once again justified – supposedly temporarily – interrupting the settlements, improvising interim solutions, and avoiding having to make compromises. This happened, as it had after the defeat of France, with a view to the opportunity for further forced emigration that was expected in the near future.

Resettlement technocrats hoped this could then be carried out without any restrictions or forbearance.

On 17 March, Frank and Hitler agreed on the idea that Konrad Meyer had already preferred 'for purely statistical reasons' in early December. 'In fifteen to twenty years,' Hitler said on this occasion, the Generalgouvernement would be 'a purely German country'. Further, Frank reported to his Krakow colleagues in the cabinet that

> we are about to experience an event, after which something new will emerge. The Generalgouvernement as we know it and have developed it will become much richer and happier, it will receive much more support, and above all, it will be de-Jewed. But it will also lose the characteristic sight of the Polish life that still prevails, for with the Jews, the Poles will go as well.

The Führer assured him that the Generalgouvernement 'will be the first to be made free of Jews [*judenfrei*]', and that in the future, 'four to five million Germans will live where twelve million Poles are now living'.[67]

The third short-term plan was *de facto* terminated on 15 March 1941. At the same time, however, it was incorporated into an incomparably more radical deportation plan that would affect not 800,000 but possibly more than 10 million people, above all – directly following the planned speedy victory – the Polish Jews. The implementation of the new General Plan for the East, which the RKF planning department had been pushing for months, was to begin directly after the territorial war of extermination against the Soviet Union, and not – in stark contrast to the third short-term plan – during the war, in competition with the Wehrmacht. Germany's political and military leaders wanted to have triumphantly concluded the war against the Soviet Union by the autumn of 1941. Until that time, 'great ethnic policy experiments . . . [would not be] feasible'. First, as Frank reiterated Göring's statement, it is 'more important to win the war than to implement racial policies'.[68]

At the same time, Göring made another promise elsewhere: 'The victorious Greater Germany will later resolve, quickly and finally, issues of *Volkstum* and racial politics that presently remain unresolved in the individual Gaus.'[69] Even the notorious antipodes, Frank and Himmler, were agreed on this point. Their opposing political interests could now – as was also the case regarding the Madagascar Plan – be overcome in the common vision of a speedy, radical solution, one which had been inconceivable up to then. They both believed this would enable them jointly to achieve their demographic goals, which were similar in principle but conflicting in practice, and end their stagnation and mutual obstruction.

Even though the practitioners of 'human deployment' were still struggling with the everyday trials and tribulations of the resettlement efforts, in March–April 1941 the strategists of the demographic new order felt euphoric optimism about the future. This was a renewed outbreak after the difficulties in 1940 forced them to face the facts, ending the first period of optimism in winter 1939–40. In autumn 1940, the Krakow planning staff was still preparing reports targeting the RKF that opposed any further mass resettlements; but now they were offering their cooperation. In the weeks of mobilization for the attack on the Soviet Union, regional and settlement planners no longer saw the Generalgouvernement as a peripheral end of the line for 'modern-day mass migration'; prospects for 'deportations eastward' were opening up.

The following examples should serve to illustrate how expectantly representatives of the German occupation forces in Krakow looked towards the future, despite the present adversity. They truly reckoned with a speedy victory over Russia. When the Institute for Research on the Jewish Question celebrated its founding on 26 March 1941 in Frankfurt am Main, Walter Gross, director of the Racial Policy Office of the Nazi Party, made a declaration on the future of Judaism: 'Eliminating the dangerous impact of its existence in Europe is only possible with absolute geographic removal.'[70] Peter-Heinz Seraphim – economics professor, 'expert on Jews', and economic command officer stationed at the time in Krakow – spoke on the subject of 'population and economic problems of a total solution of the Jewish question in Europe'. He said, 'The cities were "blocked" as it were by the Jews! Now the time to break this monopoly appears to have come!'[71] Seraphim explicitly included the cities of the Generalgouvernement in his plan; a short time later he became editor-in-chief of the Institute's publication *Weltkampf*. Fritz Arlt (staff head of the RKF in Katowice) was a friend and comrade-in-arms of Seraphim. Arlt and Wilhelm Coblitz (director of the Institute for German Activities in the East [IDO], in Krakow) were among the hand-picked guests at the ceremony. Coblitz agreed to 'closest cooperation' with his Frankfurt colleagues in 'processing' the 'question of the Eastern Jews' and they concurred that 'thorough scientific consideration of precisely this problem' was necessary as 'preparation for a final solution of this question by the Führer after the war'.[72] On 13 January, Frank had given his advisor Coblitz and research assistants the rather reactive task of developing ideas for immediate implementation on the 'influx of approximately one million Poles' and offering cultural events to the few, isolated Germans as 'spiritual support in this region, which is becoming more and more Polish'.[73] Now, however, Coblitz could offer more far-reaching hypotheses: 'The study of Jews in the institute will . . . be accomplished with the purpose of the total elimination of the Jewish problem in Europe.'[74]

A few months later, in June, his staff presented two memoranda on future population policy in the Generalgouvernement, written wholly in the spirit of Meyer, Himmler, Frank, and Hitler. Only the titles are known: 'Relocation of the Poles'[75] and 'Settlement of Ethnic Boundaries [*Volkstumsgrenzen*]'.[76] In another institute memo that survived by chance, Helmut Meinhold, IDO economics expert, wrote enthusiastically in July

1941 that 'the further military advance to the East has opened up two additional ways of solving the overpopulation problem. Either a segment of the Polish population, or all of it, can be resettled far to the East.' The young economist operationalized the plan in smaller steps, as far as the Poles were concerned. At this point in time, he already took for granted the 'resolution of the Jewish question' as a basic precondition for his ideas.[77]

IDO experts debated quite openly. In 1943, the following sentence managed to slip into a publication: 'There are only two options for solving the Jewish question: deportation or physical extermination.'[78]

## Foot march to the ghetto

In his address 'on settlement' in December 1940, Himmler declared the rapid expulsion of the Polish Jews to be the main prerequisite in coping with the whole resettlement predicament. In addition to generally abandoning new 'efforts to bring back German blood', he also promised a particular alternative: 'emigration of the Jews to make more room for Poles'. Where the deportations were headed, however, remained initially unclear. Eichmann spoke on 4 December 1940 of a 'territory yet to be determined'. Earlier, on 23 October and 6 November of the same year, a representative from the RKF 'Human Deployment' Department and Eichmann met in the Reich Security Main Office to discuss the subject of 'Jews'.[79] Although the contents of the talks are not known, it seems plausible in view of the participants that the discussion dealt with overcoming the general freeze on settlements, and especially the question: 'Where to put the Jews?'

At this time, Heydrich, Eichmann, and Fähndrich started drawing up the third short-term plan. It provided for the deportation of 770,000 Poles, including some Jews, if they directly obstructed the settlement of ethnic Germans or other goals of the third short-term plan.[80] At least in writing, the authors of the resettlement plan paid no attention to the Jews in Lodz or those interned for forced labour in Upper Silesia.[81] However, resettlement officials did additionally integrate the deportation of 60,000 Viennese Jews into their plan. This was definitely a response to promises that Hitler had made to von Schirach, the Gauleiter of Vienna, on 3 December 1940 and was an explicit exception because of the special situation in Vienna: 'deportation . . . of the 60,000 [Viennese] Jews . . . would be expedited, *i.e., implemented during the war,* due to the shortage of housing in Vienna'.[82]

Although the third short-term plan did not mention them at all, it did mean dire consequences for Jews in the Generalgouvernement and later for those in Upper Silesia. On 15 January 1941, exactly one week after the coordinating conference in Heydrich's office, Eberhard Westerkamp, head of the internal affairs administration of the Generalgouvernement, announced on the occasion of new resettlements 'that the notion is being considered that the necessary space be cleared by crowding the Jews closer together in ghettos'. Krüger referred to a plan that SS and Police Chief Globocnik had already drawn up for the district of Lublin, remarking that 'one must consider whether this could not be extended throughout the entire Generalgouvernement'.[83] On 13 December 1940, Globocnik had suggested acting 'with greater severity against the Jews in the district of Lublin'. He intended to herd them together, if possible 'in a place specially designed for this purpose, where they would be forced to perform slave labour'.[84] They would have to dig ditches, reclaim swamps, and embank rivers and make them navigable.[85]

Globocnik's plans were initially intended only for local implementation, but a few weeks later, they intersected with the concrete needs of a new situation. On 15 January 1941, the administrative head of the district of Warsaw had referred 'with great earnestness to conditions in the ghetto'. Only five days later, the director of the resettlement department there announced that another 72,000 Jews would be confined to the Warsaw ghetto, since 'room for 62,000[86] evacuated persons'[87] was needed in the western part of the district. This referred to Poles who were to be deported to the district as part of phase one of the third short-term plan.

On the same day, an order was issued on when the Jewish residents of the rural towns on the left bank of the Vistula would be forced into the Warsaw ghetto, where they were to be brought by rail or 'on foot'.[88] On 3 March, the German authorities ordered the ghettoization of the Jews of Krakow. Some of the abandoned Jewish businesses and homes were to be left for the Poles who had been forced to relocate.[89]

In fact, all Jews from the western section of the district were also forced into the Warsaw ghetto during February, March, and April. This was a direct consequence of the third short-term plan.[90] In *Scroll of Agony: The Warsaw Diary of Chaim A. Kaplan*, Kaplan, who was himself confined in the Warsaw ghetto, described the reality of that expedient solution:

26 January 1941

. . .

Today new tidings reached us. Once again hundreds of families have been uprooted from their homes and are coming to Warsaw on foot. Another expulsion in the midst of a bitter winter. There is a rumour circulating that another 72,000 people have gone into exile, and all of them will be coming to the Warsaw ghetto. . . . Further, there may be a plan behind all this barbarism, for we hear that the murderers have decided to set up three 'concentrations' of Jews: the Warsaw, Lublin, and Radom concentrations. Except for these three concentrations, no Jews will remain throughout the area of the General

Government. This will make it easier for the murderers to destroy them, not one by one but wholesale. . . .

## 31 January 1941

Today three thousand new exiles from Pruszków and other Polish cities entered the Warsaw ghetto and it was our obligation to furnish a new shelter for the unfortunates. . . .

The exiles were driven out of their beds before dawn, and the Führer's minions did not let them take money, belongings, or food, threatening all the while to shoot them. Before they left on their exile, a search was made of their pockets and of all the hidden places in their clothes and bodies. Without a penny in their pockets or a covering for the women, children, old people, and invalids – sometimes without shoes on their feet or staffs in their hands – they were forced to leave their homes and possessions and the graves of their ancestors, and go – whither? . . .

## 8 March 1941

I have a document before me. . . . It is written by the representatives of the people of Grodzisk to the 'Central Committee for Refugee Affairs' in Warsaw . . . and [it] is dated 3 March 1941. Here is its text:
'The Grodzisk delegation will operate in Warsaw after 6 March 1941. It encompasses the Jews of Grodzisk-Mazowiecki and its environs (Brwinów, Nadarzyn, Podkowa-Leśna, and Milanówek), five thousand people in all.
'The neighbouring towns were the first to receive the expulsion order, and told to move to Grodzisk. We therefore made the necessary preparations to receive the guests; we were almost certain that we, the householders of Grodzisk, would not be moved from our place. . . .
'But how great was our sorrow and distress when it was made known to us on the third of February that an expulsion order had been issued for us as well, which required us to evacuate our city by the fourteenth of February. . . .
'the last group (of six hundred people), which remained in Grodzisk until the twelfth of February, was taken to Warsaw like a transport of freight.'[91]

Human freight brought to the ghetto – that was the final part of the third short-term plan, in fact the part implemented to the greatest extent. Bringing the ethnic Germans 'home to the Reich' from distant Bessarabia, Bukovina, and Dobruja had been carried out with utmost haste in the interest of power politics and the 'European new order'. That and the 'exigencies' of the military and war economy always had the same effect as a consequence of the ethnic domino effect: the further ghettoization and impoverishment of the Polish Jews. This was accomplished according to the tried and true procedure of expelling Polish families from the incorporated eastern territories and assigning ethnic Germans to their farmsteads, and then, in turn, deporting the not yet ghettoized Jews in the Generalgouvernement and assigning the homes they left behind to deported Poles. The beginning of a long chain of resettlements was triggered in 1939 not by the 'Jewish question', but by German–Soviet treaties and the policies of the military and economic 'new order'. At the end of that chain were the not yet ghettoized Jews in the General-gouvernement. They alone were robbed of almost all means of survival and, on top of that, pressed within ghetto walls, their presence there – aside from their own hardship – further reducing the chances of survival of those already living in the ghetto.

The same procedure was used in winter 1942–43 in the Zamość region within the scope of the third expanded short-term plan, but the conditions were different. The former Jewish villages and marketplaces were con-verted to 'pensioner villages' for Poles who – though spared both slave labour and deportation to a concentration camp – were displaced to make room for ethnic German settlers.[92] The Jews had not been evacuated to ghettos and camps, however, but were murdered in Belzec a short time earlier.

As of spring 1941, gas chambers did not yet exist. At that time, the building of numerous slave labour camps was still on the agenda. Walde-mar Schön, head of the Warsaw resettlement department, said on 21 January that soon 200,000 'Jews who are presently unemployed as a result of ghetto formation' could 'march in brigades to work' outside the ghetto. In the near future, he continued, '100 per cent utilization of this workforce' could be achieved.[93] Preparations for this project began a short time later. In February, the water supply inspector in the Generalgouvernement requested 22,000–25,000 Jewish slave labourers.[94] On 2 March, Chaim A. Kaplan recorded, 'A notice was posted in the Aryan quarter [i.e., the Polish section of Warsaw] inviting Polish, Ukrainian, and Byelorussian youths to apply for jobs as supervisors of the barracks being erected for the Jews.'[95]

The camps were built by private companies that received 'a kind of concession for the exploitation of Jewish workers'.[96] They became a hell on earth. The external conditions, the shortage of food and tools, housing, and adequate work clothes made it impossible even to test whether some of the prisoners could be 'made to work' in this way. The reality of the project is reflected in the diary of Adam Czerniaków, head of the Warsaw *Judenrat*:

April 26, 1941 – . . . The news from the labor camps is very sad. Very little food and much abuse. . . .

May 5, 1941 – . . . According to their list 91 people died in 10 camps. . . .

May 10, 1941 – . . . The workers were to receive $6\frac{1}{2}$ ounces of bread, 2.2–2.9 pounds of potatoes, sugar, marmalade, meat, coffee, etc. There are no potatoes and they receive $4$–$5\frac{1}{2}$ ounces of bread. There is no fat whatsoever. . . . The camp huts have spoiled straw to sleep on and wind is blowing through the walls. The workers are shivering at night. There are no showers and rest rooms. The workers' boots were ruined in wet sand and clay. There are no drugs or bandages. . . .

May 21, 1941 – . . . A call from Rozen. They visited Lekno and one other camp. The conditions are horrendous. Nobody can stand it for a month. The firms which supply the food are stealing it from the workers. The beating of the workers is to cease. The efficiency of the work, admittedly hard, is low.[97]

In June, most of the camps were closed. It was a success credited to the economists who had been complaining of the low labour productivity from the very beginning.[98] In 1942, Friedrich Gollert, head of the Department for Regional Planning in the Warsaw district, wrote his own retrospective account of the disaster of the slave labour camps:

> Further proposals to ensure a sufficient labour force to get through the following year were submitted and tested in winter 1940–41. Large numbers of Jews were taken from the Jewish ghetto in Warsaw in 1941 and put to work for the water works. . . . The work productivity of the remaining Jews was so low that even the costs for their food were higher than the pay they earned. In the future, instead of Jews, Russian prisoners of war will be utilized for labour purposes.[99]

Himmler's announcement in December 1940 of plans for 'emigration of the Jews to make more room for Poles' thus initially led in practice to forced ghettoization and then to the development of slave labour projects. The latter proved early on to be a mistake, because of the inadequate organizational prerequisites, if nothing else. Moreover, since they were to serve to make long-term improvements in the infrastructure, like the third short-term plan, they had to be discontinued in view of preparations for the war against the Soviet Union. One of Frank's economic advisors had already succinctly prophesied back in March, when the camps were first being built, that 'through the special conditions expected in 1941, transport and communications in particular will be subjected to extraordinary strain. . . . Consequently, a series of projects scheduled for 1941 will probably not be implemented.'[100]

Rudolf Gater, the man who wrote that, worked as an efficiency expert in

Frank's administration. The sentences were taken from his – devastating – report on the 'economic balance' of the Warsaw ghetto. The report opposed the continued ghettoization of the Jews and classified the slave labour projects as inefficient and virtually impossible to carry through. Hence the contradictions that existed between economic experts and executors of plans for resettlements and forced labour were contradictions between theory and practice. Whereas the practitioners wanted to deport as many people as possible from the incorporated eastern territories to the Generalgouvernement, resorting to 'ghettoization' and 'slave labour', which for them were the most obvious solutions, economists did a few calculations and quickly determined that that was not the way out of the dilemma.

One essential determinant in the decision-making process leading to the Holocaust was an aspect of the political structures that started becoming visible in previous chapters and will gain additional contours in the following section. It was not a uniform strategy or similar goals pursued by the various projects and perspectives that led to genocide but, quite the contrary, their divergence.

## Jews unfit for work

Instead of the 'expedited' deportation of 60,000 Viennese Jews that Hitler had ordered, Heydrich provided for the deportation of only 10,000 in the first sub-programme of the third short-term plan. Of these, only 5031, most of them sick and/or elderly, were actually deported to the eastern Generalgouvernement as of 15 March.[101] One report mentioned that 'the transport [of 15 February] involved 1034 people; of these more than 60 were women. Most of the transport was made up of old, ailing people over 60 years of age, including one who was totally blind, and war invalids who were totally helpless in face of the situation.' The deportees were brought to Opole in the Lublin district.[102]

Fritz Woehrn, a member of Eichmann's staff, commented on 17 March 1941 that the first deportations were evidently the Jewish women and men of Vienna who 'were unfit for resettlement'. Woehrn informed Paul Eppstein, administrative director of the Reich Association of Jews in Germany (a compulsory association starting in 1939), that 'considerable means would be necessary for a planned emigration of the entire Jewish population that is *fit for settlement,* so that the Reich Association would not have all their assets at their own disposal'.[103]

If the pair of opposites 'fit for settlement vs. unfit for settlement' is understood as 'fit for work vs. unfit for work', which is realistic, then it is obvious that the selection of the Jewish population coincided with plans for the slave labour projects. In the Warthegau, too, relevant officials assumed corresponding changes in ghetto policies. On 31 January 1941,

Walter Moser, deputy provincial chief responsible for Lodz, assumed 'with certainty, . . . that a major portion of the ghetto residents unfit for work will be evacuated to the Generalgouvernement in the spring of 1941 and might be replaced by Jews from the Gau area who are fit for work'.[104] On 7 March, Rolf-Heinz Höppner, Eichmann's staff member in Posen, wrote:

> In order to comply with the orders of the Gauleiter [Greiser] not to deport Jews who are fit for work to the Generalgouvernement, it was decided . . . that the Jews fit for work should first be brought temporarily to the Litzmannstadt ghetto and that they be deployed from there. The rest of the Jews will be evacuated, even if this means that families will be torn apart.[105]

Officials in the Reich Auditing Office started a 14-day audit of the ghetto administration in Lodz on 23 January 1941, on orders of the Minister of Finance. The Reich Finance Minister had issued the order in November 1940, since he feared that the moment was drawing near 'in which the costs for maintaining the Jews would become a public burden'. In their final report, in February, the auditors recorded that

> the responsible local German authorities were well aware that the problem of pacification and Germanization as well as that of building up the economy of the city could only be achieved in connection with the complete relocation of the Jews or temporarily with their isolation. . . . No conclusive statement can presently be made about what conditions will be like in the future.[106]

But the auditors did make one thing very clear: costs for maintaining ghetto residents amounted to at least 2.5 million Reichsmarks per month. This money was officially lent to the ghetto administration as credit, but 'repayment of the amount, including interest, should be seen as a mere matter of form'.[107] The representatives from the auditing office assumed that 'a major portion of the ghetto residents unfit for work [would] be evacuated to the Generalgouvernement in the spring of 1941'. In addition, the auditors called for 'all skilled tradesmen and unskilled workers in the ghetto to be put to work . . . as a basic condition for the self-maintenance of the Jewish community'. According to information from the Reich Auditing Office, there were 38,221 people in the ghetto who were unemployed but fit for work.[108]

As has already been suggested, the situation in Warsaw was similar. In mid-January, efficiency expert Rudolf Gater, head of the Generalgouvernement section of the Reich Committee for Efficiency (*Reichskuratorium für Wirtschaftlichkeit*, or RKW),[109] was assigned to prepare a report on the Warsaw ghetto. In spring 1941, the administration of the Generalgouvernement started using this expert's report as the basis for consultations on future ghetto policy. Gater had calculated that if the ghetto were to remain in existence, it would swallow up huge state subsidies within a short period of time. Consequently, he made the following proposals:

> If this subsidy is to be avoided or at least reduced, the following options are available:
>
> 1. Permit undersupply without regard to the consequences.
> 2. Accelerate procedures through which organizations responsible for the exploitation of the Jewish workforce in the Jewish ghetto be put in a position to successfully utilize larger numbers of Jews for these purposes.
> 3. Relax restrictions in the Jewish ghetto in Warsaw somewhat, so that Jewish tradesmen in certain fields once again have the chance to work directly for the outside world – albeit to a modest extent.[110]

In fact, all three of Gater's suggestions were attempted during the summer months. While the number of deaths by starvation in the ghetto immediately rose drastically, measures to create jobs were generally unsuccessful. Gater envisioned two possible scenarios in this situation: either transfer an annual subsidy of 55 million Reichsmarks to the ghetto, if the Jews were to be kept alive, or 'view the Jewish ghetto as a means of liquidating the Jewish people'.[111]

This was discussed quite rationally by the experts on the ground. The plan pursued by practitioners in the RSHA was slightly different, yet the same in principle. Such reports served inevitably to radicalize it. All in all, the documents paint the general picture that in the spring of 1941, experts for Jewish matters in the RSHA and the Generalgouvernement intended to utilize 'brigades' of Jews fit for work;[112] the new slave labour projects were supposed to help make 'room' in the ghettos of the Generalgouvernement, which Heydrich, Eichmann, and Höppner then wanted to fill with Jews unfit for work who were deported from the regions of Lodz, Dąbrowa, and Ciechanów.

From this point on, Jews no longer all suffered the same form of persecution and maltreatment, and the same deportations were no longer planned for all. Rather, the Jews were divided into two groups – those fit for work and those unfit for work – who were to receive different treatment.[113] The latter, as the deportations from Vienna show, were to die quickly of hunger and hardship. It was no longer a very large step from this passive form of killing to the active murder of 'unproductive Jews', especially since the 'elimination of useless eaters' – i.e., 'Operation T-4' – had long since taken on assembly-line proportions. Himmler and Brack had already agreed back in March to murder concentration camp prisoners who were unfit for work or particularly undesirable – a disproportionately large number of whom were Jews – in the T-4 gas chambers. The project was coded 'Operation 14f13' and was a form of cooperation among authorities in which the 'euthanasia' practitioners came to the aid of their RSHA colleagues by murdering a total of 20,000 concentration camp prisoners by June 1942.

## Marshlands, White Sea, Siberia

Neither forced ghettoization nor forced labour were scheduled to go on for ever. Those in Posen, Lodz, and Krakow who carried out the anti-Jewish measures did not view them as final, but as interim steps on the road to 'the final solution of the Jewish question in Europe'. In spring 1941, they still firmly reckoned with future 'options in the East'.

Although there are few extant documents and little attention has been paid to this time period in works on the Holocaust,[114] it is possible to sketch an approximate outline of these plans. On 21 January 1941, Eichmann's staff member Theodor Dannecker wrote that 'according to the will of the Führer, after the war a final solution to the Jewish question within the parts of Europe under German rule or control will be implemented'. To this end, Heydrich received orders from Hitler – via Himmler and Göring – to 'submit a proposal for the final solution'. Dannecker's description of the project is both vague and activistic:

> The implementation will definitely comprise a huge project, the success of which can only be guaranteed through the most careful of preparations. This preparation must include the preliminary work necessary for a general deportation of all Jews, as well as detailed plans for resettlement measures in a territory yet to be determined.[115]

On 20 March 1941, Eichmann announced to representatives of the Propaganda Ministry that Heydrich 'was assigned by the Führer the task of planning the final evacuation of the Jews' and that 'he [had] submitted a proposal about 8–10 weeks [earlier]'. The proposal was reportedly not accepted 'because the Generalgouvernement was not in a position at the time [to accept] a single Jew or Pole'.[116]

Both statements indicated that around New Year 1941, Hitler had ordered Heydrich (according to Dannecker, via Göring and Himmler) to develop a plan to deport all Jews within the German sphere of influence. It was intended to replace the Madagascar Plan. On 4 December, Eichmann had estimated the number to be deported at 5.8 million. While in January, Dannecker assumed the deportations would be to 'a territory yet to be determined', using the same wording as Eichmann did six weeks earlier, Eichmann's wording on 20 March pointed the way: to the Generalgouvernement or, generally speaking, to the East. On 25 March, Franz Halder, chief of the General Staff of the Army, made notes about a meeting with Eduard Wagner, general quartermaster of the Army, on 'discussion topics for the meeting with Heydrich in view of impending issues regarding the East'.[117] It is generally assumed that this referred solely to the scope of action of the *Einsatzgruppen* (Special Units) that were formed later. But the next day, Heydrich noted the following immediately after a meeting with Göring:

> 10) Regarding the solution of the Jewish question, I gave the Reich Marshal [i.e., Göring] a brief report and submitted my proposal to him, which he approved after making a change with respect to Rosenberg's responsibilities and he ordered its resubmission.

Points 11 and 12 are also significant in this context:

> 11) The Reich Marshal told me that we should prepare a brief, 3- to 4-page manual for a military operation in Russia that the troops could be given, instructing them on the threat of the GPU apparatus, the political commissars, Jews, etc., so they basically know who to stand up against the wall.

> 12) In this context, the Reich Marshal announced that under no circumstances was the Wehrmacht to receive executive authority like that of the military administration. Instead, behind the advancing troops the Reich Marshal himself would be given complete overall authority through the edict (which the Führer had already approved), especially because of the appropriation of the necessary industries.[118] Of course he would let the Reichsführer SS act largely on his own in this matter.[119]

This document shows the extent to which Göring – in addition to Himmler, Hitler, and the Wehrmacht generals – was involved in drawing up the notorious 'commissar order'. Furthermore, Heydrich's note clearly states that he submitted a proposal 'regarding the Jewish question', not that he was ordered to do so by Göring. This happened in late March 1941, which serves to relativize the assumption of many historians that the famous letter of 31 July 1941 – in which Göring ordered Heydrich in writing 'to draw up comprehensive plans to implement the desired total solution of the Jewish question'[120] – was a crucial moment on the road to the Holocaust.

The memo of 26 March 1941 also confirms that Heydrich had already received the order at an earlier date. Only then could he 'submit a proposal' to Göring. The official written form of this order was necessary in late July only in order to increase Heydrich's scope of action with respect to other authorities. In any case, Heydrich later used Göring's letter to do just that.

Heydrich sent his original memorandum to Himmler and copies to Heinrich Müller, director of Department IV – 'also for Eichmann's information' – Walter Schellenberg, Bruno Streckenbach, Alfred Filbert, and Otto Ohlendorf, as 'confidential, top secret information'.[121] The fact that Heydrich informed Eichmann suggests that Heydrich and Göring had also spoken about deportations. Göring's reference to 'Rosenberg's responsibilities' is an indication of the direction, since at this time Rosenberg had already been designated minister of the civilian administration in the later-occupied Soviet territories.[122] It follows from this that Heydrich's proposal for the 'solution of the Jewish question' pertained, as of March 1941 at the latest, to the territory of the Soviet Union. The fact that Rosenberg was given very little real power from the outset, and that he had to relinquish authority in economic, police, and settlement policy matters to Göring and Himmler, supports this conclusion.

Thus, in March at the latest, Heydrich started preparing the deportation of all European Jews living west of the German–Soviet border. This occurred parallel to, and in the same context as, his ideas for the later formation of the *Einsatzgruppen* of the security police and the SD. There are also some indications that Heydrich had already drawn up this plan at the very end of 1940 and had already received Hitler's and Himmler's approval. Thus when he presented the third short-term plan on 8 January 1941, he divided it into subplans from the start, unlike previous plans. On that day, he mentioned only the 'first sub-programme' in concrete terms. It was to be concluded by 1 May and was to involve the deportation of 'a total of 238,500 people, . . . plus another 10,000 Jews to be deported from Vienna'.[123]

It is apparent that Heydrich took into consideration the original schedule for mobilization and invasion in the war against the Soviet Union, which was later delayed because of the war against Yugoslavia and Greece.[124] In addition, the preparatory documents for the implementation of the third short-term plan contain no clues as to how the expulsion was to continue after the conclusion of the first sub-programme. I believe that Heydrich did not want to negotiate about further deportations to be carried out within the scope of the third short-term plan until after the attack on the Soviet Union; at that time, he also planned to discuss the long-delayed 'evacuation' of the Jews.

Evidently, from then on Heydrich and Eichmann favoured the option of a dynamically conceived 'further deportation to the East', the destination of which was as yet unspecified. The goals of the plan corresponded only superficially to the Madagascar Plan; at bottom, it was dramatically different. Although the Madagascar Plan, too, was characterized by the genocidal principle of 'natural decimation through resettlement', it did not even begin to suggest the complete extermination of the deportees.

In contrast, plans with respect to the new 'options in the East' that were developed in early 1941 among the Reich Security Main Office (RSHA), the Reich Commissioner for the Consolidation of German Nationhood (RKF), the Wehrmacht, and Göring's administration for the Four-Year Plan bore the marks of something altogether different. Himmler, Heydrich, and Eichmann imagined that the Jews who were unfit for work – those who were still alive, at any rate – would be concentrated in 'death reservations' and so-called 'pensioner ghettos' at the eastern periphery of the Generalgouvernement. After the intended victory over the Soviet Union, they would be transferred to the bordering marshes in what were formerly eastern Poland and White Ruthenia. Jews fit for work were to start reclaiming these swamps in summer 1941. In addition – as it is stated in the records of the Wannsee Conference – they were to be 'brought' to the newly conquered regions of the Soviet Union to 'build roads in large brigades of workers' and would be annihilated through barbarous slave labour, in the frigid White Sea region, for example.

There are very few extant documents on the planning process from January to July 1941. Many of them were obviously written some time later, when SS leaders no longer took such plans literally. Instead, they used the terminology of these plans – which was still taken literally in the spring and early summer – as a type of code through which to euphemize the 'final solution of the Jewish question', meaning firing squad commandos and gas chambers. This was also done with respect to use of the codename 'Madagascar', i.e., by reference to a plan that had without a doubt really existed. Hitler was doing this on 22 July 1941 when he said, 'It does not matter where the Jews are sent, whether to Siberia or Madagascar.'[125]

For this reason I believe that relevant sentences in the minutes of the Wannsee Conference must be understood as reflecting intentions that had developed at an earlier stage, though here they were used as camouflage. As Burrin notes, 'Heydrich told Goebbels, whom he met at Hitler's headquarters on 23 September, that, as soon as the military situation permitted, the Jews would be transported to camps built by the communists along the White Sea canal.'[126] Goebbels had been pressuring for the deportations in his capacity as Gauleiter in Berlin. Directly following the Wannsee Conference, Heydrich reiterated the 'White Sea' option. They wanted to 'take over the Russian concentration camps,' he said, and despite all assumptions to the contrary, the region had 'extraordinarily concentrated, good agriculture and an excellent raw material base'. It would be 'an ideal future homeland for 11 million European Jews'.[127] In 1946, Frank's state secretary Josef Bühler explained during interrogations in Nuremberg that Heydrich had told him in early 1942 that Himmler had 'received orders from the Führer to consolidate all of Europe's Jews and settle them in northeastern Europe, in Russia'.[128] The records of the Wannsee Conference and Bühler's active participation – especially his 'request to solve the Jewish question [in the Generalgouvernement] as soon as possible' – were not yet known in 1946, and Bühler fell back on half-truths.

This option had also already taken on a camouflaging function in a letter that Walter Föhl, a leading Krakow resettlement organizer, wrote to his SS comrades in June 1942. Only in retrospect can this be seen as an intermediate step on the road to the Holocaust. In the letter, Föhl wrote:

Every day, trains are arriving with over 1000 Jews each from throughout Europe. We provide first aid here, give them more or less provisional accommodation, and usually deport them further towards the
White Sea to the White Ruthenian marshlands, where they all – if
they survive (and the Jews from Kurfürstendamm or Vienna or
Pressburg certainly won't) – will be gathered by the end of the
war, but not without having first built a few roads. (But we're not
supposed to talk about it.)[129]

Also in the summer of 1942, the Germans transported 3000 Jews from the
Eastern Galician town of Drohobycz to the Belzec death camp. Here, too,
they used the excuse that the deportees 'were needed for the reclamation of
the Pripet marshes'.[130]

The project of deporting the Jews to the formerly eastern Polish Pripet
marshes, extending to White Russia, was most likely developed at the same
time as the White Sea project in the Generalgouvernement, possibly with
the cooperation of the RKF. Two articles that appeared in Karl Haushofer's
journal *Zeitschrift für Geopolitik* allude to such plans in spring and early
summer 1941. In December 1941, the journal published Richard Bergius's
statement on 'The Pripet Marshes as a Drainage Problem'[131] and, in June
1942, a comprehensive essay by Hansjulius Schepers on the subject of
'Pripet-Polesie, a Land and its People'.[132]

Whereas Bergius believed that 'the issue of reclaiming the Pripet
marshes' offered agrarian hydrotechnicians 'a difficult, yet rewarding
task', Schepers concluded emphatically:

In a hundred-year utilization plan, two million tons of peat can be
extracted annually. How might this economy look, considering that
in-depth studies conclude that 'the real success of a comprehensively
implemented improvement of Polesie is expressed in an increase in
the total amount of arable land by roughly two million hectares [five
million acres]'!

Schepers was Director of the Office for Regional Planning in Krakow. Long
before the essay was published, on 19 July 1941, Frank announced that
Schepers would give an expert oral presentation to Lammers, head of the
Reich Chancellery, to explain why 'the marshlands of the Pripet and its
tributaries' should be annexed to the Generalgouvernement. Frank
commented that

in its present state, this region has minimal value, but with a
thoroughly implemented programme of drainage and cultivation,
considerable value can without a doubt be extracted from this region.
I am suggesting that this area be included, primarily because I believe
it is possible to engage certain population elements (especially Jewish
ones) in a productive activity serving the Reich. You are well aware
that in this regard I cannot complain of shortages of labour.[133]

It is unclear whether or not Schepers presented these ideas in person in the Reich Chancellery. In any case, Frank enclosed with his letter to Lammers a statement by Schepers, in which he put the case for 'the colonizational task' in the marshlands of the Pripet.[134] On 22 June 1941, the Reich Office of Regional Planning had already submitted a report on the future eastern border of the Generalgouvernement, in which the Pripet marshes were classified 'as arable land yet to be cultivated'.[135] This report was also in Lammers' possession in July. If one assumes that it had been commissioned at least four weeks earlier, there can be no doubt that the planners in Krakow and Berlin had already discussed it seriously in April or May.[136] The practitioners made related statements. In event report (*Ereignismeldung*) no. 52, Otto Rasch, the head of *Einsatzgruppe* C, presented his ideas for the 'solution of the Jewish question' on 14 August: 'The superfluous Jewish masses can be excellently exploited and used up, namely by cultivating the great Pripet marshes as well as the marshes at the northern Dnieper and the Volga.'[137]

A trace of such a debate can also be found in a July 1941 report by Helmut Meinhold, economic expert in the Krakow Institute for German Activities in the East. Meinhold wrote that 'the conceivable use of a large number of workers in the reclamation of the marshes (and a similar project in the region of the Rokitno marshes) cannot be carried out until the climatic impacts are examined as precisely as possible'.[138] Ten weeks later, on 28 September, Hitler expressed similar ecological reservations. This suggests that he had dealt with the project: 'Then we wish to leave the marshes as they are, not only because we need the area for manoeuvres, but also because of the weather, to deal with the danger of desertification.'[139]

By spring 1941, Jews fit for work and those unfit for work were separated more and more often. For this reason, plans for the deportation of European Jewry to the territory of the Soviet Union that the Germans planned to occupy soon must be viewed as a two-pronged comprehensive plan for medium-range biological extermination. It was therefore fitting that Jews 'were separated according to sex', as was stated in retrospect in the Wannsee Conference minutes, that they were to be used for labour, and that the forced sterilization of all Jewish women was often considered, 'so that the Jewish problem can be solved once and for all in this generation'.

Although the deportation of the Jews was postponed for the time being in spring 1941, this was only because all those involved assumed that by autumn they would face virtually no restrictions in carrying out all their publicly and secretly formulated plans. The deportees were supposed to die a 'natural' death, some starving or freezing to death in ghettos and camps, others worked to death under a barbaric police regime. The programme developed in spring 1941 aimed at the extermination of European Jewry, going far beyond the scope of the Madagascar Plan. In view of the planned mass resettlement, especially the desired, inconceivable cruelty of the circumstances, our sense of morality resists making any further conceptual differentiation. Nevertheless, a clear distinction must still be drawn between this and the later form of assembly-line extermination.[140]

Like previous deportation projects, the new plan was tied to a tight time schedule. Accordingly, as in the preceding months, further action could be taken as a means to overcome conflicts of interest. Precisely these circumstances yielded the necessary prerequisites to the final steps towards the murder of European Jewry by means of gas chambers.

# Notes

1 This figure also included a small number of Jews; see p. 163.

2 The number 'as of 1 April 1941' can be derived from the 21 April 1941 letter from the Old Reich/*Ostmark* settlement staff to Himmler; BAK, R49/2639.

3 Note from Meyer to Himmler, 3 December 1940, reprinted in Heim and Aly, *Struktur*, 29ff.; emphasis by the author. I presume that the actual annexation of the district of Bialystok in the autumn of 1941 was a consequence of this memorandum.

4 Telex from Krumey to Eichmann, 6 January 1941; AGK, Greiserprozeβ/36, 546ff.

5 Note by Dolezalek, 12 February 1941: 'Re: The Gauleiter and his personal staff assistant, Oberregierungsrat Siegmund, on future settlement in the Warthegau (large estate issue)'; BAK, R497Anh. I/34, 43–7. Dolezalek attributed Greiser's position to the 'influence of his reactionary agrarian advisors'. See also Müller, 94.

6 On 25 March 1941, after the third short-term plan was terminated, Frank then said, 'We must also remember that such heavy use was made of the General-gouvernement within the scope of the resettlements, not because of the malicious intentions of those involved, but rather because it became imperative due to the need to bring German people back from the East.' Frank diary, quoted in FGM, 64.

7 Frank diary, 319.

8 The military called for the accelerated deportation of 202,000 people from the incorporated eastern territories and 200,000 people within the Generalgouverne-ment. See Chapter 6 (8 January entry).

9 Frank diary, 319.

10 Kreidler, 118.

11 Secret correspondence from the Vomi to all camp commanders, 26 February 1941; BAK, R59/184, 2. The reason given was: 'Language competence, possibly also interpreters are needed for the intensifying economic relationship between the Greater German Reich and the USSR.'

12 OKW war diaries, vol. 1, 361; see also Tippelskirch, 201; Hillgruber, *Carol*, 129ff.; Hillgruber and Hümmelchen, 29.

13 Nolte, *Faschismus*, 436.

14 Frank diary, 338; Pohl, 86. Some of the Jews were ghettoized in Lublin; others were forced into the surrounding villages.

15 Frank diary, BAK, R52/II/238.

16 Müller, 23. For an implicitly critical view, see Pohl, 85ff.; Grabitz and Scheffler, 283ff.

17 Pohl, 87.

18 Grabitz and Scheffler, 283, though the authors' description of the general context of the third short-term plan is very vague.

19 The invitation to the meeting was sent by express mail on 11 March 1941; BAK, R69/388, 247ff. A draft of the letter states that the responsible inspectors of the security police and the SD were 'also invited to a meeting'. This parallel meeting with Heydrich most certainly took place, but I was unable to locate any relevant documents.

20 BAK, R69/571, 257F.

21 Letter of 21 March 1941 from Höppner (Posen) to Krumey (Lodz), in which Höppner also passed on the text of a telex from Ehlich (RSHA) from earlier that same day; AGK, UWZ/P/146, 37ff.

22 Report of a meeting on 19 March 1941 in Greifelt's office (author not identified); BAK, R69/571, 257ff.

23 Note by Stier on a meeting on 19 March 1941; BAK, R49/2604.

24 See, for example, the memo that Krumey sent to the field offices of the 'UWZ Litzmannstadt' on 31 March 1941; StA Poznań, UWZ/P/2, 10ff.

25 Note by Butschek, who attended the meeting, 20 March 1941; BAK, R49/Anh. III/26, 104ff.

26 Express letter of 26 March 1941 from Greifelt, on the outcome of the 19 March 1941 meeting; BAK, R69/388, 251ff.; excerpts reprinted in Adler, 440. These plans did not mean anything in practice. The transit and selection camps of the UWZ were converted to long-term 'Polish camps'. They were overflowing within days, so that on 31 March – despite the special wanted list that had since appeared – 'all evacuations and searches for Poles who had escaped before the evacuation' were stopped, to be resumed 'at a later date' (StA Lodz, UWZ/L/L-3636, 241).

27 Letter from Krumey to the UWZ field offices, 7 May 1941, 'Re: Evacuation of Poles for the purpose of settling Bessarabian Germans'; StA Poznań, UWZ/P/2, 24.

28 Note by Main Department (HA) I of the RKF (signed by Schröder) on a 10 April 1941 meeting with SS Oberführer Döring in Posen; BAK, R49/2639.

29 Report on the living conditions of ethnic Germans in the Munich–Upper Bavaria Gau; BAK, R59/28, 292ff.

30 Note by Dolezalek, 16 January 1941; BAK, R49/Anh. III/26, 3. Thus Müller is incorrect that 'immediately after the attack [on the Soviet Union] started, Himmler ordered that an initial contingent of 3000 of the Bessarabian Germans who had been settled in the Warthegau be removed for service in Russia' (97). The settlement had by no means been completed. Like many other authors, Müller does not pay adequate attention to the failure of RKF plans and the dynamics of the extermination politics that developed as a result.

31 Report by Butschek, 20 May 1941; BAK, R49/Anh. III/26, 114ff.

32 Report by Butschek 'on the development and activities of the settlement department (in Upper Silesia) for the period from 10 July 1940 to 31 May 1941'; BAK, R49/Anh. III/26, 120ff.

33 Danzig (Gdańsk) UWZ, minutes of 22 March of the meeting with the Higher SS and Police Chief on 21 March 1941; BAK, R75/13, 168ff.

34 Notes by Arlt on the meeting on 14 March 1941; BAK, R49/Anh. III/26, 79ff.

35 Ibid.

36 Memorandum by Butschek on 'the possibility of settlement in 1941', n.d. (the date 17 March 1941 can be derived from the contents of the file), reprinted (and incorrectly dated, owing to insufficient research at that time) in Heim and Aly, Struktur, 34–8.

37 Note by Butschek, 20 March 1941, 'Re: Meeting in Berlin on 19 March 1941';

BAK, R49/Anh. III/26, 104ff. On the extent to which the resettlements aided the expansion of the Auschwitz concentration camp, see Czech, 81ff.

38 Letter from the district chief of the gendarmerie in Sieradz to the commander of the gendarmerie in the administrative district of Litzmannstadt (Lodz), 22 March 1941; AGK, UWZ/P/126, 3f.

39 Report from the Bełchatów gendarmerie to the district gendarmerie chief in Pabianice, 18 March 1941; AGK, UWZ/P/126, 4ff. This new form of expulsion had already been implemented in Belchatow on 13 March, i.e., before the central offices officially adopted the procedure. Actually, this type of procedure had already been discussed earlier; it had long since been tested in the Generalgouvernement and was discussed for the Warthegau in December 1940 (see Chapter 6, 21 December).

40 Aside from these official forced evacuations, there were evidently also so-called 'private evictions', i.e., Poles directly expelled by their (new) German neighbours. In any case, the Reich governor in Posen had to 're'enact a corresponding ban, and 'people who carried out illegal evictions faced criminal proceedings'. (Final report on the work of the UWZ within the scope of the expanded third short-term plan in the Warthegau for the year 1942; BAK, R75/9, 3.)

41 For a certain time at least, Höppner intended to stamp 'evacuated' in the identification papers of these slave labourers, so that 'after the end of their work detail they would go to the Generalgouvernement instead of back to the incorporated eastern territories'. (Letter from Höppner to Ehlich, 14 March 1941, quoted in *Biuletyn* 12 [1960], 136Ff.)

42 See note 40, BAK, R75/9, 2.

43 Letter from Damzog to the UWZ field offices, 29 May 1941; StA Poznań, UWZ/P/2, 41f.

44 See Chapter 11, 'Total biologism'.

45 Letter from the head of security police and the SD (IVB4a/Müller) to Heinrich Himmler, 31 October 1941, quoted in Aly and Heim, 434.

46 Note by RKF Main Department I (signed by Schröder) on a meeting with SS Oberführer Döring in Posen, 10 April 1941; BAK, R49/2639.

47 Frank diary, entry of 11 May 1941, 373.

48 Letter from Greiser's personal advisor, Siegmund, to Koppe, 10 May 1941; StA Poznań, UWZ/P/2, 36. To some extent contradicting his own eviction edict, Greiser issued an order on 2 May 1941 in his capacity as RKF representative to the SS settlement staffs to see 'if there were an area in their jurisdiction, closed off if possible (reforestation area, etc.), for temporary accommodation of Poles to be evacuated'. He explicitly urged that care be taken, since there was no telling 'when the Poles crowded into the reservation areas could be deported'. Since the security police expressed misgivings about closed-off areas, however, the practice of 'eviction' continued, even though – from a police perspective – this was just as problematic (ibid. 25ff.).

49 Report by Butschek, 7 June 1941, 'on the development of the settlement department for the period from 10 July 1940 to 31 May 1941'; BAK, R49/Anh. III/26, 120ff. As an example for the Warthegau, see the report of 8 October 1941 by the UWZ field office in Kolmar ('The Polish residences are crowded to the absolute limit'); StA Poznań, UWZ/P/2, 50ff.

50 On this subject, see the very interesting report 'on a meeting of the VDA managing directors in Posen on 6–7 April 1941'; BAK, R59/28, 338–47.

51 Express letter from Greifelt to the RKF representatives in the incorporated eastern territories, 26 March 1941; BAK, R75/3, 12ff. Contrary to all planning stipulations, the average size of the farms allotted to the settlers was *de facto*

only 32–37 acres (note by Butschek on the meeting of 19 March 1941; BAK, R49/Anh. III/26, 104ff.).

52 Note by Butschek, head of the 'South' office of the RKF settlement staff in Upper Silesia, 19 February 1941; BAK, R49/Anh. III/26, 73ff.

53 Express letter from Greifelt to the RKF representative in the incorporated eastern territories, 26 March 1941; BAK, R75/3, 12ff.; emphasis is my own.

54 Adler, 440, quoted in Safrian, 98.

55 Letter from Department III of the RKF to the deputy Gauleiter of Thuringia, 28 April 1941; BAK, R49/2639.

56 Report by DUT managing director Alfred Kulemann, at the Advisory Council session of 20 March 1941; BAP, 17.02/34, 1–18. According to the report, the DUT employed 1150 people at the time.

57 Express letter from Greifelt to the RKF representatives in the incorporated eastern territories, 26 March 1941; BAK, R75/3, 12ff. The letter was based on RKF order no. 27/I of 20 March 1941 on 'temporary employment of the settlers'.

58 RKF order no. 26/I of 21 January 1941; BAK, R59/100, 4.

59 Report by DUT managing director Kulemann at the Advisory Council session of 20 March 1941; BAP, 17.02/34, 4.

60 Letter from the Old Reich/Ostmark settlement staff to Himmler, 21 April 1941; BAK, R49/2639.

61 Letter from Leo Reichert (RKF staff main office) to the RKF baggage centre in Lodz, 30 September 1941; BDC, SS-HO/51039.

62 Note by Stier about the meeting on 19 March 1941; BAK, R49/2604.

63 Order no. 456 from the Ethnic German Liaison Office in Posen (signed by Doppler), 25 March 1941; BAK, R59/222, 39ff.

64 Order no. 459 from the Ethnic German Liaison Office in Posen (signed by Doppler), 25 March 1941; BAK, R59/222, 43.

65 Abbreviated minutes of the meeting of VDA directors in Posen on 6–7 April 1941; BAK, 59/28, 339ff.

66 Extensive correspondence on this project can be found in AGK, EWZ/L/838/1/2 passim; BAK, R69/554, passim; photographs of at least some of the exhibition panels can be found in BAK, Bild/100.

67 Report by Frank on a 90-minute meeting 'behind closed doors' with Hitler; Frank diary, 332, 335ff.; Eisenblätter, 201. On 27 March, Kulemann (DUT) had written to Greifelt that starting on 1 April, no more ethnic Germans would be resettled from the Generalgouvernement to the Warthegau (BAP, 17.02/215). This corresponds to the fact that Krüger, Higher SS and Police Chief in Krakow, was referred to as 'Representative of the Reich Commission for the Consolidation of German Nationhood (RKF)' for the first time in a letter of 18 April 1941 written by the RKF staff main office (BAK, R49/2605).

68 Comments by Frank on a corresponding statement by Göring, Frank diary, 336.

69 Edict issued by Göring, 18 February 1941, 'Re: Labour deployment and population, Volkstum, or racial politics', quoted in Maier, 87.

70 Report by Otmar von Verschuer on the founding of the institute, in Der Erbarzt 9 (1941), 91ff.

71 Peter-Heinz Seraphim, 'Bevölkerungs- und Wirtschaftsprobleme einer europäischen Gesamtlösung der Judenfrage', Weltkampf 1: 1–2 (1941), 45.

72 These sources can be found in Aly and Heim, 220.

73 Frank diary, 322ff.; on the function of the institute, see Heim and Aly, Berater.

74 Wilhelm Coblitz, 'Das Institut für Deutsche Ostarbeit in Krakau', Der Deutsche im Osten 4: 2 (1941), 90.

75 The title is verified in Helmut Meinhold, 'Die Erweiterung des Generalgouvernements nach Osten', A: Allgemeines, July 1941; BAK R52/IV/144a. A

footnote states, 'cf. the report on the resettlement of the Poles, Krakow, June 1941'.

76 Existence of the source is verified in *Die Burg* 3: 3 (1942), 357; listed as authors are Helmut Meinhold (IDO economics expert) and Anton Plügel (IDO *Volkstum* expert).

77 Helmut Meinhold, 'Die Erweiterung des Generalgouvernements nach Osten', July 1941, quoted in Aly and Heim, 251.

78 Josef Sommerfeldt, '200 Jahre Abwehrkampf gegen das Ostjudentum', *Deutsche Post aus dem Osten* 15: 2–3 (1943), 12, quoted in Volkmer. Sommerfeldt headed the IDO 'Section for Research on Race and *Volkstum*'.

79 Present at the meetings were, for the RSHA, Eichmann and Walter Jagusch (Section IVA5, Emigrant and Jewish Affairs) and, for the RKF, at least Schreiber (Main Department I, 'Human Deployment'). Dates, participants, and topics discussed are known only from Schreiber's statement of transportation expenses (statement of 11 November 1940 for reimbursement of transportation outlay; BAK, R49/2603). On Jagusch's later career as expert for Jewish affairs for the security police in *Ostland*, see Hilberg, 364.

80 However, 'the expected number of Jews to be evacuated' was supposed to be listed separately, since the deported Jews in the Generalgouvernement without a doubt received worse treatment than the deported (non-Jewish) Poles (telex from Krumey to Eichmann, 6 January 1941; AGK, Greiserprozeβ/36, 546ff.)

81 A large number of Jews from the administrative district of Zichenau (Ciechanów, East Prussia) were evidently supposed to be deported within the scope of the third short-term plan, to make room for either Lithuanian Germans or a military training ground. A report on such a deportation, from Płock-Mława to the Częstochowa ghetto, appears in Gilbert, *Holocaust*, 142ff; see also Gutman, *Encyclopedia*, 'Częstochowa' entry, 336–7; Benz and Golczewski, 432.

82 Letter from Lammers to von Schirach, quoted in Pätzold, 279; emphasis is my own. See Rosenkranz and Burrin. The latter correctly emphasizes (p. 87) that at that time the deportation plan had to be seen as an exception to the general rule of not deporting German and Austrian Jews during the war.

83 Frank diary, 328. Before this procedure was suggested, the participants at the meeting had mentioned other ways to 'accommodate the settlers', but these were rejected for a variety of reasons. On the slave labour camps for Jews in the district of Lublin, see, for example, the service certificate of SS Untersturmführer Langner, 20 January 1941; BDC, PA/Langner; Pohl, 81ff.; FGM, 213ff.

84 Frank diary, 311.

85 This plan was in line with expert reports by the IDO; see Helmut Meinhold, 'Die Eckpfeiler des Weichselverkehrs', *Deutsche Forschung im Osten* 1: 4 (1941), 18–27; 'Die Weichsel im europäischen Wasserstrassennetz', July 1941, MS; BAK, R52/IV/144a. Meinhold had already reported on this subject in late March; Heim and Aly, *Berater*, 43, note 6.

86 Since Heydrich referred to a total of 248,500 people in the first phase of the third short-term plan, the people to be relocated were evidently to be equally divided among the four districts of the Generalgouvernement.

87 Report by Waldemar Schön on the erection of the Warsaw ghetto, 20 January 1941; quoted in *Okkupationspolitik in Polen*, 194.

88 See documents nos. 20, 22, and 23 in FGM, 61ff.

89 *Krakauer Zeitung*, 20–21 March 1941.

90 Reitlinger, 50; Gilbert, *Atlas*, 53; Gilbert, *Holocaust*, 139ff.

91 Kaplan, 238–9, 251–2.

92 Wasser, 134.

93 Report by Schön 'on the erection of the Jewish quarter in Warsaw', 20 January 1941, quoted in Aly and Heim, 313.
94 Pohl, 83ff.; Frank diary, 343, 348, 360 (entries on 3 and 19 April 1941).
95 Kaplan, 249.
96 This is how Rudolf Gater described the procedure, quoted in Aly and Heim, 319.
97 Czerniaków diary, 226, 230, 233, 239.
98 See Aly and Heim, 326ff.
99 *Warschau unter deutscher Herrschaft. Deutsche Aufbauarbeit im Distrikt Warschau* (Krakow, 1942), 201.
100 'Die Wirtschaftsbilanz des jüdischen Wohnbezirks in Warschau', reprinted in Heim and Aly, *Struktur*, 106.
101 Benz and Moser, 69.
102 For details, see Rosenkranz, 255–62.
103 Note by Eppstein, 17 March 1941, quoted in Adler, 83; emphasis is my own.
104 BAK, R58/240, 89; Aly and Heim, 307ff.
105 Note by Höppner on 7 March 1941 about a meeting he led on 4 March in Posen with SS Obersturmbannführer Ernst Kendzia (director of the Labour Department in the Reichstatthalterei [regent's office] in Posen), Leopold von Funcke (Reich Labour Administration in Berlin), and Krumey. 'Re: Selection of Poles fit for work in Litzmannstadt'; AGK, UWZ/P/146, 26ff. (I would like to thank Dieter Maier for information about the positions held by those who participated in the meeting.)
106 See Aly and Heim, 309, 307.
107 Ibid. 303.
108 See ibid. 300–11. The report appears in Heim and Aly, *Struktur*, 39–73.
109 Today the office is called the Efficiency Committee for the German Economy (*Rationalisierungskuratorium der deutschen Wirtschaft*, RKW).
110 Quoted in Aly and Heim, 320. The report appears in Heim and Aly, *Struktur*, 74–138.
111 Quoted in Aly and Heim, 319.
112 Eichmann and representatives of the labour administration even thought of forcing Jews from Lodz to work within the territory of the Old Reich. This plan failed owing to Hitler's vehement objections on purely racist grounds. For details, see Maier, 89–95. However, although Hitler expressly prohibited the using of Jewish slave labourers in the Old Reich, existing camps in Lower Silesia for Jewish slave labourers from annexed eastern Upper Silesia were maintained, and in addition, new ones continued to be established. In the end, 52 such camps, albeit small ones, existed in the region between Breslau and Görlitz (Konieczny, 100ff.).
113 My statements can be researched more thoroughly. This would require a systematic examination of the politics of ghettoization and slave labour in the Generalgouvernement and the incorporated eastern territories. Open questions include when, where, and which Jewish communities were dissolved and their members sent to other ghettos; if, and if so how, deportees were selected according to the criterion of fitness for work; and who received their residences, workshops, and other property. Wolfgang Scheffler has correctly drawn attention to this gap in Holocaust research (see Scheffler, 'Ghettos').
114 Breitman's study represents an exception to this; in this context, see especially 151ff.
115 Note by Dannecker on the establishment of a 'Central Office for Jewish Matters' in France, 21 January 1941, quoted in Klarsfeld, 361ff.
116 Note of 21 March 1941, quoted in Adler, 152ff.

117 Halder war diary, vol. II, 328; Krausnick, *Einsatzgruppen*, 116; Jacobsen, 512–21.
118 The 'authorization' for this was issued by Hitler in late February (war diary-WiRüAmt/Stab, entry on 26 February 1941; BA-MA, RW19/164, 180).
119 Memo by Heydrich on 'today's presentation to the Reich Marshal', 26 March 1941; ZASM, 500/3/795.
120 IMG, vol. 26, 11ff.
121 On the roles played by the persons named here and their later production of legends and lies, see Krausnick, *Einsatzgruppen*.
122 He did not officially assume this position until Hitler signed the decree on the 'administration of the newly occupied eastern territories' on 17 July 1941. It is generally assumed that Rosenberg was unofficially named by Hitler on 2 April 1941 (Dallin, 24ff., 51ff.); in fact, however, as Heydrich's memo suggests, he was verbally named at an even earlier date.
123 See Chapter 6, entry of 8 January 1941, p. 138.
124 The invasion was scheduled for 15 May 1941. 'In order to conceal the intention to attack', the final phase of the advance was to begin as late as possible, on 24 April according to the original plan, and was to be completed by 15 May (Kreidler, 117ff.).
125 Minutes of the meeting between Hitler and Slavko Kvaternik, head of the Independent State of Croatia, on 22 July 1941; ADAP, series D, vol. 13, appendix III, 838.
126 Burrin, 129.
127 Secret address by Heydrich, 4 February 1942 in Prague, quoted in Kárný and Milotová, 220. Heydrich mentioned this subject while explaining to his audience – 'off the record' – that in the best case, the non-Germanizable Czechs could be used for 'pro-German jobs such as guards, foremen, etc.'. Since Heydrich used third-party information with respect to the 'concentrated, good agriculture' in the freezing Polar Sea region (including the White Sea), it could be that a study on Siberia that was prepared in July 1941 by the RSHA's Wannsee Institute had been commissioned within the context of these deportation plans. This cited passage appears there (Wannsee Institute: Siberia, July 1941; BA-MA, RW19/Anh. I/1551, 23f. See Roth, *Gesamtplan*, 38; however, the document does not corroborate the far-reaching conclusions reached by the author).
128 Testimony by Bühler, 23 April 1946, quoted in Pätzold and Schwarz, 131, 135.
129 Quoted in Aly and Heim, 215f. Föhl was deputy director of the Population and Welfare department in the Generalgouvernement at the time. On this department in the Internal Affairs Administration of the Generalgouvernement, see Aly and Heim, 207–16.
130 Gilbert, *Holocaust*, 307.
131 'Die Pripjetsümpfe als Entwässerungsproblem', *Zeitschrift für Geopolitik* 18 (1941), 667ff.
132 'Pripet-Polesien, Land und Leute', ibid. 19 (1942), 278–87; on such plans, see also Wilhelm, *Rassenpolitik*, 25.
133 Letter from Frank to Lammers, 19 July 1941; BAK, R6/21, 136ff.
134 Ibid. 138ff.
135 Memorandum ('The Generalgouvernement and the border along the Bug') of the Reich Office for Regional Planning, 22 June 1941; ibid. 150ff.
136 Commissioned by the Planning Department of the RKF, the Reich Office for Regional Planning had already drawn up district plans for the settlement zones in the incorporated eastern territories; that project took five months (Müller, 94).
137 Quoted in Wilhelm, 628; see also Bauer, 170ff.

138 Meinhold, 'Erweiterung'; see note 77, this chapter.

139 Monologe, 74. Later, after the Jews had already been murdered, drainage of the marshes was once again considered. Instead of a biotope in need of preservation, it was regarded as a main partisan base – 'a constant element of political uncertainty'. The mere thought of the area made the German generals nervous. Thus it is understandable why Friedrich Trampedach, head of the Policy Department in the administration of the Reichkommissariat of *Ostland* (the Baltic states), and regional planner Gottfried Müller offered the following suggestion in November 1942 – after the battle of Stalingrad had begun: the 'deployment' of people who were very knowledgeable in hydro-technics and considered part of an 'active and reliable nation [*Volkstum*]', i.e., a million Dutchmen at the southern periphery of their 'planning territory', in the Pripet marshes (Seckendorf, 180, 196).

140 In a recent work, Zámecník has drawn similar conclusions. He summarizes:

> Sources confirm that the Holocaust was preceded by the intention to deport European Jewry to the territory of the conquered USSR. In summer 1941, Hitler had not yet ordered the final solution, though he promised it in connection with the expected lightning victory in the East. Deportation to the northern territories of the USSR would have been the simplest form of genocide. Under the murderous working and climatic conditions, the Jews would have died en masse, just like the millions who were deported under Bolshevik rule. None of the deportees were supposed to survive.
>
> (p. 94)

This, too, could be researched in greater detail. It is possible to determine which Jewish deportations and slave labour projects were planned and possibly even implemented in a rudimentary form right at the beginning of the campaign against Russia. In this context, the activities of *Einsatzgruppe z. b. V (the Einsatzgruppe* for special use), for example, should be examined more closely. It was formed within the first few months of the war against the Soviet Union, led by Eberhard Schöngarth, commander of the security police and the SD in the Generalgouvernement, and was active in the 'occupied peripheral areas,' i.e., in the part of 'Poland formerly belonging to Russia'. Members of the *Einsatzgruppe* executed several tens of thousands of people, especially Jews, within a short period of time (see Krausnick, *Einsatzgruppen*, 157, 320; Wilhelm, *Rassenpolitik*, 175ff.).

# 8

# War of extermination and Lebensraum

## Chronology: 1 May–31 July 1941

**1 May 1941:** Herbert Backe, state secretary in the Ministry of Food and Agriculture, informs Goebbels that the weekly meat ration for the so-called normal German consumer must be reduced from 500 to 400 grams.[1] The reduction is to begin on 2 June.

**2 May:** Discussion between Göring's two state secretaries, Paul Körner and Erich Neumann, Backe and Thomas on the economic goals of the war against the Soviet Union. They conclude, 'Without a doubt, umpteen million people would starve if we take what we need out of the country.'[2]

**6 May:** Goebbels notes, 'Backe lays out the food supply situation. . . . If only the harvest this year is good. And then we'll line our pockets in the East.'[3]

**9 May:** Gauleiter Greiser inspects the Lodz ghetto.[4]

The RKF settlement planners are concerned with 'Eastern settlement' in the period following victory over the Soviet Union; with Himmler's agreement, they prepare to bring in Dutch and Flemish tradesmen and businesspeople – rare occupations among Germans – who will 'form a desirable counterweight to the unavoidable taking in of Slavic workers'. In this way, the population economists at the RKF hope at the same time to reduce 'overpopulation' in Holland and Flanders.[5] (In October 1941, the RKF will determine that 'gaining more space in the East' would facilitate concrete 'preparation for the settlement of Dutch and Flemish people in the East'.[6])

**14 May:** Initial preparations for resettlement of 60,000 to 70,000 ethnic Germans from occupied France in Alsace and Lorraine.[7]

The same day, Claussen, of the Reich Ministry of Food and Agriculture, explains, 'The Ukraine, the breadbasket of Russia, harvests 40 million tons of grain annually, that is, 40 per cent of the total Russian harvest. . . . The

Ukrainian population itself could survive on 10 to 15 million tons of grain, so that this land represents an area of great surplus.'[8]

**15 May:** Greifelt, head of the RKF staff main office, once again refuses to resettle 1500 Bulgarian Germans, as 'it is only possible to house them in camps'. He advises that representatives of that ethnic group be 'informed with emphasis that they must plan to remain in Bulgaria for an additional one to two years'.[9]

Conclusion of the German–Croatian border agreement for the annexation of 'Lower Styria' (that is, northern Slovenia) to Germany.[10]

**20 May:** The Reich Security Main Office stipulates that the emigration of Jews from France and Belgium must be prevented 'in view of the definitely imminent final solution of the Jewish question'.[11]

**23 May:** Regarding future occupation policy in the Soviet Union, the economic policy guidelines for the Economic Organization in the East/ Agricultural Group state, 'Many tens of millions of people will become superfluous in this region and will die or have to emigrate to Siberia.' Attempts 'to save the population there from death by starvation' and feed them with grain from the Ukraine 'neutralize Germany's staying power in the war'.[12]

Göring later explains the consequences of these guidelines as follows: 'This year, 20 to 30 million people in Russia will starve. Perhaps this is a good thing, as certain peoples must be decimated.'[13]

The same day, Himmler orders that Kočevje (Gottschee) Germans living in the Italian-annexed parts of Slovenia be resettled as a group, without any racial selection, to 'Lower Styria' (northern Slovenia). The reason for refraining from 'racial screening' in this way is that, due to lack of housing and real estate, so-called 'Old Reich cases' can be neither accommodated nor compensated.[14] Contrary to Himmler's original intention, the RSHA then does in fact insist on a selection of the settlers.[15]

On 31 August, the German and Italian governments conclude a treaty for the resettlement of the Kočevje Germans. The resettlement takes place from November 1941 to February 1942 and involves a total of 13,500 people.[16]

On 6 April, the date of the German attack on Yugoslavia and Greece, the RKF and Security Police had already formed a resettlement staff for removal of the Slovenian minority from heretofore German and Austrian Lower Styria. On 16 April, this is followed by the establishment of a corresponding resettlement staff for the areas of northern Yugoslavia annexed by Germany.[17] Some 220,000 to 260,000 Slovenes are to be relocated in three 'waves'.[18] By the end of 1942, the following result is achieved: 'The property of 17,000 anti-German Slovenes was confiscated and they were evacuated to rump Serbia; 37,000 Slovenian and Wind border residents were brought to the Old Reich, some as people suitable for Germanization (11,000), some as ethnic alien labourers.'[19]

**27 May:** In the United States, Roosevelt announces a full-scale national emergency. He thus incontrovertibly sets the economic stage for the United States' later entry into the war.[20]

**29 May:** Hitler issues regulations 'on the utilization of the appropriated assets of enemies of the Reich', which establish, with an eye towards the later deportation of the Jews, that confiscated property will largely be 'transferred free of charge' to local authorities.[21]

**6 June 1941:** The Supreme Command of the army conveys the 'commissar order' to the units designated for action in the war against the Soviet Union.[22] According to the order,

> In the struggle against Bolshevism, the enemy *cannot* be expected to behave according to the principles of humanity and international law. In particular, we can expect from the *political commissars of all types* – as actual bearers of resistance – hate-filled, cruel and in-human treatment of our prisoners. . . . The initiators of barbaric, Asiatic methods of battle are the political commissars. . . . When captured in *battle* or *resistance*, therefore, they are to be shot at once.[23]

Himmler inspects the Lodz ghetto and views the tailor shop there.[24] At the same time, he is informed about the 'reconstruction' and 'redevelopment of the city of Litzmannstadt'. Himmler orders that 'the scheduled planning be carried out' and the necessary 'freedom of action' ensured. Greiser uses this to formulate the following edict:

> The basic principle behind the renovation and reconstruction of the city of Litzmannstadt must be generosity in the distribution of the accrued Jewish and Polish property. Bureaucratic and accounting objections must not place any obstacles in the path of the planned project. I request that all participating offices be fully and completely faithful to these principles of the Reich Commissioner for the Consolidation of German Nationhood.[25]

**Early June:** Within the scope of the so-called 'remaining resettlement from Romania', a further 8000–10,000 ethnic Germans are to be transported out. Because the project is halted on 15 June in the face of new plans for the eastern territory, only 4532 people are brought by boat to Vienna via the Danube.[26]

**9 June:** A new murder operation begins in the psychiatric hospitals in the incorporated eastern territories. On this date, 58 men and women are deported from the Gostynin hospital and killed by the Lange Special Commando Unit, using gas vans. The same fate is suffered on 16 June by 82 patients from the Warta institution. During July, they are followed by 150 patients in the Kochanówska facility and 158 from the Tiegenhof hospital near Gniezno. On 29 July, approximately 55 patients in the psychiatric hospital of the Jewish community in Lodz are murdered, after a commission from the Race and Settlement Department had made inquiries about the hospital in Lodz on 8 July.[27] On 22 July, the transport division of T-4 sends 171 men and 339 women from the West Prussian hospital of Konradstein (Kocborowo) to the gas chamber in Pirna ('Sonnenstein').[28]

**14 June:** A conference is held in Warsaw on experiences with the slave labour camps created for Jews in March and April. The same month, the camps are dismantled due to their inefficiency.[29]

**16 June:** The Reich Ministry of the Interior announces that Jews in the annexed eastern territories will 'soon [become] stateless'.[30]

**17 June:** Heydrich orders the instigation of pogroms by the *Einsatzgruppen* standing by for the occupation of the Soviet Union. This is followed by the assignment that they liquidate all Jews in party and government offices, as well as other 'radical elements'.[31]

**18 June:** The *autobahn* administration desires 'the urgent replacement' of 500 Jews working on construction sites in the Warthegau: 'The Jews were assigned to us from the ghetto in Litzmannstadt, but most are ill and threaten to spread epidemics. Replacement by Poles is sought.'[32] (In late December 1940, '1300 Jews and Jewesses' were still working on construction of the *autobahn* from Frankfurt an der Oder to Posen. They lived in barracks camps, and the ghetto received – at least theoretically – 80 per cent of their wages, 'made available for Jews remaining behind'.[33])

**19 June:** Hitler assures Frank that 'the Jews [will be] removed from the Generalgouvernement in the foreseeable future', and the Generalgouvernement would then 'be merely a transit camp, as it were'.[34]

**20 June:** Frank reports to Goebbels that the Generalgouvernement is already looking forward to the fact that 'they can deport the Jews. Jewry in Poland is gradually degenerating.'[35] To his closest colleagues, Rosenberg explains, 'We do not accept the responsibility of helping feed the Russian people from the (south Russian) areas of surplus production. We know that this is a harsh necessity, lying beyond of any emotion.'[36]

**Mid-June:** The Institute for German Activities in the East completes an expert report on the subject, 'Relocation of the Poles'.[37]

**21 June:** Himmler formally instructs the planning division of the RKF to draw up a 'General Plan for the East'. It should include an outline of settlement policies in the parts of Eastern Europe that are already occupied or whose conquest is imminent.[38]

**22 June:** Start of the war against the Soviet Union.

**28 June:** Goebbels notes, 'Supply situation in Berlin is very poor. . . . The situation is even worse in the occupied territories. In some places there is actual famine.'[39]

**June:** Because there have been plans to Germanize the Generalgouvernement since March 1941, Frank orders that no further resettlements be authorized for ethnic Germans wishing to emigrate from the Generalgouvernement to the Reich.[40]

**1 July 1941:** Goebbels notes,

> Yesterday: Incoming planes to [i.e., British bombardments of] Hamburg, Bremen, Kiel. This time with some success. We are not doing much in England. Eastern front: . . . Things in general look good; however, the Russians are offering more resistance than at first expected. . . . Jewish question in Berlin pursued further. There is still much to do and so much to pay attention to.[41]

**2 July:** Goebbels:

> No incoming planes in the East, 120 in the West, with some success. But the feared major English attack has not occurred as yet. But what has happened so far is plenty. In Cologne, slight drop in mood, which comes from constant sleep deprivation.[42]

**3 July:** Franz Halder, chief of the general staff of the army, states, 'It is thus probably not saying too much if I maintain that the campaign against Russia was won in fourteen days.'[43]

**8 July:** In a discussion of the military situation, Hitler emphasizes his 'fundamental' intention of 'levelling' Leningrad and Moscow, in order to prevent people from remaining there 'whom we would then have to feed through the winter'. The aim is to cause a 'national disaster' that would 'rob not only Bolshevism, but also Muscovitedom [*Moskowitertum*], of their centres'.[44]

**14 July:** The Economic Command Staff East demands 'rapid ghettoization' of Jews in the newly occupied parts of the Soviet Union, so that 'reliable non-Jews have a chance'.[45]

**15 July:** Meyer, director of planning for the RKF, presents the General Plan for the East that had been requested three weeks earlier.[46] The plan is discussed and augmented in the coming weeks and months; soon it provides for the resettlement of at least 31 million people. Himmler says in June 1942:

> There would be no point to the war if, after the war . . ., Bohemia and Moravia, the eastern German Gaus, southeastern Prussia, Danzig–West Prussia, Warthegau, Upper Silesia, the Generalgouvernement, Ostland [i.e., the Baltic states], the Crimea, and Ingermanland [i.e., the region around St Petersburg] were not completely settled by Germans in twenty years. . . . If we do not make the bricks here, if we do not fill our camps full of slaves – in this room I am speaking very clearly and very plainly – full of slave labourers who build our cities, our villages, our farms without regard to losses, then we will not have the money, not even after years of war, to equip the settlements such that real Germanic people can live there and put down roots in the first generation.[47]

**16 July:** Meeting between Hitler, Rosenberg, Lammers, Keitel, Göring, and Bormann. It is decided that (Eastern) Galicia should be added to the Generalgouvernement. Göring emphasizes the urgency of 'ensuring our food supply'. Hitler declares, 'The motives before the world for our steps must be guided by tactical considerations. All necessary measures – execution, deportation, etc. – shall be taken nevertheless and can be taken nevertheless.' In addition to other areas of settlement, the Crimea has to be 'cleared of all aliens and settled with Germans'.[48]

The same day, Höppner, head of the Central Resettlement Office in Posen, reports to his superior, Eichmann, that in view of the scarcity of food to be expected in the coming winter, the officials dealing with the Jewish question in the Warthegau had considered 'finish[ing] off the Jews unfit for labour through some fast-acting means'.

**17 July:** Frank declares that 'he desires no further creation of ghettos [in the Generalgouvernement], since according to the Führer's express declaration on 19 June of this year the Jews would be removed from the Generalgouvernement within the foreseeable future'.[49]

On the basis of an agreement with the Wehrmacht, Heyrich stipulates that active Communists, members of the Soviet intelligentsia, and 'all Jews' are to be taken from the camps for Soviet prisoners of war and executed.[50] By early 1942, some 140,000 prisoners of war will have been murdered on these grounds.

**19 July:** Lammers informs Frank by telephone that Eastern Galicia is being made part of the Generalgouvernement.[51]

**20 July:** During his second visit to Lublin, Himmler orders the establishment of an SS and police district in the city and the creation of an immense concentration camp, and discusses ideas for the rapid Germanization of the region with Globocnik.[52]

**21 July:** A staff member of the RKF writes to Himmler's personal staff:

> On the occasion of his last inspection tour of the Wartheland Reichsgau, the Reichsführer SS apparently placed $1\frac{1}{2}$ million Reichsmarks at the disposal of Gauleiter Greiser for special purposes. It has not yet been possible to obtain confirmation of this directive. We most humbly request instructions as to whether this sum may be paid out.[53]

(I have been unable to determine the purpose for which Himmler promised this sum. I note the fact for the sake of later research. In any case, this much may be stated: the fact that the amount in question was to be paid to Greiser by the RKF indicates a connection to resettlement policy, and the phrase 'special purposes' permits the assumption that it was not harmless.)

**22 July:** Hitler rejects Frank's suggestion for expanding the Generalgouvernement by adding the Pripet marshes.[54] As has been his way previously in a number of border decisions, Hitler does not make a final decision: 'The possibility has been reserved', Frank writes on 22 July 1941, 'that additional zones could go to the Generalgouvernement.' At the same time, the Führer's Chancellery confirms the fact that 'Jews and other asocial elements will soon be [deported] to the East.'[55]

**28 July:** Krumey, head of the Central Resettlement Office in Lodz, notes on the resettlement situation:

> The third short-term plan, which took effect in February 1941, was interrupted by the events in the East at the behest of the OKW on 15 March 1941, after the nineteenth transport. At the order of the Reichsführer SS, however, the settlers from Bessarabia and Buchenland [Bukovina] housed in the Vomi camps must be settled this year, to avoid further harm. To carry out this order, the UWZ camps were occupied by up to 5000 Poles at the instructions of the Higher SS and Police Chief, SS Gruppenführer Koppe. The responsible offices could not yet give even an approximate date when the

transport ban will be lifted and the trains to the Generalgouvernement can be resumed.[56]

**31 July:** Meeting between General Thomas of the Armament Economy
Office and Göring's state secretary Körner (of the office of the Four-Year
Plan) on 'organizational questions in Russia'. They conclude, 'quarter
Jews in barracks and utilize them in the form of work brigades'.[57] In a
meeting of the Economic Command Staff East the same day, Backe repeats
that 'only very small amounts [of food] are available' to feed the urban
population of the USSR.[58]

Göring instructs Heydrich in writing to prepare 'a comprehensive solution to the Jewish question in the German sphere of influence in Europe',
and to 'supply it with the most favourable solution that time permits, in
the form of emigration or evacuation'.[59]

# Notes

1  Goebbels diaries, vol. I/4, 617.
2  IMG, vol. 31, 84.
3  Goebbels diaries, vol. I/4, 625ff.
4  *Chronicle*, 52.
5  Draft RKF report 'on preliminary work to gain Dutch and Flemish settlers for
   the new eastern territories', 9 May 1941; BAK, R49/2605.
6  Letter from Stier, on 17 October 1941; BAK, R49/2607. In November, the first
   Dutch 'pioneers' arrived in Posen; see 'Siedlung für holländische Handwerker',
   *Ostdeutscher Beobachter*, 1 November 1941; 'Bauernwacht im Osten. Die
   Niederländer sind die ersten Pioniere', *Deutsche Zeitung in den Niederlanden*,
   5 December 1941. See Bosma, 200ff.
7  Note by Kulemann; BAP, 17.02/202.
8  Note by Eicke (WiRüAmt) on a discussion with ministerial official Claussen
   (Reich Ministry of Food and Agriculture), 14 May 1941; BA-MA, RW19/473,
   178.
9  Letter from Greifelt to the Vomi, 15 May 1941, BAK, R49/2605. In November
   1941, the first 423 'economically deprived' Bulgarian Germans were transported to the Reich. The compensation question was not posed for them.
   They were brought to the Reich *de facto* as workers and soldiers. Himmler
   thereupon decreed, 'the remainder are also to be resettled'. (Draft of directive
   on 'partial settlement of Bulgaria,' 23 December 1941; BAK, R49/2607. Letter
   from R. Brandt to W. Lorenz, 4 April 1942; BDC, 'Um- und Aussiedlung'
   [Resettlement and Removal] file, 17.)
10 Hillgruber and Hümmelchen, 72.
11 Quoted in Adler, 29.
12 IMG, vol. 36, 135–57. The guidelines had, as they said, 'received the approval
   of the highest offices'. At the time, the German leadership assumed that 30
   million Russians would starve in the coming winter if they succeeded in cutting
   the Ukraine off militarily from the industrialized north of the Soviet Union.
   Herbert Backe, undersecretary in the Reich Ministry of Food and Agriculture,
   presented this plan to Hitler verbally at the end of January. He opposed the
   comparatively moderate ideas of General Thomas, head of the Armament

Economy Office. In February, Thomas had written a memorandum on the 'impact of an operation in the east on the military economy', in which he predicted that he would only require two and a half to three million tons of grain for the Soviet Union. (KTB-WiRüAmt/Stab, BA-MA, RW19/164, 235, ibid./189, 226; Aly and Heim, 'Herrschaft', 93; Müller, 'Ausbeutungskrieg', 113ff.; Müller, *Wirtschaftspolitik*, 387–401.)

13 Göring on 25 November 1941 in discussion with the Italian Foreign Minister Galeazzo Ciano, quoted in Madajczyk, 92. This concept had been common among the German leadership and its agricultural experts since May 1941. (See Aly and Heim, 365ff.)

14 Letter to the head of the RSHA, Hofmann, 28 May 1941 (signature illegible); letter from Hofmann to Litzmannstadt EWZ, 23 May 1941; AGK, EWZ/L/838/79, 1ff. The 'Old Reich cases' ('Altreich', thus 'A cases', in contrast to 'E[ast] cases') were those ethnic Germans who were considered unworthy of settlement in the east due to age, unfitness for work, or 'genetic or political handicap'.

15 Report 'on treatment of A cases' within the scope of the 'Gottschee [Kočevje] resettlement', n.d.; AGK, EWZ/L/838/80, vol. 2, 1–38.

16 BAK, R59/233, 19; Wehler, 73ff.

17 *Okkupationspolitik, Südosteuropa*, 139.

18 Ibid. 171.

19 RKF activity report (status at end of 1942); BAK, R49/26, 34; Wehler, 69.

20 This US step placed Hitler and the Wehrmacht leadership – whose strategic planning was already cutting it close in terms of time owing to limited resources – under even greater pressure to actually win the campaign against the Soviet Union, which was designed as a blitzkrieg, within a few weeks. See Hillgruber, *Strategie*, 398ff.

21 RGBl. I (1941), 303. In 1943, Bormann made the decree more precise: 'Recently, the Führer has repeatedly emphasized that the economic strength of the Reichsgaus is to be increased through allocation of their own assets to fulfil their cultural and other tasks. It is his will, therefore, that appropriated assets of enemies of the state flow in large quantity to the self-administrating bodies' (letter from Bormann to the Reich Minister of Finance, 3 June 1941; BAK, R2/032109).

22 On the background, see Jacobsen, *passim*; Krausnick, *Einsatzgruppen*, 97ff.; Streit, 44ff.

23 Quoted in Streit, 48, emphasis in original.

24 *Chronicle*, 59.

25 Decree by Greiser on 'the restructuring of the city of Litzmannstadt', 20 June 1941, quoted in Gutschow, 252.

26 This figure comes from a statement by the Waterways Commission (*Wasserstrassen-Direktion*) Vienna, 31 July 1941; BAK, R5/817.

27 *Chronicle*, 63ff.

28 The dates mentioned and the respective number of murder victims are found in the sections on specific institutions in Zagłada. On the hospital in the Lodz ghetto, see also *Chronicle*, 67ff.

29 Berenstein, 170.

30 Express letter from Reich Minister of the Interior to the high Reich offices, 16 June 1941, 'Re: citizenship in the incorporated eastern territories', quoted in Pätzold, 289ff.

31 Streim, 117.

32 Activity report by the UWZ office in Grätz, quoted in a letter from the Posen UWZ, 24 July 1941; AGK, UWZ/P/146, 70.

33 Report from Reich Auditing Office on the Lodz ghetto, February 1941, quoted in Heim and Aly, *Struktur*, 56.

34 Frank diary, 386.
35 Goebbels diaries, vol. I/4, 705.
36 Nbg. Docs., PS-1058.
37 See Chapter 7, p. 162.
38 Müller, 96. As a reminder, the planning department had already determined in November 1940 that the incorporated parts of Poland and the General-gouvernement were not enough to accommodate all German settlers. See Chapter 7, p. 150.
39 Goebbels diaries, vol. I/4, 721.
40 Quoted in Greifelt's decree (no. 37/I), 2 July 1941; PAA, R/100630, 48ff.
41 Goebbels diaries, Reuth, 1615ff.
42 Goebbels diaries, Reuth, 1620.
43 Halder war diary, vol. 3, quoted in Goebbels diaries, Reuth, 1638 (note).
44 OKW war diaries, vol. 1, 1021.
45 Assessment of the situation in key words; BA-MA, RW/31/11, 49f.
46 Müller, 96; Aly and Heim, 408ff.
47 Speech by Himmler to senior department heads and headquarters chiefs, 9 June 1942; Himmler, *Geheimreden*, 158f. On the discussion of various planning variants in the period 1941–42, see Roth, 'Gesamtplan', 41ff.
48 Note by Bormann on the meeting on 16 July 1941, IMG, vol. 38, 86ff.
49 Frank diary, 386.
50 Quoted in Pätzold, 296ff.
51 Letter from Frank to Karlernst Lasch, 26 July 1941; StA Lviv, R-35/2/12, 5b.
52 Note by Himmler on the orders he gave in Lublin, 21 July 1941; BDC, SL/54. See Pohl, 95ff.
53 Letter from RKF – I/21.7.41/Sch/Hy – to the Reichsführer SS/Personal staff, 21 July 1941; BAK, R49/2606.
54 Frank diary, 389.
55 Frank diary; BAK, R52/II/184.
56 Note by Krumey, 28 July 1941; AGK, UWZ/P/146, 71f.
57 Note on discussion; BA-MA, RW/12/189.
58 Note on discussion; BA-MA, RW/31/11, 104ff.
59 IMG, vol. 26, 11ff.

# 9

# *Frustrated expectations of victory*

## Jews in Europe and Northern Africa

Within only 19 months – between September 1939 and March 1941 – Heydrich had formulated four increasingly broad deportation plans, paralleling the increasingly expansive military goals. First, in autumn 1939, came the project known as 'Generalgouvernement–Jewish Reservation of Lublin', which Heydrich changed in June 1940 to the as yet indefinite demand for a 'territorial final solution'. Up to this point, his intention had been to deport the German, Austrian, Czech, and Polish Jews. The Madagascar Plan followed in July–August 1940; it included all Jews in the countries occupied so far by Germany, as well as those in the dependent states of Slovakia and Vichy France – approximately 4 million people. This plan was replaced in late autumn 1940 by the project with which the RSHA intended to deport 5.8 million Jews. I was unable to find a document in which this overall figure was broken down into individual countries. Because it included 1.8 million more Jews than the Madagascar Plan, and no new war had been fought in the interim, my assumption is that nearly all European Jews living west of the German–Soviet demarcation line were supposed to be victims of this deportation project – not only those in the occupied and directly dependent countries, but all those living within the 'economic sphere of the German *Volk*', a concept which Eichmann used here for the first time.

That is why the project must have been developed before December 1940, at a time when the idea of a wider European economic sphere had taken on concrete form, but a rapid defeat of Britain had already been ruled out. Hitler had not yet decided in favour of war against the Soviet Union, much as he was already considering it. However, in late October, he and the German naval command were planning, albeit hesitantly, for 'Operation Felix'; this was 'a German intervention on the Iberian peninsula', the goal of which was the conquest of Gibraltar to gain some military leeway in the Mediterranean, which was largely dominated by the British fleet. Vichy France was to be a passive participant. Thus I would date the genesis of the plan drawn up by Eichmann on 4 December 1940 for the deportation of 5.8 million Jews to early November.[1] The vague announcement that the 'relocation of the Jews' would take place 'to a territory yet to be determined' corresponded to the crisis into which Hillgruber admitted 'Hitler's overall strategic concept had fallen' by October and November.[2]

The figures provided for France in the minutes of the Wannsee Conference are especially perplexing. Almost 600,000 more Jews were listed there than in the Madagascar Plan. Apropos of this, the *Frankfurter Zeitung* daily of 4 December 1941 reported that the Jews 'in France's possessions in Northern Africa' were also subject to the new law forcing all French Jews to become members of the 'Federation of Jews in France'. The report contained the following figures: 165,000 Jews in the occupied part of France, 170,000 in the unoccupied part, 160,000 in Morocco, 150,000 in Algeria, and 50,000 in Tunisia – a total of 695,000.[3] I suspect that the Jews of Algeria, Morocco, and Tunisia were already included in deportation planning in November 1940. This belief arises, first of all, from an attempt to break down the figure of 5.8 million by countries and, second, from an awareness of the existence of an obvious connection between military planning and the options for racial policy. Thus it may be assumed that the 'Felix' undertaking – which was first laid to rest in favour of 'The Move Eastward', but remained an element of strategic planning – also affected the scope of the planned deportation of the Jews.

The strategists of Jewish policy developed their project on 'evacuation to the East' in winter 1940–41, when concrete preparations for Operation Barbarossa had eliminated the German–Soviet demarcation line from the mental map of the German military. The project encompassed all the European Jews – more than 11 million people.[4] From the beginning, the plan aimed not at the marginalization of a persecuted minority on the periphery of the empire, but at biological extermination. The geographically clearly limited goal that had still characterized the Madagascar Plan was replaced by a less geographically well-defined concept, in which only deportation itself remained concrete: it was to take place in an easterly direction, and was both means and ends.

In autumn 1941, on the basis of their last resettlement plan, the participants formulated the 'final solution' in the same form in which it was implemented as the systematic murder of millions in the occupied areas of the Soviet Union and in the extermination camps. The execution of all able-bodied Jewish men in the Soviet Union, in the spirit of rooting out the 'Jewish–Bolshevik enemy', was thus considered part of the fighting itself in the 'war of worldviews'. It paved the way, as had the 'euthanasia' murders, for systematic extermination, although, like those killings, it was not from

**Table 2** Jews in Europe and North Africa

| | 'Territorial Solution', June 1940 | Madagascar Plan, August 1940 | Continental Block concept, Nov. 1940 | 'European Final Solution', June 1941 |
|---|---|---|---|---|
| Rounded-off figure for each: | 3,250,000 | 4,000,00 | 5,800,000 | 11,000,000 |
| Specific figures: | | | | |
| Reich and Protectorate | 320,000 | 320,000 | 315,000[5] | 249,700 |
| Incorporated eastern territories | 500,000 | 500,000 | 500,000 | 420,000 |
| Generalgouvernement | 2,300,000 | 2,300,000 | 2,300,000 | 2,284,000 |
| Total: | 3,120,000 | | | |
| Slovakia | | 95,000 | 95,000 | 89,000[6] |
| France | | 270,000 | [!] 800,000 | 865,000[7] |
| Luxembourg | | 2,500 | 2,500 | 0 |
| Belgium | | 80,000 | 80,000 | 43,000 |
| Netherlands | | 160,000 | 160,000 | 160,800[8] |
| Denmark | | 7,000 | 7,000 | 5,600 |
| Norway | | 1,500 | 1,500 | 1,300 |
| Total: | | 3,735,500 | | |
| Hungary | | | 742,800 | 742,800 |
| Romania | | | 300,000 | 342,000 |
| Bulgaria | | | 48,000 | 48,000 |
| Greece | | | 69,600 | 69,000 |
| Yugoslavia | | | 75,000 | 50,000 |
| Albania | | | 200 | 200 |
| Italy | | | 58,000 | 58,000 |
| Spain | | | 6,000 | 6,000 |
| Portugal | | | 3,000 | 3,000 |
| Total: | | | 5,563,600 | |
| Switzerland | | | | 18,000 |
| Sweden | | | | 8,000 |
| Finland | | | | 2,300 |
| Ireland | | | | 4,000 |
| Turkey (European part) | | | | 55,500 |
| Britain | | | | 330,000 |
| Latvia, Lithuania, the European part of the parts of eastern Poland formerly annexed by the Soviet Union (excluding Eastern Galicia)[9] | | | | 5,480,500 |
| Total: | | | | 11,335,700 |

the beginning an intentional element of a 'strategy' of murder of the European Jews.

The minutes of the Wannsee Conference contain an appendix with some statistics. These include figures on Jews in various countries which were extrapolated from previous projects, but also meticulously updated: several hundred thousand people who had been deported or murdered by *Einsatzgruppen* commandos by the time the conference took place were indirectly acknowledged, in that they had already been subtracted from the older initial figures. Even though Eichmann's precise calculations cannot always be entirely reconstructed,[10] as shown in Table 2, the statistical picture emerges for the four successive deportation projects.

These figures are taken essentially from the Madagascar Plan and the records of the Wannsee Conference. Individual differences arise from changes in borders and from the deportations and murders of Jews from various countries that occurred in the interim. This is true for the General-gouvernement only to a limited extent. Eastern Galicia had already been added to it in summer 1941, and several tens of thousands of Jews had already been shot there by the date of the conference; nevertheless, some 350,000 additional Jews should have gone into Eichmann's statistical accounting. The opposite in fact occurred: Eichmann subtracted those who had died so far in the ghettos and camps; in addition, as in other statistics, he probably calculated the 'natural death surplus' arising from the massive reduction in births; and finally, now that the German author-ities had frequently ghettoized the Jews of the Generalgouvernement and subjected them to numerous censuses, he revised the overestimated figures of summer 1940.

# Heydrich's assignment

The statistical appendix to the minutes of the Wannsee Conference raises additional questions. Specifically, it documents the fact that not only were the Jews of French North Africa to be deported 'to the East', but also those of Great Britain, Ireland, and the European part of Turkey. In face of the military losses, by 20 January 1942 such deportation plans were no longer being given serious consideration. Rather, at bottom the statistics corresponded precisely with the Wehrmacht leadership's June 1941 strategic blueprints, which are barely comprehensible now, in hindsight; the statistics had probably already been drafted at this point in time, and were later corrected only for countries in which the 'Final Solution' had already begun. At the time, Hitler and a considerable number of German generals quite seriously believed that they would be able to bring the war with the Soviet Union to a victorious conclusion within eight weeks. German forces were expected to conquer the 'European–West African base position against the

English–American coalition' by the autumn, for the military 'cleansing of the Mediterranean'.[11]

According to Hillgruber, the following was also planned:

> As the last step in the battle against Great Britain, the Army chief of staff and the general staff of the army [on 4 and 11 June 1941] considered a landing on the British Isles. However, this was to be merely the *coup de grâce* against an already-crumbling British empire. . . . The return of surplus infantry divisions [from the Soviet Union] was already to begin in early August, according to lecture notes of the operations division on 15 July. In early September, the withdrawal of armoured and motorized divisions above a set number was to begin to Germany or to the planned zones of deployment for the [intended] operations through Turkey to Syria and from south-western France through Spain to northwestern Africa.[12]

Hillgruber continues that Hitler and his general staff assumed at the beginning of the campaign 'that the majority of the German army and air force would already be fully available for new tasks by late autumn of 1941'.[13]

This scenario could have been the original basis for the column of figures that was introduced in the Wannsee records with the sentence, 'In the course of the final solution of the European Jewish question, 11 million Jews come under consideration, distributed among the various countries as follows.' If we take this list seriously, it indicates the date of the statistics, in which only details were later corrected. They correspond precisely to the strategic options and the expectations of victory in June–July 1941.

Taking this as the basis, we can also determine which trains Heydrich and Himmler planned to use to deport the European Jews to the Soviet Union: those which would otherwise have departed empty to pick up more than 90 divisions and millions of tons of grain at the end of August.[14] If we follow this interpretation, which I deduce entirely from the internal logic of overall resettlement policy and military planning, a whole series of seemingly disparate facts can be more easily understood. For example, it would explain why the otherwise so lively correspondence between Eichmann, Günther, Novak, and Krumey on scheduling conferences and train and locomotive availability completely ceased after 15 March 1941; nowhere is there any indication that transportation for the deportations, which had merely been postponed, was being prepared – as it was, for example, for the Madagascar project.[15] Against the background of strategic planning 'for the period following Barbarossa', it is then understandable why Heydrich announced 'the definitely imminent final solution of the Jewish question' with such certainty in May 1941, and internally informed the Reich Ministry of the Interior that the Jews would 'soon [become] stateless'. It also becomes clear why, in July 1941, Heydrich assigned jurist Friedrich Suhr to ensure the connection between the RSHA and the Foreign Office and gave him the title of 'Officer for the Final Solution of the Jewish Question, especially Abroad'.[16] Finally, such an interpretation also permits a convincing explanation of why, at a discussion on 'organizational issues in Russia', General Thomas of the Armament Economy Office and Göring's state secretary Körner decided on 31 July exactly that Jews would be 'quarter[ed] in barracks and utilize[d] in the form of work brigades'.[17]

On 31 July, Heydrich's task of implementing 'a comprehensive solution of the Jewish question in German spheres of influence in Europe', long since assigned verbally, was finally confirmed in writing by Göring. Now the time seemed ripe to 'supply [the Jewish question] with the most favourable solution that time permits, in the form of emigration or evacuation'. Apparently even the impatient deportation experts took their cue from this time frame. This is exactly why they announced new, long-postponed requests for population shifts in July and August, as though on command, as will be shown.

Not until military conditions appeared to be fulfilled did Heydrich need such a letter from Göring, in order to soften up other 'central institutions'. Heydrich now had in his pocket the 'assignment', formulated as vaguely and ambiguously as hundreds of Führer's orders and authorizations. But he could show it to no one. Not until four months later, on 29 November, did he have this opportunity, while inviting participants to the Wannsee Conference.[18]

# The 'underestimated' Red Army

Heydrich had received his written assignment on 31 July. But it became increasingly clear, from the following day on, that the war against the Soviet Union was progressing differently than the military, Hitler, Himmler, and his ethnic resettlement policy-makers had assumed in any of their scenarios. All hope of resuming in August the 'evacuations' that had abruptly broken off in March vanished within a few weeks. Over the short term – and that was what the men carrying out the resettlements were most interested in – 'The Move Eastward' was proving illusory. Heydrich had placed his hopes in this alternative back in January; he had announced only an initial, partial programme for the third short-term plan and had projectively connected everything else, especially the 'solution of the Jewish question', with the 'opportunities in the East'. Awareness that this plan, too, would be infeasible dawned on the various participants with varying degrees of rapidity and led to various reactions; however, the following situation began to emerge starting in early August (and was impossible to ignore within a few weeks):

- On 1 August, Goebbels noted, 'It is now also openly admitted that we were somewhat in error in estimating Soviet fighting strength. The Bolsheviks are offering stronger resistance than we suspected. . . . We will take care of them nevertheless, mainly because we must take care of them.'[19]
- On 4 August, the SD reported, 'The wait for special reports of new major successes on the Eastern Front, which never took so long in any previous campaign', was causing a 'gradual decline in the expectant mood of the population'; it was being assumed 'that the Red Army has succeeded in bringing the German advance largely to a halt'.[20]
- On 11 August, even Halder, the army general chief of staff, who only a month earlier had maintained that the war would be won in 14 days, registered the fact that the strength of the enemy had been 'under-estimated'.[21]
- On 19 August, Goebbels remarked, 'The Führer is very annoyed at himself for letting himself be fooled about the potential of the Bolsheviks by reports from the Soviet Union. His underestimation of the enemy's armoured divisions and air force, in particular, has meant an extraordinary amount of trouble for our military operations. He has suffered greatly as a result. It is a serious crisis.'[22]

How deep the shock went can be judged only if one is aware of how heavily the German leadership had wagered on the risky card of speedy victory. As the military's castles in the air dissolved into nothing during August, so did those of the ethnic resettlement policy-makers. Not only had all prospects for resettlement policy proved to be nothing but gambles by autumn 1941; the dream of a grab for the Ukrainian breadbasket had also faded beyond reach. Claussen, the same ministerial official who had calculated in May that 25 million tons of grain were available from the Ukraine to meet German and Western European needs, determined more soberly in September that the German army on the eastern front – 3 million men – could only 'satisfy two-thirds of its needs with bread grain and meat from the occupied Russian territories'. The situation worsened steadily. Claussen was forced to acknowledge that the autumn planting in the Ukraine – where, for climatic reasons, there was no spring planting – had taken place on only some 20 per cent of the fields. As a result, vast areas were 'overgrown with weeds', and damage had taken place 'that [would] remain irreparable for years'. By December, the Wehrmacht could no longer obtain even two-thirds of its supplies, but only 'a very small portion, from the occupied territories of the Soviet Union'. This meant 'only around 10 per cent of grain for bread (200,000 tons) and roughly 30 per cent of meat (also 200,000 tons)'. In fact, 'most of the required bread and meat . . . [had to] be delivered from the homeland'.[23]

Yet the trains full of wheat, sunflower oil, and meat should actually have been going in the other direction, in order to guarantee the German 'average consumer' better rations and prevent the outbreak of famine and rebellion in Spain, France, Italy, Greece, and Norway. Though it is difficult to imagine today, in 1939 continental Europe required foreign imports of 12 to 13 million tons of grain per year to supply food to 25 million people. This deficit already existed in peacetime; in wartime, it was bound to increase. There was a shortage of workers, horses, diesel fuel; nitrogen was no longer processed into artificial fertilizer, but made into gunpowder. The British naval blockade prevented necessary imports, and the road from the euphoria of victory to defeatist recollections of the famine of winter 1917–18 was a short one.[24]

Of course, Hitler, his Wehrmacht generals, and his agricultural experts stuck to their intention of starving the Russian population in the north – as they had planned in spring 1941: 'It cannot be doubted,' according to the army general quartermaster, 'that Leningrad, in particular, must starve.'[25] But this did not serve to better the German food situation, despite the intentions behind it. This miscalculation necessarily left its mark upon policies within the German sphere of influence.

In 1940, Frank had repeatedly pointed out that he could only take additional settlers into the Generalgouvernement if the central offices in Berlin ensured that the deportees would be fed. Due to the division of territory, the harvest in the occupied area, a region with poor economic prospects from its creation, could never suffice to supply its own population, let alone feed additional Wehrmacht soldiers and settlers. In the first fiscal year of wartime supply, 1939–40 (calculated from harvest to harvest, that is, from 1 August to 31 July), 150,000 tons of bread grain were sent to Warsaw from the Reich. By 21 May 1940, agricultural experts had already determined that 'deliveries' would have to take place in the opposite direction by the second year of wartime supply, that is, from 1 August 1940.[26] Frank was largely able to avoid this situation in 1940–41; in 1941–42, the deliveries totalled around 100,000 tons of grain, and in 1942–43, 500,000 tons, which corresponded to the needs of a million and a half people.[27]

The tides of war had turned. This was reflected even in the passwords Krumey assigned to his resettlement commandos in the Warthegau.[28] In the week of 21–27 July 1941, they were 'Minsk', 'Kiev', 'Vitebsk', 'Smolensk', 'Odessa', 'Petersburg', and 'Moscow'; in the week of 8–14 September, they were 'Strength', 'Honour', 'Struggle', 'Courage', 'Obedience', 'Loyalty', and 'Industriousness'.[29]

## Concentrating the *Volk*

Among Hitler's initial reactions to the altered strategic situation was the sudden cessation of the 'euthanasia' operation, which took place on 24

August 1941. The decision took the men of T-4 by surprise, and to later observers it appeared a paradox.

It is now possible to document at least two considerations, based strongly in *realpolitik*, that led to this step. One linked the difficulties on the eastern front to the risk that any controversy over 'euthanasia', however secret it might be kept, could place an additional strain on the 'mood' of the German public. In this vein, Goebbels noted on 15 August:

> I must ask the Führer whether he wishes a public debate on the euthanasia problem at this moment. We could perhaps have this debate follow the new Liebeneiner film 'I Accuse' [*Ich klage an*].[30] I myself am against it, at least for the present. We would only inflame passions with such a debate. This is extraordinarily impractical in a critical period of the war. At the moment, we should keep any inflammatory material away from the people. The nation is so preoccupied with the problems of the war that other issues simply cause heat and friction. Also, in this way the people's concentration on the actual issue of the war, that is, the achievement of victory, loses its cogency.[31]

The political background to such considerations was formed by the difficulties faced by the German armies on the eastern front and the famous 3 August sermon by the Bishop of Münster, Clemens August Graf von Galen. Von Galen publicly described the euthanasia programme as 'pure murder'. Even worse, he linked it to an additional, equally delicate political point: in the same sermon, he spoke of the latest British bombardments and their disastrous aftermath in Münster. Von Galen did not interpret them, as official jargon prescribed, as 'cowardly aerial terror', but as 'God's judgement'. He said this punishment had to strike the city's Christians because innocent, defenceless people were continuously being murdered in their midst, violating the divine commandment, 'Thou shalt not kill'.

In addition to the eastern front, which required all the 'people's concentration', a second military problem increasingly preoccupied the German leadership at the time: the attacks by the Royal Air Force. For geographic reasons, they targeted the mainly Catholic population of northwestern Germany, of whose loyalty the Nazi leadership had never been quite certain from the outset. The bombardments targeted cities such as Cologne, Krefeld, Rheydt, and Mönchengladbach, as well as Münster. They led to massive 'setbacks in mood', regularly documented by the SD, which crystallized around the lack of medical care for the wounded. Because Hitler and his advisors tended to be sensitive to such reports, they found themselves forced to make additional auxiliary hospitals available. Only the psychiatric hospitals could be considered for this; thus they had to be 'cleared'. However, at this point in time, this increased the risk of placing a further strain on the people's already shaken confidence. For T-4 was in the process, in the summer of 1941 of all times, of deporting patients from Westphalian psychiatric hospitals to the murder centres.[32]

The impact of the sermon by the 'lion of Münster' unfolded within a specific context. Hitler and his ilk must have understood what Galen was doing as sheer defeatism, since he judged the destruction of cities by British bombers to be a 'judgement' – one which 'a just God must and will impose on anyone who does not support that which is God's will'.

The dilemma of politics and legitimation in which Hitler found himself as a result of Galen's complex argumentation is quite clearly described in the following document. It refers directly to the meeting of 24 August, in the course of which the provisional – but immediate – cessation of 'euthanasia' was decided. The text was circulated as an internal Nazi party memorandum, thus reaching a wide audience. It was signed by Karl Brandt, who, after Bouhler, was Hitler's second 'euthanasia' representative.

> Due to emerging necessity, the Führer ordered on 24 August 1941 that buildings be made available or built to replace damaged hospitals in certain cities threatened by air raids. . . . These additional buildings must be annexed to mental hospitals and the like, which are favourably located in terms of grounds and in respect to distance from the specific cities threatened by air raids. Such facilities will be made available in collaboration with the special representative in the Reich Ministry of the Interior (Dr Linden). The costs of transferring patients to free up these facilities will be borne by the public transport company in Berlin, pending later settlement with the Reich.
>
> The purpose of this measure is thus, first of all, to maintain hospitals for certain cities in locations that are safe from aerial attack, and also to use existing facilities as the basis for expansion in the form of barracks, in order to avoid technical and sanitary facilities that are difficult to procure. These new hospitals shall serve, in addition to the usual types of illness, above all for the recuperation of children and to offer expectant mothers a quiet place for the delivery.

Herbert Linden, responsible for the bureaucratic procedures of Operation T-4 in the medical department of the Ministry of the Interior, was to determine which hospitals were to be cleared for victims of the aerial war. In so doing, Linden had to utilize the only available, effective, and well-established organization, the Public Hospital Transport Organization, Inc. (*Gemeinnützige Krankentransport Organisation GmbH*, GEKRAT). This was the transport department of Operation T-4, which normally 'transferred' those patients selected for death to the murder centres by bus.

Now, however, according to Hitler's decision, the patients would no longer die in gas chambers, but, because of the precarious situation, were in fact to be transferred. The very fact that this was to occur using the same organizational means was sure to arouse the suspicions of a well-informed public. 'The general belief' was that patients were only transferred to other facilities in order to be 'intentionally killed' (von Galen). Thus Hitler, Brandt, and Bouhler decided upon the following, in every respect unusual, procedure:

> This expedient measure will engender a degree of disquiet among certain segments of the population as a result of the transfer of patients from mental institutions to other hospitals. However, because the patients are in fact only being transferred for the duration of the war, their relatives will also be informed of their location beforehand. It shall also be made possible that the patients still be allowed to receive visitors to a correspondingly meaningful extent. Increased travel costs, etc. are to be borne by the Reich in these cases. . . . It seems desirable that, in the local daily press of the cities involved, the reasons for this overall measure be discussed propagandistically. . . . Under these circumstances, it will be possible through provision of this information to reduce any pre-existing disquiet and defuse rumours, since the public can be entirely involved in monitoring the measures mentioned above.[33]

Considering this Party memorandum and Goebbels diary entries, the 'Führer order' on cessation of the 'euthanasia' murders comes to seem both an understandable and a pragmatic consequence. On 24 August 1941, Hitler was reacting to a situation that had emerged a short time earlier as a result of very varied factors that came together only by chance. The already apparent stagnation on the eastern front and the increasingly frequent British bombings of the large cities in the west of the Reich had strained the nerves of the German public. Additional 'inflammatory material', as Goebbels put it, seemed 'extraordinarily impractical in [this] critical period of the war'. Further, Brandt's letter suggests the way in which a conflict of purpose arose between the suddenly necessary medical care of air raid victims, on the one hand, and the relatively rigid – in fact, 'planned economy-like' – 'euthanasia' programme, on the other.[34] In fact, the German leadership reacted subtly and flexibly to the public 'mood'. Conversely, this meant that Hitler, Himmler, and Heydrich felt sure of the support, or at least the passivity, of the overwhelming majority when they began the comprehensive murder of European Jewry a few weeks later. We can do no more than pose the question here, as the apparatus of authority is the focus of this book. A study on what the Germans thought of the 'solution of the Jewish question' in 1941 has yet to be written. It would be methodologically difficult, but should without question be attempted – employing, for example, the method used by Walter Kempowski for his Stalingrad documentation, *Das Echolot. Ein kollektives Tagebuch Januar bis Februar 1943* (The Echo-Sounder. A Collective Diary from January to February 1943).

# 'Untenable situation' II

On 18 July 1941, Hans Frank, still gripped by the excitement of victory and full of optimism, declared before his assembled economists and food supply experts:

> If we now develop a food supply and reconstruction plan, it is clear that certain questions with which we have ceaselessly dealt in these nearly two years will no longer concern us to the same degree. I believe that now an improvement in conditions in Warsaw and the other large cities will occur. . . . In the coming days, I will give the order to clear the Warsaw Ghetto. At all events, we must ensure that we remove the Jews from the Generalgouvernement. Because, in the Führer's own words, the Generalgouvernement will in the future no longer be a final destination, but exclusively a transit camp.[35]

Two days later, on 20 July, Frank petitioned to annex the sparsely settled 'marshes of Pripet' – in addition to Galicia, which had just been added to the Generalgouvernement and was rated as 'overpopulated' – because he claimed to see in it a possibility of 'providing elements of the population (especially Jewish) with productive activity that serves the Reich'.[36] The following day, Jost Walbaum, Head of the Health Administration of the Generalgouvernement, was informed by Frank of his 'decision to take on the dissolution of the Warsaw ghetto as [his] first task', given the increased incidence of spotted fever.[37]

Frank reckoned at the time with the rapid deportation of the Jews to a not too distant destination 'to the east' – but not with gas chambers. Despite all experience to the contrary, his staff reacted to his simple declaration of intent as though it were hard fact. For example, a preliminary administrative report on Galicia on the subject of 'population' stated:

> In terms of non-German national groups in the Galicia district, we have: Ukrainians, 63.6 per cent; Poles, 22.4 per cent; Jews, 14 per cent. Because the Jews are not taken into account by the German administration, the ratio of Ukrainians to Poles shifts as follows: Ukrainians, 70.6 per cent, Poles, 29.4 per cent.[38]

The report is dated 28 August 1941. On 2 September, the creation of 'Jewish collection areas' in the Generalgouvernement was ordered.[39]

The head of the Warsaw *Judenrat* or Jewish Council, Adam Czerniaków, was not unaware of these intentions. His diary contains the entry, 'A meeting of the grocers about the reserves for the winter, food substitutes, etc. One of the Poles has commented that there has been a change in the official policy towards the Jews.' In response to Czerniaków's questions, Heinz Auerswald, the German ghetto commissioner, 'said that rumours about the resettlement include not only the Jews but also the Poles'.[40]

Auerswald meant this to be reassuring, but the rumours were grounded in fact. Talk of the General Plan for the East had got about. The contents of the strictly confidential papers of Höppner, Mayer, and Greifelt did not remain secret. While Rosenberg had informed his closest colleagues on 8 May that 'the entire area between Narva and Tilsit' was to be 'transformed into part of the greater German Reich',[41] and while Hitler, in a 'top secret Reich matter' on 16 July, had 'emphasized that the entire Baltic area had to become a Reich territory', on 9 August the 'rumour' on the streets of Liepāja (German: Libau) was 'that even the region up to Minsk is to go to the Reich, and that the Latvians will be settled in the latter area, that is, will be deported from Latvia', and that 'German farmers are to be settled' in Latvia itself.[42] The fears of the people of Liepāja, and Czerniaków's impressions, corresponded to the expansionist plans being debated at the same time behind closed doors by the vanguard of the Greater German territorial planners in Riga,[43] Krakow, and Berlin, in the expectation of imminent victory – an illusion that was to last only a few weeks.

This was followed, as usual, by mutual obstruction and haggling over each of the long-scheduled deportations, and thus by the very same 'untenable situation' that the top politicians and police experts of the Generalgouvernement and the Warthegau had complained to each other about in summer 1940.

The conflict between the administrative leadership of the Warthegau and that of the Generalgouvernement over additional mass deportations had been developing since January 1940. The many compromises described in the preceding chapters remained as fragile as the political framework within which they achieved temporary validity – not because Nazi infighting came to a head there and the image neuroses of Gauleiters, governors, and generals were worked off around them, but because real and, at bottom, incompatible interests faced off against each other. Hitler, Frank, and Himmler believed in mid-March 1941 that they had overcome this stalemate (which, despite brief detours, constantly recurred) in the common prospects of the war of conquest, territory, and extermination against the Soviet Union. From that point on, they assumed – unanimously as never before – that the deportations 'to the east' could actually be accomplished in autumn of the same year. When it became apparent by August that the Red Army could not be defeated in a blitzkrieg, as all plans had presupposed, the constellation of summer 1940 was repeated – though under far more tense conditions created by frustrated expectations of victory and the prospects of a possibly long war fraught with casualties.

One symptom was the rapid increase in the already great tension prevailing in the camps for ethnic Germans. On 1 October 1941, the Ethnic German Liaison Office complained that among the Bukovinian and Dobruja Germans, 'petitions for return to Romania have recently taken on pathological proportions'. Once the problem had been thus ascertained, guidelines for response soon followed: petitions were to be 'immediately' rejected by camp directors if 'usable workers are found' in the settler family. The petitions could be considered if applicants 'are worthless to us, and we have an interest in deporting them'.[44] Ten days later, the Ethnic German Liaison Office had already developed a procedure 'for the return of Romanian German settlers to Romania'. It was now 'intended, as a rule, to permit the return of persons belonging to selection category IV'.[45]

Ethnic Germans, like Poles, were also divided into selection categories by the racial examiners of the Reich Security Main Office. As with all 'ethnic aliens', this was always done secretly, on the pretext of a medical examination.[46]

The disquiet, frustration, and annoyance among the interned settlers were not limited to those in the lowest 'selection category'. On 14 October, 'Mobile Commission No. VII' reported to the Central Immigration Office that 250 Dobruja Germans in a Franconian resettlement camp had actually refused naturalization. The reason given was homesickness. 'This refractory behaviour of individual settlers', according to the report, 'or the majority of settlers is so obvious that it must be assumed . . . that they are not willing to change their opinion.' And this despite the fact that they were, 'from a racial point of view, on average usable and valuable peasants'.[47] Attempts followed to get the settlers to change their minds, but to no avail.[48] On 19 January 1943, Fritz Arlt, director of the RKF branch in Katowice (Kattowitz), reported on the 'concluding work on settlement in Upper Silesia': the 'possibilities of settlement' for farmers were exhausted, but '1809 people' still remained in his camps. These included some 400 'settlement resistors' who had been brought together in the Zator camp. According to Arlt, it had been agreed 'to transfer the ringleaders to a concentration camp', while the others 'would be deprived of their eastworthiness'. 'I wish to ensure', wrote Arlt to Greifelt, 'both the transfer to a concentration camp and the most rapid possible transfer to an Old Reich camp.'[49]

In autumn 1941, the organizers of 'human deployment' had reacted more helplessly. On 24 October 1941, they had formally proposed that the Dobruja and Bessarabian Germans be settled in a further expanded East Prussia.[50] But the neighbouring General Commissioner of Lithuania, Theodor A. von Renteln, had long since heard about this. In the Führer's headquarters, he voiced his 'concern' over the ideas that were coming to him from Himmler's circles. Von Renteln had heard that he might have to 'give up the Memel bend as well, and a certain "hinterland" for Memel, to the East Prussian Gau'. Further, he understood there was a plan to 'settle [ethnic Germans] there even before the start of winter [!] and to remove the same number of Lithuanians in exchange, only they do not yet know where to put them'. In his indignation, von Renteln announced that he intended 'to go directly to the Reich Marshal and the Führer, whom he knows well from his Party activities'.[51]

The plan for 'rapid settlement' of the refractory Dobruja Germans was dismissed before the men of the 'human deployment' programme even had a chance to consider it out loud. Therefore, on 11 December 1941 Greifelt again turned to Himmler in the matter: 'Now that the Reichsführer SS has decided', he began, 'that the Crimea and the adjacent Black Sea region are intended for later settlement as an East Goth Gau,' the question arose whether it was not possible for 'around 10,000 Dobruja Germans and more or less the same number of Bessarabian Germans' to be settled there. True, they were not of 'East Gothic extraction', but they were more familiar with the Black Sea climate than with that of Lithuania and 'their German consciousness was impeccable'; thus they 'could form an initial starting point for the later settlement of the Crimea'.[52]

The old situation had returned: vague plans for the future were offered up instead of concrete, immediate settlement opportunities – except that it was no longer the second, but now the third winter of the war. This required a harsh response. In an appeal to 'all settlers who are presently employed in mining in Saxony or the Sudetenland', Greifelt threatened 'further measures'. 'Some settlers', he said, referring obliquely to outright strikes, had 'not yet taken up the work assigned to them.'[53] Greifelt drew up this appeal on 9 December 1941. On 23 December, his representative, Stier, wrote to the Danzig office of the RKF, 'Re: Malicious Settlers'. Stier suggested a 'consultation with the SD', as it would 'in fact prove necessary to issue a general ruling on this'.[54] On 15 April 1942, the staff main office of the RKF finally drew up 'instructions for all [ethnic German] settlers'; they were apparently to be signed by Himmler, but then – as far as I am aware – were never distributed after all. Nevertheless, the text characterizes the situation. The settlers were called upon to thank the 'dearly beloved Führer' for rescuing them 'from the terror of the Bolsheviks'; to forget the promise of rapid resettlement; and to accept reality – a combination of threat and promise:

> To those who are constantly dissatisfied and often unjustly annoy officials and offices with their complaints and petitions, I must make it perfectly clear that, at a time when the entire German people is waging a battle for its existence or non-existence, there is no place for personal wishes and complaints. . . . Thousands of settlers are still waiting to be settled in the east or in the Old Reich. . . . All this will change once the war is brought to a victorious conclusion.

After the 'final victory', promised the appeal in closing, everyone would receive 'his due' – 'every last settler who has done his duty'.[55]

# Notes

1 Breitman, 141 comes to the same conclusion using different arguments.

2 Hillgruber, *Strategie*, 325.

3 The figures match those in a report for the German embassy in Paris on 18 February 1942. See *Okkupationspolitik in Frankreich*, 52. For a summary of legislation on Jews in Tunisia, Algeria, and Morocco, see Benz and Wetzel, 113ff. The question remains why Eichmann raised this figure by another 170,000. This might have been based on an estimate by the Reich Security Main Office on the number of foreign Jewish refugees in France and the large number of assimilated Jews there. After all, the German ambassador in Paris, Otto Abetz, reported on 28 February 1941 that 'conscientious countings were being carried out by the SD', according to which, in Paris alone 'one must reckon with some 200,000 Jews' (Klarsfeld, 365ff.) In any case, Steinberg is wrong to write (13), 'Le protocole de Wannsee mentionne la présence de 165,000 Juifs en France occupée, et de 700,000 Juifs dans la zone non occupée. Si le premier chiffre est vraisemblable – il prenait en compte les chiffres du recensement des Juifs – celui de la zone Sud relève de la fantaisie.'

4 In fact, the resettlement experts of the Reich Security Main Office were expecting an even higher number, since, according to the minutes of the Wannsee Conference, the 'figures provided for the various foreign countries' referred 'only to religious Jews, as the definition of Jews according to racial principles is to some extent still lacking there'.

5 Here Eichmann included the statistical outcome of the as yet limited possibilities for forced emigration and the 'death surplus'.

6 The special census of Jews that took place on the occasion of the census of 15 December 1940 indicated a figure of 88,951; Aly and Roth, 82.

7 Steinberg, 13.

8 According to the statistical overview drawn up by the Reich Inspector for Population Registration for 13 June 1941, the number of Jews, including '*Mischlinge*' (those of mixed race), came to 159,508; Aly and Roth, 64.

9 These figures (and also those for Serbia) actually did refer to the date of the conference; at the time, several hundred thousand Jews had already been murdered. Estonia, for example, was 'free of Jews'.

10 Individual deportations within the German sphere of influence are not taken into account here. In any case, they seemed to be a zero-sum game to the strategists of Jewish policy after each new expansionist step.

11 Hillgruber, *Strategie*, 378ff.

12 Ibid. 379, note 10; 542. (The method of citation that combines the two greatly divergent sources is justified by a cross-reference by the author.) See Schüler, 453ff.

13 Hillgruber, *Strategie*, 377ff.

14 For the transport of an infantry division, 68–72 trains were generally needed; 90–100 were required for an armoured division; Schüler, 237ff.

15 The recently published special study by Kurt Pätzold and Erika Schwarz on the role of Eichmann's Officer for Transport Matters, Franz Novak, implicitly confirms this. Here too, no documents exist for the period in question in which any preparatory, logistical planning for the Jewish deportations can be found. The same is true for the fundamental work of Klaus A. Friedrich Schüler on the logistics of the Russian campaign. (See Schüler; Pätzold and Schwarz, *Auschwitz, passim*.)

16 The month that Suhr received this assignment is mentioned in his recommendation for a medal, 21 October 1944; BDC, PA/Friedrich Suhr.

17 Meeting notes; BA-MA, RW12/189.
18 See Broszat, 'Erklärung', 251f. Here he states similarly, but with less conviction, that in spring and summer, Hitler had 'promised generously, though foolishly', that various

> regions could shortly be made *judenrein* – promises that apparently occurred in this period in connection with the war in Russia, which was being prepared for or had already been set in motion, but still went on the assumption that this war would be successfully concluded by the onset of winter, and that, so to speak, unlimited opportunities would then exist to deport the Jews to a far distant region beyond the German empire in the East.

19 Goebbels diaries, Reuth, vol. 4, 1645.
20 Meldungen aus dem Reich (4.8.1941) [Reports from the Reich (4 August 1941)], 167.
21 Halder war diary, vol. 3, 170.
22 Goebbels diaries, Reuth, vol. 4, 1656ff.
23 Report by Eicke (WiRüAmt) on the meeting with Claussen, 7 January 1942; BA-MA, RW19/73, 92ff.
24 On the planning, see the summary in Aly and Heim, 365–93.
25 Eduard Wagner, 13 November 1941; quoted in Streit, 157ff.
26 Minutes of meeting between General Thomas and a group of experts on 'the situation in agriculture and options for food supply over the longer term', 21 May 1940; BA-MA, RW19/2453.
27 The drastic increase in the contingent for 1942–43 was undoubtedly related to the murder of Jews in the Generalgouvernement. See correspondence between Backe, Himmler, and Krüger; BAK, NS19/1995, 174ff.; Frank diary, 544ff.
28 The commandos worked mainly at night, and thus needed passwords. At the time, they were involved in 'evicting' Poles within the Warthegau.
29 AGK, UWZ/L/147.
30 On the origins of the film and the story of its treatment, see Roth's excellent discussion; Roth, 'Film', 147–70.
31 Goebbels diaries, Reuth, vol. 4, 1652ff.
32 This might have been by chance. Perhaps, however, the planners in the Führer's Chancellery delayed the murder of psychiatric patients in this region for so long because they considered the risk there to be especially high and wished to avoid prematurely endangering their overall murder operation.
33 BAK, NS6/335, 108.
34 The note that appeared here in the first edition of the book has been omitted, as the document mentioned was erroneously dated 28 August 1941, due to a typographical error, instead of 28 July 1941. As a result, it was incorrectly placed in this context.
35 Frank diary; BAK, R52/II/184 (economic conference of 22 July 1941); Frank diary, 389 (Regeste).
36 Letter from Frank to Lammers, 19 July 1941; BAK, R6/21, 136ff.; see Frank diary, 387.
37 Frank diary, 389.
38 Report of the Department of Population and Welfare, 28 August 1941 (signed [Alfred] Bisanz); StA Lviv, R-35/12/30, 28–30.
39 Chronology of the Warsaw Ghetto (author: Hanns von Krannhals); Sta. Hamburg, 141 Js 192/60 (investigation of Dr Ludwig Hahn).
40 Czerniaków diary, 269, 272, entries of 20 and 28 August 1941.
41 Quoted in Seckendorf, 179.

42 Report of a trip by Hans von Payr (WiRüAmt/Stab), 11 August 1941; BA-MA RW19/473, 131.

43 Seckendorf, 181ff.; Aly and Heim, 425ff.

44 Memorandum from Vomi/Lower Silesia operations command 'To all Camp Directors!', 1 October 1941; BAK, R59/199, 15ff.

45 Note on 11 October 1941; BAK, R69/136, 180. Collection camps for the 'returnees' were set up in Gleiwitz and Ratibor. The 'return of [ethnic German] settlers from Romania' – a total of 2362 people out of 6159 who had 'applied for return' – took place under the seal of a 'Secret Reich Matter' in January–February 1943. The destination of the four transports was Czernowitz (letter from Himmler/personal staff to Greifelt, 29 January 1943; BAK, NS19/3763; report by Arlt ['Development, Organization, Work of the Office of the Gauleiter and Senior President as Plenipotentiary of the Reichsführer SS, Reich Commissioner for the Consolidation of German Nationhood in Upper Silesia, from Sept. 1939 to Jan. 1943']; BAK, R49/Anh. III/1, 50. Train availability was organized by Eichmann as part of the overall deportation train schedules. The unannotated train schedules, together with the destinations Auschwitz and Treblinka, are published in Hilberg, *Railroads*). In the period from 28 May to 12 November 1941, 5912 supposed 'Romanians or Ukrainians by blood' whom the racial examiners of the Central Immigration Office had located among the Romanian German resettlers had already been 'sent back to Romania . . . in special transports' (Arlt report, ibid.).

46 It was expressly ordered that any public 'reference to the racial screening and selection' of ethnic Germans was 'to be absolutely avoided' (press guidelines of the Lodz EWZ, 12 April 1940; AGK, EWZ/L/838/2, 6). During this selection by the suitability evaluators of the Main Race and Settlement Office of the SS, the 'main decision' – that is, the size and quality of the future farms for the settlers – was made (letter from the RuSHA, Litzmannstadt subsidiary, 17 February 1941; BAK, R69/554, 44.)

47 Letter from 'Mobile (Naturalization) Commission' VII of the EWZ to the EWZ leadership staff in Litzmannstadt (Lodz), 14 October 1941; BAK, R69/136, 181ff.

48 Letter from von Malsen to Ehlich and Fähndrich, 2 December 1941; BAK, R69/136, 219.

49 Letter from Arlt to Greifelt, 19 February 1943; BDC, SS-HO/4701.

50 Note by the RKF, 24 October 1941; BAK R49/2607.

51 Koeppen's notes in the Führer headquarters (entry for 8 October 1941); BAK, R6/34a, 44f. In addition, the RFK department for 'human deployment' had already suggested that the Lithuanian Germans who had been resettled seven months previously be transported 'back to their old farms', if they were considered 'eastworthy' (*ostwürdig*, referring to certification as being of good 'Aryan' stock and therefore fit for settlement in the East) (suggestion by Stier to Greifelt 'to be presented to the Reichsführer SS', 10 September 1941; BAK, R49/2606.)

52 Letter from Greifelt to Himmler, 11 December 1941; BAK, R49/2607. A mention in passing: from this constellation, Himmler and the planning experts of the RKF soon developed the 'Zamość' settlement project, which has since been quite thoroughly described in the relevant literature. They attempted to implement it with tremendous brutality during the battle for Stalingrad. In all relevant works – by Madajczyk, for example, and Wasser – this relocation crime is portrayed as a voluntaristic act of Himmler's. However, for a satisfactory analysis it would be necessary also to describe the internal side of the act: the pressure from the resettlement camps, the many empty promises made by

Himmler, and the pressure for justification into which he had manoeuvred himself.

53 Appeal by Greifelt, 9 December 1941; AGK, EWZ/L/838/148, 38–40, and also BAK, R49/2756.

54 Letter from Stier to the representative of the RKF in Danzig, 23 December 1941; BAK, R49/2609. Twelve months later, Himmler's directive was already going into force that settlers who 'lack the desire for good work performance' were to be placed in jobs with 'particular physical requirements' (memorandum from the RKF and Vomi, Pomerania operations command, 7 December 1942; BAK, R59/183, 112).

55 Instructions for all ethnic German settlers, draft, unsigned, 15 April 1942; BAK, R49/2609.

# |10|

# 'The Jews have got to go'

## Local 'solutions'

Höppner's extensive experience led him to evaluate the options for evacuation much more sceptically than did Frank.[1] He had sent his (multi-page) proposal to Eichmann at the early date of 16 July 1941. It contained a sophisticated concept for the 'solution of the Jewish question in the Wartheland Reichsgau', one that could be implemented in the form of an intermediate-term provisional solution coordinated by Höppner himself, independent of transport capabilities. Höppner continued the debate of the previous year. He used the approach of winter as an argument, at a time when prevailing attitudes were still confident of victory.[2] However, he no longer waited for 'a basic decision' on the issue from Hitler or Himmler, as Frank and Greiser had done the year before, when despite all reservations they had agreed to leave the Jews where they were for the time being.

Now Höppner was circulating a concrete proposal:

> There is a danger that, in the coming winter, it will become impossible to feed all the Jews. It must seriously be considered whether the most humane solution is to finish off the Jews unfit for labour through some fast-acting means. This would definitely be more pleasant than letting them starve to death.[3]

This was not the first time Höppner had brought up the notion of murdering individuals he considered useless. As previously mentioned, in October 1940, when he did not know what to do with Poles who could not be deported for health reasons, he noted in the margin of a letter of complaint, 'It is possible that different measures must be taken for persons unfit for transport.'[4] As the 'official in charge of resettlement affairs' in Posen, he had also long since gained practical experience in the matter. Starting in winter 1939–40, he had been involved at least indirectly in the murder of several thousand of the mentally ill in the Warthegau. At the time he wrote his letter, the (Herbert) Lange Special Commando Unit – which like Höppner was part of the Posen security police and SD apparatus – was combing the institutions in the Warthegau for a second time to find 'useless eaters' to kill by means of the gas van. None the less, on 16 July Höppner was not considering killing *all* Jews. This is absolutely clear from his remark. He proposed killing Jews who were unfit for labour and concentrating those able to work in a camp. There, he continued, 'all Jewesses who could still be expected to bear children' should be sterilized, 'so that the Jewish problem can be solved once and for all in this generation'.[5]

As much as Höppner was arguing here 'from the bottom', it should not be overlooked that, at the same time, the upper echelons of the hierarchy had gone through corresponding opinion-forming processes. This is confirmed by fragmentary documentation of the relations between organizers of the deportation of Jews, on the one hand, and those of the 'euthanasia' programmes, on the other. Starting in the autumn of 1939, the agents of the T-4 operation had been working together with chemists at the Forensics Institute, i.e., members of the RSHA, to develop suitable methods by which to kill the mentally ill. During discussion of the Madagascar Plan, they had offered the logistical services of their 'smoothly run transport organization'; at the same time, in the gas chambers of T-4, they murdered almost all Jewish patients in German institutions who were potentially unfit for transport. This could not have happened without consultation with Himmler and Heydrich.[6] In the autumn of 1940, the men of T-4 helped their RKF and Vomi colleagues save face by 'clearing' dozens of institutions for them so they could be converted to reception camps for ethnic Germans.

In January 1941, Himmler asked Bouhler, who was in charge of the 'euthanasia' department, to help him 'free' the concentration camps of 'human ballast'.[7] This led to the so-called 'Operation 14f13'.[8] Starting in early April, T-4 doctors visited the concentration camps, selecting a portion of those prisoners categorized by local camp commandants as 'asocial' or sick for transport to the T-4 gas chambers. By the summer of 1941, 2500 prisoners had died in this manner from the concentration camps at Mauthausen, Buchenwald, Auschwitz, and Sachsenhausen.[9] A distinction was made here among the prisoners; for German, Polish, or Czech prisoners the selection doctors carried out an admittedly very superficial physical examination, whereas the Jewish prisoners were selected on the basis of their file alone.[10]

At the same time, in January 1941, Himmler requested that Viktor Brack, second-in-command to Philipp Bouhler, examine the technical feasibility of mass sterilization of the Jews. Brack reported on 28 March 1941 on a method based on X-rays and asked Himmler to decide 'if and what should be done in the matter, theoretically or actually'. Himmler's response did not come until six weeks later; he informed Brack that he was very interested in his report and would speak with him about it as soon as possible. On 27 May, someone else – gynaecologist Carl Clauberg – proposed a competing project to Himmler. Clauberg was also concerned with developing a method of non-operative mass sterilization of individuals deemed 'unworthy of or undesirable for reproduction'. Himmler's health policy advisor Ernst Grawitz enthused over the 'unheard-of significance . . . that such a procedure would have on negative population policies'.[11]

In the decision-making process leading up to the murder of much of European Jewry, it must thus be noted that Himmler, Brack, and Clauberg considered a proposal in early 1941 that can be related to the intention at that time to biologically exterminate European Jewry. Not until after the Wannsee Conference did Himmler give the go-ahead for both sterilization projects, which used different methods. The victims were then no longer to be Jews, but rather German–Jewish 'hybrids' (*Mischlinge*),[12] in particular the 'Eastern ethnic groups' (*Ostvölker*). Both Carl Clauberg and T-4 physician Horst Schumann worked on the project in open competition – as Himmler presumably wanted – in the same place, namely, Auschwitz. Clauberg, at least, was supported by Fritz Arlt, head of the RKF branch office in Katowice.[13]

When on 16 July, Höppner, head of the Central Resettlement Office (UWZ) in Posen, brought up the notion of sterilizing all Jewish women in the Warthegau who were fit for work, he was taking up ideas that had been discussed in various institutions for at least six months. It is likely that this kind of parallelism – with a certain delay – existed with respect to plans for mass extermination as well. This is substantiated by the fact that approximately 100 participants in Operation T-4 later built and operated the extermination camps at Belzec, Sobibór, and Treblinka. It is difficult to say when the first, preliminary consideration of this took place. In any case, discussion was already under way in October 1941,[14] if not still earlier.

In the Nazi Party file on T-4 physician Curt Schmalenbach, an entry on 21 June 1941 might be related to options that were to extend far beyond the sphere of Operation T-4 up to that point. According to the file:

> He [Schmalenbach] was only recently appointed a senior government councillor [*Regierungsrat*], and is constantly rushing off on secret assignments (for example to Paris, Warsaw, Prague, Vienna, etc.). In addition, he has an identification card from the Führer's private office (Bouhler), with which he is authorized to refuse [to give] any information on his activities and the purpose of his trip.[15]

Schmalenbach's destinations indicate that the 'Jewish question' might have been the subject of a secret mission. This is also suggested by the categorical secrecy regarding the purpose of his trips, which was unusual for representatives of the state and party apparatus involved in 'euthanasia'-

related projects. Moreover, Schmalenbach's position was an interesting one: first he ran the operation of the T-4 gas chambers in Pirna; then he was promoted to Viktor Brack's 'medical adjutant', responsible for 'special tasks'.[16]

Since Himmler did not seriously pursue the forced sterilization project, I think it possible that the official in the Führer's Chancellery responsible for 'euthanasia' had already planned the active mass murder of Jews even before the war against the Soviet Union had begun. In any case, there is reason to assume on the basis of extant documents that at this early point in time, Bouhler, Brack, and Schmalenbach – like Höppner – were not considering murdering all Jews, but only those unfit for work. This is borne out by a later note by Erhard Wetzel, in charge of Jewish matters in the East Ministry, who determined at the end of October 1941 that 'given the current state of affairs, I have no reservations against eliminating Jews who are unfit for labour using the Brackian devices'. He continued that Brack had declared his willingness 'to participate in the production . . . of the gassing apparatus'.[17]

In accordance with his sphere of authority, Wetzel was referring to the extermination of Soviet Jewry. Yet the question of fitness for work was not in fact central to the issue here. Under the paradigm of racial war, from which followed the ruthless annihilation of the 'Jewish–Bolshevik enemy', the commandos of the security police and the SD, supported in many instances by Wehrmacht units, were primarily concerned with shooting Jewish men fit for military service. This generally left women, children, and the elderly, i.e. those 'unfit for labour' from a German perspective. Their elimination 'through some fast-acting means' had been a subject of discussion for quite some time in the Warthegau, in consideration of the food supply situation and economization of the ghettos. On 15 August, the commandos of the *Einsatzgruppen* (Special Units) in the Soviet Union started murdering even those who had previously been spared. They gave high priority to shooting 'unproductives'. There is now general agreement that this was a direct outcome of Himmler's visit to the eastern front on 15 and 16 August.[18]

Here, too, the unexpected obstacles that confronted the military campaign definitely had a significant impact on the decision. For the first time, the *Einsatzgruppen* recorded in their so-called event reports (*Ereignismeldungen*) the 'liquidation' of 'Jewish men, women, and children', and the 'extermination of Jews of both sexes and all age groups'.[19] While the murder commandos killed approximately 50,000 Soviet Jews in the first eight weeks of the war, the number had risen to 500,000 within the next four months.[20]

As unambiguous as Himmler's command was, it should not be interpreted as an isolated, authoritative act. As early as 8 August, while on an inspection tour to the Baltic states, an official of the Armament Economy Office was informed that 'several thousand Jews have been "liquidated" in

Libau [Liepāja]. . . . Jewish women have not been shot up to now. There was talk that they would be eliminated later by gassing.'[21] Himmler evidently had not simply ordered the expansion of the genocide on 15 August; it had previously been discussed and demanded by the officers and teams of the murder commandos, and to some extent it was already practised.[22]

The rapid radicalization of anti-Jewish policy in the occupied areas of the Soviet Union must be seen, in retrospect, as part of the Holocaust. From the perspective of the perpetrators, however, it was part of the foundation of practical experience that contributed – within only a few weeks after the failure of the last major deportation project – to the decision leading up to the construction of large extermination camps. Thus, 15 August 1941 cannot be interpreted as the date of a decision to undertake comprehensive, general extermination, as the following documents will demonstrate.

## Remote 'final reception sites'

On 3 September 1941, Höppner again contacted Eichmann. He sent him a 15-page memorandum on the 'organization of the Central Resettlement Office (UWZ)', in which he developed ideas on how to logistically manage the new, colossal deportation plans that extended far into the Soviet Union. It is evident from the memo that Eichmann had verbally requested such a statement. Höppner had also 'discussed in detail' his 'basic ideas' with Krumey, head of the UWZ branch office in Lodz, in order to ensure that 'actual practical experience' had been taken into consideration. Höppner also sent the outlined plan to Hans Ehlich, his second superior in the RSHA. He always informed Ehlich on issues of 'ethnically alien elements' in general (i.e., not only Jews), including questions of so-called racial selection. Höppner began:

> After the end of the war a large-scale deportation of population groups that are undesirable for the Greater German Reich will be necessary in the various territories taken over by Germany. This concerns not only the final solution of the Jewish question, which will pertain to, in addition to the Greater German Reich, all states under German control; in addition, it includes above all the deportation of racially not re-Germanizable members of primarily eastern and southeastern peoples within the German settlement sphere. This task is the responsibility of the Reichsführer SS, in his capacity as Reich Commissioner for the Consolidation of German Nationhood; it must be assumed by him, as it was previously by the Chief of Security Police and the SD, since it is essentially a security police issue.

Following an enclosed diagram, Höppner suggested setting up branches of the UWZ in the Generalgouvernement and the Protectorate of Bohemia and Moravia, as well as in the various Reich Commissariats into which the Soviet Union was and would be further divided. In short, he intended to 'establish a tight, thoroughly organized office' that would set up branch offices in all those 'territories out of which ethnically alien elements flow and into which they are again settled'. 'For the sake of expedience', the branches were to be established 'at human transfer points, where camps are set up and where transports have to be organized'.

After completing his multi-page presentation of the organization and bureaucratic details of a future Central Resettlement Office (UWZ) based on the models developed in Posen and Lodz, Höppner concluded with a caveat:

The ideas I have presented here remain incomplete since I know neither the intentions of the Führer and the Reichsführer SS, nor those of the Chief of the Security Police and the SD with respect to plans for these territories. I could imagine making available vast areas that are presently part of Soviet Russia for population groups that are undesirable in the Greater German settlement sphere; they would be totally under the administration of the chief of the security police and the SD, or at least that of the Reichsführer SS and the chief of the German police. I imagine an SS and police official at the head of such an area, who has a staff to carry out his orders that might resemble that of a military commander in the occupied territories. . . . Further, it might be useful to delegate a man from the Four-Year Plan to serve as financial expert to the staff of the SS and police chief.

Höppner's memorandum on further resettlement politics, prepared at Eichmann's request, corresponded without a doubt to similar considerations by the planning department of the RKF within the scope of the General Plan for the East; some of the relevant documents have survived. Höppner's basic ideas also appeared in a note of 21 August written by SS Sturmbannführer and legation counsellor Carltheo Zeitschel. Zeitschel wrote the following for his superior, Ambassador Otto Abetz in Paris, on the 'solution of the Jewish question in all of Europe':

In establishing the new order of the eastern territory, these six million Jews [living in the Soviet Union] would have to be somehow consolidated, probably on a separate territory created for them. It should not prove all that difficult to use this opportunity to add all the Jews [from] all the other European states and to deport those Jews herded together in ghettos in Warsaw, Litzmannstadt, Lublin, etc. . . . We could then make all of Europe empty of Jews [judenfrei] within a short period of time.

Unlike Höppner and Eichmann, Zeitschel was of the opinion that 'the problem of transporting the Jews to the eastern territories would be possible, even during the war'. Zeitschel, however, had no practical experience in resettlement. He proposed discussing the subject with the 'Reich Minister for the Eastern Territories, Reichsleiter [Alfred] Rosenberg', and with Himmler; he also advised 'suggesting this idea' to Göring, since he felt Göring was 'very receptive to the Jewish problem at the present time'.[23]

Heydrich could at least boast of an organizational success on 12 September 1941. He wrote to Pohl of

the extraordinary significance of the decision of the Führer that the responsibility of the Reichsführer SS, in his capacity as the Reich Commissioner for the Consolidation of German Nationhood, has now been made effective and valid in the occupied eastern territories as well.[24]

This gave Himmler free rein in all (re)settlement policy matters, both in the Generalgouvernement and the occupied Soviet Union. In other words, Rosenberg, Reich Minister for the Eastern Territories, and his Reich commissioners were required – in theory, that is, since the Führer decision for now did not mean much more – to bow to Himmler's population policy orders.[25] The 'solution of the Jewish question' was within his jurisdiction.

From 13 to 15 September, the 135 staff members of cluster IIIB of the RSHA held a meeting, presided over by their director, Ehlich, to discuss the 'situation of ethnic and racial policies'. Since the content of the addresses and discussions was confidential, 'only those matters accessible to the public [were] recorded with file references'. Lecture topics included 'The organization and future development of work on nationhood [*Volkstumsarbeit*]', 'The minorities question and its resolution', 'The resettlement of ethnic Germans and settlement tasks in the East', and 'The state of ethnic policy in the East'.[26]

On 7 October, Heydrich enacted comprehensive administrative instructions 'on setting up and organizing the immigration and emigration offices of the security police'. The explanation corresponded to both the RKF's General Plan for the East and Höppner's memorandum: 'The occupation of additional territories has considerably expanded the tasks of the security police in the area of immigration and emigration.' Mention of relocation in the closing paragraph 28 is succinct and quite threatening: 'The activities of Department II – Relocation – and Department III – Police Action – are subject to special orders issued by the Chief of the Security Police and the SD.'[27]

Höppner responded in a similarly imprecise manner in his memorandum on the subject of relocation and evacuation. However, unlike Heydrich's semi-public order, Höppner's memo contained an explicit justification:

It would be sheer fantasy to discuss further organization in these intake areas [of the occupied Soviet Union], since fundamental decisions must first be made. Aside from that, it is essential that we be totally clear from the outset as to what is to be done in the end with these displaced populations that are undesirable for the Greater German settlement areas. Is the goal to permanently secure them some sort of subsistence, or should they be totally eradicated?[28]

To judge by this memo, Höppner still assumed in early September that 'the final solution of the Jewish question' was an essential initial step in the general evacuation programme and that it would affect Jews living in all states 'under German control'. He did not view systematic murder as having already been agreed upon. He did indeed know that discussion of it was largely a result of his own initiative. His own combination of proposal and demand forced a fundamental decision to be made. His motives are obvious: first of all, Höppner knew all too well how time-consuming and hopeless plans for mass deportations could be. Second, in view of the stagnating German invasion on the eastern front, he must have been aware that there would be hardly any possibility for him to organize transports until the following summer. Third, he made reference to his own proposal of 16 July – even if he did not mention it explicitly – and expanded upon it. Whereas at that time, six weeks earlier, Höppner had considered using a 'fast-acting means' on the approximately 100,000 Jews in the Warthegau who were unfit for work, he was now demanding that a decision be made whether the term 'evacuation' should continue to mean the deportation of many millions of people into wretched conditions, or should instead mean their immediate death. The response to Höppner's questions tended to pertain to all 'populations . . . undesirable for the Greater German settlement areas', first and foremost – and now in its entirety – European Jewry.

## Disparate documents

Some sources cannot be easily incorporated into the latest developments in research. Nevertheless, I would like to introduce them here. Perhaps their classification will become possible at a later date. Right now, they merely serve to demonstrate how difficult it is to make concrete statements about the course of discussion in the latter half of 1941 on methods for the 'final solution of the Jewish question', and about the alternatives introduced into that discussion.

# Ships

Commissions from the concentration camp administration inspected the resettlement camps in the late summer of 1941. A memorandum of 11 September announced that they came 'for the purpose of registering ethnic Germans . . . who were to be used in guard units in the concentration camps'.[29] At the same time, these commissioners from Berlin were seeking 'inland waterway navigators in the camps with detailed knowledge of Russian currents and canals'.[30] The memorandum can be seen as marking the turning point in the war on the Eastern front. The Wehrmacht had enormous supply problems – hence the search for inland waterway navigators – and the delay in deportations initially led to the plan to expand the system of concentration camps as quickly and consistently as possible – hence the recruitment of guard units.

The concentration camp administration's search for navigators could also have something to do with the transport problems faced by the RSHA and the RKF after their original deportation plans failed in August. There is in fact a second document that mentions ships. On 18 October 1941 Franz Rademacher, officer for Jewish matters in the German Foreign Office, and Friedrich Suhr, Eichmann's staff member in charge of the 'solution of the Jewish question in Europe', travelled to Belgrade.[31] The aim of their mission was to gain an impression 'on the ground' of the difficulties that arose in solving 'the Jewish and Gypsy problems'. 'The situation' appeared to the Berlin delegation to be 'very precarious'. Local offices demanded quick deportation; Rademacher, on the other hand, examined the reasons 'why the Jews [could be transported] neither to Romania nor to the Generalgouvernement or the East'. Agreement was finally reached on the following points:

1. Male Jews will be shot by the end of this week, thus eliminating the problem mentioned in the delegation's report.
2. The remaining approximately 20,000 Jews (women, children, and the elderly), as well as approx. 1500 Gypsies, of whom the men shall likewise be shot, . . . shall initially be consolidated in the Gypsy quarter and then transported at night to the Serbian (Danube) island of Mitrovica.

Food for the winter had been 'secured in meagre amounts', according to the report. 'As soon as logistically feasible,' Rademacher closed his report, 'within the scope of the overall solution of the Jewish question, the Jews will be deported by ship to the reception camps in the East.'[32]

Here once again, ships were spoken of. Ever since the Baltic Germans were brought 'home to the Reich' via the Baltic Sea, officials of the resettlement programme had known waterways to be the simplest and least expensive form of 'modern mass migration'. In the autumn of 1940, the

Ethnic German Liaison Office – with the help of the Danube Steamship Company of Vienna – transported more than 100,000 'settlers' to Belgrade from Russian and Romanian harbours along the Danube. There, in the harbours of Prahovo and Semlin, they built reception camps for a total of 15,000 people.[33] In the summer of 1941, as part of plans to evacuate children from urban areas, almost 30,000 youths were brought by ship to remote camps from areas of the Reich that were in risk of being bombed.[34]

## Mogilev

Albert Widmann, chemist at the Forensics Institute in Berlin, arrived in Mogilev on 18 September 1941. There he carried out gassing experiments at the psychiatric institution, killing at least 20 patients. Whereas the Operation T-4 gas chambers and the gas vans of the Lange Special Commando Unit used carbon monoxide discharged from gas canisters, these deaths represented a further development of the procedure, 'since it was impossible to transport CO canisters to Russia'.[35] Widmann channelled the exhaust of two running automobile engines into a provisionally sealed laboratory room for his experiment in Mogilev. The patients died after approximately 15 minutes. This procedure was deemed especially feasible, 'because any random room could be used for this procedure, and motor vehicles were available everywhere'.[36] Arthur Nebe, head of *Einsatzgruppe* B, was also chief of the Reich Criminal Police Office in civilian life and thus Widmann's superior. Nebe had ordered and observed the experiment. In mid-August Himmler had directed him to do so and to 'report' back to him on the results.[37] The experiment led to the construction of a new generation of gas van, which was then used starting in December 1941 in the Warthegau, the occupied parts of the Soviet Union, and – somewhat later – in Serbia.

It is perhaps no coincidence that the experiment took place in the Novinki psychiatric institution near Mogilev, as Himmler had visited precisely this institution on 15–16 August.[38] On 9 September, *Einsatzkommando* (Task Force) 8 set up operations in Mogilev as its 'final' site – a rather unusual step in fast-moving mobile warfare. The Higher SS and Police Chief of Central Russia, Erich von dem Bach-Zelewski, also resided there.[39] An SS unit entered Novinki in late October, and all patients who had survived to that point were shot on 5 November.[40] In mid-November, the SS Main Office for Budget and Construction ordered a huge crematorium for Mogilev. It was to comprise 32 cremation chambers, for a daily cremation capacity of more than 2000 corpses. The ovens were to be fired with wood instead of the usual coke.[41] On 30 December 1941, the first four chambers arrived in Mogilev. Additional parts of the planned facility were later redirected to Auschwitz.

The plans to set up such a crematorium in Mogilev have only recently become known, since information on it was found in the files of the building administration of the Auschwitz concentration camp, which were long hidden away in Moscow. Jean-Claude Pressac evaluated this material in his book *Les Crématoires d'Auschwitz* (The Crematoriums of Auschwitz). However, I believe the author erred in taking too literally the reason for sending the crematoriums to Mogilev, as stated in the contract between the SS building administration and the manufacturer in Erfurt. The customer had claimed it urgently needed the huge crematorium to burn the remains of tens of thousands of victims of a typhus epidemic, including their clothing and the lice, i.e., the cause and carriers of the disease.[42] I consider this a pretext. The airtight box-shaped superstructure for the previously mentioned gas vans, in which without a doubt hundreds of thousands of Jews were to be murdered, had been ordered from a special company in Berlin by SS technicians under exactly the same pretext a short time earlier; they claimed they needed these special trucks to transport the corpses of those who had died from an alleged typhus epidemic.[43]

I believe this raises the question whether a centre for the extermination of European Jewry was to be set up in Mogilev in the autumn of 1941. If that is the case, then it is obvious that this project was already reduced in scope in December, shortly after it was started, and abandoned in favour of camps situated farther west. This would not have happened all of a sudden. The 'Mogilev' alternative would not be definitively abandoned until it was proven in practice that sufficient options existed to murder the Jews undisturbed in occupied Poland.

## Dnieper

These considerations accord with the aforementioned ship transports. Mogilev lies 200 kilometres east of Minsk at an altitude of 144.6 m (474 ft) above sea level, at the northeastern edge of the Pripet (Pinsk) Marshes. The city had a population of 60,000 in 1941. Its railway connection to the west was insignificant,[44] but it did have a river harbour on the upper Dnieper (see map 3, on p. xi).

The river, as a specialist in inland navigation determined in 1941, drops gradually and is unusual for Russia in that it remains ice-free, even in the upper reaches, for an average of 240 days per year. In 1939 it took ships about 150 hours for the upstream passage from the Crimean Black Sea port; travel was not difficult, thanks to the 60-metre-high dam built southwest of Dnjepropetrovsk, completed in 1932.[45]

If this description of the river is examined in conjunction with the planned construction of the crematoriums in Mogilev, the result is an outline of a plan for the deportation and extermination of the Jews of southeastern Europe. In any case, drawing such a conclusion would correspond with Rademacher's statement of 25 October, in which he assured the transport of Jewish women and children the following spring, 'by ship, to the reception camps in the East'.

There is yet another indication of such a project; according to one – albeit controversial – source, Hitler authorized Himmler on 2 October 1941 'to remove' the 50,000 Jews from the northern Greek city of Salonika.[46] One must ask why Himmler had the deportation of Jews from the remote city of Salonika authorized at this early point in time, since, first of all, he was confronted with the much more urgent resettlement demands of his colleagues at the RKF and the UWZ; second, the Gauleiters of Berlin and Vienna – Goebbels and von Schirach, respectively – were repeatedly pressuring Hitler to deport the 120,000 Jews of these two cities preferentially; and third, Heydrich had already announced that he would make the Protectorate of Bohemia and Moravia 'free of Jews . . . within the year'. A possible answer might be that Himmler saw ship logistics to be certain, operating independent of the Reich railway system and any possible failures of the Wehrmacht. This would provide him with the opportunity to start a not merely rhetorical, but real 'solution of the European Jewish question'. From this perspective, Jews of the port city of Salonika were the ones in Himmler's direct sphere of influence that he could most easily transport by ship via the Crimean peninsula to Mogilev.

The description of inland navigation routes in the western Soviet Union cited above reveals yet another perspective. It states that one of the most important secondary rivers of the Dnieper is, 'because of its significance for passage to central Europe, without a doubt the Pripet'. It 'facilitates navigation' due to its minimal drop and 'substantial water volume'. 'The Dnieper–Bug Channel built by the Bolsheviks in 1939–40 increased shipping considerably starting in the summer of 1940. Not only were export shipments bound for Germany routed to Brest Litovsk, but shipping also greatly assisted the Bolshevik offensive.'[47]

If the description is read another way, it could explain what Himmler was thinking of when he promised Greiser on 18 September 1941 that the additional 60,000 Jews he had wanted to crowd into the Lodz ghetto would be 'deported further east next *spring*'.[48] For one thing, at this time it was relatively certain that the Wehrmacht was to begin a new, second offensive on the eastern front the following spring, thus blocking the railway lines; moreover, the Ethnic German Liaison Office had specifically sought inland navigators familiar with Russian rivers and channels.

## 'Preliminary considerations'

On 3 September 1941, when Höppner asked the RSHA whether the 'populations that are undesirable for the Greater German settlement areas' were to be 'permanently [secured] some sort of subsistence' or 'totally eradicated', Fähndrich had also turned to Eichmann. Fähndrich, head of the 'Human Deployment' Department of the RKF, wanted to know when the 'evacuations' were finally going to resume.

At the same time, he started creating facts on the ground. Without waiting for a response from Eichmann, Fähndrich wrote to the four RKF representatives in the incorporated eastern territories the next day:

> Since the reasons that led at the time to an interruption of evacuations to the Generalgouvernement to some extent no longer exist, I intend – together with the Chief of the Security Police and the SD – to obtain permission from the Generalgouverneur for the evacuations to be resumed, even if to a limited degree. Hence I request an exact report of the extent to which evacuations are needed for the near future. Please list only those evacuations that are urgently needed to enable resettlements. An overview of additional, desired evacuations can be attached.[49]

Höppner used the same method. On 20 August he had already ordered, within the scope of a 'general inspection' of Poles, the selection of those 'who must be first and immediately relocated when evacuations are resumed (those who are especially unsound racially, in particular those with the blood of Asian peoples, and asocials, in particular criminals and those unfit for work)'.[50]

Zeitschel, too, as liaison between the German embassy in Paris and the commander of the security police there, was not interested merely in far-reaching visions of the future; three weeks after presenting his statement on the 'Jewish question in all of Europe', he demanded that the Reich Foreign Minister get Himmler to approve the deportation of 10,000 Jews in camps 'to the newly occupied eastern territories as soon as possible, in order to clear the few wretched camps we have for additional Jews'.[51]

On 9 September 1941 Greifelt, head of the RKF staff main office, demanded that 'the areas around Ciechanów, Bialystok, the Beskids, or the northwestern region of the Generalgouvernement' be 'cleared' for the settlement of a total of 30,000 Dobruja, Bessarabian, and Bukovinian Germans.[52]

One day later, Fähndrich of Greifelt's 'Human Deployment' Department suggested transporting the Lithuanian Germans, who had been resettled eight months earlier, 'back to their old farms'.[53] Greifelt saw himself 'forced', as he put it, 'to reach agreement with the royal Italian government that another contingent of South Tyroleans be removed, as provided for in the German–Italian treaty';[54] that is, a total of 30,000 people were to be resettled within a few weeks from South Tyrol to Germany.[55]

As though by tacit agreement, all demands for 'evacuation', 'making room', and 'clearing' that had been temporarily deferred since March 'in view of the impending events in the East' were resumed in July–August 1941. Eichmann, who otherwise often replied within hours, did not respond to Fähndrich's request – which was followed by two similar telex messages from Höppner and Krumey – until 29 September, i.e., four weeks later.[56]

In 1960 in Jerusalem, Eichmann described, under the rubric 'My Memoirs', the problems he experienced in the summer 1941: 'Like the earlier situation regarding emigration, . . . increasing difficulties [arose] with the evacuations'; on the one hand, he felt pressured, and 'on the other, the project died from bureaucratic inactivity and true difficulties'.[57] Despite numerous reservations about the source value of such a document, it is true that on 29 September Eichmann answered Fähndrich, Höppner, and Krumey in just this tone: 'Although not underestimating the difficulties surrounding the resettlement,' he began, 'a resumption of evacuations *at this time* cannot be reckoned with.' He continued:

> in view of the current situation, the Generalgouvernement is not in a position at this time to facilitate the influx of Poles and Jews. Even a request to accept Jews returned from the district of Warsaw who illegally entered the government district of Zichenau [Ciechanów, located in the 'incorporated' part of East Prussia] has been initially rejected by the office of the Generalgouverneur. . . . In addition, I would like to add in this context that in view of my efforts to find another territory that could serve as a provisional alternative to take in the contingent of evacuees – the occupied Soviet Russian territories were considered – it has been decided that we should wait until the transport situation improves. Under the present circumstances, there is no telling when a resumption of the relocations to the incorporated eastern territories can once again be considered.[58]

This letter is noteworthy in several respects. Eichmann drew a direct correlation between 'difficulties in the resettlement' of ethnic Germans and the 'evacuation of the Jews', just as Himmler did on 10 December 1940 to Reich and Gau leaders. In his explanation, Eichmann described how the old conflict with the administration of the Generalgouvernement had reignited with regard to attaining authorization for each and every resettlement – the well-known 'untenable situation'. Furthermore, he reported on his 'efforts . . . to find . . . a provisional alternative' in occupied Soviet Russian territories. Was Eichmann referring to Mogilev as a deportation destination? Why did he emphasize the words 'at this time' at the beginning of his letter? Was he already working on concrete alternatives? Presumably, yes. However, were these actual assignments or a product of his own initiative? Was Eichmann still counting on a 'solution of the Jewish question' after winning the war, or was it to be implemented during the war? The option of mass murder had certainly already been considered at this point in time; Höppner's memorandum of 2 September

1941 is evidence of this. Nevertheless, it is uncertain how far the consensus on this subject extended and whether the sites and methods had already been decided upon at the time Eichmann composed his response to Fähndrich. Questions can merely be posed in this regard.[59]

It is, however, clear what Eichmann failed to include in his letter. On the same day, 29 September 1941, he obtained approval from the Reich Ministry of Transport for the transport of 20,000 Jews and 5000 Gypsies out of the territory of the Reich. The trains were not destined for the conquered 'territory' of the Soviet Union, as had been planned for months, and they were not even headed to eastern Poland, to the former German–Soviet demarcation line. Instead, their destination – albeit temporary, as Himmler promised – was the Lodz ghetto.[60] This is precisely where, under the aegis of Fähndrich, Höppner and Krumey had demanded massive deportation of 'undesirable population groups'. Eichmann had worked out this deportation schedule at the request of Himmler and implemented it a short time later, since 'the Führer' had requested 'that, from West to East, the Old Reich and the Protectorate [be] emptied and freed of Jews as soon as possible'.[61]

Himmler passed this 'request' of Hitler's on to Greiser, Gauleiter responsible for Lodz, on 18 September. It led to the deportation of Jews and Gypsies to the Lodz ghetto, 'as an initial step', as Himmler promised. But this decision resulted in massive protests from the Lodz ghetto administration, the economic command generals, and the mayor and provincial head of the government there. Nevertheless, the transports began on 15 October.

Orders to deport a large portion of the German-Jewish population were issued by Himmler in his position as Reichsführer SS. As Reich Commissioner for the Consolidation of German Nationhood, he ordered via Wilhelm Koppe, his representative in Posen, the 'speedy settlement' of the approximately 30,000 Bessarabian and Bukovinian Germans 'still remaining' in transit camps in the Warthegau.[62]

Complying with Himmler's wishes, Koppe explained to the men of the SS settlement staff in Posen what they had to do. He started by describing 'the tragic fate of the settlers in the camps, who were broken down both mentally and physically and almost incapable of being resettled'. Then he gave a 'binding order' that the settlement of the peasants among the ethnic German internees 'must be implemented by 1 December 1941' and that city dwellers were to be settled 'by 31 December 1941'. Koppe brushed aside critical questions whether 'this had not become irresponsible'. Instead, he sent all those present on their way with the following advice: the SS men of the settlement staffs had to be 'the eternally restless element, stirring people up . . . and putting pressure on all offices involved in the settlements'; they had to 'be inventive with regard to the means used to support the settlement process'.[63]

Since settlements always required prior evacuations, to be on the safe side, Krumey was present at the meeting. Since deportations 'to the East' were not an option, as Eichmann had just confirmed, the only remaining alternative was to 'force' the Poles into the quarters still inhabited by Jews in the Warthegau region. Thus, it was convenient that the ethnic Germans were supposed to be settled in the eastern part of the Warthegau (the West had been 'free of Jews' since early 1940). On 26 September, Krumey had already sent 900 Jewish women and children by train from Włocławek (German: Leslau) to the Lodz ghetto. A second transport with more than 1000 people from the same area followed three days later, 'again almost exclusively women and children'.[64] There was also a third transport.[65] All of this was done to make room for Poles, who in turn had to make way for German settlers. This action was carried out against the express wishes of the Lodz mayor, Werner Ventzki. At the same time, he had had the homes of 2000 Jews at the edge of the ghetto torn down 'for the purpose of improved police surveillance and in the course of city planning', and he now feared 'a danger of epidemic'.[66]

The first systematic murder of Jews in the Warthegau took place within this context. Neither the exact date nor the method of extermination – gas van or firing squad? – is known. There is nevertheless agreement that it took place in late September or early October. If we follow the principles by which Höppner, Krumey, and others like them acted, this crime would have taken place just when it became clear – after the Włocławek Jews were put into the Lodz ghetto – that any additional deportations would fail due to resistance by the local authorities.

A report by Isaiah Trunk described the events as follows:

> The entire Jewish population of the district of Konin, approximately 3000 people, [had been] concentrated in Sagurawe. Prior to this, all men between 14 and 60 and all women between 14 and 50 had to receive a medical examination, which cost four Reichsmarks per person. This was supposed to determine fitness for labour, so they said. After that the evacuation began, which we were told was supposed to be by truck to the neighbouring city of Koil and from there by train to Lodz. In fact, however, 60 people were loaded onto each truck and taken to the nearby forests of Kazimierz [Biskupi], where they were murdered.[67]

Thus before this first systematic murder of the Jews of an entire community in the Warthegau took place, Himmler had for a variety of reasons already had Jews transported to the Lodz ghetto or had announced their transport. Of course, Heydrich also participated, simultaneously pursuing his own interests. After taking over the office of 'deputy' Reich protector in Prague on 27 September because of the growing Czech resistance movement, and thus *de facto* becoming the Reich protector himself, Heydrich declared the 'solution of the Jewish question' there to be one of the most important items on his agenda. On 10 October he had already held a consultation with his new offices in the Hradcany on the 'solution of the Jewish question in the Protectorate and partly in the Old Reich'. This provided for the 'evacuation' of the approximately 88,000 Czech Jews, starting on 15 October, and for the transport of 5000 Prague Jews 'to start moving little by little until 15 November'. The destination of these transports was also the Lodz ghetto. Since according to Heydrich's data, however, 'for now, much consideration [had to be shown to] the Litzmann-stadt authorities', an additional 50,000 – the 'most troublesome Jews' – were to be selected and deported to Minsk and Riga, where Nebe and Rasch, heads of the *Einsatzgruppen*, would put the Jews 'in the camps for communist prisoners'.[68] The 'Gypsies to be evacuated' from the Protectorate, i.e., *all* of them, were to 'be brought to Stahlecker in Riga'.

Since these camps did not exist, and prisoners of war assumed to be communists were executed without exception at this point in time, Heydrich's wording implied that the Czech Jews and Gypsies there were to be treated in exactly the same manner.[69] Heydrich wanted initially to concentrate all those who, according to this plan, could not yet be deported 'to the East', approximately 30,000 people, in two isolated ghettos, each one divided into a 'work camp' and a 'supply camp'.[70] These were not to produce for the wartime economy; rather, they were only supposed to produce 'small objects without the use of machinery'. 'The "Council of Elders" was supposed to collect these objects and, in return, they would receive a minimum of foodstuffs with the calculated minimum of vitamins, etc.' This form of ghettoization was to lead to the death of the majority of inhabitants within a very short time.

> The Jews will have to dig themselves a place to stay. . . . Precautionary measures should be taken to prevent epidemics developing in the ghetto from endangering the surroundings. . . . The Jews are by no means to be buried; instead, bodies are to be burnt locally in small crematoriums in the ghetto.

These ghettos were to be 'temporary camps' until the inhabitants were evacuated to 'regions in the East'. They were to lead to a 'greatly decimated' ghetto population by the time of deportation.[71]

## Constructing the extermination machine

The record of the Prague meeting of 10 October 1941 documents how little, in these days and months, the notion of murderous deportation still differed from that of immediate and, if possible, trouble-free extermination of European Jewry; and how the term 'evacuation' became a synonym for murder. From this point on, the outward description of the last remaining – minuscule – steps in the building of a complete extermination machine has been verified in many sources. If – beyond private conversations between Hitler, Göring, Himmler, Frank, Greiser, and Heydrich – there were ever any official documentation of the programme, and not merely a command, through which the long wished-for biological eradication of European Jewry would be implemented in the form of a fast, industrialized process of extermination, then it would most likely be dated in the first two weeks of October.

On 6 October, Hitler modified his 'request' that the Jews be temporarily deported to the Lodz ghetto. He then demanded that 'all Jews be removed from the Protectorate, and not merely to the Generalgouvernement [and the incorporated eastern territories], but directly farther East'. This, how-ever, was deemed 'not feasible at the present moment due to the great demands for transportation by the military'.[72] It might very well be that at this time, Hitler did not yet use such wording to mean the construction of gas chambers; we simply do not know.[73]

A description of the concrete facts appears more significant to me. As indicated by the sequence of events, there must have been some political transformation during these few days. Himmler and Heydrich now ordered the construction of several large extermination facilities. This thus opened up for them the opportunity to implement the deportation demands and promises that had been repeatedly postponed, without any complicated negotiations with the authorities of 'receiving districts', and involving only relatively minor logistical and material expenses.

I assume that the final step between making the political decision and actually carrying out the plans was an extremely small one, which was possible under the conditions of this dictatorship as long as it was not confronted with any conflicting interests. The technological prerequisites for mass extermination had long since been tested on the mentally ill and had been developed further since Widmann's experiment in Mogilev. Regarding the actual course of events, my ideas are supported by the confusing, varied decision on policies towards the Jews between August and late September/early October 1941. This was followed by a phase of rapid, carefully targeted individual decision-making in mid-October and November. The following chronology emerges from the facts themselves.

In the second half of October, Globocnik's staff chose Belzec as the location for the extermination camp to be built in the Generalgouverne-ment; construction began in early November.[74] After some delays, the first eastern Polish Jews were murdered there on 17 March 1942. The Sobibór and Treblinka concentration camps were built later. Technically and logis-tically, they were subcamps of Belzec, built to increase extermination capacity and reduce transport distances. After Heydrich's assassination in May 1942, they were referred to collectively as the camps of 'Operation Reinhard'.

On 21 October 1941, i.e., right after preparations had been made for the construction of the Belzec extermination camp, a prohibition against building new ghettos came into force in the Generalgouvernement. The explanation was that 'there is hope that the Jews will be deported within the foreseeable future'.[75] Four days later, the head of the Warsaw *Judenrat* noted, 'In conference of *Bevölkerungswesen* [Population Division of the German administration] in Kraków, there was a feeling that plans exist which go beyond the mere reduction of the ghetto area (could it be resettlement?).'[76] On 11 November, advertising that had begun in August for contracts involving the employment of Jews in the Warsaw ghetto was stopped.[77] On 22 October, the officer for *Volkstum* issues of the Krakow Institute for German Activities in the East (IDO) found that continued anthropological field research on Jewish families was threatened: 'We do not know', he wrote to a staff member, urging her to act quickly, 'what measures for the relocation of the Jewish population have been planned for the next few months; we might lose valuable material if we wait too long.' On 3 November, the two researchers for the project agreed to anthropologically survey '100 [Jewish] families, in order to save at least some of the material, should any measures be taken'.[78]

On 20 November, Kurt Eimann, the SS man who led the first mass executions of the mentally ill in 1939 in the West Prussian city of Wejherowo (German: Neustadt), was made area commander of the SS in Lublin.[79] On 27 and 28 November, members of the technical staff of Operation T-4 met in Pirna 'to discuss the future'.[80] Brack definitely mentioned sending some of the murder specialists to Belzec; this began a short time later.

Parallel to these events, initial discussions took place on 21 and 22 October about the construction of a crematorium with 15 chambers at Auschwitz. Theoretically, 1440 corpses could be cremated in it within 24 hours. In mid-November the same members of the SS building administration ordered a similar facility with 32 cremation chambers for Mogilev.[81] In December, the concentration camp commandant at Auschwitz carried out the first experiment in killing prisoners with the Zyklon B pesticide.[82]

After construction of the first series of six small gas vans intended for the *Einsatzgruppen* in the Soviet Union, a 'trial gassing' was carried out on 3 November in the Sachsenhausen concentration camp. In December, the department for technical matters within the Reich Security Main Office ordered the production of 30 special containers for gas vans, with which 100 people could be killed per trip.[83] The first series, which was considerably smaller and whose six vans had a total capacity of 30 to 50 people per trip, had been ordered in early October. A clear, qualitative leap separates the two orders; the December order raised the killing capacity of the gas vans twelve-fold.

Mass extermination of the Jews began on 8 December. The Chelmno extermination camp was equipped first with two and later with three gas vans. It was located 50 kilometres north of Lodz. Although no further deportations to the Generalgouvernement or the Soviet Union were considered at this time, the UWZ in Lodz set up a special 'Department

II – Relocation' on 19 November. This evidently involved an administrative reorganization in view of the impending 'evacuation' of Jews to Chelmno.[84]

## German consensus

Only after all these technical and organizational preparations had been made did Heydrich organize what was then called the 'consultation of the state secretaries', held on 29 November on the banks of the Grosser Wannsee. He referred to his written orders of 31 July 1941 from Göring, and enclosed a photocopy of this order with each invitation, for 'joint discussion'. The conference had to be postponed; it finally took place on 20 January 1942. Heydrich sought and needed the political consensus of 'all . . . central institutions directly involved with these issues with respect to bringing their goals into line'.[85] After briefly summarizing German policy towards the Jews over the last nine years, Heydrich then came to the main topic on the agenda: 'Instead of emigration,' he began, 'an additional solution, after prior authorization by the Führer, has now become the evacuation of the Jews to the East.' He closed the session 'with a request [to those present] . . . to lend him the appropriate support in carrying out the tasks necessary for the solution'.[86]

The record of the conference of 20 January 1942 is merely a pale reflection of a process of discussions and decisions by the civilian, police, and military elites of the German Reich. How did these men converse with each other on the telephone? What comments were made; what complicit glances were thrown to each other in passing at their countless formal and informal meetings? The record is worded in the usual coded language of the 'top secret Reich matter', which preferred expressions such as 'deport', 'resettle', or 'move through' to explicit mention of killing. This language did not serve to ensure secrecy. It aimed, through the use of aseptic terminology, to make mass murder easier to administer and – this was the intention and achievement of the conference – it helped incorporate the 'final solution' into the daily bureaucratic and political routines of the German state and organize a division of labour. The procedure made it possible for each person to avoid any individual responsibility, instead entering into partly active, but generally passive, complicity with the government. Nothing more was demanded of the individual. Nothing more was necessary in Germany.

Heydrich had largely already built a consensus among the various participating authorities during the weeks prior to the conference. The Justice Ministry and the Reich Chancellery were already dealing with the issue of where to draw the line 'regarding what people are to be affected by the measures under consideration'.[87] The conference participants resolved to defer the deportation of so-called *Mischlinge* (i.e., those of 'mixed blood') and of Jews in mixed marriages, since they could not agree on where to draw the line. They considered 'the impact of such a measure on the German relatives' and also feared that the complicated task of 'settling issues of mixed marriages and mixed blood' could lead to 'never-ending administrative paperwork'. The Wehrmacht, too, had submitted a statement supporting the deportation of Jewish men who had received honours in the First World War to Theresienstadt, the so-called 'ghetto for the aged', instead of to the extermination camps. Economic command specialists insisted 'that Jews presently employed in industries necessary for the war effort cannot be evacuated as long as replacements are not available'. The German Foreign Office developed 'requests and ideas . . . for the planned overall solution of the Jewish question in Europe'.[88]

Greifelt, chief of the RKF staff main office, had also been invited to the conference. He did not participate, however, since on 20 January he was busy trying to pacify the Italian government concerning a new delay in the resettlement of South Tyroleans.[89] Earlier, he had demanded that newly available Jewish real estate be placed at the disposal of the ethnic German settlers classified as 'Old Reich cases'. After 20 January 1942, he expressed his satisfaction that the Higher SS and Police Chief in Krakow had 'already come to an agreement with the Reich Security Main Office' about how the 'evacuation' of the Jews there should proceed.[90] Individual Gauleiters felt it was important to deport the Jews as quickly as possible, 'if only for housing reasons and other sociopolitical exigencies'. The Reich Ministries for Internal Affairs, Finance, and Labour worked together with the Reichsbank to determine how to distribute real estate and other property and, ultimately, the pension rights of those who would soon 'transfer their residence outside the country'.

In the Warthegau, Heydrich had to convince neither the Gauleiter, Greiser, nor his resettlement staff of the 'planned measure'. He faced somewhat more difficulty in the Generalgouvernement.[91] But there, as well, consensus existed within the civilian administration on the decision to murder the Jews to the same degree as the hoped-for rapid deportation to the East proved impracticable.

On 15 October 1941, Viennese bank director Max Bischof, economic specialist for the Warsaw ghetto, determined that the number of workers 'was insignificant in comparison with the mass of 500,000 people'. One day later, the Director of the Economy Department indicated 'that the ghetto could not support itself financially, could not survive without subsidies, if the aim were to maintain the viability of the Jewish population'. 'This', he continued, 'has nothing to do with the justification for the ghetto. It is an interim concentration camp until the time when the Jews can be deported.'[92]

At exactly the same time, from 13 to 16 October, approximately 100 public health, Wehrmacht, and SS physicians in Bad Krynica were working to combat epidemics in the Generalgouvernement. Jost Walbaum, head of the Health Department in the Frank government, had determined that

> there are only two ways. We sentence the Jews in the ghetto to death by hunger or we shoot them. Even if the end result is the same, the latter is more intimidating. We cannot do otherwise, even if we want to. We have one and only one responsibility, that the German people are not infected and endangered by these parasites. For that any means must be acceptable.

The minutes note at this point, 'applause, clapping'.[93]

Frank's representative at the Wannsee Conference, Josef Bühler, made a presentation expressing the sentiments of his staff experts. He suggested 'resolving the Jewish question' in the Generalgouvernement 'as soon as possible', because 'the Jew as a carrier of disease is an eminent danger' and 'moreover, the majority of cases are unfit for labour'.

On 16 December 1941 Frank informed his cabinet members of the planned mass extermination in a speech that suggests how, and with what line of reasoning, the conference participants discussed their decision to murder European Jewry:

> As an old National Socialist I must say, if the Jewish tribe were to survive the war, whereas we sacrificed our best blood for the preservation of Europe, then this war would represent only a partial victory. Therefore, as regards the Jews, I start from the basic assumption that they shall disappear. They have got to go.

Frank asked rhetorically,

> But what is to happen to the Jews? Do you think they will actually be resettled in villages in the eastern territories? We were told in Berlin: why all this trouble; we have no use for them in the eastern territories or in the Reich Commissariat [Ukraine] either. Liquidate them yourselves!

Perhaps in response to a questioning glance, Frank added some comments on how this was to be done.

> Ordinary conceptions cannot be applied to such gigantic and singular events. At any rate, we will have to find a means which will lead to the goal. . . . Where and how this is going to happen is a task for the agencies we will have to create and establish here, and I am going to tell you how they will work when the time comes. . . . The following thought, however, must stand above all else: directly following the process of re-Germanizing the eastern territories of the Reich, this territory of the Generalgouvernement will become the next part of Europe to be subject to absolute German penetration. We will build great Reich *autobahns* clear across our country. Along these Reich

*autobahns*, settlement villages inhabited by Germans will grow up. . . . Since this also gives us the opportunity to pass on to the East the ethnically alien populations we have no use for, it will not lead to insurmountable difficulties to let the German national element become more and more rooted and increasingly force out the ethnically alien element.[94]

In his speech, Frank also made this demand: 'The Generalgouvernement will have to become just as free of Jews [*judenfrei*] as the Reich.' That was obviously not the case on 16 December 1941. The deportations had just begun. But Frank suggested to himself and his listeners that the Jews had already 'disappeared'.

# Notes

1 Höppner's scepticism was confirmed in a note of 28 July 1941 by his staff member Krumey, which states:

> The third short-term plan, which started in February 1941, was interrupted by the OKW [Wehrmacht Supreme Command] on 15 March 1941 after the nineteenth transport, due to events in the East. On order of the Reichsführer SS, however, the settlers in the Vomi camps [in the Warthegau district] from Bessarabia and Buchenland [Bukovina] [approx. 30,000 people] must be settled this year in order to avoid further damages. In order to comply with this order, the UWZ camps were filled with up to 5000 Poles, on request of SS Gruppenführer Koppe, the Higher SS and Police Chief. The responsible offices were not able to name even an approximate date when the transport ban would be lifted and trains to the Generalgouvernement would resume running.
>
> (AGK, UWZ/P/146, 199f.)

2 The fact that Höppner pressed forward could be viewed as a contradiction to my interpretation of Göring's written order to Heydrich. Aside from Höppner's distrust of all too extensive deportation plans, a further argument should also be considered: Höppner might already have been informed that the Jews in sealed ghettos would be the last to be deported. This would correspond to the later order of transports to the extermination camps.

3 Quoted in Pätzold, 295.

4 Report by the SD main field office in Posen on the 'impact of resettlement in the district of Posen', 19 October 1940; AGK, UWZ/P/195, 4f. A similar report on 25 October 1940 is located ibid./225, 5.

5 Letter from Höppner to Eichmann, 16 July 1941; quoted in Pätzold, 295ff.

6 This is confirmed by the circumstances under which the last mentally ill Jews from Baden were transferred to T-4 in February 1941; see Faulstich, 258.

7 Quoted in Dressen, 78ff.

8 The name came from the relevant file reference used by the concentration camp inspector.

9 See Grode, 82ff.

10 Aly, 'Medicine', 45.

11 Grawitz's note and Clauberg's related planning outline; BDC, PA/Clauberg, quoted in Aly and Heim, 417.

12 See Hilberg, 417ff.

13 Ibid., 1007ff.; Bock, 452–6; Aly and Heim, 408–21.

14 For a summary, see Pohl, 97ff.

15 BDC, PA/Schmalenbach; quoted in Aly, 'Medicine', 45.

16 This is how Friedrich Mennecke referred to the position of his colleague Curt Schmalenbach in his letter of 25 November 1941 (quoted in Chroust, vol. 1, 242, and Chroust, 'Selected Letters', 253).

17 Wetzel's draft memorandum for Lohse and Rosenberg, 25 October 1941; quoted in Adler, 87; see Hilberg, 873ff.

18 Burrin, 111ff.; Beer, 407.

19 Streim, 114.

20 Burrin, 113; see also Adam, 303ff.

21 Travel report by Major von Payr, on his visit to the Northern Economic Inspectorate, 11 August 1941; BA-MA, RW 19/473, 124–32.

22 Mass executions in Liepāja were carried out by Special Commando Unit 1a, led by Martin Sandberger, whose main position was chief of the Central Immigration Office (EWZ). Sandberger had the appropriate expertise. He played a leading, active role when the psychiatric institutions in northeastern Germany and the annexed portion of Poland were 'evacuated' in 1939–40 for resettlement purposes. (Sandberger's deputy in the EWZ, Karl Tschierschky, had a similar career as head of Special Commando Unit 1c; see Wilhelm, *Rassenpolitik*, 198ff.).

23 Report by Zeitschel to Abetz, 22 August 1941, quoted in Klarsfeld, 367ff.; Safrian, 110ff.

24 Letter from the Chief of the Security Police and the SD to SS Gruppenführer Pohl, head of the administrative main office of the SS, 12 September 1941, Main Historical Archives of Riga, R-70/5/8, 4.

25 As can be seen from Heydrich's letter of 18 September 1941 to Lammers and the enclosed draft edicts, the extension of Himmler's power as head of the RKF lacked an important prerequisite; namely, a corresponding authorization by the security police to issue directives to the heads of the civilian administration in the occupied territories (see Kárný and Milotová, 121ff.).

26 BAK, R69/1152, *passim*. The meeting took place in the SD leadership school in Bernau, near Berlin.

27 *Befehlsblatt des Chefs der Sicherheitspolizei und des SD* (Command Gazette of the Chief of the Security Police and the SD) 2: 42 (31 October 1941), 219–41.

28 Memo of 2 September 1941 from Höppner to Eichmann and Ehlich, with a letter of 3 September; BAP-DH, ZR 890 A 2, 222–38. In the files of the Lodz UWZ, there is an outline on the subject of this memo that has a somewhat different structure; the document is neither dated nor signed (AGK, UWZ/L/3, 1).

29 By 1 October 1941, explicit instructions had already been issued for the 'registration of settlers as guards for concentration camps': 'The applicants, between the ages of 18 and 45, must be at least 1.65 m [5′4″] tall and may not be registered for military service or belong to a military unit.' By 5 October 1941, lists were to be submitted of 'any settlers . . . who could be considered for such operations' (memorandum of 1 October 1941 from the Vomi/Operations command of Lower Saxony, addressed 'to all camp commanders!'; BAK, R59/199, 15ff.).

30 Memorandum of the Ethnic German Liaison Office (Vomi)/Operations command, Baden Gau, 11 September 1941; BAK, R59/100, 93.

31 Also present was SS Untersturmführer Franz Stuschka of the 'Main Office for Jewish Emigration' in Vienna; Safrian, 113ff.

32 Rademacher's report for Luther, 25 October 1941; ADAP/D/XIII.2, 5790ff., quoted in Longerich, 288ff. On 8 September 1941, representatives of the

Foreign Office in Belgrade had 'sent a joint dispatch' proposing 'that 8000 Jewish men be removed from Serbia, perhaps in barges moving downstream on the Danube to [an island in] the delta of the river in Romania' (Veesenmayer and Benzler to the Foreign Office, 8 September 1941; NG-3354, quoted in Hilberg, 685).

33 'Die Donauschiffahrt im Dienste der Umsiedlung', *Zeitschrift für Binnenschiffahrt* 73 (1941), 55–8. (The former camp run by the Ethnic German Liaison Office was converted to an extermination camp in March 1942. There, approximately 16,000 Jews and 1500 Gypsies were murdered by means of a gas van. See Browning, *Fateful Months,* 70ff.; Hilberg, 690ff.)

34 Gerhard Dabel, 'Kinderlandverschickung mit Fahrgastschiffen', *Zeitschrift für Binnenschiffahrt* 74 (1942), 121ff.

35 Widmann's testimony of 11 January 1960, quoted in Beer, 407. (Gassing procedures were also developed in the autumn of 1939, involving the participation of the Forensics Institute.)

36 Judgment of the Stuttgart (jury) court of 15 September 1967 (Ks 19/62) in Widmann's trial, quoted in Ebbinghaus and Preissler, 88.

37 Widmann's testimony, quoted in Beer, 408.

38 Testimony of N. N. Akimova, a physician at the institution, of 18 November 1946 in the trial of the 'crimes of the German-fascist conquerers in the White Russian SSR', in Minsk, quoted in Ebbinghaus and Preissler, 88.

39 Krausnick, *Einsatzgruppen,* 158.

40 Akimova's testimony, quoted in Ebbinghaus and Preissler, 90ff.

41 Pressac, 38ff. Mogilev was also the site of three SS construction supervision offices in the occupied part of the Soviet Union. They had their own building supplies depot, vehicle fleet, etc. (ibid. 40; Hilberg, 866–7).

42 Pressac has written a commendable book, but on this point the fact that he is a pharmacist seems to have got the better of him. His statements on the typhus epidemic on the German eastern front are incorrect and his sources are weak (38ff.). From an epidemiological and practical perspective, it is not a good idea to transport 2000 typhus corpses daily to a distant, central crematorium.

43 Beer, 410.

44 Kreidler, 397ff.

45 Although the dam was partly blown up as the Red Army withdrew, this had a greater impact on power generation than it did on navigation (see Müller, *Wirtschaftspolitik,* 233).

46 Engel, 111. The Jews of Salonika were not actually deported until 1943, and the destination was Auschwitz (see the impressive description in Safrian, 225–60).

47 The passages cited have all been taken from the book by Friedrich Ross, which was designated 'for official use only': *Die verkehrs- und raumpolitische Bedeutung der europäisch-sowjetrussischen Wasserstrassen* (The significance of European-Soviet Russian waterways for transport and territorial policy) (*Schriften des Ostsee-Instituts für Wirtschaftsforschung in Danzig*) (Danzig, 1943), esp. 86ff., 95ff. The work was prepared 'in collaboration with the Central Association for German Inland Navigation, the German Institute for Economic Research, and the Reich Association for Territorial [*Raum*] Research'. Preliminary versions – also by Ross, presumably excerpted from a report – can be found in *Zeitschrift für Binnenschiffahrt* 73 (1941), 105–17; 74 (1942), 54–77.

Since Ross was an expert not only in inland navigation, but specifically in questions of population and *Volkstum* (see BDC, PA/Ross), having published on the subject, one can reasonably ask if the following comment should not be read as suggesting a slave labour project:

From a territorial policy perspective, the system of canals connecting Danzig, Königsberg, Memel, and Riga are superbly suited to be trade routes between the Baltic and Black Seas. They are gateways to the East, leading the way to new transportation directions, the expansion of which will be one of the major transport policy tasks of the post-war years.

(ibid. 59)

48 Letter from Himmler to Greiser, 18 September; BAK, NS19/2655, 3 (my emphasis).

49 Fähndrich's letter on 'evacuations from the newly incorporated eastern territories' to the representatives of the RKF in Königsberg, Posen, Danzig, and Katowice, 3 September 1941; BDC, SS-HO/5038. The heads of the local offices of the criminal police also started pressuring the Reich criminal police office in November 1940 in a similar manner, increasing pressure in the summer of 1941. They demanded the deportation of Gypsies. The delayed responses and varied information on possible evacuation deadlines correspond – also in terms of the data – to the ups and downs of resettlement policies in general (see Kenrick and Puxon, 80).

50 Memo by Höppner, 20 August 1941; BAK, R75/7, 2. The project then started in October 1941 with a 'trial registration of Poles in the district of Wollstein [Wolsztyn]' (note by Krumey, ibid. 3).

51 Letter from Zeitschel to Abetz, 10 September 1941, quoted in Klarsfeld, 32. Abetz spoke to Himmler about this in early October. He was told that 'the Jews in the concentration camps in the occupied territory could be deported as soon as transportation means allow' (letter from Zeitschel to Dannecker, 8 October 1941, quoted in Pätzold, 309ff.).

52 A note written for Greifelt by Stier, 'for presentation to the Reichsführer SS', 9 September 1941; BAK, R49/2606.

53 Stier's proposal to Greifelt 'for presentation to the Reichsführer SS', 10 September 1941; BAK, R49/2606. It was approved and later partially implemented (letters of 3 and 27 March 1942; ibid./2609).

54 Greifelt's letter to Jury: 'Re: Increase in the number to emigrate from South Tyrol', 21 September 1941; BAK, R49/2606. In all, 10,000 people were involved in addition to the resettlements already under way. Greifelt had given the appropriate assurance in Rome on 2 August 1941; ADAP, series D, 13: 1, 231ff. See also Greifelt's memorandum on the 'Increase in the number to emigrate from South Tyrol', 10 November 1941. In a 'highly confidential' letter, explicit reference was made to 'foreign policy grounds', and to the fact that 'the [location of the] group settlement area for the South Tyroleans could not yet be determined' (reprinted in Der Menscheneinsatz, 1st supplement, 5ff.).

55 Greifelt had only agreed to resettle an additional 10,000 South Tyroleans; the resettlement of 20,000 – from previous agreements – was still unresolved (note on a meeting from 13–15 September 1941 of the staff of cluster IIIB on the 'Volk and racial policy situation'; BAK, R69/1152, 8).

56 Letter from Eichmann to the RKF staff main office, 29 September 1941; AGK, UWZ/L/1, 110. Fähndrich's letter to Eichmann is not extant, but its existence can be assumed on the basis of this reply, which mentioned it in the subject reference: 'your letter of 2 Sept. 1941 – I – 1/5 – 1/30 Aug. 1940; Dr. F/Klu.' Eichmann sent a copy of his letter to Höppner 'with reference to the telex of 13 September 1941 from Posen, no. 11881, and that of 17 September 1941 from Litzmannstadt, no. 9143, for your information'.

57 Quoted in Pätzold and Schwarz, 160ff. (The authors' comment that this was 'an invention' of Eichmann's is incorrect.)

58 Letter from Eichmann to Fähndrich (cc sent to the UWZ in Posen), 29 September 1941; AGK, UWZ/L/1, 110; emphasis in the original.

59 In any case, some documents indicate that at this time, on the one hand, Eichmann had to reject all requests for deportation, and he had not yet incorporated extermination camps as a given into his calculations; on the other hand, he proposed (partial) mass executions of Jews even outside the Soviet Union. This was noted by Rademacher, responsible for Jewish affairs in the German Foreign Office, on 13 September 1941 on the margin of a telegram demanding the 'immediate deportation' of 8000 Jewish men from Belgrade. 'According to information from Sturmbannführer Eichmann, bringing them to Russia and the Generalgouvernement is impossible. It is not even possible to accommodate the Jews from Germany there. Eichmann suggests shooting them' (quoted in Safrian, 113).

60 Telex from Friedrich Uebelhoer, provincial chief of Litzmannstadt (Lodz), to Himmler, 9 October 1941; BAK, NS19/2655, 35ff.

61 Letter from Himmler to Greiser, 18 September 1941, ibid. 3. Even if Himmler later expressly denied this and offered 'fundamental considerations' as the reason for the sudden deportation 'from West to East', it can be assumed that one of the reasons was to quickly obtain living space in the 'Western air raid risk areas' (correspondence of 8 and 11 October 1941 between Thomas and Himmler, ibid. 44, 48). At the same time, Eichmann's Vienna staff boasted that it had obtained authorization for the 'evacuation' of 5000 Jews to Lodz, 'even though Vienna was not within the air raid risk area' (letter from Alois Brunner to the deputy Gauleiter of the Vienna Gau, 6 October 1941, quoted in Safrian, 120). In November, the Reich Minister of Finance wrote the following on the deportation of German Jews: 'The newly available residences' had to be evacuated quickly, particularly in the cities, 'where they have been designated as accommodation for bombed out national comrades.' The letter continued that the deportations had already begun in Berlin, Hamburg, Bremen, Kassel, Cologne, and Düsseldorf (express letter from the Reich Minister of Finance [signed by Walter Schlüter] to the chief finance officers, 4 November 1941; BAK R2/Anh/7/032109).

62 The fact that not much came of this, as often was the case, indicates the growing self-created pressure facing the resettlement politicians. In March 1943, Himmler spoke realistically of '20,042 persons of German nationality living [!] in the Litzmannstadt camps', whom he now wanted to resettle in Zamość as soon as possible (letter from Himmler to Krüger, 28 March 1943, quoted in Okkupationspolitik in Polen, 258).

63 Krumey's report of 7 October 1941 on the meeting of the SS settlement staff of Posen and Litzmannstadt on 2 October 1941; StA Poznań, UWZ/P/2, 169ff.

64 Chronicle, 77f.

65 The total number is reported by Benz and Golczewski (440) as 3100.

66 Letter from Ventzki to Uebelhoer, 24 September 1941; BAK, NS19/2655, 4.

67 Trunk, 252ff.; Benz and Golczewski, 447.

68 In late 1941 and early 1942, more than 65,000 German, Austrian, and Czech Jews were in fact deported to Minsk, Riga, and Kovno (Kaunas). Prior to this, most of the Jews already in the ghettos there were murdered. This was done for several reasons, one major reason being to 'make room' for deportees from the West. See the extensive presentation by Safrian, 134–68.

69 The later practice was different; most of these deportees were not shot immediately, but were murdered little by little (cf. ibid.).

70 According to reports, Theresienstadt was considered for Bohemia and 'an existing Jewish village [was to be expanded] into a ghetto for Moravia'. Only 'Theresienstadt' was implemented. Initially, '347 Germans and 3498

Czech nationals' had to be evacuated. Since this went 'hand in hand with the internment of the Jews', Heydrich had 'no great difficulty' acquiring the 'necessary residential and commercial space for the settlers' (Heydrich's letter to Frick, 21 February 1942). 'After total evacuation of all Jews' from this ghetto as well, Theresienstadt, according to Heydrich, was to be 'settled by Germans through perfect planning, thus [becoming] the centre of German life'. This would become 'another outpost', created in exemplary fashion according to the ideas of the Reichsführer SS in his capacity as the Reich Commissioner for the Consolidation of German Nationhood (Heydrich on 17 October 1941 'on future plans for the Protectorate'). It is apparent how much Heydrich adopted the 'ideas' of the RKF in the passages in his secret Prague inaugural address of 2 October 1941 that very clearly deal with settlement policy. A letter from Lammers on 14 November 1941 is evidence of the fact that, at this time, Hitler ordered 'that the decree of 7 October 1939 for the consolidation of German nationhood be extended to apply to the Protectorate of Bohemia and Moravia as well'. On 19 October 1941, Heydrich explained to his staff that he intended to 'have the Führer' extend the RKF decree to apply to the Protectorate 'within the next few days' (All documents mentioned here can be found in Kárný and Milotová, 98–113, 128–48, 176, 228ff.)

71 Notes on the meeting of 10 October 1941 in Prague 'on the solution of the Jewish question', quoted in Kárný and Milotová, 128ff. Present at the meeting were Heydrich, K. H. Frank (Reich Protector), Horst Böhme (Commander of the Security Police, Prague), Maurer (presumably Böhme's economic advisor), Karl von Gregory (Dept. IV of the office of the Reich Protector in Prague), Eichmann, Hans Günther (Central Office for Jewish Emigration, Prague), and Wolfram von Wolmar.

72 Koeppen's memo of 6 October 1941, quoted in Kárný and Milotová, 97.

73 It is possible, however, that just at this time he had associated certain illusions with the second blitzkrieg offensive on the eastern front, which had just begun under the codename 'Typhoon'. 'The Führer is convinced', Goebbels wrote on 4 October 1941, relieved, 'that if the weather remains somewhat favourable, the Soviet army will be essentially destroyed in fourteen days.' On 11 October, Goebbels had already come to terms with the fact that 'barring a miracle, it might be necessary to continue fighting through the entire winter' (Goebbels diaries, Reuth, 4: 1675, 1686).

74 Pohl, 105.

75 Frank diary, 436.

76 Czerniaków diary, 293.

77 Letter from the Reich Labour Ministry to the Association of Chambers of Commerce in the Reich Economic Chamber, 11 November 1941; BAK, R11/1220, 237. See Aly and Heim, 328ff.

78 Letter from Anton Plügel to Dora Maria Kahlich, 22 October 1941, and Kahlich's reply to Plügel, 3 November 1941, quoted in Aly and Heim, 198ff.

79 BDC, PA/Eimann.

80 Letter from Mennecke to his wife, 25 November 1941, quoted in Chroust, vol. 1, 242ff., and Chroust, 'Selected Letters', 253ff.

81 Pressac, 152f.; see also the section on Mogilev in this chapter.

82 Pressac, 41ff. In the experiment, 250 prisoners classified as 'terminally ill' and 600 Soviet prisoners of war classified as 'fanatic Communists' were killed. Up to now, according to Pressac, this experiment has been mistakenly thought to have taken place in early September.

83 Beer, 414ff.

84 An order from Krumey, 19 November 1941; StA Lodz, UWZ/L/L-3636; 278. Hermann Püschel, Krumey's deputy, became head of the 'relocation'

department. It accorded with the logistics of resettlement policy that deportations to Chelmno begin, not in the Lodz ghetto, but in the rural eastern towns of the Warthegau, where they had to quickly 'make room' to settle ethnic Germans and at the same time 'evict' the Poles.

85 This was the wording in the records of the Wannsee Conference.
86 The records are reprinted, e.g., in Pätzold and Schwarz, 102–12.
87 A later document on this subject can be found in Chapter 12, p. 266.
88 Luther's notes of 8 December 1941, reprinted in Pätzold and Schwarz, 91.
89 Monthly report of the DUT for January 1942; BAP, 17.02/300, 2. Reference was also made in this report to the discussions between DUT, RKF, and the Reich Finance Ministry, the aim of which was for 'Jewish real estate in the Reich to also be made available for A [Old Reich] cases' (4).
90 See Chapter 11, Total 'biologism'.
91 See Eichmann's note on a meeting of 28 November between Heydrich and Krüger, 1 December 1941, reprinted in Pätzold and Schwarz, 90ff.
92 Quoted in Aly and Heim, 445ff. The head of the Warsaw Jewish Council was correct in his suspicions when he glued a newspaper clipping about this meeting into his diary. The report, obviously disguising its true meaning, said that 'the presence of more than 600,000 Jews in the District of Warsaw gave rise to wide-ranging discussions' (Czerniaków diary, 289).
93 Quoted in Browning, 'Genocide', 158.
94 Frank diary, 457ff.

# |11|

# *Elements of the decision to carry out the Holocaust*

## An open secret

Although Hitler had discontinued the murder of German psychiatric patients owing to domestic political considerations, the German leadership could look back positively on this first programme of mass extermination. Until summer 1941, the murder of patients in psychiatric institutions went off almost without a hitch, and the secrecy of the project helped contribute to this. That was the path taken quite deliberately from the very beginning, as shown in a memorandum on the 'euthanasia question' written by Hitler's personal physician, Theo Morell, in summer 1939.

In the memorandum, Morell investigated, at Hitler's request, whether 'mercy killing' should be legally regulated or practised as an 'official secret'. He based his arguments on a survey conducted in the early 1920s among the overwhelmingly proletarian parents of seriously disabled children. The parents were posed the 'purely hypothetical' question whether they would consent to a 'painless shortening of your child's life'. They answered overwhelmingly in the affirmative. However, Morell did not conclude from this that one might simply begin and carry out the planned crime in a completely public, legally regulated fashion. Rather, he referred to a minority of the parents questioned whom he felt were important. They had said they were unwilling to be made judges over their own children, but would welcome it if doctors would make such a decision. Thus Morell wrote in his report to Hitler:

> Many parents express the following: If you had simply done it and said that our child died from some illness. One could take this into account. We should not think that we cannot undertake beneficial measures without the approval of the people, our sovereign.[1]

It was reasons like these that led Hitler to prefer an 'officially secret' procedure and later to refuse to publish a law 'on assisted death for the incurably ill'.[2] However, this was not really intended to prevent information on the murders from rapidly leaking out. Instead, such official secrecy gave the public and those who indirectly shared in the crime the opportunity to give their tacit consent to government measures. If the relatives did not entirely reject the government offer to 'relieve' the suffering of their severely disabled children or mentally ill wives or husbands, then at least it must have been important to them not to know too much about the circumstances of their deaths. A similar process was also at work among the doctors involved in the bureaucratic preparations, who 'were told nothing about the operation officially; unofficially it was assumed that everyone had somehow already been sufficiently informed',[3] as a doctor from a Rhine facility wrote in her diary in winter 1940–41. A secretary from Eichmann's Section IVB4 later testified to the same thing:

> I did not know any details of the events in the concentration camps, but I knew that the final solution of the Jewish question consisted of the extermination of the Jews. . . . I had already learned the word 'special treatment' during my time in Berlin. No one ever spoke about it in the office, not even with friends. . . . But everyone who dealt with it knew what the whole thing meant.[4]

This form of 'secret Reich matter', which was actually public, can be understood as an offer to Germans in general, and to the indirect participants in particular, to avoid responsibility and enter into an unconfessed, passive complicity that did not weigh on the conscience.

Aside from a very few, easily controlled exceptions, there was not the least bit of opposition among the many thousands of officials involved in the bureaucratic process of the 'euthanasia operation'. Looked at in this way, it is pointless to ask, 'How much did they know?' The question should be, 'Why did the Germans want to know so little?'

The experience of Operation T-4 remained crucial for the later organizers of the 'final solution of the Jewish question'. It gave them the certainty that systematically planned mass murder, organized according to a division of labour, was essentially possible to achieve with the German government apparatus and the German public. The sermon by Bishop Galen of Münster remained an – if not the – exception to the rule. Until summer 1941, occasional acts of resistance could be dealt with. In March, Brack spoke to the assembled state supreme court presidents and general prosecutors of the Third Reich about the 'euthanasia programme'. He explained that 'in 80 per cent of the cases, the relatives [of those killed] agree; 10 per cent protest, 10 per cent are indifferent'.[5]

Even if the minority of those who protested had been larger, their opposition did not have an effect until two other crises of legitimacy placed the political system under additional strain: the difficulties on the eastern front and the increase in British air raids.

The protagonists were aware of the connections. Thus even after the sudden cessation of Operation T-4, they could look back on the development of their murder programme as a success. Top German officials, ministers, and leaders had gained the expertise essential to later decisions; the logic of the 'secret Reich matter' lay in the certainty that euphemisms would not be investigated and would not only be gratefully accepted, but even expected as an opportunity for denial and indifference.

# Total biologism

The common images of an insane, racist state and a central, or long since determined, plan for extermination correspond to the self-image of the Greater German 'Führer state', but not to reality, which obeyed different laws. The internal logic of the Nazi state developed between the poles of great plans for change and expansion, unstable interim solutions, and limited resources. These were followed by practical constraints, expectations, and the necessity for action – all under the condition of a state-implemented (racist) order of values that was firmly grounded in German society. Most of this does not seem so remote from us that it cannot be described. The event is accessible to analysis, using conventional historiographic methods.

The decision on the 'final solution of the Jewish question' was unquestionably interwoven with the anti-Semitic doctrine of the German state at the time. Goebbels' diary entry for 19 August 1941 is a good example of this: 'I will not rest or repose until we, too, have drawn the final conclusions with regard to Jewry.' And on 20 August, he wrote, 'We must approach this problem without any sentimentality.' On 2 November, 'The Jews are the lice of civilized humanity. They must somehow be exterminated. . . .'[6]

This element was also central to the decisions that led to the Holocaust. Nevertheless, any analysis will miss the mark if it is based only on the explanations offered time and again by Hitler and his Propaganda Minister and if it takes them at face value. For an investigation of the murder of the European Jews, critical reserve is also necessary, given the illusory nature of all ideologies. Furthermore, the processes of decision-making in a dictatorship are, as a rule, murky, especially from an ideological perspective. They must be examined all the more conscientiously to reveal their substantive core.

Nazi ideology gained its effectiveness not from isolated, government-controlled hatred of Jews or the mentally ill, Gypsies or Slavs, but from the totalitarian unity of so-called negative and positive population policies. Zygmunt Bauman has interpreted these mechanisms as an expression of modernity, which to him is a 'garden culture'. He attempts to describe the politics of the totalitarian state using the metaphor of the great gardener, as described by Nazi ideologist Walther Darré, who wishes the garden of society 'to lift itself above the harsh rule of natural forces', create 'suitable conditions for growing', keep away 'harmful influences', 'tend what needs tending', and 'eliminate the weeds which would deprive the better plants of nutrition, air, light and sun'.[7]

Because the retrospective interpretation of Nazism as a rule follows the perspective of the victim, the obviously negative aspect of racial politics is generally regarded as an absolute. As understandable as this is, such a one-sided view leads historical analysis astray and causes it to almost ignore the 'positive' aspects of Nazi population policies. Thus the following is a brief summary of the closed overall biologist system of the Nazi state.

In it, all people – including the Master Race – were biologically unequal. They were therefore separated on an open scale into those of greater and those of lesser value. The mixing of the one with the other was to be prevented, because those of lesser value were perceived as a threat. The number of people of inferior worth had to be kept as low as possible through state control. Marriage and reproduction among those of superior worth were to be encouraged, according to biological criteria, regardless of any traditional social barriers. Anything serving the interests of those of greater value might and should be done – if necessary, to the disadvantage of the inferior.

What was true for the individual was even more true for the collectives, the races. Races differed more or less in their basic biological character-istics and because the respective share of persons to be classified as of superior or inferior worth fluctuated greatly. Two collectives were seen to be of lesser value overall: the Jews and the Gypsies – although the Jews also counted as a world enemy, the so-called anti-race *per se*.[8]

This was the construct that Heinrich Himmler liked to call the 'social-ism of good blood'. It was not the ideology itself that was historically unique, but the fact that it succeeded within a short time in becoming the central principle of a modern state, and apparently achieved this position easily under the specific conditions prevailing in Germany. The restructur-ing of the entire legal system, basically every administrative act, was guided by this body of rules. Two examples help illustrate this.

- On 18 July 1940, the Reich Ministry of the Interior published formal guidelines that would be used to divide the German population into four categories. The lowest group comprised 'asocial persons' who were to be 'excluded from receiving any assistance', any welfare aid. A step above them was the category that included those Germans classed as 'still acceptable'. A family in this category 'cannot be seen as an asset to the national community [*Volksgemeinschaft*]', but it would probably be 'no serious burden on it' either. While the guidelines expressly provided for the possibility of forcibly sterilizing people in this category, no such directive existed for the 'asocials'. More far-reaching 'measures of negative population policy' – namely, deportation, slave labour, and extermination – were actually intended for them, though this was not explicitly spelled out in the guidelines.[9] The two 'lower' groups were followed in this biological hierarchy by the majority of the 'average population'; towering above them were those Germans who – at least theoretically – were considered 'genetically especially valuable', regardless of class or origin, and who stood out through 'professional achievement and social advancement', because of which they were to receive special support.[10]

- In 1942, the Reich Security Main Office set up a biological reprieve for Polish or Russian slave labourers arrested for 'prohibited sexual relations' with German women (*'Volksgenosinnen'*), and who were all, at Himmler's wishes, to be 'sent to the gallows'. Now the delinquents were selected for their fitness to be Germanized, on the basis of a special series of questions. It may be that this occurred because of the shortage of labour or as a result of the rapid spread of this sort of 'criminality'; that is not the issue here. Himmler and Heydrich did not handle their system rigidly. What is important is that, in evaluating the slave labourers, the very same 'racial questionnaire' was used that was commonly employed internally to evaluate SS members. The graphic layout of the questionnaire corresponded in all its details with a standardized defect inspection report now familiar in Germany.[11] However, the evaluation system differed significantly; along with the defects of the inspected object, it also recorded its merits. Both together were used to calculate an 'overall rating' – universal, sterile, and morally neutral – employing a formula that varied according to racial group affiliation.

Unlike the Germans, Poles, Russians, or Czechs, the Jews were not subject to such an internal selection,[12] as they were classified as generally inferior. Nevertheless, their situation worsened precisely under these conditions of general selection. Thus pressure at the margins of the overall system increased progressively, from the inside out, and was constantly reapplied. 'Emigration of Jews to make more room for Poles', Himmler had said when explaining how he would accomplish the long-overdue resettlement of the ethnic Germans.

The Reich Commissioner for the Consolidation of German Nationhood cultivated the basic biologist principle in its purest form. 'Quarantine' camps, train routeing plans, and selection bodies characterized the external process. Hardly had the ethnic Germans settlers 'returned home' when specially trained selectors at the Central Immigration Office – Josef Mengele worked in this capacity for a time in 1940 – checked their physical, social, and vocational qualities. They refused naturalization to mentally ill and crippled settlers and those married to 'inferior aliens', distinguishing them with an 'S' for 'special case'. The others were separated into 'A' (*Altreich* or Old Reich) and 'O' (*Ost*, or East) cases, generally in a ratio of one to four. The 'Old Reich cases' had been classified by the racial examiners as inferior additions to ethnic blood; the RKF resettled them on a case-by-case basis in Germany for the purpose of assimilation. The 'East cases' were considered of sufficiently high value to 'survive the nationality [*Volkstum*] struggle in the newly acquired eastern territories'. The selection experts of the Central Immigration Office assigned 'characteristics' to the top-secret personal dossiers of the 'O cases'. These served as criteria in allocating farms; in practice, therefore, it was a question of money. This is more or less how it went: 'Heinrich V., one of the best carpenters, respectable family'; 'Johann F., negligent farmer, slovenly family, 10 to 15 hectares on a trial basis'; 'Josef G., very capable worker, very industrious, although he has a gammy leg'; 'Georg E., capable wife, somewhat slow, mediocre'; 'August S., shoemaker, small workshop with little land, man weakly, wife bad foot, otherwise respectable family'.[13]

The majority of 'O cases' among the ethnic German peasant families remained in camps in southern Germany anyway. When they were finally 'called away', as it was termed, after a year and a half, they first found themselves in a temporary camp in Lodz; from there, they were supposed to be 'placed' on new (stolen) land in the eastern Polish region of Zamość. The trains made several rounds. Romanian German 'O cases' were exchanged for Lithuanian German 'A cases' – simple labourers:

> The transport of these settlers from Lithuania will occur immediately following the deportation of the present internees of the camp; the trains are scheduled to travel from Main-Franconia to Litzmannstadt and from there, empty, to Mecklenburg, to be loaded in Mecklenburg with settlers from Lithuania and then sent on to the now-empty camps in Main-Franconia.[14]

New train routeing plans were drawn up for settlement in Zamość in eastern Poland, which was to have begun after the harvest but, as usual, was delayed. On 25 January 1943, a freight train left Zamość for Berlin with 1000 young Polish men and women 'without unproductive dependants', as it was put. They were to take the jobs of 'armaments Jews', who were deported to Auschwitz on the same train, along with their 'unproductive' family members. There, the train was loaded with luggage for the ethnic German settlers and sent back to Zamość. At the same time, the ethnic Germans arrived in passenger trains, where they were received by the SS settlement staff and settled in the areas 'evacuated' by Poles and, before that, by Jews. There they were assigned approximately 50-acre farms, each created out of five ('unproductive') Polish peasant farms. From Zamość, the train departed once again for Auschwitz, loaded with 1000 Poles who had been designated by the security police and the racial examiners as particularly 'undesirable' ('selection category IV').[15]

Even though 1000 Jews and 1000 Poles were 'deported' to Auschwitz according to this train schedule, their fates even there varied greatly. The director of one of these transports, an employee of the Central Resettlement Office in Lodz, reported on a discussion with an SS colleague who had received one such transport in Auschwitz:

> With reference to fitness for labour deployment, SS Hauptsturmführer Haumeier explained that only able-bodied Poles should be supplied, in order to prevent as far as possible any unnecessary strain on the camp and the feeder traffic. Imbeciles, idiots, cripples and sick people must be removed from the camp as quickly as possible through liquidation to relieve pressure on the camp. However, this measure is made more difficult to the extent that, according to RSHA instructions, unlike the measure applied to the Jews, Poles must die a natural death.[16]

The train routeing plans between Zamość, Berlin, and Auschwitz document the meshing of resettlement and removal, selection and genocide, the intrinsic logic of 'human deployment', and the planning and organizational unity of so-called positive and negative population policy. The support and preferential treatment granted those of 'superior worth' went hand in hand with the marginalization of the 'inferior'.[17] Only within this relationship did total biologism gain the dynamic that led to the murder first of German psychiatric patients and then of European Jews and Gypsies. Operation T-4 was fundamental to the Holocaust not only for the concrete experience it provided, but also because it served as an example: it legitimized the notion of biological 'elimination' as an immanent principle of life for the Master Race itself, making it that much easier for it to be directed outward and transferred to other collectives.

# The Heydrich system

Three weeks into the war, on 21 September 1939, Reinhard Heydrich issued his first set of guidelines on the 'Jewish question in the occupied territories'.[18] They were directed to the leaders of the *Einsatzgruppen* of the security police and SD, which were deployed in 1939 and carried out mass executions during the war against Poland, though plainly to a lesser degree than later in the Soviet Union. The guidelines contained three elements that would remain crucial to the later decision-making process culminating in the 'final solution'. Heydrich no longer sought forced Jewish emigration abroad, but instead favoured deportation to the new periphery of the area under German control;[19] at the same time, he divided this 'long-term goal' into 'short-term goals'. Further, he encouraged his colleagues on the ground to offer their ideas and criticize directives from headquarters whenever they deemed this necessary as a result of the concrete difficulties they experienced in practice. The guidelines are a good example of the 'Heydrich system'.

Not only in Jewish policy, but soon also in the entire policy of 'ethnic cleansing', Heydrich regularly distinguished between short-term and long-term goals. He made distinctions between 'steps towards fulfilment of this final goal', which could be realized in the short term, and a medium-term 'overall measure', which demanded 'the most thorough preparation, in both technical and economic respects'. 'As the first preliminary measure', in September 1939, the western Polish provinces intended for annexation were to be 'made free of Jews, or at least, we should aim to create only a few cities of concentration'. In the future Generalgouvernement, 'as few concentration points as absolutely necessary [were to] be established' for the Jewish population: at railway junctions, or at least on railway lines, 'to facilitate later measures'.

'With regard to short-term goals', Heydrich demanded 'total utilization of all forces'. The final goal, on the other hand, remained vague and 'top secret'. According to Heydrich, it required 'longer periods'. In this way, the agents of Jewish policy justified every shortcoming and all brutality with the provisional nature of their actions. They acted in the conviction that their improvisations were an element of a 'planned overall measure', an 'ultimate solution', and thus a greater, and soon achievable, design for a new order.

In his guidelines, Heydrich also established a basic principle:

> It goes without saying that the impending tasks cannot be set down here in all their details. The following instructions and guidelines at the same time serve the purpose of encouraging the leaders of the *Einsatzgruppen* to think practically.

Heydrich knew how to avoid schematic thinking. Each active participant was to describe his own concrete experiences and thereby help adapt the always-preliminary guidelines to practice. To some extent, the functionaries of the Führer state, even in the SS, cultivated an open, cooperative style of leadership and thus minimized the tension inherent in any administrative body between general instructions and practical application in everyday bureaucratic practice.

Difficulties always arose on the ground, at the widely dispersed grass roots of the resettlement authorities. There, endless compromises were necessary, and ever more comprehensive 'overall solutions' were therefore required. Heydrich's open method of proceeding, with an eye to ongoing corrections, remained typical of the later transition from deportation to systematic murder of the European Jews.

Any planning must remain open to correction, to a certain degree. It is more efficient to mark off the general framework, while at the same time leaving room for practice-oriented suggestions and initiatives 'from the bottom up'. Heydrich and Himmler consciously utilized this modern administrative insight and trained their new SS elite in this way. As early as 1937, the following problems appeared on the final examinations for the future SS aristocracy: 'How would you go about checking and proving a person has Jewish relations?', 'Put together a Reich report on "Jews in the cattle trade" and make some suggestions for eliminating the evils you describe', and 'How do you envision the solution to the Jewish question?'[20]

Such approaches within the SS, predicated on flexibility and cooperation, correspond to Raul Hilberg's insight on the entire German bureaucracy at the time:

> Thousands of proposals were introduced in memoranda, presented at conferences, and discussed in letters. The subject matter ranged from dissolution of mixed marriages to the deportation of the Jews of Liechtenstein or the construction of some 'quick-working' device for the annihilation of Jewish women and children at Łódź and the surrounding towns of the Warthegau. At times, it was assumed that the moment had come, even if there was no definite word from above. . . . The bureaucratic network of an entire nation was involved in these operations, and its capabilities were being expanded by an atmosphere facilitating initiatives in offices at every level.[21]

The famous letter that Höppner wrote to Eichmann on 16 July 1941 was based on 'discussions' that had taken place – and, it may be assumed, continued to take place – in Posen among representatives of the regional authorities. Thus Höppner began his letter with the following sentence: 'The following solution has been suggested', including, as mentioned above, the use of 'some fast-acting means' to 'finish off' the Jews of the Warthegau who are 'unfit for labour'. Thus it was the lowest ranks of the resettlement apparatus that thought up 'things' which, it was said, 'sometimes [sounded] fantastic'. They did not, for example, pass their suggestions on to the next-highest level of the hierarchy for decision, but instead offered them for discussion, in the spirit of teamwork: 'I would be grateful', Höppner told Eichmann, 'for an opinion at your convenience.'

Such facts qualify the simple concept of the Führer state and of a central decision to exterminate the Jews that was passed down through the chain of command and then carried out, in the Prussian tradition of blind obedience. Instead, the murderous ideas that were developed in Posen, and probably also in Globocnik's circles in Lublin, corresponded to similar considerations and practices at the top levels of the dictatorship. The protagonists at the lower, local level were thoroughly aware of this. They did not formulate their suggestions at random. They knew what options and suggestions had a chance of being carried out at any particular point in time.

How this must often have played out is demonstrated by an exchange of correspondence between Höppner and Krumey in 1943 that is one of the rare ones to have survived. At the time, the two subordinate Obersturmbannführers were not permitted to take part in the conference of SS generals in Posen on 4 October 1943 at which Himmler also discussed 'the final solution'. Nevertheless, both soon knew exactly what had been said. Himmler had said:

> I wish, here before you, quite openly to mention a very difficult chapter. . . . I am talking about the evacuation of the Jews, the extermination of the Jewish people. It is one of those things that is easily said. 'The Jewish people will be exterminated,' says every Party comrade, 'of course, it's in our programme, elimination of the Jews, extermination, we'll do it.' And then they all come, those worthy 80 million Germans, and each one has his own decent Jew. Of course, the others are swine, but this one is a great Jew. Of all who talk that way, none of them has watched, none of them has gone through it. Most of you know what it means to see 100 bodies lying there, 500 lying there or 1000 lying there. To have got through this and, aside from exceptions due to human weakness, to have remained decent, that has made us tough.[22]

On 11 November, Höppner wrote to Krumey:

> Enclosed I am sending you the speech by the Reichsführer SS. I am depending on you to use it only for your personal information, as I am not really allowed to pass the speech on. I would even be grateful if you would destroy it when you no longer need it.

Five days later, Krumey responded, 'My sincerest thanks for sending me the document. I will act in accordance with your wishes.'[23]

## Historians' debate

The present study leaves some questions open; however, the results make it possible to describe certain elements of the decision to murder the European Jews that have not been known until now. It may also be stated that the dynamic that developed out of resettlement policies was an essential factor. The most important new documents, presented in the previous pages, are part of the written legacy of the administrative apparatus set up from the beginning of the war to organize 'ethnic redistribution'. These documents allow us to fill certain gaps in our knowledge of the increasing radicalization of the persecution of the Jews in the years 1939 to 1941, or at least plausibly to bridge them. A range of contentious issues that have existed until now among various historians and historical schools and have dominated the discussion may become less important, while new ones could emerge.

Nevertheless, our knowledge of the Holocaust remains fragmentary. Similarly, it is still difficult consistently to weigh the various factors significant to the decision to exterminate the Jews. The empirical clarification of one uncertainty leaves others open, and often enough makes it necessary for new questions to be asked. Some may be deciphered with the help of individual studies, based on the theories presented here or with the help of quite different ones.

Although it is certainly no longer possible to explain every dimension of the crime, it is nevertheless still possible to come closer to the historical truth. That is also the reason for this study. Its aim is to make the Holocaust historically comprehensible. This does not mean denying or qualifying it, but rather comprehensively imagining the considerations that ultimately led to its implementation.

Historians have long wondered when the decision was made to murder European Jewry. Some believe it occurred in March 1941, while others insist on certain dates in July, September, or November.[24] Arguments and counterarguments can be found for every such assessment. Because probative documents, in black and white, remain rare, and the surviving perpetrators, to the extent they were later asked (and asked sensibly), systematically lied,[25] there is considerable room for differences of opinion. Apodictically juxtaposed, each assumption rules out the other. But we come closer to the truth if we understand the various times that must be included in the analysis not as the dates of a single act of decision-making, but as qualitative steps in the course of a broad-based, internally contradictory process of political opinion formation.

This much is certain, according to the sources and findings offered here: there was no voluntaristic 'decision' on the systematic, industrialized murder of the European Jews. There is only the assumption of later analysts that the horrible deed must have been decided upon in a completely extraordinary manner. Typical of this is the opinion of Eberhard Jäckel, who maintains that 'a joint discussion or decision', perhaps even a comparatively longer decision-making process, can be 'ruled out': 'No important decisions in this state were made by a body. At the highest level, Hitler made decisions alone and then announced them.'[26]

In contrast, the previous chapters demonstrate the extent to which the conventional rules of state bureaucratic procedure applied even to the 'final solution'. Political decisions generally are not made in a day, nor are they carried out in linear fashion; and they are not exclusively positively determined. It remains crucial to the results which options prove suitable or unsuitable in the debate and the test phases of trial and error. Thus the course of political opinion formation – even under the conditions of the Nazi dictatorship – can be viewed as a more or less open process. The transitions between planning, decision-making, and practice were fluid, the boundaries between the participants and interested institutions permeable.

Those who participated in such processes could do this in various, sometimes contradictory, but overall equally supportive ways. They could favour one solution or another, present detailed suggestions for improvement, or simply declare themselves indifferent – a statement whose weight should not be underestimated. Another possibility was to state that one was neither competent to solve, nor responsible for solving, the tiresome problem, but thought it important that a way finally be found to eliminate it. All these possible behaviours became part of the decision-making process on the 'final solution'; they led to a consensus and, seen in this way, contributed equally to the implementation of the Holocaust. It seems helpful to me to emphasize the differences, the distinctive expediency of the various arguments, rather than heedlessly assuming an overarching, intentional wish for extermination on the part of the participants.

A Führer order was not needed for this; in fact, it would have been counterproductive. Hitler took part in building the consensus, made demands, and let the implementors know that they did not need to conform to any traditional norms; rather, they could carry out any type of 'solution' at all. But he did not give orders. In fact, this was an open decision-making process between the top representatives of the relevant institutions, on the one hand, and their subordinates, on the other. They worked on various plans, wrote up proposals for decisions, submitted them through official channels, and got them back for revision and resubmission.

The ongoing linkage between practice and planning was characteristic of the attempts to deport the Jews right from the start. Even in their first weeks on the job, the bureaucrats in Himmler's 'resettlement' institutions had resorted to mass murder. For their immediate purposes, they had patients in Pomeranian, Polish, and West and East Prussian psychiatric hospitals 'cleared out' to 'accommodate' ethnic Germans. If we add the several thousand mentally ill Jews in German psychiatric facilities who were killed in anticipation of the 'solution of the Jewish question', and the 10,000 to 15,000 German patients in institutions who were deported to the gas chambers of Operation T-4 starting in autumn 1940 to 'free up' space for interim camps for southeastern European and South Tyrolean settlers, then we can safely say that those who had carried out 'ethnic redistribution' at Himmler's behest had had at least 30,000 people killed by July 1941, within the scope of their authority and 'necessities'. They were long familiar with the practice of executing and gassing those they held to be useless, as a means to cope with the bottlenecks that arose in the course of carrying out their tasks.

With the start of the Russian campaign, a second important practice joined the almost two years of practical experience of murder: the mass executions of Soviet prisoners of war, Jews, and suspicious civilians on the eastern front.[27]

Nevertheless, even though the date makes it seem likely, Göring's request to Heydrich on 31 July 1941 did not simply obey the logic of this practical development. Instead, it followed on the above-mentioned discussion that the two had held on 26 March, about which Heydrich had noted, 'Regarding the solution of the Jewish question, I gave the Reich Marshal a brief report and submitted my proposal to him, which he approved after making a change with respect to Rosenberg's responsibilities and he ordered its resubmission.' Thus Wolfgang Scheffler falls short of the truth when he writes, 'Hitler's expectations of victory in July 1941 led directly to Göring's order of 31 July 1941 . . . '[28] Christopher Browning makes a similar argument.[29] In any case, there can be no question of an order – Göring himself used the verb 'charge' (*beauftragen*).

Unlike Scheffler and Browning, Andreas Hillgruber[30] and Richard Breitman[31] – employing differing approaches but concentrating strongly on the persons of Hitler and Himmler, respectively – arrived at the insight that the essential basic decisions about the extermination of European Jewry were made in spring, and that the threshold from deportation to extermination was crossed at that time. But Breitman, in particular, who takes this theory much further than Hillgruber, is wrong to assume that the extermination plans of spring 1941 already corresponded to the later option of murdering the European Jews totally, as quickly as possible, with the help of a specially developed technique of mass annihilation. Both portrayals, however, lack a description of how the plans of spring 1941 differed from the earlier Madagascar Plan, on the one hand, and the later practice of extermination, on the other.

The third position is most pointedly offered by Arno J. Mayer:

> Accordingly, the escalation and systematization of the assault on the Jews was an expression not of soaring hubris on the eve of victory, but of bewilderment and fear in the face of possible defeat. Indeed, the decision to exterminate the Jews marked the incipient debacle of the Nazi Behemoth, not its imminent triumph.[32]

In contrast, the present study produces a different picture. In connection with the plan of attack against the Soviet Union, and against the backdrop of the self-created 'constraints' of resettlement policy, it was decided in March 1941 at the latest to deport the European Jews 'to the East'. Heydrich's March plan provided for extermination of the Jews through the 'natural' means of hunger, cold, and slave labour – in the northeastern regions to be conquered in the Soviet Union. The deportation itself, 'the foot march', was also to be employed as a means to this end. To this extent, the concrete geographic destination was of secondary importance. Hitler, Göring, Himmler, Heydrich and his closest associates knew this plan in detail and therefore saw no reason to make important 'Jewish policy' decisions over the following months. The plan was an expression of the expectation of victory of early 1941, which seemed to be confirmed in the first few weeks of the Russian campaign. Göring's assignment of 31 July 1941 marked the point at which the deportation plan was originally supposed to begin.

More or less from that day on, the military difficulties on the eastern front began to become apparent. From then on, various departments and offices in the Reich Security Main Office, in Hitler's Chancellery, in Posen,

Lodz, and Warsaw were working on alternative 'solutions'. That, too, occurred step-by-step, accelerated in the same measure that the situation on the eastern front became not only difficult, but hopeless. In other words, Heydrich's plan in spring 1941 was inextricably linked to a successful blitzkrieg against the Soviet Union. Against the backdrop of its defeat, the project was changed to what we describe today as the Holocaust. Thus it is correct to argue using the concepts 'expectation of victory' and 'defeat' – but only when they are understood in their historical context, as frustrated expectations of victory. Not until this situation arose was rapid, uncomplicated extermination designed. This option was preceded by the cumulative failure of all the deportation projects, which was in turn connected with a self-created, cumulative straitjacket.

Even in the perpetrators' own perception, the original 'territorial solution to the Jewish question' differed plainly from the form of the 'final solution' from March 1941 (at the latest), first planned in the form of mass deportations 'to the east' and later manifested in the extermination camps. While wide-ranging discussions on the intention to 'reduce' the Slavic population by many millions were held well into 1944, frequently with minutes kept and guidelines widely circulated, such concrete discussions on the 'final solution of the Jewish question' were the exception after the beginning of 1941.

With the idea of biologically exterminating European Jewry, the regents and police chiefs of the Third Reich went far beyond the methods that seemed to them the most extreme possibilities permitted within the framework of the normal European degree of discrimination and violence.[33] In accordance with this, there emerged a new, incomparably stricter form of secrecy and euphemism than in the years 1939–40. The perpetrators were aware of the singularity of their crime and covered their tracks as best they could.[34] Himmler himself issued the maxim that the 'final solution of the Jewish question' should 'never' be spoken of publicly – that it should be a 'never written, never to be written' chapter of our history.[35]

# Projective conflict resolution

The deportation of the European Jews 'to the east' had been conclusively agreed upon since March 1941. Hitler and Göring had delegated the logistical preparations for the undertaking to Himmler and Heydrich. One may well imagine that, once a fundamental decision on the 'Jewish question' had been made and the military prerequisites seemed satisfied by late July, Hitler could indeed have expressed the wish 'not to hear any more on the issue'.[36] Given other statements made by Hitler, we can guess the wording he might have used in the winter of 1940–41 to clothe his 'authorization', referred to now and again by Himmler and Heydrich, 'to solve the Jewish question' quickly and ruthlessly immediately following victory over

the Soviet Union.[37] A statement by Hitler on 22 July 1941 points the way:
'If there were no more Jews in Europe, nothing would any longer stand in
the way of the unity of the European countries. It does not matter where
the Jews are sent, whether to Siberia or Madagascar.'[38] Six days earlier, in
his discussion with Rosenberg, Lammers, Keitel, Göring, and Bormann,
Hitler had spoken less guardedly but no more concretely in regard to the
Jewish question. Bormann noted the Führer's opinion as follows: 'The
motives before the world for our steps must be guided by tactical
considerations. All necessary measures – execution, deportation, etc. –
shall be taken nevertheless and can be taken nevertheless.'[39] And when, in
summer 1942, Gauleiter Greiser of the Warthegau pressured Hitler to make
a decision on what was to happen to Jews in the regions he administered,
Hitler responded that he 'should use his own discretion in dealing with
this'.[40]

Hitler's role, if we consider the totality of the documents presented in
this book, cannot be described as that of an inexorable giver of orders, but
as that of a politician who gave his people free rein, encouraged them to
develop the imagination to make the apparently impossible possible, and
backed them unconditionally. Early on, a resettlement official in Posen
explained the challenge posed him by tasks that he had 'not known so
far' in his life. No Führer's orders helped him to 'master even the most
difficult situations'; there was only a type of general authorization with
which he was to prove himself a ruthless man of action, undisturbed by
even the most objectionable reality – that is, 'the Führer's words: to strike
from the dictionary of the German people the word "impossible"'. This
alone 'made it possible for the individual to solve the problem assigned
him'.[41]

Raul Hilberg speaks of the 'flow of administrative measures', which at
'the threshold of the killing phase . . . was unchecked', and of a political
'atmosphere facilitating initiatives in offices at every level'.[42] In his 1993
book, *Die Eichmann-Männer* (Eichmann's Men), Hans Safrian comes to
the conclusion that Section VIB4 of the Reich Security Main Office was a
'liaison and coordinating office' that

> for one, coordinated the demands made of it for mass deportations,
> and for another, in the search for placement possibilities, received
> and checked far-reaching, in some cases murderous proposals from
> subordinate and lateral offices, passed them on to superiors, and
> ensured permission to carry out the proposed measures.

In Safrian's view, it was individuals who, 'within the scope of their more or
less vague instructions, made decisions, put in place activities for which
there were no express orders (as yet), and thus set the entire process in
motion and kept it going'.[43]

My empirical findings confirm Hilberg's and Safrian's overall views. In
addition, they allow recognition of the way in which the constraints that

arose from German warmaking, the home-to-the-Reich programme for ethnic Germans, and the associated evacuations and resettlements repeatedly influenced the respective form of the 'solution of the Jewish question' project and led to increasingly radical ideas. From this perspective, it also becomes clear the extent to which the plans of Himmler, Heydrich, and Eichmann were bogged down by conflicting realities just at the time they were supposed to be carried out. The study shows how complete was the dead end into which the men of the Reich Security Main Office and the RKF – often made to appear so all-powerful in post-war literature – had manoeuvred themselves by 1940–41. They had created facts on the ground that they were at no point able to control, despite all the force and criminal energy at their disposal. They had made promises, issued promissory notes that they never paid off. The lords of the 'organized mass migration' had turned into lords of camps for ethnic Germans and Poles, of ghettos and barracks.

The history leading up to the Holocaust can only be adequately treated if it includes the uninterrupted cutbacks in and modification of all resettlement projects and brings home the pressures that increased daily as a result of the home-to-the-Reich programme for ethnic Germans. Even the violent death of the Polish Jews, described euphemistically as 'evacuation', documents the failure of the deportation projects: the Jews of the Warthegau, the Generalgouvernement, and Upper Silesia died where they were – in Chelmno, in Belzec, Sobibór, and Treblinka, in Auschwitz.

Hans Mommsen early on found a workable concept for the type of decision-making process described above, in his theory of a 'system of cumulative radicalization'.[44] The fact that Mommsen at first assumed a largely isolated policy towards the Jews as his starting point does not detract from it.[45] The concept, like similar 'functionalist' ideas of Martin Broszat's, takes aim at the assumption of 'intentionalism', of which Eberhard Jäckel is a prominent adherent, that Hitler's omnipotence and will alone led to the Holocaust, and that these sufficiently explain the crime.

The functionalists pursue the insight that the 'Führer state', despite what the contemporary label and the later collective defensive strategy of the Germans involved would lead one to believe, was not monocratically, but polycratically structured. Thus in 1977, Broszat wrote:

> It appears to me, however, that no comprehensive order for the extermination existed and that the 'program' for the extermination of the Jews developed through individual operations and gradually attained its institutional and factual character by spring 1942 after the construction of the extermination camps in Poland (between December 1941 and July 1942).[46]

Unlike Broszat, I do not agree that the 'final solution' 'developed' more or less successively. Rather, as my results show, one can discern clear leaps in development in March, July, and October 1941. However, I agree with Broszat – and some documents in the following chapter indicate this – that the extermination programme was at first experimental, until sometime in May 1942. This point of view strengthens the significance of the consensus achieved by Heydrich at the Wannsee Conference and poses the question whether the machinery of extermination would not have been stopped, or at least slowed, had serious opposition and difficulties in legitimation arisen in the initial weeks and months. This leads to questions about the behaviour of the Germans, in particular. These questions are not the subject of this book, but must be posed in the same measure that we take leave of the exculpatory idea of a 'Führer order.'

The polycratic structure of the National Socialist state cannot be doubted. Yet it should not be misunderstood – as occasionally happens, with unjustified reference to Broszat – as a conglomerate of vanities, jealousies, and intrigues by powerful Nazi figures. It represented real conflicts of interest. A 'Führer order', a 'Führer decision', became necessary when the conflicts between Frank or Greiser, Himmler or Göring had to be settled or mediated. Nevertheless, Franz Neumann was only partially correct when he wrote in *Behemoth* in 1942 that 'the decisions of the Leader are merely the result [of] compromises between' competing interests and authorities.[47]

The concept of 'compromise' needs to be explained. The conflicts of interest between the various power centres of the Third Reich, which were constantly losing or gaining importance and influence, arose out of the tension between differing and generally hypertrophied goals (of conquest), sanitized social utopias, and the notorious scarcity of the materials necessary for these. Even when the representatives of the various institutions pursued conflicting, mutually exclusive interests, they were willing to work together to resolve the conflicts necessarily produced by their divergent strategies – especially the intended speed of their implementation – with the help of theft, slave labour, and extermination. From this emerged the logic of the 'special authorization by the Führer' desired by all the participants and often enough presumed in advance. Until autumn 1941, this was not characterized by a decision preferring one or another variant, nor was it compromise, as Neumann believed; it was an attempt to give equal consideration to contradictory interests, plans, and 'necessities' and to resolve the conflict of purpose in maximalist form, in the sense of a 'final solution'. In other words, the more radical and far-reaching the various plans, resettlement projects, and war aims became, the larger the least common multiple (to put it mathematically) had to become into which all these plans were resolved.

The practice of projective conflict resolution required rapid – very rapid – implementation of ever-expanding plans. Hitler, the top leaders of the Reich, and their advisors and henchmen linked this with the concept of completely new conditions for action in which their discretionary leeway – the space and raw materials at their disposal – would be so enormous and vast that the German leadership would not need to accept any scarcity or limitations, any conflicts of purpose or compromises. Then, within this framework, the 'Jewish question' would be the first to be 'settled'.

In late summer and autumn of 1941, it quickly became apparent that the fourth project 'for a final solution' would not be implemented either. From this followed a search for some perspective in which as many of the divergent interests as possible could be realized at the same time. Those who had repeatedly postponed the deportation of the dispossessed, ghettoized Jews now openly discussed the possibility of systematic, rapid extermination. They understood mass murder as the simplest way of carrying out the short- and long-term plans that they had been developing and redeveloping for nearly two years, but could never put into practice. The representatives of all other institutions agreed to the new 'solution' because it would not infringe upon their interests, and because they had all long since integrated the disappearance of the Jews solidly into their calculations; they had taken their property, crowded them together, and generally treated them as though they were already gone.

# Notes

1  Quoted in Aly, 'Medicine', 31.
2  The law, including an accompanying decree, was drawn up at the end of 1940 at the initiative of the psychiatrists involved in 'euthanasia', with Heydrich's collaboration. See Roth and Aly. Hitler had refused to have it published; however, the organizational section of the law, which governed the creation of a central institution, was published as a decree on 23 October 1941 in the Reich Legal Bulletin. See Aly, 'Progress', 165ff.
3  Quoted in Aly, 'Medicine', 31.
4  Testimony of witness Erika Scholz at the trial of Franz Novak, 11 December 1969, quoted in Pätzold and Schwarz, *Auschwitz,* 168.
5  Quoted in Aly, 'Medicine', 44. It was certainly not without reason that, on April 1941, a decree made visits by pastors to psychiatric institutions dependent on the express wish of the patients (most of whom were not allowed to make their own decisions), and thus effectively forbade them. (General decree by the Reich Ministry of the Interior on 'Activity by Religious Communities in Public Hospitals and Mental Institutions' of 9 April 1941; RMBLiV 6 [1941], col. 647).
6  Goebbels diaries, Reuth, 1660ff., 1695ff. On Goebbels' role, see Jäckel, 114. Despite such martial statements, one should not be deceived about the fact that government anti-Semitism in the Third Reich was a combination of many varied prejudices. It was not only 'right-wing extremist', but also integrated the resentments of conservatives, liberals, and the left, sometimes referring to the Jews' supposed lust for revolution and modernization, sometimes to the unwillingness of Eastern European immigrants to assimilate, and sometimes to 'Jewish capital'.
7  Bauman, 92, 113–14.
8  This was reflected in the various areas of responsibility in the RSHA: The

'solution of the Gypsy plague' was the task of the criminal investigation department (Department V), the 'solution of the Jewish question' was assigned to 'Research on and Control of Adversaries' (Department IV).

9 See Aly and Roth, 105ff.

10 Richtlinien für die Beurteilung der Erbgesundheit (Guidelines for the Assessment of Genetic Health), drawn up by the department for 'Health System and Cultivation of the Volk' in the Reich Ministry of the Interior, printed in RMBliV 5 (1940), column 1519ff. For an interpretation, see Aly and Heim, 163ff. In his famous 'A Plea for the Historicization of National Socialism' (1990, German 1985), Broszat ignored the aspect of general, biologist hierarchization. Only by so doing could he write that the legislation of the Nazi period 'brought with it . . . a series of social policy innovations'; for example, 'improvements in the protection of minors, equalizing the status of white- and blue-collar wage earners'. It is true that we now take many of these laws for granted – but under different conditions. Child benefits, for example, are no longer only for 'genetically healthy Aryan families'. In the history of the genesis of such laws, that which Broszat urges is exactly what should not be done: they should not be isolated from the 'fact that this epoch was in general one of infamy', in order to then simply give them credit for the 'many social, economic and civilizing forces and efforts at modernization' that nevertheless existed (Broszat, 'Plea', 86–7). These forces did exist. Nevertheless, an investigation of the social advances cited by Broszat – for example, the improvement in the legal status of out-of-wedlock children – regularly leads back to Himmler's staff, which was also quite active in this regard. The context of this book involves the flip side, the 'infamy' of the epoch. This, too, can be adequately investigated only if one includes the 'progressive', 'positive' aspects of Nazi demographic and social policy in the analysis.

11 Such a form is reprinted in Aly and Roth, 19.

12 This is true if one ignores the relatively late, and only sporadic, separation of Jews into those fit and those unfit for work, which then also determined the order in which they were murdered. Only the course of the war – that is, the premature end to the 'final solution' – allowed the average chance of survival of a 25-year-old, single Jewish specialized worker to be higher than that of a 40-year-old mother of several children.

13 'Preassignment list [*Vorzuweisungsliste*] for the village community of Sbu [South Bukovina] – 12 – Kornuluncze', undated (1941); BAK, R49/Anh. I/37, 34ff. (There are hundreds of thousands of such files on selections of Germans. However, they were never presented by scholars as part of a total system in which – in contrast to the official ideology of the '*Volksgemeinschaft*', or national community – people were atomized to an almost incredible degree, and thus made accessible.)

14 Memo from the Ethnic German Liaison Office, Operational Gau of Main-Franconia, to all camp leaders, 16 June 1942; BAK R59/114, 24.

15 Aly and Heim, 437. See also Krausnick and H.-G. Adler, who called attention early on to these concrete relationships, though he did not undertake a broader investigation.

16 Report by SS Untersturmführer Heinrich Kinna 'on the transport of 644 Poles (from Zamość) to the work camp Auschwitz on 10 December 1942', quoted in *Biuletyn* 13 (1960), 18Ff.

17 Michel Foucault analysed this mechanism as a new technique of power that he called biopower. It consisted of regulating life, the biological processes of the human species, politically:

> The [ancient power of] sovereignty . . . caused death or let live. . . .
> Now a power emerged . . . that consisted, in contrast, of fostering life
> or allowing death. . . . In Nazi society, there was this extraordinary
> thing: it is a society which absolutely generalized biopower, but at the
> same time generalized the sovereign right to kill. The two mechanisms
> coincide: the classic, archaic one which gave the state the power of life
> or death over its citizens, and the new mechanism, which is organized
> around discipline, regulation – in short, the new mechanism of bio-
> power. So that one can say that the Nazi state allowed the field of a life
> which it forms, protects, guarantees, and biologically cultivates, and at
> the same time the sovereign right to kill someone – not only the
> others, but its own – to become absolutely coexistent.
>
> (Michel Foucault, 'Leben machen und sterben lassen',
> [1976 speech address], in *Lettre International* 20 [1993], 63, 67)

18  Express letter from Heydrich to the heads of the *Einsatzgruppen* of the security
    police on the 'Jewish question in the occupied territory', 21 September 1939,
    reprinted in FGM, 37ff.
19  Though restricted, the policy of forced emigration of German, Austrian, and
    Czech Jews continued until autumn 1941. As Peter Witte informs us, the last
    group emigration was documented as taking place on 15 October 1941. Some
    50,000 people were able to save themselves in this way even after 1 September
    1939 – many, however, only temporarily; in the course of the war, they would
    again fall into the clutches of the Germans.
20  Note on 20 February 1937 'Re: Tasks for SS-Junkers', quoted in Heim, 53ff.
21  Hilberg, 997, 1002.
22  Speech by Himmler at SS Gruppenführer meeting in Poznań on 4 October 1943,
    quoted in IMG, vol. 29, 145.
23  Correspondence between Höppner and Krumey, 11–16 September 1943
    (emphasis in original); AGK, UWZ/L/196, 12ff.
24  For a summary up to 1985, see Jäckel and Rohwer; later, Mayer (1989), Breitman
    (1991), Safrian (1993), Burrin (1994).
25  Eloquent examples of this are the statements made to prosecutors in Bonn by
    Höppner and Koppe in the 1960s. Neither was ever convicted in the Federal
    Republic of Germany.
26  Jäckel, 105.
27  See Browning (*Ordinary Men*), Förster, Friedrich, Heer, Krausnick, Messersch-
    midt, Streim, Streit, Wilhelm.
28  Scheffler, 'Endlösung', 204.
29  Browning, *Fateful Months*, 8–38.
30  Hillgruber, 'Endlösung', 140; similarly, Krausnick, 59–124.
31  Breitman, 145ff. See also S. Friedländer, 30.
32  Mayer, 235.
33  The same is true of the strategy of a war of extermination against the Soviet
    Union, which also – deliberately – deviated from the norms of 'normal
    European warfare', to which the German leadership had heretofore felt itself
    bound. The 'operations' against Poles by the security police during the war
    were also, at first, the exception. Internally, they were highly controversial,
    precisely because they deviated from the rules of 'normal warfare'.
34  In this context, Ernst Nolte deserves a more sober appraisal. His attempt to
    integrate the murder of European Jewry into the thoroughly oppressive conti-
    nuum of European resettlement and extermination policy in this century, under
    the chapter heading 'Genocide and the "Final Solution of the Jewish Question"'
    (Ernst Nolte, *Der europäische Bürgerkrieg 1917–1945. Nationalsozialismus und*

*Bolschewismus* [Frankfurt am Main and Berlin, 1987], 499–517), has a number of arguments in its favour, up to the Madagascar Plan. But this project was not implemented. It is interesting for an analysis of the Holocaust; however, no final historical judgement can be based on it. Discussions on a 'territorial solution of the Jewish question' formed an ephemeral interim stage on the road to increasingly radical decisions that have no parallel in history.

35 Speech by Himmler to SS Gruppenführers in Posen (Poznań), 4 October 1943, quoted in IMG, vol. 29, 145 (Himmler used the word *Ruhmesblatt* – a 'glorious chapter').

36 In any event, this is exactly what Hitler said when assigning Himmler the task of finding a 'final solution' to the 'South Tyrol problem', which he was finding very annoying.

37 I imagine that Hitler's words at the time were analogous to those he used when calling on the responsible Gauleiters, on 25 September 1940, to report within ten years' time that Alsace-Lorraine was 'German, purely German', and saying that he would not ask later 'what methods they had applied in making the region German' (see Chapter 4, 25 September).

38 Minutes of a meeting Hitler held with the head of the independent state of Croatia, Kvaternik, on 22 July 1941; ADAP, series D, vol. 13, Anh. III, 838.

39 Note by Bormann on the general meeting with Hitler, Rosenberg, Lammers, Keitel, and Göring, 16 July 1941; IMG, vol. 38, 86ff.

40 This was, in any event, how Greiser put it in a letter to Himmler, 21 November 1942, quoted in Sta. Bonn, 8Js103/65, note of 10 May 1973, 27.

41 Speech by the head of the Litzmannstadt (Lodz) operational unit (*Einsatzstab*) of the Ethnic German Liaison Office, Obersturmbannführer Doppler (undated, winter 1939–40); BAK, R49/20, 11–28, here 15.

42 Hilberg, 994f., 1002f.

43 Safrian, 11–21.

44 Mommsen, 'Radikalisierung'.

45 More recently, see Hans Mommsen, 'Umvolkungspläne'.

46 Broszat, 'Genesis', 93.

47 Neumann, 469, 521–2.

# |12|

# The murderers' postscripts

## Bilfinger (RSHA) to Wetzel (East Ministry)

'When taking measures regarding the Jewish question in the occupied eastern territories, it must always be kept in mind that the Jewish question has to be solved generally for all of Europe. Measures taken in the occupied eastern territories that serve the final solution of the Jewish question and thus the elimination of Judaism should not be hindered in any way whatsoever. A speedy solution of the Jewish question is to be striven for in the occupied eastern territories in particular.'[1] (29 January 1942)

## Eichmann to the State Police headquarters

'The evacuation of Jews to the East that has been being carried out in certain areas represents the beginning of the final solution of the Jewish question in the Old Reich, the *Ostmark* [i.e., Austria], and the Protectorate of Bohemia and Moravia. These evacuation measures were initially restricted to especially urgent plans. . . . New intake site possibilities are presently being arranged with the aim of deporting additional contingents of Jews.'[2] (31 January 1942)

## Greifelt (RKF) to Krüger (Krakow)

'The current displacement [of ethnic Germans within the Generalgouvernement] can be of a provisional nature only and will not be all too significant for the final settlement of the region. . . . As I have been informed, you have already come to an agreement with the Reich Security Main Office regarding the evacuation and resettlement of Poles and Jews.'[3] (21 February 1942)

# Hitler's proclamation to the members of the Nazi Party (NSDAP)

'Today the ideas of our National Socialist and fascist revolution have conquered great and mighty states, and my prophecy shall hold true that it is not the Aryan race that will be destroyed in this war, but rather it is the Jew who will be exterminated. Whatever comes with the struggle, however long it will last, this shall be its final outcome. And only then, after the elimination of these parasites, will a long period of international understanding and thus true peace spread over the suffering world.'[4] (24 February 1942)

# Meeting between Eichmann and the chiefs of the State Police (Stapo)

According to the official record, 'in order for individual Stapo offices to no longer be "tempted to deport difficult, elderly Jews along with the others", SS Obersturmbannführer Eichmann explained reassuringly that these Jews remaining in the Old Reich would most probably already be deported in the course of this summer or autumn to Theresienstadt, which was designated as a "Ghetto for the Aged". This city has been cleared and initially 15,000–20,000 Jews from the Protectorate can already be settled there. This is being done to "save face to the outside world".'[5] (6 March 1942)

# Reuter's notes on a conversation with Höfle (both in Lublin)

'1. It would be helpful if the Jews arriving on transports in the district of Lublin were separated at the dispatch station into those fit for work and those unfit for work. . . . 2. All Jews unfit for work will be sent to Belzec, the most remote border station in the district of Zamość. . . . In closing [Höfle] said he could receive four to five transports destined for Belzec daily, containing 1000 Jews each. These Jews would cross the border and never return to the Generalgouvernement.'[6] (16 March 1942)

# Rademacher (German Foreign Office) to the Personnel Department

'The greater the certainty of a German victory, the greater and more urgent become the tasks of the department, because the Jewish question must be resolved in the course of the war; that is the only way it can be taken care of without a general outcry from around the world. After the Jewish question is resolved in Germany, it will become necessary to tackle the problem in other European countries one after another, as is now being done in Slovakia and Croatia.'[7] (24 March 1942)

## Goebbels' diary entry

'The Jews are now being deported to the East from the Generalgouvernement, starting around Lublin. . . . By and large, one can say that 60 per cent of them must be liquidated, while only 40 per cent can be used for work. The former Gauleiter of Vienna [i.e., Globocnik], who is carrying out the operation, is proceeding quite judiciously, using a method that is not all too conspicuous. The Jews are facing a judgment which, although it is barbaric, they totally deserve. The prophecy the Führer made for them for starting a new world war is beginning to come true in the most terrible manner. . . . The ghettos that are being emptied in the cities of the Generalgouvernement are now being filled with Jews deported from the Reich. The procedure will then repeat itself after a certain period of time.'[8] (27 March 1942)

## Weekly report from the Generalgouvernement

'The Jews were transported by rail to the East. . . . The evacuation of the Jews has proven that the operation can also be implemented on a large scale; that is, for all of the Generalgouvernement.'[9] (28 March 1942)

## State Secretary in the Reich Justice Ministry

'The final solution of the Jewish question requires that a clear and authoritative line be drawn regarding what people are to be affected by the measures under consideration. Such a line can only be drawn if, from the outset, hybrids [Mischlinge] who are only one-quarter Jewish are excluded from the regulation.'[10] (5 April 1942)

## Population and Welfare Department in Lublin

'My proposal has offered basic clarity that Jews are to be deported out of here at the same rate, if possible, as Jews from the West are brought in. The present status of settlement movements is that about 6000 have been

settled here from the Reich; about 7500 have been deported out of the
district and 18,000 from the city of Lublin. In particular, 3400 have been
evacuated from Piaski, in the district of Lublin, and so far 2000 Reich Jews
have been brought in; 2200 have been deported from Izbica, in the district
of Krasnystav, and so far 4000 Reich Jews have been brought in; 1950 have
been evacuated from Opole and Wąwolnica, in the district of Puławy.'[11]
(7 April 1942)

## Greiser to Himmler

'The operation for the special treatment of approximately 100,000 Jews
in the area of my Gau, which you authorized in agreement with SS
Obergruppenführer Heydrich, Chief of the Reich Security Main Office,
can be completed within the next two to three months. I request authorization to be permitted, after completion of the Jewish operation, to use
the available, trained, special commando unit in averting a risk to the
district that is growing by catastrophic proportions every week. Here in
the district there are thus far approximately 230,000 recognized cases of
TB among those with Polish ethnicity. Of these, approximately 35,000
Poles are estimated to have open tuberculosis. . . . In view of the urgency
of this proposal I request your basic authorization as soon as possible so
that now, during the present operation against the Jews, preparations can
be made for all precautionary measures for the start of the operation
involving Poles with open TB.'[12] (1 May 1942)

## German Foreign Office to the German Ambassador in Pressburg (Bratislava)

'Please report the following to the Slovakian government: The Reich
government guarantees that Jews accepted during the de-Jewing
[*Entjudung*] of Slovakia will remain permanently in the eastern territories
without any chance of returning to Slovakia. Germany shall make no
claims regarding the property that these Jews of Slovakian citizenship
left behind in Slovakia, other than the fee of 500 Reichsmarks to be paid
for each Jew received.'[13] (2 May 1942)

## Administrative head of the Lublin district to Frank

'About 40,000 Jews were recently taken from the city of Lublin. . . . It is
hoped that over the course of time the district will be totally cleansed of
Jews. It turns out that especially in the district of Lublin the Jew is a

parasite, and the population is happy to be rid of these elements weighing upon them.'[14] (31 May 1942)

## Himmler to his SS generals

'The third task is mass migration in Europe, which we are in the process of implementing. We will certainly complete the migration of the Jews within a year; then there will be no more migrations.'[15] (9 June 1942)

## Progress report of the Lodz State Police Office

'In the course of forming the Gau ghetto, it proved necessary to make room for the Jews to be settled. For this purpose, a large number of Jews unfit for work were evacuated from the ghetto and handed over to the special commando unit. A total of 44,152 Polish Jews have been evacuated since 16 January 1942. Of the 19,848 Jews brought to the ghetto in October 1941 from the Old Reich, the Ostmark, and the Protectorate of Bohemia and Moravia, 10,993 have been evacuated, so that space has been made for approximately 55,000 Jews.'[16] (9 June 1942)

## Brack to Himmler

'On orders from Reichsleiter Bouhler, I placed a portion of my men at the disposal of Brigadeführer Globocnik quite some time ago to carry out his special task. In response to his renewed request, I have now detailed additional personnel. Brigadeführer Globocnik's opinion in this matter is that we should carry out the entire Jewish operation as quickly as possible, to avoid getting caught in the middle some day when problems arise making it necessary to abort the operation.'[17] (23 June 1942)

## Deputy State Secretary in the German Foreign Office

'At a meeting on 20 January 1942 I ordered that all questions relating to foreign countries be first cleared through the Foreign Office. This was approved by Gruppenführer Heydrich, and he complied with the regulation faithfully from the outset, as did the office of the Reich Security Main Office in charge of Jewish matters, working on all measures in smooth cooperation with the Foreign Office. The Reich Security Main Office proceeded in this area in an almost overly cautious manner.'[18] (21 August 1942)

## Government session in Krakow on questions regarding food supply

'Food for the Jewish population, estimated up to now at 1.5 million, is to be discontinued, except for an estimated 300,000 Jews working as manual labourers or in some other capacity in the service of the Germans.'[19] (24 August 1942)

## Confidential information from the Nazi Party Chancellery

'In the course of efforts towards the final solution of the Jewish question, there has recently been discussion within the population in various parts of the Reich on "very severe measures" being carried out against the Jews, especially in the eastern territories. It has been concluded that such remarks – largely in distorted and exaggerated form – were passed on by vacationers from the various groups stationed in the East who were able to observe such measures. . . . In order to be able to avoid the spreading of such rumours, which are often deliberately biased, the following statements on the present state of affairs have been provided: The struggle against Judaism has been going on for around 2000 years, up to now unsuccessfully. Not until 1933 did we begin to seek the ways and means of facilitating the total separation of Jewry from the German national body. . . . In view of the severely limited *Lebensraum* presently available to the German people, we hoped to solve this problem essentially by accelerating the emigration of the Jews. Since the beginning of the war in 1939, emigration options have steadily declined; also, the economic sphere of the German people is consistently growing in addition to its living space, so that in view of the large number of Jews living in these regions, emigration is no longer a sufficient means by which to force them back totally. Since our next generation will not be able to experience this issue with such immediacy or see it clearly enough, due to past experiences, and since the matter, now that it is under way, is pressing for a conclusion, the problem as a whole must be solved by the present generation.'[20] (9 October 1942)

## Speer to Himmler

'I have been informed that a major resettlement operation is under way in the district of Bialystok. Roughly 40,000 Jews are to be evacuated from the Bialystok ghetto. In order to eliminate the last partisan strongholds remaining in the forests around Bialowitze, the White Ruthenians living there – also about 40,000 people, predominantly peasants – are to be evacuated and transferred to the dwellings in Bialystok that used to house Jews. Because these are insufficient for the rural population, the additional housing shortage is to be alleviated by a wooden housing scheme, or barracks, with a capacity of 20,000 people. . . . '[21] (1 February 1943)

## Meeting between Greifelt and Himmler

'The Reichsführer SS has ordered that settlement measures [i.e., the settlement of ethnic Germans in the Zamość region] be continued as part of existing options, whereby efforts must be made to find other accommodation for the evacuated Poles. It is an urgent task to remove the 300,000–400,000 Jews still remaining in the Generalgouvernement.'[22] (12 May 1943)

## Globocnik on 'Operation Reinhard'

'Valuables from Operation "Reinhard" were submitted to the SS Main Office for Economic Administration in Berlin to be forwarded to the Reichsbank or to the Reich Ministry of Economics. This included . . . a total of RM 100,047,983.91.' 'The total material expenses, travel expenses, fees, etc. that accrued from the operation' were first subtracted from the cash. 'An additional regular amount was allotted the concentration camp [i.e., Maidanek] for construction of buildings, establishment of business operations, and to procure necessary agricultural machinery. . . . Spun fabrics, clothing, linens, blanket feathers, and rags were collected and sorted according to quality. The sorted objects then had to be examined for hidden valuables, and finally disinfected. More than 1900 railroad cars were then made available to the offices named by the Reich Ministry of Economics on orders of the SS Main Office for Economic Administration. Not only were these supplies used to clothe ethnically alien labourers, but a large amount of it was respun. . . . On orders of the Reichsführer SS, the best articles of clothing were separated out for use by ethnic Germans. . . . Valuable furnishings and household goods were repaired and most of them given to ethnic German settlers. Inferior goods were either destroyed or given to the [Polish] population as a premium for good work in the harvest.
' . . . The evacuations . . . have been carried out and the operation concluded. The prerequisite was to register the people with the least possible economic burden on war production through methodologically correct action, despite the limited personnel available. By and large this has been achieved.'[23] (March/November 1943)

# Notes

1 Express letter from Rudolf Bilfinger (RSHA, Dept. IIA 'Organization and Law') to Erhard Wetzel, 29 January 1942; BAK, R6/74, 94.

2 Express letter from Eichmann to the relevant security police (Sipo) offices and the SD in the Old Reich, Vienna, and Prague, 31 January 1942; quoted in *Biuletyn* 12 (1960), 30Fff.

3 Letter from Greifelt to Krüger, 21 February 1942; BAK, R49/2608.

4 Quoted in Pätzold, 345ff.

5 Note by the Stapo headquarters in Düsseldorf 'about the meeting on 6 March 1942 in the Reich Security Main Office – Section IVB4', 9 March; quoted in Kárný and Milotová, 232.

6 File memo by Fritz Reuter (Population and Welfare Department officer in the administration of the Generalgouvernement in the Lublin district), about a conversation on 16 March 1942 with Hans Höfle (Globocnik's chief of staff for the organization of the extermination of the Jews); quoted in *Okkupationspolitik in Polen*, 218.

7 Letter written by Franz Rademacher to prevent some of his staff from being drafted into the Wehrmacht, 24 March 1942; PAA, Inland IIA/B347/3, quoted in Döscher, 249.

8 Goebbels diaries, Reuth, 1776ff.

9 Report of the District Propaganda Department in Lublin, 28 March 1942; quoted in Pohl, 115 ('Evacuations' to the Belzec extermination camp started in the Lublin ghetto on the evening of 16 March).

10 Letter from Franz Schlegelberger, state secretary in the Reich Justice Ministry, to the participants at the Wannsee Conference, 5 April 1942, quoted in Mommsen and Obst, 476ff.

11 March progress report by Richard Türk, head of the Population and Welfare Department in the district of Lublin, 7 April 1942, quoted in FGM, 271.

12 Letter from Greiser to Himmler, 1 May 1942, quoted in *Doc. Occ.*, vol. 13, 40ff. Himmler initially approved the proposal – at the urging of Höppner and Krumey – but then rejected it because of 'reservations' expressed by Kurt Blome, deputy Reich health director. Blome referred to possible resistance by Poles and the possible protests of the Catholic Church, since it was impossible to keep such actions secret, as 'experience [had] shown' (letters of 18 November and 3 December 1941, respectively, from Blome and Himmler to Greiser; ibid., 42ff.).

13 Telex from Deputy State Secretary Martin Luther to the German embassy in Pressburg (Bratislava), 2 May 1942; quoted in Longerich, 301ff.

14 Lecture given by Wilhelm Engler, administrative head of the district of Lublin, at the government session of 31 May 1942; Frank diary, 500.

15 Himmler's speech to senior department heads and main administrative chiefs on the occasion of Heydrich's death, 9 June 1942, quoted in Himmler, *Geheimreden*, 159.

16 Quoted in Safrian, 122.

17 Letter from Brack (Führer's Chancellery, in charge of organizing the 'euthanasia' programme starting in 1939) to Himmler, 23 June 1942, quoted in Longerich, 371.

18 Notes by Martin Luther, Deputy State Secretary in the German Foreign Office, 21 August 1942, quoted in Pätzold and Schwarz, 127ff.

19 Minutes of the government session of 24 August 1942, Frank diary, 549.

20 Confidential information of the Party Chancellery, series 66 ('access only for Gau and district heads'), 9 October 1942, quoted in Pätzold, 351ff. The aim of

this was to provide information to pass on to subordinate officers and Germans who asked questions.

21 Letter from Speer to Himmler, 1 February 1943, quoted in Longerich, 223. On the actual events, see Grossman, 143, 405 (n. 22), 197, 407 (n. 28).

22 Notes on Greifelt's report to Himmler, 12 May 1943, quoted in *Biuletyn* 12 (1960), 84F.

23 From Globocnik's progress reports 'on the administrative conclusion of "Operation Reinhard"', March and November 1943; BAK, NS19/2234, 2, 35ff.

# Glossary

**Abteilung Erb- und Rassenpflege**  Department of Hereditary and Racial Maintenance

**Altreich**  'Old Reich', i.e. Germany within its 1937 borders, before annexations

**Amt für die Umsiedlung von Polen und Juden**  Office for the Resettlement of Poles and Jews. Renamed *UWZ* (q.v.) in April 1940

**Amt für Volkswohlfahrt**  Office for Public Welfare

**Aussiedlung**  Resettlement from one territory to another

**Auswanderungs- und Räumungsangelegenheiten**  Emigration and Evacuation Matters

**Auswärtiges Amt**  German Foreign Office

**Bevölkerungswesen**  Population Division of the German administration

**Deutsches Auslandsinstitut**  German Foreign Institute

**Deutsche Volksliste**  List of ethnic Germans, which provided for four categories of Germanization, ranging from full Reich citizenship to a form of Reich 'protection', with limited rights

**Einsatzgruppe**  Special units of Security Police *Sipo* (*see Sicherheitspolizei*) or SD (*see Sicherheitdienst*) in occupied territories, whose primary task was to kill (above all) Jews in the wake of the invading German army

**Einsatzkommando**  Task force – subdivision of an Einsatzgruppe

**Endlösung**  'Final Solution': the Nazi euphemism for the elimination of Europe's Jews, evolving in meaning in the course of the war from deportation to mass murder

*EWZ Einwandererzentralstelle*   Central Immigration Office. Under the direction of Reinhard Heydrich, its functions derived from the *Heim ins Reich* (q.v.) programme. Many of its tasks overlapped with those of the *UWZ* (q.v.)

*Fremdstämmige*   Those of alien descent

*Fremdvölkische, fremdvölkisch*   Ethnic aliens, ethnic alien elements, ethnically alien

*Gauleiter*   Leader of *Gau* (main territorial unit of the Nazi party), responsible directly to Hitler

*Gemeindetag*   Conference of Mayors

*Generalgouvernement*   'Government-General': comprised the eastern part of Poland not incorporated into the Reich but ruled as a satellite territory. The *Generalgouverneur* was Hans Frank

*Gestapo*   *Geheime Staatspolizei* (Secret State Police), involved in surveillance of the regime's political and ideological enemies, and in the maintenance of industrial order

*HA*   Hauptamt (Head Office)

*Heim ins Reich*   'Home to the Reich': Nazi policy of resettling ethnic Germans living abroad within the Greater German Reich

*Inländer*   The lowest of the four categories of Germanization for those regarded as ethnic Germans – i.e., protected members of the German Reich with limited [*Inländer*] rights

*Institut für Deutsche Ostarbeit*   Institute for German Activities in the East, located in Krakow

*IV B4*   A subdivision of the *RSHA* (q.v.). Led by Adolf Eichmann. See pp. 64–5 for further description of *IV B4* and associated sections

*judenfrei*   An area free of Jews

*Judenrat*   Council of Jews: compulsory Jewish 'self'-administrations set up by the Nazis in Jewish ghettos

*Kripo*   Kriminalpolizei (crime police)

*Lebensraum*   'Living space', i.e. the territory to be taken from Jews and Slavs in Eastern Europe and Russia for German settlement; *see also Ostraumlösung*

*Menscheneinsatz*   Human Deployment, department of the *RKF* (q.v.)

*Mischlinge*   Nazi term for people of mixed race, particularly with mixed Jewish and non-Jewish backgrounds

***Oberabschnitt*** Major regional division of the SS

***Ostjuden*** Eastern European Jews

***Ostmark*** Austria

***Ostraumlösung*** 'The Move Eastward': Germany's planned imperial expansion to the East; *see also Lebensraum*

***Polentum*** The 'Polish nation'; literally, 'Polendom'

***Räumung*** Evacuation

***Regierungsrat*** A bureaucratic ranking

***Reichsbürgerschaft*** Reich citizenship

***RFSS Reichführer SS*** (*und Chef der deutschen Polizei*) Heinrich Himmler's official title

***RKF Reichskommissar für die Festigung deutschen Volkstums*** An office held by Himmler from 1939: in that capacity he brought 'home to the Reich' some half a million ethnic Germans living abroad; *see also Heim ins Reich*

***RSHA Reichssicherheitshauptamt*** Reich Security Main Office. An SS and government organization that controlled offices responsible for intelligence, security, and criminal police work, and including the Gestapo and SD. Under the overall command of Heinrich Himmler, it was run by Reinhard Heydrich until his death and then by Ernst Kaltenbrunner

***RuSHA Rasse und Siedlungs-Hamptamt*** Race and Settlement Head Office; an SS organization

***Schutzstaffel*** (*SS*) Originally the security organization of the NSDAP, under Heinrich Himmler it became the single most powerful organization in the Nazi state

***Sicherheitsdienst*** (*SD*) The security and intelligence service of the SS and inextricably linked to the *Sipo* and German police organizations

***Sicherheitspolizei*** (*Sipo*) The German security police, comprising *Gestapo* and *Kripo* (qq.v.)

***Siedlungsraum*** Settlement space

***Staatlichkeit*** State entity

***Stabshauptamtes*** Staff Main Office

***Streudeutsche*** Ethnic Germans living among the native population of an area, rather than in a block of German settlement

***UWZ Umwandererzentralstelle*** Central Resettlement Office. As coordinator of this office (in Posen and Lodz), Adolf Eichmann deported or placed in ghettos Jews and Poles whose property and businesses were needed for 'ethnic German settlers'

*Verdrängung* Eviction

*Volk* Literally, 'people': carries connotations of nation or race

*Volksdeutsche Mittelstelle, or Vomi* Ethnic German Liaison Office. It was founded in 1936 in order to better integrate ethnic Germans into Nazi policy. With the change in policy in 1939, it became *de facto* one of Himmler's many resettlement offices. In June 1941, the *Vomi* then officially became a main SS office

*völkisch* [adjective] Nationalist (where the nationalism is defined according to racial or ethnic criteria)

*völkische Flurbereinigung* Ethnic redistribution: derived from an agricultural term for the consolidation of splintered landholdings, the Nazi distortion referred to the territorial consolidation and mutual separation of different ethnic groups

*Volksboden* German ethnic region

*Volksgemeinschaft* 'National community'. Nazi concept of a harmonious society founded on racial purity and transcending class conflict

*Volksgenossen* 'National comrades'. Term to describe members of the *Volksgemeinschaft* (q.v.)

*Volksgenossinnen* Female form of the above, i.e., German women

*Volkstum* Denotes ethnicity or national cultural identity, nationhood

*Waffen-SS* Term introduced in 1940 to describe militarized units of the SS

*Wehrmacht* The German armed forces

*Wirtschaftsverwaltungshauptamt* (*WVHA*) Economic-Administrative Central Office of the SS. Part of its remit was to oversee economic activities at concentration and extermination camps

# List of abbreviations

| | |
|---|---|
| AA | *Auswärtiges Amt*, Foreign Office |
| ADAP | *Akten zur Deutschen Auswärtigen Politik*, Files on German Foreign Policy |
| AGK | *Archiv der Hauptkommission zur Untersuchung der hitleristischenVerbrechen, Warschau*, Archive of the Main Commission to Investigate the Hitler Crimes, Warsaw |
| Anh. | *Anhang*, appendix |
| BAK | *Bundesarchiv (Koblenz)*, Federal Archive, Koblenz |
| BA-MA | *Bundesarchiv-Militärarchiv (Freiburg)*, Federal Archive/ Military Archive, Freiburg |
| BAP | *Bundesarchiv (Außenstelle Potsdam)*, Federal Archive, Potsdam branch |
| BAP-DH | *Bundesarchiv (Potsdam), Zwischenarchiv Dahlwitz-Hoppegarten*, Federal Archive (Potsdam), Temporary Archive Dahlwitz-Hoppegarten |
| BDC | Berlin Document Centre |
| DAF | *Deutsche Arbeitsfront*, German Labour Front |
| DAG | *Deutsche Ansiedlungsgesellschaft*, German Settlement Company |
| DAI | *Deutsches Auslandsinstitut (Stuttgart)*, German Foreign Institute, Stuttgart |
| Doc., Docs. | Document(s) |
| DUT | *Deutsche Umsiedlungs-Treuhand GmbH*, German Resettlement Trusteeship Company |
| DVL | *Deutsche Volksliste*, list of ethnic Germans; *see* glossary |
| E.K. | *Eisernes Kreuz*, Iron Cross |
| EWZ | *Einwandererzentralstelle*, Central Immigration Office |
| EWZ/L | *Einwandererzentralstelle/Litzmannstadt (Lodz)*, Litzmannstadt [Lodz] Central Immigration Office |

| | |
|---|---|
| FGM | *Faschismus, Getto, Massenmord*, Fascism, Ghetto, Mass Murder; *see* bibliography |
| 14f3 | The business reference and code name for the murder of concentration camp prisoners with the help of 'Operation T-4' |
| GEKRAT | *Gemeinnützige Krankentransport Organisation GmbH*, Public Hospital Transport Organization, Inc. |
| Gen.Gouv., GG | *Generalgouvernement* |
| Gestapo | *Geheime Staatspolizei*, secret state police |
| GHTO | *Grundstücks-Haupttreuhandstelle Ost*, Main Trusteeship Office for Real Estate in the East |
| HA | *Hauptabteilung*, Main Office |
| HTO | *Haupttreuhandstelle Ost*, Main Trusteeship Office in the East |
| IDO | *Institut für Deutsche Ostarbeit (Krakau)*, Institute for German Activities in the East, Krakow |
| IfZ | *Institut für Zeitgeschichte (München)*, Institute for Contemporary History, Munich |
| IMG | *Internationaler Militärgerichtshof (Nürnberg)*, International Military Tribunal at Nuremberg, *see* bibliography |
| jW. | *jüdischer Wohnbezirk (Warschau)*, Jewish quarter of Warsaw; Nazi euphemism for the Warsaw ghetto |
| KTB | *Kriegstagebuch*, war diary |
| KZ (KL) | *Konzentrationslager*, concentration camp |
| NAW | National Archives (Washington, DC) |
| Nbg. Doc. | Documents from the trials before the American military court at Nuremberg |
| NL | *Nachlaß*, personal archive |
| NSDAP | National Socialist German Workers' Party (Nazi Party) |
| NSV | *Nationalsozialistische Volkswohlfahrt*, National Socialist Public Welfare |
| OA | *Oberabschnitt*; *see* glossary |
| OKH | *Oberkommando des Heeres*, Supreme Command of the Army |
| OKW | *Oberkommando der Wehrmacht*, Supreme Command of the Wehrmacht |
| PA | *Personalakte*, personnel file |
| PAA | *Politisches Archiv des Auswärtigen Amts (Bonn)*, Political Archive of the Foreign Office, Bonn |
| R | *Bestände von Reichsbehörden im BA*, documents from Reich offices in the Federal Archives |
| RABl. | *Reichsarbeitsblatt*, Reich Labour Bulletin |
| Rep. | Repositorium |
| RGBl. | *Reichsgesetzblatt*, Reich Legal Bulletin |
| RKF/RKFDV | *Reichskommissar für die Festigung deutschen Volkstums*, |

|  | Reich Commission(er) for the Consolidation of German Nationhood |
| RKO | Ostland Reichskommissariat |
| RKW | *Reichskuratorium für Wirtschaftlichkeit*, Reich Committee for Efficiency (Today the office is called the *Rationalisierungskuratorium der deutschen Wirtschaft*, or Efficiency Committee for the German Economy) |
| RM | Reichsmark |
| RMF | *Reichsministerium der Finanzen*, Reich Ministry of Finance |
| RMBLiV | *Ministerialblatt des Reichs- und Preußischen Ministeriums des Innern*, Ministerial Bulletin of the Reich and Prussian Ministries of the Interior |
| RMdI | *Reichsministerium des Inneren*, Reich Ministry of the Interior |
| RSHA | *Reichssicherheitshauptamt*, Reich Security Main Office |
| RuSHA | *Rasse- und Siedlungshauptamt der SS*, SS Main Office for Race and Settlement |
| RV | *Reichsvereinigung der Juden in Deutschland*, Reich Association of Jews in Germany |
| SD | *Sicherheitsdienst*, Security Service |
| Sipo | *Sicherheitspolizei*, Security Police |
| SS | Schutzstaffel |
| SS-HO | SS hanging files at the BDC |
| StA | *Staatsarchiv*, State Archives |
| Sta. | *Staatsanwaltschaft*, government prosecutor's office |
| T-4 | code name for the offices at Tiergartenstraße 4, Berlin, responsible for murdering mentally handicapped Germans |
| Tgb | *Tagebuch*, diary |
| UTAG | *Umsiedlungs-Treuhand-Aktiengesellschaft, Riga*, resettlement trusteeship stock company, Riga office |
| UWZ | *Umwandererzentralstelle*, Central Resettlement Office |
| UWZ/L | *Umwandererzentralstelle/Lodz*, Central Resettlement Office in Lodz |
| UWZ/P | *Umwandererzentralstelle/Posen*, Central Resettlement Office in Posen |
| VDA | *Verein für das Deutschtum im Ausland,* League for Germandom Abroad |
| VJP | *Vierjahresplan*, Four-Year Plan |
| VZG | *Vierteljahrshefte für Zeitgeschichte*, Quarterly Journal of Contemporary History |
| Vomi | *Volksdeutsche Mittelstelle*, Ethnic German Liaison Office |
| Vomi/P | *Volksdeutsche Mittelstelle/Posen*, Ethnic German Liaison Office in Posen |
| WiRüAmt | *Wehrwirtschafts- und Rüstungsamt*, Armament Economy Office |
| YIVO | Yiddish Scientific Institute (New York) |

ZASM    *Zentrum zur Aufbewahrung historisch-dokumentarischer Sammlungen, Moskau,* Centre to Preserve Historical Documentary Collections, Moscow

ZSg    *Zeitgeschichtliche Sammlung,* Contemporary History Collection

ZStL    *Zentrale Stelle der Landesjustizverwaltung zur Aufklärung nationalsozialistische Verbrechen, in Ludwigsburg,* Central Federal Justice Administrative Office Regarding Nazi Crimes, in Ludwigsburg

# Bibliography

Ackermann, Josef, *Heinrich Himmler als Ideologe* (Göttingen, Zurich, Frankfurt, Musterschmidt, 1970).

Adam, Uwe Dietrich, *Judenpolitik im Dritten Reich* (Düsseldorf, Droste Verlag, 1979, 2nd edn).

ADAP: *Akten zur Deutschen Auswärtigen Politik 1918–1945*, Series D and E 1937–1945 (Baden-Baden, Imprimerie Nationale, 1950ff.) (cited as ADAP).

Adler, Hans-Günter, *Der verwaltete Mensch. Studien zur Deportation der Juden aus Deutschland* (Tübingen, Mohr, 1974).

Aly, Götz, 'Hinweise für die weitere Erforschung der NS-Gesundheitspolitik und der "Euthanasie"-Verbrechen', in *Arbeitsmigration und Flucht. Vertreibung und Arbeitskräfteregulierung im Zwischenkriegseuropa [Beiträge 11]* (1993), 195–204 (cited as Aly, 'Hinweise').

Aly, Götz, 'Medicine against the Useless', in Aly, Chroust, and Pross, 22–98 (cited as Aly, 'Medicine').

Aly, Götz, 'Pure and Tainted Progress', in Aly, Chroust, and Pross, 156–237 (cited as Aly, 'Progress').

Aly, Götz (ed.), *Aktion T 4 1939–1945. Die 'Euthanasie'-Zentrale in der Tiergartenstraße 4* (Berlin, Edition Heinrich, 1989, 2nd edn) (cited as Aly, *Aktion T4*).

Aly, Götz, Chroust, Peter, and Pross, Christian, *Cleansing the Fatherland: Nazi Medicine and Racial Hygiene*, trans. Belinda Cooper (Baltimore and London, Johns Hopkins University Press, 1994).

Aly, Götz and Heim, Susanne, *Vordenker der Vernichtung. Auschwitz und die Pläne für eine neue europäische Ordnung* (Hamburg, Hoffmann und Campe, 1991; Frankfurt a.M., Fischer Taschenbuch Verlag, 1994, 3rd edn) (cited as Aly and Heim).

Aly, Götz and Heim, Susanne, 'Deutsche Herrschaft "im Osten". Bevölkerungspolitik und Völkermord', in Peter Jahn and Reinhard Rürup (eds),

*Erobern und Vernichten. Der Krieg gegen die Sowjetunion* (Berlin, Argon, 1991) (cited as Aly and Heim, 'Herrschaft').

Aly, Götz and Roth, Karl Heinz, *Die restlose Erfassung. Volkszählen, Identifizieren, Aussondern im Nationalsozialismus* (Berlin, Rotbuch Verlag, 1984).

Arendt, Hannah, *The Origins of Totalitarianism*, rev. edn (New York, Harcourt Brace Jovanovich, 1973).

Bach, Dieter and Jacobsen, Hans-Adolf (eds), *Mißtrauische Nachbarn und Hindernisse auf dem Weg der Verständigung Bundesrepublik Deutschland–Sowjetunion* (Mühlheim/Ruhr, Evangelische Akademie, 1987).

Bauer, Yehuda, 'Auschwitz', in Jäckel and Rohwer, 164–73.

Bauman, Zygmunt, *Modernity and the Holocaust* (New York, Cornell University Press, 1989).

Beer, Matthias, 'Die Entwicklung der Gaswagen beim Mord an den Juden', *VZG* 35 (1987), 403–17.

*Beiträge zur nationalsozialistischen Gesundheits- und Sozialpolitik*, vols 1–11 (vols 1–10: Berlin, Rotbuch Verlag, 1985–1992; from vol. 11 [1993], Verlag der Buchläden Schwarze Risse [Berlin] and Rote Strasse [Göttingen]) (cited as *Beiträge*).

Benz, Wolfgang (ed.), *Dimension des Völkermords. Die Zahl der jüdischen Opfer des Nationalsozialismus (Benz)* (Munich, Oldenbourg; 1991). (Individual essays by Ino *Arndt* and Heinz *Boberach* [German Reich], Jonny *Moser* [Austria], Ino *Arndt* [Luxembourg], Juliane *Wetzel* [France and Belgium], Holm *Sundhaussen* [Yugoslavia], László *Varga* [Hungary], Eva *Schmidt-Hartmann* [Czechoslovakia], Frank *Golczewski* [Poland] and Gerd *Robel* [Soviet Union] cited, respectively, as *Benz and Arndt* etc.).

Berenstein, see Brustin-Berenstein.

Bernhardt, Heike, *Die Anstaltspsychiatrie in Pommern 1939 bis 1946. Ein Beitrag zur Aufhellung nationalsozialistischer Tötungsaktionen unter besonderer Berücksichtigung der Landesheilanstalt Ueckermünde* (Leipzig, PhD dissertation, 1993).

*Biuletyn Głównej Komisji Badania Zbrodni Hitlerowskich w Polsce* 12 (Warsaw, Wydawnictwo Prawnicze, 1960) (cited as *Biuletyn*).

Boberach, Heinz (ed.), *Meldungen aus dem Reich 1938–1945. Die geheimen Lageberichte des Sicherheitsdienstes der SS*, vol. 1 (Herrsching, Pawlak, 1984) (cited as *Meldungen aus dem Reich* [Reports from the Reich]).

Bock, Gisela, *Zwangssterilisation im Nationalsozialismus. Studien zur Rassenpolitik und Frauenpolitik* (Opladen, Westdeutscher Verlag, 1986).

Bosma, Koos, 'Verbindung zwischen Ost- und Westkolonisation', in Rössler and Schleiermacher, 198–214.

Bracher, Karl Dietrich, *The German Dictatorship: The Origins, Structure, and Effects of National Socialism*, trans. Jean Steinberg (New York, Holt, Rinehart & Winston, 1970).

Breitman, Richard, *Architect of Genocide: Himmler and the Final Solution* (New York, Alfred A. Knopf, 1991).

Broszat, Martin (ed.), *Kommandant in Auschwitz. Autobiographische Aufzeichnungen des Rudolf Höss* (Stuttgart, Deutsche Verlags-Anstalt, 1958) (cited as *Höss*).

Broszat, Martin, *Nationalsozialistische Polenpolitik 1939–1945* (Stuttgart, Deutsche Verlags-Anstalt, 1961) (cited as Broszat).

Broszat, Martin, 'Hitler and the Genesis of the "Final Solution": An Assessment of David Irving's Thesis', *Yad Vashem Studies* 13 (1979), 73–125 (cited as Broszat, 'Genesis') [Also in Hannsjoachim W. Koch, *Aspects of the Third Reich* (London and Basingstoke, Macmillan, 1985), 390–429, 559–67.]

Broszat, Martin, 'Zur Erklärung des nationalsozialistischen Massenmords an den Juden', in Jäckel and Rohwer, 179–84, 239–42; quoted from Broszat, *Hitler*, 245–55 (cited as Broszat, 'Erklärung').

Broszat, Martin, *Nach Hitler. Der schwierige Umgang mit unserer Geschichte* (Munich, DTV, 1988) (cited as Broszat, *Hitler*).

Broszat, Martin, 'A Plea for the Historicization of National Socialism', trans. Thomas Ertman, in Peter Baldwin (ed.), *Reworking the Past: Hitler, the Holocaust and the Historians' Debate* (Boston, Beacon Press, 1990), 77–87 (cited as Broszat, 'Plea').

Browning, Christopher R., *The Final Solution and the German Foreign Office: A Study of Referat D III of Abteilung Deutschland 1940–1943* (New York, Holmes & Meier, 1978) (cited as Browning, *Final Solution*).

Browning, Christopher R., *Fateful Months: Essays on the Emergence of the Final Solution* (New York, London, Holmes & Meier, 1985) (cited as Browning, *Fateful Months*).

Browning, Christopher R., 'Nazi Ghettoization Policy in Poland, 1939–1941', *Central European History* 19 (1986), 343–68.

Browning, Christopher R., 'Nazi Resettlement Policy and the Search for a Solution to the Jewish Question, 1939–1941', *German Studies Review* 9 (1986), 497–519.

Browning, Christopher R., 'Genocide and Public Health: German Doctors and Polish Jews, 1939–1941,' in Christopher R. Browning, *The Path to Genocide: Essays on Launching the Final Solution* (Cambridge and New York, Cambridge University Press, 1992), 145–68 (cited as Browning, 'Genocide').

Browning, Christopher R., *Ordinary Men: Reserve Police Battalion 101 and the Final Solution in Poland* (New York, HarperCollins, 1992) (cited as Browning, *Ordinary Men*).

Brustin-Berenstein, Tatiana, 'Die jüdische soziale Selbsthilfe', *Arbeitsamt und Sondererlaß. Menschenverwertung, Rassenpolitik und Arbeitsamt* [*Beiträge* 8] (1990), 156–74 (cited as Berenstein).

Buchheim, Hans, 'Rechtsstellung und Organisation des Reichskommissars für die Festigung deutschen Volkstums', *Gutachten des Instituts für Zeitgeschichte* 1 (Munich, Institut für Zeitgeschichte, 1958).

Burleigh, Michael, *Germany Turns Eastwards: A Study of Ostforschung in the Third Reich* (Cambridge, Cambridge University Press, 1988).

Burrin, Philippe, *Hitler and the Jews: The Genesis of the Holocaust*, trans. Patsy Southgate (London, Arnold; New York, Routledge, Chapman & Hall, 1994).

*Chronicle*, see Dobroszycki.

Chroust, Peter (ed.), *Friedrich Mennecke. Innenansichten eines medizinischen Täters im Nationalsozialismus. Edition seiner Briefe 1935–1947* (2 vols, Hamburg, Hamburger Institut für Sozialforschung, 1987) (cited as Chroust).

Chroust, Peter, 'Selected Letters of Doctor Friedrich Mennecke', in Aly, Chroust, and Pross, 238–95 (cited as Chroust, 'Selected Letters').

Ciano, Count Galeazzo, *Tagebücher 1939–1943* (Bern, Alfred Scherz, 1946) (cited as Ciano diary).

Conquest, Robert, *The Nation Killers: The Soviet Deportation of Nationalities* (London, Macmillan, 1970).

Conquest, Robert, *The Harvest of Sorrow: Soviet Collectivization and the Terror-Famine* (London, Melbourne, Hutchinson, 1986).

Czech, Danuta, *Das Kalendarium von Auschwitz*, trans. Jochen August, Nina Kozlowski, Silke Lent, and Jan Parcer (Reinbeck, Rowohlt, 1989).

Czerniaków, Adam, *The Warsaw Diary of Adam Czerniaków: Prelude to Doom*, ed. Raul Hilberg, Stanislaw Staron, and Josef Kermisz, trans. S. Staron and the staff of Yad Vashem (New York, Stein & Day, 1979).

Dallin, Alexander, *German Rule in Russia 1941–1945: A Study of Occupation Policies*, 2nd edn (London and Basingstoke, Macmillan, 1981).

Dawidowicz, Lucy S., *The War against the Jews 1933–1945* (New York, Bantam Books, 1975).

Dobroszycki, Lucien, *The Chronicle of the Lodz Ghetto 1941–1944* (New Haven, London, Yale University Press, 1984) (cited as *Chronicle*).

*Documenta Occupationis Teutonicae*, vols 5, 6, 8, 13 (Poznań, Instytut Zachodni, 1952, 1958, 1969, 1990, resp.) (cited as *Doc. Occ.*).

*Dokumenty i Materiały do dziejów okupacji niemieckiej w Polsce* (Getto łódzkie), vol. 3 (Warszawa, Łódź, Kraków, 1946) (cited as *Dokumenty*).

Döscher, Hans-Jürgen, *Das Auswärtige Amt im Dritten Reich. Diplomatie im Schatten der 'Endlösung'* (Berlin, Siedler, 1987).

Dressen, Willi, 'Euthanasie', in Kogon *et al.*, 27–80.

Drobisch, Klaus, 'Die Judenreferate des Geheimen Staatspolizeiamtes und des Sicherheitsdienstes der SS 1933 bis 1939', *Jahrbuch für Antisemitismusforschung* 2 (1993), 230–54.

Ebbinghaus, Angelika and Preissler, Gerd, 'Die Ermordung psychisch kranker Menschen in der Sowjetunion. Dokumentation', *Aussonderung und Tod. Die klinische Hinrichtung der Unbrauchbaren* [*Beiträge* 1] (1985), 75–107.

Ebbinghaus, Angelika and Roth, Karl Heinz, 'Vorläufer des "Generalplans Ost". Eine Dokumentation über Theodor Schieders Polendenkschrift vom 7. Oktober 1939', 1999. *Zeitschrift für Sozialgeschichte des 20. und 21. Jahrhunderts* 7, no. 1 (1992), 62–94.

Eichholtz, Dietrich, *Geschichte der deutschen Kriegswirtschaft 1939–1945*, vol. 1 (Berlin, Akademie, 1984).

Eisenblätter, Gerhard, *Grundlinien der Politik des Reichs gegenüber dem Generalgouvernement, 1939–1945* (Frankfurt a.M., PhD dissertation, 1969).

*Encyclopedia*, see Gutman.

Engel, see *Heeresadjutant*.

Faulstich, Heinz, *Von der Irrenfürsorge zur 'Euthanasie'. Geschichte der basischen Psychiatrie bis 1945* (Freiburg i.Br., Lambertus, 1993).

Ferenc, Tone, *Quellen zur nationalsozialistischen Entnationalisierungspolitik in Slowenien 1941–1945* (Maribor, Zalozba Obzorja, 1980).

FGM, see Jewish Historical Institute of Warsaw.

Förster, Jürgen, 'Der Angriff auf die Sowjetunion', *Das Deutsche Reich und der Zweite Weltkrieg* 4 (1983), 1030–78.

Foucault, Michel, 'Leben machen und sterben lassen' [Address given in 1976], *Lettre International* 20 (1993), 62–7.

The Diary of Hans Frank, an official log, in Nuremberg document PS-2233; excerpts reprinted in International Military Tribunal, *Trial of the Major War Criminals*, vol. 29 (Nuremberg, 1947–49), 356–724. Citations in this book were translated from Präg and Jacobmeyer (eds), see below.

Friedlander, Henry, 'Jüdische Anstaltspatienten in Deutschland', in Aly, *Aktion T4*, 34–44.

Friedländer, Saul, 'From Anti-Semitism to Extermination: A Historiographical Study of Nazi Policies toward the Jews', *Yad Vashem Studies* 16 (1984), 1–50.

Friedrich, Jörg, *Das Gesetz des Krieges. Das deutsche Heer in Rußland 1941 bis 1945. Der Prozeß gegen Oberkommando der Wehrmacht* (Munich, Zurich, Piper, 1993).

Fröhlich, Elke (ed.), *Die Tagebücher von Joseph Goebbels. Sämtliche Fragmente*, part I: 1924–1941 (Munich, London, New York, Paris, Saur, 1987) (cited as Goebbels diaries).

Gebel, Hans Georg and Grießhammer, Heinrich, *Dokumentation zu den Krankenverlegungen aus den Neuendettelsauer Anstalten 1941, dem Verhalten von Innerer Mission und Kirche 1936–42 und der heutigen Reaktion von Kirche und Diakonie auf die Nachfrage nach den Ereignissen* (Berlin, self-published, 1977).

Gilbert, Martin, *The Macmillan Atlas of the Holocaust* (New York, Macmillan, 1982).

Gilbert, Martin, *The Holocaust: A History of the Jews of Europe during the Second World War* (New York, Holt, Rinehart & Winston, 1985) (cited as Gilbert, *Holocaust*).

Goebbels diaries, see Fröhlich.

Goebbels diaries, Reuth, see Reuth.

Goshen, Seev, 'Eichmann und die Nisko-Aktion im November 1939', *VZG* 29 (1981), 74–96.

Grabitz, Helge and Scheffler, Wolfgang, *Letzte Spuren* (Berlin, Edition Heinrich, 1988).

Grode, Walter, *Die 'Sonderbehandlung 14f13' in den Konzentrationslagern des Dritten Reiches. Ein Beitrag zur Dynamik der faschistischen Vernichtungspolitik* (Frankfurt, Bern, New York, Peter Lang, 1987).

Grossman, Chaika, *The Underground Army: Fighters of the Bialystok Ghetto* (New York, Holocaust Library, 1987).

Gutman, Israel (ed.), *Encyclopedia of the Holocaust* (3 vols, New York, Macmillan, 1990).

Gutschow, Niels, 'Stadtplanung im Warthegau 1939–1944', in Rössler and Schleiermacher, 232–58.

Halder, Franz, *Kriegstagebuch* (3 vols, Stuttgart, Kohlhammer, 1962–64) (cited as Halder war diary).

Heer, Hannes, 'Killing Fields', *Mittelweg* 36: 3 (1994), 7–31.

*Heeresadjutant bei Hitler 1938–1943. Aufzeichnungen des Majors Engel*, ed. and commentary by Hildegard von Kotze (Stuttgart, Deutsche Verlagsanstalt, 1974) (cited as Engel).

Hehn, Jürgen von, *Die Umsiedlung der baltischen Deutschen – das letzte Kapitel baltischdeutscher Geschichte* [*Marburger Ostforschungen* 40] (Marburg, Herder Institut, 1982).

Heiber, Helmut, 'Der Generalplan Ost', *VZG* 6 (1958), 281–325.

Heim, Susanne, *Gibt es eine Ökonomie der 'Endlösung'? Wirtschaftsrationalisierung und Vernichtungspolitik im besetzten Polen 1939 bis 1945* (Berlin, PhD dissertation, 1991) (cited as Heim, *Ökonomie*).

Heim, Susanne, '"Deutschland muß ihnen ein Land ohne Zukunft sein". Die Zwangsemigration der Juden 1933 bis 1938', in *Arbeitsmigration und Flucht. Vertreibung und Arbeitskräfteregulierung im Zwischenkriegseuropa* [*Beiträge* 11] (1993), 48–81 (cited as Heim).

Heim, Susanne and Aly, Götz, *Ein Berater der Macht. Helmut Meinhold oder der Zusammenhang zwischen Sozialpolitik und Judenvernichtung* (Hamburg, Berlin, self-published, 1986) (cited as Heim and Aly, *Berater*).

Heim, Susanne and Aly, Götz (eds), *Bevölkerungsstruktur und Massenmord. Neue Dokumente zur deutschen Politik der Jahre 1938–1945* [*Beiträge* 9] (cited as Heim and Aly, *Struktur*).

Heim, Susanne and Aly, Götz, 'Staatliche Ordnung und "organische Lösung". Die Rede Hermann Görings "Über die Judenfrage" vom 6. Dezember 1938', *Jahrbuch für Antisemitismusforschung* 2 (1993), 378–405.

Herbert, Ulrich, *Fremdarbeiter. Politik und Praxis des 'Ausländer-Einsatzes'* *in der Kriegswirtschaft des Dritten Reiches* (Berlin, Bonn, J. H. W. Dietz, 1985).

Hilberg, Raul, *The Role of the German Railroads in the Destruction of the* *Jews*, published as a manuscript and presented in 1976 as a study at the annual meeting of the American Sociological Association (cited as Hilberg, *Railroads*).

Hilberg, Raul, *The Destruction of the European Jews*, rev. edn (3 vols, New York, Holmes & Meier, 1985) (cited as Hilberg).

Hilberg, Raul and Söllner, Alfons, 'Das Schweigen zum Sprechen bringen. Ein Gespräch über Franz Neumann und die Entwicklung der Holocaust-Forschung', in Dan Diner (ed.), *Zivilisationsbruch. Denken nach* *Auschwitz* (Frankfurt a.M., Fischer Taschenbuch Verlag, 1988), 175– 200 (cited as Hilberg and Söllner).

Hillgruber, Andreas, *Hitler, König Carol and Marschall Antonescu. Die* *deutsch–rumänischen Beziehungen 1938–1944* (Wiesbaden, Steiner, 1954) (cited as Hillgruber, *Carol*).

Hillgruber, Andreas, *Hitlers Strategie. Politik und Kriegführung 1940–1941* (Frankfurt a.M., Bernard & Graefe, 1965) (cited as Hillgruber, *Strategie*).

Hillgruber, Andreas (ed.), *Staatsmänner und Diplomaten bei Hitler.* *Vertrauliche Aufzeichnungen über Unterredungen mit Vertretern des* *Auslandes 1939–1941* (2 vols, Frankfurt a.M., Bernard & Graefe, 1967 [vol. 1], 1970 [vol. 2]) (cited as Hillgruber, *Staatsmänner*).

Hillgruber, Andreas, 'Die "Endlösung" und das deutsche Ostimperium als Kernstück des rassenideologischen Programms des Nationalsozialismus', *VZG* 20 (1972), 133–53 (cited as Hillgruber, 'Endlösung').

Hillgruber, Andreas and Hümmelchen, Gerhard, *Chronik des Zweiten* *Weltkrieges. Kalendarium militärischer und politischer Ereignisse* *1939–1945*, rev. and exp. edn (Düsseldorf, Droste, 1978).

Himmler, *Geheimreden*, see Smith and Peterson.

*Höss*, see Broszat.

IMG: *Der Prozeß gegen die Hauptkriegsvebrecher vor dem Internationalen* *Militärgerichtchof.* Quotations have been translated from, and page numbers cited according to, the German edition (cited as IMG). See also the English edition: *International Military Tribunal, Trial of the Major* *War Criminals*, 14 November 1945–1 October 1946 (Nuremberg, 1947–49).

Immenkötter, Herbert, *Menschen aus unserer Mitte. Die Opfer von* *Zwangssterilisierung und Euthanasie im Dominikus-Ringeisen-Werk* *Ursberg* (Donauwörth, Auer, 1992).

Jachomowski, Dirk, *Umsiedlung der Bessarabien-, Bukowina-, und* *Dobrudschadeutschen. Von der Volksgruppe in Rumänien zur* *Siedlungsbrücke an der Reichsgrenze [Buchreihe der Südostdeutschen* *Historischen Kommission* 32] (Munich, Oldenbourg, 1984).

Jäckel, Eberhard, *Frankreich in Hitlers Europa. Die deutsche Frankreich-*

*politik im Zweiten Weltkrieg* (Stuttgart, Deutsche Verlags-Anstalt, 1966) (cited as Jäckel, *Frankreich*).

Jäckel, Eberhard, *Hitlers Herrschaft* (Stuttgart, Deutsche Verlags-Anstalt, 1986) (cited as Jäckel).

Jäckel, Eberhard and Rohwer, Jürgen (eds), *Der Mord an den Juden im Zweiten Weltkrieg. Entschlußbildung und Verwirklichung* (Frankfurt a.M., Fischer Taschenbuch Verlag, 1987).

Jacobsen, Hans-Adolf, '"The *Kommissarbefehl*" and Mass Executions of Soviet Russian Prisoners of War', trans. Dorothy Long, in Krausnick *et al.*, 505–35.

Jewish Historical Institute of Warsaw (ed.), *Faschismus, Getto, Massenmord* (Berlin, 1962) (cited as FGM).

Jochmann, Werner (ed.), *Monologe im Führerhauptquartier 1941–1944. Die Aufzeichnungen Heinrich Heims* (Hamburg, Knaus, 1980) (cited as *Monologe*).

Kaplan, Chaim A., *The Warsaw Diary of Chaim A. Kaplan*, ed. and trans. Abraham I. Katsh, rev. edn (New York, Collier, 1973) [originally published as *Scroll of Agony* (New York, Macmillan, 1963)].

Kárný, Miroslav and Milotová, Jaroslava (eds), *Protektoráni politika Reinharda Heydricha* (Prague, Tisková, edicni a propagacni sluzba, 1991).

Kenrick, Donald and Puxon, Gratton, *The Destiny of Europe's Gypsies* (London, Heinemann Educational Books for Sussex University Press, 1972).

Kettenacker, Lothar, *Nationalsozialistische Volkstumspolitik im Elsaß während des Zweiten Weltkrieges* (Stuttgart, Deutsche Verlags-Anstalt, 1973).

Klarsfeld, Serge, *Vichy–Auschwitz: Le Rôle de Vichy dans la Solution Finale de la Question Juive en France 1942; 1943–44* (2 vols, Paris, Fayard, 1983 [vol. 1], 1985 [vol. 2]). Quotations in this book were translated and cited from the German edition: Sege Klarsfeld, *Vichy–Auschwitz. Die Zusammenarbeit der deutschen und französischen Behörden bei der 'Endlösung der Judenfrage'*, trans. Ahlrich Meyer (Nördlingen, Greno, 1989).

Klee, Ernst, *'Euthanasie' im NS-Staat. Die 'Vernichtung lebensunwerten Lebens'* (Frankfurt a.M., S. Fischer Verlag, 1983) (cited as Klee).

Klee, Ernst (ed.), *Dokumente zur 'Euthanasie'* (Frankfurt a.M., Fischer Taschenbuch Verlag, 1985) (cited as Klee, *Dokumente*).

Koehl, Robert L., *RKFDV: German Resettlement and Population Policy 1939–1945* (Cambridge, MA, Harvard University Press, 1957).

Kogon, Eugen *et al.* (eds), *Nationalsozialistische Massentötungen durch Giftgas. Eine Dokumentation* (Frankfurt a.M., Fischer Taschenbuch Verlag, 1986).

Konieczny, Alfred, 'Die Zwangsarbeit der Juden in Schlesien im Rahmen der "Organisation Schmelt"', in *Sozialpolitik und Judenvernichtung. Gibt es eine Ökonomie der Endlösung? [Beiträge 5]* (1987), 91–110.

Král, see *Vergangenheit*.

Krausnick, Helmut, 'The Persecution of the Jews', trans. Dorothy Long, in Krausnick *et al.*, 1–124 (cited as Krausnick).

Krausnick, Helmut, *Hitlers Einsatzgruppen. Die Truppen des Weltanschauungskrieges 1938–1942* (Frankfurt a.M., Fischer Taschenbuch Verlag, 1985) (cited as Krausnick, *Einsatzgruppen*).

Krausnick, Helmut, Buchheim, Hans, Broszat, Martin, and Jacobsen, Hans-Adolf, *Anatomy of the SS State*, 2 vols (London, Collins, and New York, Walker & Co., 1968).

Kreidler, Eugen, *Die Eisenbahnen im Machtbereich der Achsenmächte während des Zweiten Weltkrieges. Einsatz und Leistung für die Wehrmacht und Kriegswirtschaft* [*Studien und Dokumente zur Geschichte des Zweiten Weltkrieges* 15, ed. Arbeitskreis für Wehrforschung in Stuttgart] (Göttingen, Frankfurt, Zurich, Musterschmidt, 1975).

Kroeger, Erhard, *Der Auszug aus der alten Heimat. Die Umsiedlung der Baltendeutschen* [*Veröffentlichungen des Instituts für Nachkriegsgeschichte* 4] (Tübingen, Verlag der deutschen Hochschullehrer-Zeitung, 1967) (cited as Kroeger).

Kroeger, Jürgen Ernst, *So war es. Ein Bericht* (Michelstadt/Odw., Neuthor, 1989).

Kursell, Otto von, 'Begegnungen mit Esten und Russen', in Henning von Wistinghausen (ed.), *Zwischen Reval und St. Petersburg. Erinnerungen von Estländern aus zwei Jahrhunderten* (Weissenhorn, Konrad, 1993).

Lochner, Louis P. (ed.) *The Goebbels Diaries 1942–43* (Garden City, NY, Doubleday, 1948). Citations in this book were translated from more comprehensive multi-volume German editions; see Fröhlich (ed.) 1987 and Reuth (ed.) 1992.

Loeber, Dietrich A. (ed.) *Diktierte Option. Die Umsiedlung der Deutsch-Balten aus Estland und Lettland 1939–1941* (Neumünster, Wachholtz, 1972).

Longerich, Peter (ed.) *Die Ermordung der europäischen Juden. Eine umfassende Dokumentation des Holocaust 1941–1945* (Munich, Zurich, Piper, 1989).

Madajczyk, Czesław, 'Generalplan Ost', *Polish Western Affairs* 3 (1962), 391–442.

Madajczyk, Czesław, *Die Okkupationspolitik Nazideutschlands in Polen 1939–1945* (Berlin, Akademie, 1987) (cited as Madajczyk).

Maier, Dieter, *Arbeitseinsatz und Deportation. Die Mitwirkung der Arbeitsverwaltung bei der nationalsozialistischen Judenverfolgung in den Jahren 1938–1945* [*Publikationen der Gedenkstätte Haus der Wannsee-Konferenz* 4] (Berlin, Hentrich, 1994).

Majer, Diemut, *'Fremdvölkische' im Dritten Reich. Ein Beitrag zur nationalsozialistischen Rechtssetzung und Rechtspraxis in Verwaltung und Justiz unter besonderer Berücksichtigung der eingegliederten Ostgebiete und des Generalgouvernements* (Boppard, Boldt, 1981).

May, Johannes *et al.*, *'Euthanasie' in den Staatlichen Heilanstalten Zwie-falten und Schussenried* (Zwiefalten, 1991).

Mayer, Arno J., *Why Did the Heavens not Darken? The 'Final Solution' in History* (New York, Pantheon, 1988).

*Der Menscheneinsatz. Grundsätze, Anordnungen und Richtlinien*, ed. Hauptabteilung I des Reichskommissars für die Festigung deutschen Volkstums [RKF Main Dept. I] (Berlin, 1940) (cited as *Menscheneinsatz*). Among other locations, there is a copy of this in the BAK, RD/10/4/1.

Messerschmidt, Manfred, *Die Wehrmacht im NS-Staat. Zeit der Indok-trination* (Hamburg, von Decker, 1969).

Messner, Reinhold (ed.), *Die Option. 1939 stimmten 86 Prozent der Südtiroler für das Aufgeben ihrer Heimat. Warum? Ein Lehrstück in Zeitgeschichte* (Munich, Zurich, Piper, 1989).

Mitscherlich, Alexander and Mielke, Fred, *Medizin ohne Menschlichkeit. Dokumente des Nürnberger Ärzteprozesses* (Frankfurt a.M., Fischer Taschenbuch Verlag, 1983).

Mommsen, Hans, 'Der Nationalsozialismus. Kumulative Radikalisierung und Selbstzerstörung des Regimes', in *Meyers Enzyklopädisches Lexikon*, vol. 16 (Mannheim, Vienna, Zurich, Bibliographisches Institut, 1976), 785–90 (cited as Mommsen, 'Radikalisierung').

Mommsen, Hans, 'The Realization of the Unthinkable: The "Final Solution of the Jewish Question" in the Third Reich', trans. Alan Kramer and Louise Willmot, in Gerhard Hirschfeld (ed.), *The Policies of Genocide: Jews and Soviet Prisoners of War in Nazi Germany* (London, Allen & Unwin, 1986), 97–144; also in Hans Mommsen, *From Weimar to Ausch-witz: Essays in German History*, trans. Philip O'Connor (Cambridge, MA, Polity Press, and Oxford, Blackwell, 1991) (cited as Mommsen).

Mommsen, Hans, 'Umvolkungspläne des Nationalsozialismus und der Holocaust', in Helge Grabitz, Klaus Bästlein, and Johannes Tuchel, *Die Normalität des Verbrechens. Bilanz und Perspektiven der Forschung zu den nationalsozialistischen Gewaltverbrechen* [Festschrift for Wolfgang Scheffler on his 65th Birthday] (Berlin, Edition Hentrich, 1994), 68–84 (cited as Mommsen, 'Umvolkungspläne').

Mommsen, Hans and Obst, Dieter, 'Die Reaktion der deutschen Bevölk-erung auf die Verfolgung der Juden 1933–1943', in Mommsen and Willems, 374–427.

Mommsen, Hans and Willems, Susanne (eds) *Herrschaftsalltag im Dritten Reich. Studien und Texte* (Düsseldorf, Schwann, 1988).

*Monologe*, see Jochmann.

*Mosbach im Dritten Reich* (no. 2), 'Uns wollen sie auf die Seite schaffen'. Deportation und Ermordung von 262 behinderten Menschen der Johannesanstalten Mosbach und Schwarzach in den Jahren 1940 and 1944 (Mosbach, Volkshochschule, 1992) (cited as Mosbach).

Muehlon, Wilhelm, *Tagebuch der Kriegsjahre 1940–1944* (Dornach, Edition Spicker, 1992).

Müller, Rolf-Dieter, 'Von der Wirtschaftsallianz zum kolonialen Ausbeutungskrieg', in Militärgeschichtliches Forschungsamt (ed.), *Das Deutsche Reich und der Zweite Weltkrieg 4 [Der Angriff auf die Sowjetunion]* (1983), 98–189 (cited as Müller, 'Ausbeutungskrieg').

Müller, Rolf-Dieter, 'Das "Unternehmen Barbarossa" als wirtschaftlicher Raubkrieg', in Gerd Ueberschär and Wolfram Wette (eds), *'Unternehmen Barbarossa'. Der deutsche Überfall auf die Sowjetunion 1941* (Paderborn, Schöningh, 1984).

Müller, Rolf-Dieter, *Hitlers Ostkrieg und die deutsche Siedlungspolitik. Die Zusammenarbeit von Wehrmacht, Wirtschaft und SS* (Frankfurt a.M., Fischer Taschenbuch Verlag, 1991) (cited as Müller).

Müller, Rolf-Dieter (ed.) *Die deutsche Wirtschaftspolitik in den besetzten sowjetischen Gebieten 1941–1943* [Final Report of the *Wirtschaftsstab Ost* and notes by a member of the *Wirtschaftskommando* in Kiev] (Boppard, Boldt, 1991) (cited as Müller, *Wirtschaftspolitik*).

Neumann, Franz, *Behemoth: The Structure and Practice of National Socialism 1933–1944*, 2nd edn (New York, Octagon, 1963).

Nolte, Ernst, *Der Faschismus in seiner Epoche* (Munich, Piper, 1965, 2nd edn) (cited as Nolte, *Faschismus*).

Nolte, Ernst, *Der europäische Bürgerkrieg 1917–1945. Nationalsozialismus und Bolschewismus* (Frankfurt a.M., Berlin, Propyläen, 1987) (cited as Nolte).

*Die faschistische Okkupationspolitik in Polen (1939–1945)*, document selection and introduction by Werner Röhr et al. [*Europa unterm Hakenkreuz* 2] (Berlin, VEB Deutscher Verlag der Wissenschaften, 1989) (cited as *Okkupationspolitik in Polen*).

*Die faschistische Okkupationspolitik in Frankreich (1940–1944)*, document selection and introduction by Ludwig Nestler et al. [*Europa unterm Hakenkreuz* 3] (Berlin, VEB Deutscher Verlag der Wissenschaften, 1990) (cited as *Okkupationspolitik in Frankreich*).

*Die faschistische Okkupationspolitik in den zeitweilig besetzten Gebieten der Sowjetunion*, document selection and introduction by Norbert Müller et al. [*Europa unterm Hakenkreuz* 8] (Berlin, Akademie, 1991) (cited as *Okkupationspolitik in der Sowjetunion*).

*Die Okkupationspolitik des deutschen Faschismus in Jugoslawien, Griechenland, Albanien, Italien und Ungarn (1941–1945)*, document selection and introduction by Martin Seckendorf et al. [*Europa unterm Hakenkreuz* 6] (Berlin, Akademie, 1992) (cited as *Okkupationspolitik, Südosteuropa*).

OKW war diaries, see Schramm.

Pätzold, Kurt (ed.), *Verfolgung, Vertreibung, Vernichtung. Dokumente des faschistischen Antisemitismus* (Leipzig, Verlag Philipp Reclam jun., 1987).

Pätzold, Kurt and Schwarz, Erika, *Tagesordnung Judenmord. Die Wannsee-Konferenz am 20. Januar 1942* (Berlin, Metropol, 1992) (cited as Pätzold and Schwarz).

Pätzold, Kurt and Schwarz, Erika, *'Auschwitz war für mich nur ein Bahnhof'. Franz Novak – der Transportoffizier Adolf Eichmanns* (Berlin, Metropol, 1994) (cited as Pätzold and Schwarz, *Auschwitz*).

Pohl, Dieter, *Von der 'Judenpolitik' zum Judenmord. Der Distrikt Lublin des Generalgouvernements 1939–1944* (Frankfurt a.M., Peter Lang, 1993).

Pospieszalski, Karol Marian, *Niemiecka Lista Narodowa w 'Kraju Warty'* [*Documenta Occupationis Teutonicae 5*] (Poznań, Instytut Zachodni, 1949).

Präg, Werner and Jacobmeyer, Wolfgang (eds), *Das Diensttagebuch des deutschen Generalgouverneurs in Polen. 1939–1945* (Stuttgart, Deutsche Verlags-Anstalt, 1975) (cited as Frank diary).

Pressac, Jean-Claude, *Les Crématoires d'Auschwitz: La Machinerie du Meurtre de Masse* (Paris, CNRS Editions, 1993). Quotations in this book were translated and cited from the German edition: Jean-Claude Pressac, *Die Krematorien von Auschwitz. Die Technik des Massenmords*, trans. Eliane Hagedorn and Barbara Reitz (Munich, Piper, 1994). See also the separate work: Jean-Claude Pressac, *Auschwitz: Technique and Operation of the Gas Chambers*, trans. Peter Moss (New York, Beate Klarsfeld Foundation, 1989).

Rebentisch, Dieter, *Führerstaat und Verwaltung im Zweiten Weltkrieg. Verfassungsentwicklung und Verwaltungspolitik* (Wiesbaden, Stuttgart, Franz Steiner, 1989).

Reitlinger, Gerald, *The Final Solution: The Attempt to Exterminate the Jews of Europe 1939–1945*, 2nd rev. and augm. edn (London, Valentine, Mitchell, 1968).

Reuth, Ralf Georg (ed.), *Joseph Goebbels' Tagebücher 1924–1945* (5 vols, Munich, Zurich, Piper, 1992) (cited as Goebbels diaries, Reuth).

Rhode, Gotthold, 'Als Ortsbevollmächtigter in Neustadt (Kudirkos Naumiestis) in Litauen. Erinnerungen an die Umsiedlung der Litauendeutschen Januar bis März 1941', in Hermann Schubnell (ed.), *Alte und neue Themen der Bevölkerungswissenschaft* [Festschrift for Hans Harmsen] Schriftenreihe des Bundesinstituts für Bevölkerungsforschung 10 (Wiesbaden, Boppard, Boldt, 1981), 151–66.

Rosenkranz, Herb, *'Reichskristallnacht.' 9 November 1938 in Österreich* (Vienna, Frankfurt, Zurich, Europa-Verlag, 1968).

Rössler, Mechthild and Schleiermacher, Sabine (eds), *Der 'Generalplan Ost'. Hauptlinien der nationalsozialistischen Planungs- und Vernichtungspolitik* (Berlin, Akademie Verlag, 1993).

Roth, Karl Heinz, 'Filmpropaganda für die Vernichtung der Geisteskranken und Behinderten im Dritten Reich', in *Reform und Gewissen. 'Euthanasie' im Dienst des Fortschritts* [*Beiträge 2*] (1985), 125–93 (cited as Roth, 'Film').

Roth, Karl Heinz, 'Erster "Generalplan Ost" (1940) von Konrad Meyer', *Mitteilungen der Dokumentationsstelle zur NS-Sozialpolitik* 1, no. 4 (1985).

Roth, Karl Heinz, 'Europäische Neuordnung durch Völkermord. Bemerkungen zu Götz Alys und Susanne Heims Studie über die "Vordenker der Vernichtung"', in Schneider, 179–95 (cited as Roth, 'Neuordnung').

Roth, Karl Heinz, '"Generalplan Ost" – "Gesamtplan Ost". Forschungsstand, Quellenprobleme, neue Ergebnisse', in Rössler and Schleiermacher, 25–117 (cited as Roth, 'Gesamtplan').

Roth, Karl Heinz and Aly, Götz, 'Das "Gesetz über die Sterbehilfe bei unheilbar Kranken"', in K. H. Roth (ed.), *Erfassung zur Vernichtung. Von der Sozialhygiene zum 'Gesetz über Sterbehilfe'* (Berlin, Verlagsgesellschaft Gesundheit mbH, 1984), 101–79.

Safrian, Hans, *Die Eichmann-Männer* (Vienna, Zurich, Europaverlag, 1993).

Schaich, Ludwig, 'Kirche und Innere Mission Württembergs im Kampf gegen die "Vernichtung lebensunwerten Lebens"', in *Evangelische Dokumente zur Ermordung der 'unheilbar Kranken' unter der nationalsozialistischen Herrschaft in den Jahren 1939–1945* (Stuttgart, Innere Mission und Hilfswerk der EKD (main office), 1964).

Scheffler, Wolfgang, 'Rassenfanatismus und Judenverfolgung', in Wilhelm Treue and Jürgen Schmädeke (eds), *Deutschland 1933* (Berlin, Colloquium, 1984), 16–44 (cited as Scheffler, 'Rassenfanatismus').

Scheffler, Wolfgang, 'Wege zur "Endlösung"', in Herbert A. Strauss and Norbert Kampe (eds), *Antisemitismus. Von der Judenfeindschaft zum Holocaust* (Bonn, Bundeszentrale für politische Bildung, 1985), 186–214 (cited as Scheffler, 'Endlösung').

Scheffler, Wolfgang, 'The Forgotten Part of the "Final Solution": The Liquidation of the Ghettos', *Simon Wiesenthal Center Annual* 2 (1985), 31–51 (cited as Scheffler, 'Ghettos').

Scheffler, Wolfgang, 'Probleme der Holocaustforschung', in Stefi Jersch-Wenzel (ed.), *Deutsche-Polen-Juden. Ihre Beziehungen von den Anfängen bis ins 20. Jahrhundert*, conference proceedings (Berlin, Colloquium Verlag, 1987), 259–81 (cited as Scheffler, 'Probleme').

Schmuhl, Hans-Walter, *Rassenhygiene, Nationalsozialismus, Euthanasie. Von der Verhütung zur Vernichtung 'lebensunwerten Lebens' 1890–1945* (Göttingen, Vandenhoeck & Ruprecht, 1987).

Schneider, Wolfgang (ed.), *Vernichtungspolitik. Eine Debatte über den Zusammenhang von Sozialpolitik und Genocid im nationalsozialistischen Deutschland* (Hamburg, Junius, 1991).

Schramm, Percy E. (ed.), *Kriegstagebuch des Oberkommandos der Wehrmacht* (Herrsching, Pawlak, 1982) (cited as OKW war diaries).

Schüler, Klaus A. Friedrich, *Logistik im Rußlandfeldzug. Die Rolle der Eisenbahn bei Planung, Vorbereitung und Durchführung des deutschen Angriffs auf die Sowjetunion bis zur Krise vor Moskau im Winter 1941–42*, introd. by Andreas Hillgruber (Frankfurt a.M., Lang, 1987).

Schumann, Wolfgang and Nestler, Ludwig (eds), *Europa unterm Haken-kreuz. Die Okkupationspolitik des deutschen Faschismus* (8-volume document edition) (Berlin, 1989ff.).

Seckendorf, Martin, 'Die "Raumordnungsskizze" für das Reichskommis-sariat Ostland vom November 1942. Regionale Konkretisierung der Ostraumplanung', in Rössler and Schleiermacher, 175–97.

Seraphim, Hans-Günther (ed.), *Das politische Tagebuch Alfred Rosenbergs aus den Jahren 1934/35 und 1939/40* [*Quellensammlung zur Kultur-geschichte* 8] (Göttingen, Musterschmidt, 1956).

Smith, Bradley F. and Peterson, Agnes F. (eds), *Heinrich Himmler. Geheim-reden 1933 bis 1945* (Frankfurt a.M., Berlin, Vienna, Propyläen, 1974) (cited as Himmler, *Geheimreden*).

Steinberg, Lucien, *Un document essentiel qui situe les débuts de la 'Solu-tion Finale de la Question Juive'*, introd. by Léon Polikov, afterword by Henry Bulawko (Paris, Impr. Gelbard, 1992).

Streim, Alfred, 'Zur Eröffnung des allgemeinen Judenvernichtungsbefehls gegenüber den Einsatzgruppen', in Jäckel and Rohwer, 107–19.

Streit, Christian, *Keine Kameraden. Die Wehrmacht und die sowjetischen Kriegsgefangenen 1941–1945* (Stuttgart, Deutsche Verlags Anstalt, 1978).

Stuhlpfarrer, Karl, *Umsiedlung Südtirol 1939–1940* (2 vols, Vienna, Munich, Löcker, 1985).

Tippelskirch, Kurt von, *Geschichte des Zweiten Weltkriegs* (Bonn, Athenäum, 1951).

Trunk, Isaiah, *Lodzher geto* [*Ghetto Lodz*, in Yiddish] (New York, YIVO [Marstin], 1962).

*Die Vergangenheit warnt. Dokumente über die Germanisierungs- und Austilgungspolitik der Naziokkupanten in der Tschechoslowakei*, compiled and with an introduction by Václav Král (Prague, Orbis, 1960) (cited as Král).

Volkmann, Hans Erich, 'Die NS-Wirtschaft in Vorbereitung des Krieges', in *Das Deutsche Reich und der Zweite Weltkrieg* 1 (1979), 177–368.

Volkmer, Gerhard F., 'Die deutsche Forschung zu Osteuropa und zum osteuropäischen Judentum in den Jahren 1933 bis 1945', in *Forschungen zur osteuropäischen Geschichte* 42 (1989), 109–214.

Wasser, Bruno, *Himmlers Raumplanung im Osten. Der Generalplan Ost in Polen 1940–1944* (Basel, Berlin, Boston, Birkhäuser, 1993).

Wehler, Hans-Ulrich, *Nationalitätenpolitik in Jugoslawien. Die deutsche Minderheit 1918–1978* (Göttingen, Vandenhoeck & Ruprecht, 1980).

Wilhelm, Hans-Heinrich, 'Die Einsatzgruppe A der Sicherheitspolizei und des SD 1941/42. Eine exemplarische Studie', in Helmut Krausnick and Hans-Heinrich Wilhelm, *Die Truppe des Weltanschauungskrieges. Die Einsatzgruppen der Sicherheitspolizei und des SD 1938–1942* (Stuttgart, Deutsche Verlags-Anstalt, 1981) (Munich, PhD dissertation, 1974) (cited as Wilhelm).

Wilhelm, Hans-Heinrich, *Rassenpolitik und Kriegsführung. Sicherheits-polizei und Wehrmacht in Polen und der Sowjetunion* (Passau, Wissenschaftsverlag Richard Rothe, 1991) (cited as Wilhelm, *Rassen-politik*).

Wolfanger, Dieter, *Die nationalsozialistische Politik in Lothringen (1940–1945)* (Saarbrücken, PhD dissertation, 1977).

Wollasch, Hans-Josef, 'Geistig behinderte Menschen zwischen "Caritas" und Nationalsozialismus. Die St. Josefanstalt Herten in Baden', *Caritas 1981* [Yearbook of the German *Caritas* Association] (Freiburg i.Br., Badenia, 1981), 350–68.

*Zagłada chorych psychicznie w Polsce 1939–1945. Die Ermordung der Geisteskranken in Polen 1939–1945*, ed. Polskie Towarzystwo Psychia-tryczne Komisja Naukowa Historii Psychiatrii Polskiej (bilingual, Warsaw, 1993) (cited as *Zagłada*).

Zorn, Gerda, *Nach Ostland geht unser Ritt. Deutsche Eroberungspolitik und die Folgen. Das Beispiel Lodz* (Cologne, Röderberg, 1988, 2nd edn).

# Index of names

# Index of places